MILK STREET
BAKES

177

MILK STREET

BAKES

CHRISTOPHER KIMBALL

WRITING AND EDITING
J. M. Hirsch, Michelle Locke, Ari Smolin,
Dawn Yanagihara and Matthew Card

RECIPES
Wes Martin, Courtney Hill, Rose Hattabaugh, Hisham Ali Hassan
and the Milk Street Kitchen Cooks and Recipe Contributors

ART DIRECTION
Jennifer Baldino Cox

VORACIOUS

LITTLE, BROWN AND COMPANY
NEW YORK BOSTON LONDON

Little, Brown and Company
Hachette Book Group
1290 Avenue of the Americas, New York, NY 10104
littlebrown.com

First Edition: October 2024

Voracious is an imprint of Little, Brown and Company, a division of Hachette Book Group, Inc.

The Voracious name and logo are trademarks of Hachette Book Group, Inc.

The publisher is not responsible for websites (or their content) that are not owned by the publisher.

The Hachette Speakers Bureau provides a wide range of authors for speaking events. To find out more, go to hachettespeakersbureau.com or call (866) 376-6591.

Photography Credits: Joe Murphy except as noted by page: Channing Johnson, pages X, 500; Connie Miller of CB Creatives, pages 14, 22, 30, 31, 37 (top left), 43, 45 (left), 56, 63, 64-65, 67, 68, 70, 73, 75, 77, (top left), 81, 118, 120, 121, 122, 127, 140, 142-143, 154-155, 159, 160, 167, 184, 186, 190, 191, 192, 201, 202, 203, 205, 206, 221, 235, 260, 263, 264, 268, 270, 277, 278-279 (step shots), 280, 293, 295, 309, 311, 312, 313, 314, 316, 326-327, 328, 330, 333, 341, 342, 345, 347, 349, 351, 352-253 (step shots), 355 (top left), 357, 359, 362, 365, 367, 369, 371 (top left), 373, 375, 377, 381, 383, 384-385, 386, 388, 391, 392 (top left), 394, 399 (top left), 401, 402, 406, 408-409, 415, 417, 418, 420 (top left), 423, 424, 427, 428, 431, 433, 435, 439, 441, 442, 445, 446, 457, 460, 467, 469, 475; Jennifer Baldino Cox, page 77 (bottom right), 84, 92, 93 (right), 97, 100, 106, 110, 113, 124-125 (step shots), 130, 135, 138, 290, 322, 449 (bottom right), 499; Erika LaPresto, pages 35, 164, 188, 301, 302, 305, 319 (top left), 338, 451, 452, 465; Jeffrey Bliss, pages 28, 116 (step shots); Brian Samuels, page 298; Rick Poon, page 79; Joyelle West, page 459.

Styling Credits: Wes Martin except as noted by page: Christine Tobin, pages 14, 22, 30, 31, 37 (top left), 43, 45 (left), 56, 63, 64-65, 67, 68, 70, 73, 75, 77, (top left), 81, 118, 120, 121, 122, 127, 140, 142-143, 154-155, 159, 160, 167, 184, 186, 190, 191, 192, 201, 202, 203, 205, 206, 221, 235, 260, 263, 264, 268, 270, 277, 278-279 (step shots), 280, 293, 295, 309, 312, 313, 316, 326-327, 328, 330, 333, 341, 342, 345, 347, 349, 351, 352-253 (step shots), 355 (top left), 357, 359, 365, 367, 369, 371 (top left), 373, 375, 381, 383, 384-385, 386, 388, 391, 392 (top left), 394, 399 (top left), 401, 402, 406, 408-409, 415, 417, 418, 420 (top left), 423, 424, 427, 428, 431, 433, 435, 439, 441, 442, 445, 446, 457, 460, 467, 469, 475; Catrine Kelty, page 377; Molly Shuster, page 314; Catherine Smart, page 311; Monica Mariano, page 362.

ISBN 9780316538886

LCCN 2024933871

10 9 8 7 6 5 4 3 2 1

IM

Print book interior design by Empire Design Studio
Printed in China

Contents

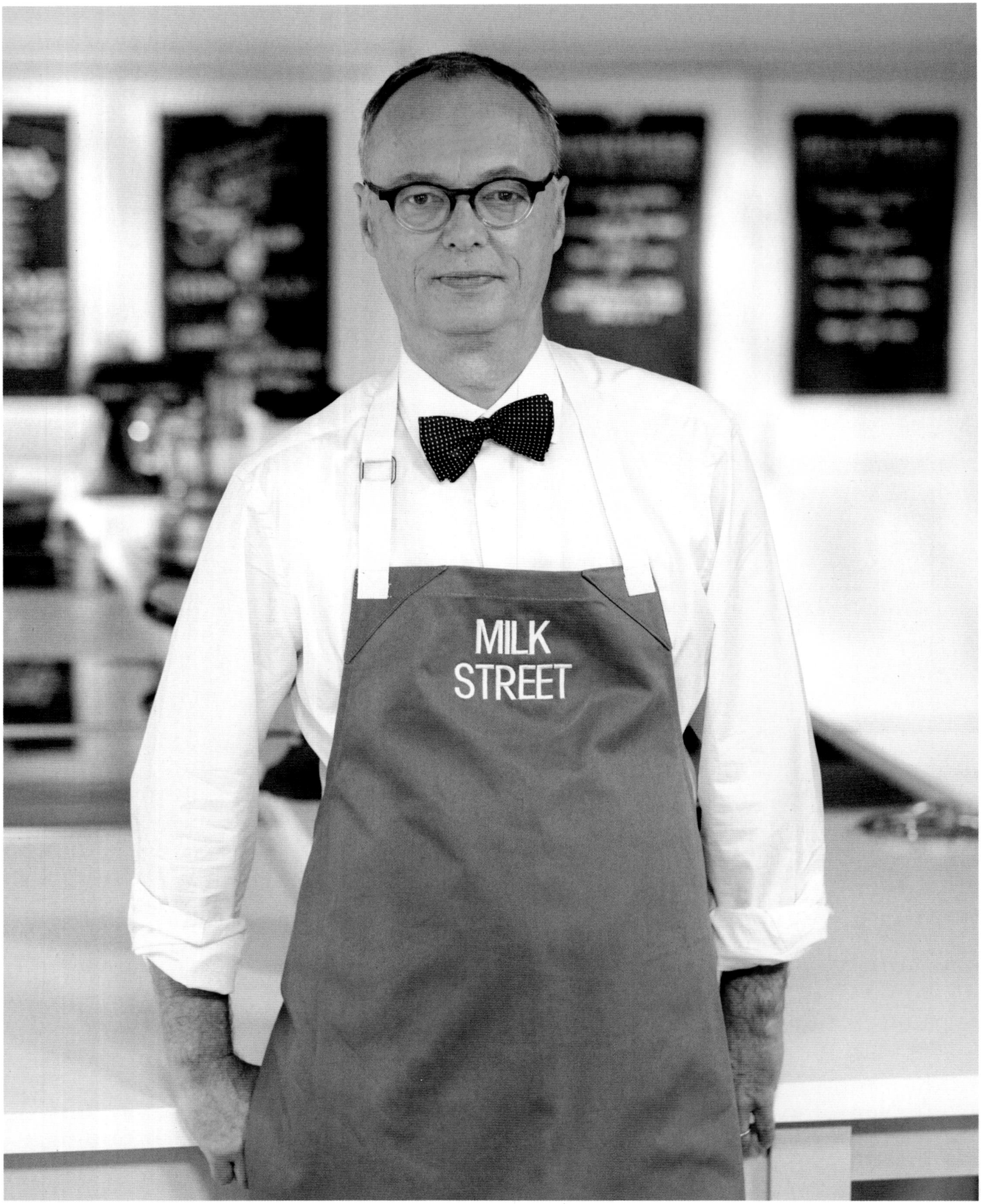
MILK
STREET

Introduction

American cooking has a strong claim to a blue ribbon for its baking repertoire. Nobody in the world does as many pies as we do, from apple to Key lime. I can't count the number of biscuit recipes available, from cream biscuits to beaten biscuits. And, of course, America is the king of cakes, from classic coconut to carrot to flourless chocolate.

But once you step off the plane in Paris, London, Copenhagen, Mexico City, Istanbul, Lisbon or Rome, you find a new world of baking. A simple Spanish almond cake that uses no wheat flour. Loaf cakes that include slightly-bitter rye flour to balance the sugar. Basque cheesecake that requires no water bath and is super-creamy and light. A Mexican sweet corn cake that is prepared in a blender, not a mixer. Or Catalan biscotti, Yelapa-style sweet corn pie, sticky chocolate cake from Sweden, kolaches from Poland, broken phyllo cake from Crete, or a spinach and cheese borek (a phyllo-encrusted savory pie) from Türkiye. And, one of my favorites, a snackable dream cake from Denmark.

In researching this book, we also found many American recipes we'd never heard of, from peanut butter banana cream pie to maple-glazed hermits. And we have gone beyond sweets to include yeasted breads, flatbreads, pizzas and savory tarts. We love the notion of upside-down pizza, pour-in-the-pan pizza, and endless varieties of flatbreads (some can be made in just minutes in a skillet).

It has been said that baking is a science. You can play around with a stir-fry, not with Swedish cardamom buns. That is why professional recipe development and testing are so important when it comes to baking. There are so many things that can go wrong, from an oven that runs hot or cold, ingredients not at the proper temperature, a lack of patience (a bigger problem than you might think), using not quite the right ingredients (such as substituting milk for buttermilk or using all-purpose flour instead of bread flour). It's the little things that count, and Milk Street is here to help you avoid the pitfalls and provide recipes that describe how baked goods should look, not just give you baking times that may not correspond to your home oven.

Though I am first and foremost a baker, I had no idea how much I would learn from the recipes in this volume. First, most of these recipes are much easier than you would think, from beer pretzels to sweet potato rolls. And so, these days, I bake bread almost every weekend because it's fun and easy. Second, one-layer cakes, including loaf cakes, are the most common style of cake in most places, and they are just as good as more complicated multi-layer cakes. (And some can be prepared in a blender!) Some recipes turn things upside down – a chocolate cake steamed on top of the stove or a spanakopita prepared in a skillet. And then, of course, there are new flavor combinations, from a salted peanut and caramel tart to a pistachio-cardamom cake.

Baking is an adventure, a pleasure and a form of alchemy. I defy you to make a loaf of bread or a cake without feeling a connection to something deeper, a tie that binds, a source of happiness that results from working with your hands. When we bake, we use all of our senses – especially touch and aroma – which grounds us to what is most important in life. I often get the feeling that modern life seems particularly ephemeral, hard to grasp. A home-baked cake is just the thing to set things right. You can get your hands on it, you can inhale the freshly baked scent, and you can taste the results of your effort.

Not bad for a square of Danish dream cake!

Chapter 1

Before You Bake

INGREDIENT INSIDER

Starting with the right ingredients is key to successful baking. From all-purpose flour to yogurt, here is a roundup of the core ingredients used in recipes throughout this book.

DAIRY

Along with flours that provide structure and fats that bring richness, dairy is an important element in baking. Liquids such as milk and semisolids like yogurt add moisture and help bind batters and doughs.

Buttermilk

Buttermilk not only lends a pleasant tanginess to baked goods, such as biscuits, soda bread and cakes, it also adds richness without weighing down textures or adding unwanted fattiness. Grocery stores usually offer either cultured nonfat or low-fat buttermilk; traditional buttermilk, made the old-fashioned way by churning, is rare. Any of these options will work in recipes that call for buttermilk. Note that buttermilk curdles easily if heated, so don't warm or scald it as you might milk. For information on buttermilk substitutes, see Best Bet For Better Buttermilk, p. 57.

Coconut Milk

Coconut milk is not a dairy product, but it often is used in the same way as cow's milk. In our recipes that call for coconut milk, purchase the type packaged in a can, not in a carton and sold in the dairy case as a beverage. We consider a 14-ounce can to be standard, but sizes vary somewhat; a tablespoon or two more or less shouldn't affect a recipe. Before use, be sure to stir well to incorporate the fat that rises to the surface. We almost always opt for regular, not light, coconut milk, but don't mistake richer, fattier coconut cream for coconut milk. For more information about coconut products see Cracking the Coconut Code, p. 261.

Eggs

In baking, eggs are a multifunctional ingredient, providing fat as well as structure while also acting as a binder, leavener and emulsifier. We use large eggs in all of our cooking and baking. When room-temperature eggs make a difference in a recipe, the ingredient list will indicate, otherwise eggs can be used straight from the refrigerator. If you need to separate eggs, keep in mind that it's easiest to do so when the eggs are cold because the yolk is relatively firm, making it more resistant to breakage. To quickly bring cold eggs to room temperature, simply submerge them in a bowl of hot water for a few minutes.

Milk

When we use milk in baking, it's almost always whole milk. Low-fat and nonfat milk are too lean and watery to deliver flavor and richness. As with eggs, if room-temperature milk makes a difference in a recipe, the ingredient list will indicate. If it does not, milk straight from the refrigerator is fine to use.

Yogurt

As with buttermilk, yogurt adds tart, tangy flavor to baked goods, as well as a richness that isn't heavy or overbearing. We often lean on yogurt to bring moisture and tenderness to quick breads, flatbreads, muffins and rustic, homey cakes. If a recipe calls for Greek yogurt, regular yogurt is not an appropriate substitute, as the two have different moisture contents.

FATS

In baked goods, fats supply richness and tenderness as well as a luxuriousness that makes a sweet a treat. In addition, fats assist with crisping and browning, which heightens textural appeal and builds flavor. Moreover, fats convey flavor, meaning they help carry taste and aromatic compounds from other ingredients.

Butter

Breaking with convention, we use salted butter in all of our cooking and baking; we prefer the flavor, as well as the convenience of stocking just one variety of butter in our kitchens. Since our recipes are developed with salted butter, the amount of additional salt in the ingredient list takes into account the salinity of the butter. If you prefer unsalted butter, consider adding a touch more salt when making recipes from this book. As a frame of reference, a full stick of butter contains approximately ¼ teaspoon salt. Also, our recipes are developed with standard butter, which contains 16 to 18 percent water; richer, higher-fat European-style butters should work fine, but may behave a little differently. Butter

readily absorbs the aromas of other ingredients, so store it tightly wrapped or in an airtight container in the refrigerator. For longer storage, wrap in foil and freeze.

Neutral Oil

Oil is the fat of choice for many quick breads, muffins and cakes. Unlike butter, which contains water and milk solids, oil is 100 percent fat and remains fluid at room temperature, so it makes for an exceptionally tender, moist and plush crumb. Neutral oils are flavorless oils that don't obscure or interfere with the flavors of other ingredients. When we reach for a neutral oil, it's usually grapeseed, but there are many options, including sunflower, safflower and peanut.

Olive Oil

In addition to neutral oil, we use a fair amount of extra-virgin olive oil in our baking—in savory breads, of course, but also in sweets. It's our go-to when we're looking for a non-butter fat with more personality than neutral oil. A fruity, smooth-tasting olive oil is ideal for sweet baked goods; savory breads can handle peppery, more assertive olive oil.

Tahini

Tahini, a paste made from ground sesame seeds, isn't your typical baking ingredient, but we are fond of its earthy, rich, pleasantly bitter flavor in baked goods. It functions as both a fat and a flavoring, and is especially good paired with dark, toasty ingredients, such as chocolate, coffee and browned butter. As with sesame oil, tahini can be made from raw or toasted sesame seeds. In a tasting, we found tahini made from raw seeds to be pasty and grainy. On the other hand, many supermarket brands were acrid from over-roasting. We prefer tahini made with gently roasted seeds; Soom, Beirut, Lebanon Valley and Sesame King (Regular Roast) were our favorites. Upon standing, the oil in tahini will rise to the surface, so be sure to stir well before use, making sure to scrape along the base of the jar to incorporate the bits that settle at the bottom. Tahini is fine for a month or so at room temperature, though we recommend refrigeration beyond that to maintain freshness.

FLOURS AND STARCHES

Flour, or starch of some sort, is the backbone of nearly every type of baked good. All-purpose flour is the kitchen workhorse, but we lean on a variety of flours, starches and ground meals to add complex, nuanced flavor and texture to muffins, cakes, cookies and breads of all sorts.

All-Purpose Flour

All-purpose flour ranges from nine to 11 percent in protein, depending on the brand. Gold Medal all-purpose flour comes in at 10.5 percent; King Arthur at 11.7 percent. Either will deliver great results. All-purpose flour may be bleached or un-bleached, and the package will indicate. We have found that only in rare instances do the two perform differently enough to warrant specifying one or the other. All-purpose flour is relatively shelf-stable, so store it in the pantry in an airtight container or canister with a wide mouth for easy scooping.

Almond Flour

Almond flour, also referred to as almond meal, is made by grinding almonds to a fine, powdery texture. If made from blanched almonds, its color is a creamy, off-white hue; if made from skin-on almonds, the flour contains brown flecks. We prefer the former. We often use almond flour to add a subtly sweet, nutty flavor to cakes and cookies, and since it does not contain gluten, it also helps produce tender, delicate textures in baked goods. To extend its shelf life, store almond flour in the refrigerator or freezer.

Bread Flour

Bread flour contains 12 to 14 percent protein and, as its name suggests, is used mainly in bread baking. The higher protein content means greater gluten development and better-structured loaves, boules, baguettes and pizza crusts. Though all-purpose flour is used to make some types of yeasted breads, the exchange does not go both ways. Bread flour should not be used in recipes that call for all-purpose flour. We have tried swapping bread flour for all-purpose in several recipes, including yellow cake and sugar cookies, and had little success. The cake turned out dense and gummy and the cookies lacked crispness. Like all-purpose flour, bread flour can be stored in an airtight container in the pantry.

Cake Flour

Cake flour is lower in protein than all-purpose flour and is almost always bleached, which also affects the flour's ability to form gluten. As such, and as its name implies, cake flour often is used to make cakes and other baked goods in which a fine, ultra-tender texture is desired. As a substitute for cake flour, sources commonly suggest mixing all-purpose flour with a small amount of cornstarch (to replace 1 cup cake flour, combine ¾ cup plus 2 tablespoons all-purpose flour with 2 tablespoons cornstarch). Our testing has shown that though this approximation works, when baked goods require it, cake flour delivers the best results.

Corn Flour

Pale yellow corn flour is made by grinding dried whole kernels of corn. Essentially, it is cornmeal taken to a finer, almost powdery texture. In the U.K., cornflour (one word) is what we in the U.S. call cornstarch, but corn flour (two words) and corn-starch are very different products and are not interchangeable.

Cornmeal

Cornmeal can be made from either white or yellow corn, and it is sold in fine, medium and coarse grinds. For baking, we tend to use fine yellow cornmeal most often because it hydrates most easily and lends a warm golden hue (coarse cornmeal is excellent for making polenta). Seek out stone-ground cornmeal, as its flavor is richer and has a cleaner, truer corn flavor than steel-ground cornmeal.

Oats

For baking, we like the hearty, sturdy texture of old-fashioned rolled oats. Before use, we often oven-toast the oats to bring out toffee-like notes, then process a portion of them in the food processor, essentially making toasted-oat flour. For our recipes, avoid instant oats and quick-cooking oats, as these more-processed varieties are finer and lack the chew of old-fashioned oats.

Rye Flour

With earthy, slightly spicy flavor notes and a subtle bitterness, rye flour often is used in bread-baking, but it also works well in cookies, brownies and cakes that feature the dark, rich notes of chocolate, spices, caramel and molasses. It is available in light, medium and dark varieties; the more bran, endosperm and germ the rye kernels retain before milling, the deeper the color of the flour and the fuller its flavor. Pumpernickel flour is made from 100 percent whole-grain. For general use in baking, we recommend sticking with medium rye flour. Rye is not gluten-free, but it does contain less gluten than wheat flour, and the liquid-absorption properties of rye flour are different from all-purpose. For more information about substituting rye flour in baking, see Up Your Baking Game with Rye (p. 303). Rye flour is best stored in the refrigerator or freezer.

Semolina Flour

Milled from high-protein durum wheat and commonly used to make dried pasta, semolina has a pale, creamy yellow hue and a granularity akin to fine cornmeal. In Italy and the Middle East, semolina often is used in breads, but its subtly nutty flavor and distinctive texture also have a place in cookies, puddings and other sweets. Semolina flour is available in different grinds, so shopping can be confusing, especially if choosing amongst imported brands. Domestically produced Bob's Red Mill semolina flour, widely available in supermarkets, has a medium coarseness that works well in many applications, but pass on any semolina labeled "coarse," as it will give baked goods an unpleasant grittiness.

Tapioca Starch

Fine and powdery tapioca starch, also known as tapioca flour, is a gluten-free starch that contributes a chewy, stretchy texture to baked goods, such as Brazilian Cheese Puffs (recipe p. 38). Look for tapioca starch alongside the flour in the baking section of the supermarket or in the international aisle. It also is sold in Latin American markets and most Asian grocery stores.

Whole-Wheat Flour

To make whole-wheat flour, the entirety of the wheat berry—the bran, endosperm and germ—is milled. Whole-wheat flour commonly is used in yeasted breads, but we also employ small amounts in quick breads, bar cookies and even tart pastry to add an earthy, complex flavor. To prolong its shelf life, store whole-wheat flour in the refrigerator or freezer.

LEAVENERS

Leaveners are the unsung heroes in many baked goods. They quietly do their job of providing lift in batters and doughs, creating light textures and open crumbs, then they get out of the way of the flour, butter, sugar and other ingredients that supply structure and flavor.

Yeast

Of the various types of yeast sold in supermarkets, we prefer instant yeast, which also is known as rapid-rise, quick-rise or bread machine yeast. It commonly is packaged in ¼-ounce envelopes that contain about 2¼ teaspoons each, but frequent bread bakers might seek out more economical 4-ounce jars. For more information about yeast and how to substitute active dry yeast for instant yeast, see Make the Most of Your Yeast (p. 229).

Baking Powder

Baking powder is a mixture of baking soda (an alkali) and an acidic ingredient plus an anti-caking agent. It's a common ingredient in quick breads, biscuits, muffins, cakes, cookies

and other baked goods that require a lift to attain a light, open texture. Double-acting baking powder is the most widely available variety. Its name refers to the two rounds of activation that take place—the first happens when liquid is introduced and the baking soda and acidic component react and cause the dough or batter to rise. The second occurs in the oven, when the heat induces additional lift. Baking powder has a shelf life that's shorter than you might expect, so check the expiration date before use.

Baking Soda

Not to be confused with baking powder (though the two look the same), baking soda is an alkali, so it's an effective leavener in baking recipes that contain an acidic ingredient, such as buttermilk, lemon juice, sour cream or yogurt. When baking soda and acid meet, a chemical reaction releases carbon dioxide that provides lift. Baking soda also assists with browning, as alkaline doughs and batters brown more readily, which translates to better, more complex flavor in baked treats.

SALT

In baking, salt is used in small quantities, but the ingredient has an outsized impact on flavor, even in goods in which sweetness is the main attraction. Salt makes foods taste better and brings flavors into sharp focus.

Flaky Sea Salt

We sometimes sprinkle flaky sea salt onto baked goods just before they go into the oven. The coarse crystals not only add texture and a complementary pop of salinity, they also make for a more polished look. We tend to favor Maldon Sea Salt Flakes, harvested in the U.K., which has a unique pyramid shape and a delicate but satisfying crunch.

Kosher Salt

In savory cooking, we prefer kosher salt because the larger granules are easier to pinch and sprinkle with your fingers. So in this book, you will find recipes that call for both kosher salt and table salt—for instance, a flatbread dough made with table salt, but kosher salt used in the flatbread filling. The two most common kosher salt brands are Morton Coarse Kosher Salt and Diamond Crystal Kosher Salt. Our recipes are developed with Morton. Grains of Morton are denser and more compact than Diamond Crystal, which are larger and fluffier, so the same volume of Morton is saltier than Diamond. If you use Diamond in our recipes, increase the amount called for by 30 to 50 percent, depending on your salt sensitivity.

Before You Bake

Table Salt

Common table salt—the kind put into salt shakers—is what we prefer to use in most baked goods as the fine, uniformly sized grains disperse evenly and dissolve readily even in low-moisture doughs, crumbles and similar mixtures. Fine sea salt has a similar grain size to table salt and can be used in its place.

SWEETENERS

Sugar supplies sweetness to baked goods, but from the delicate, floral nuances of honey to the smoky, bitter notes of molasses, sweeteners can bring flavor notes far beyond basic sugariness. Caramelization and crisping are other important attributes of sugar when it comes to baking.

Brown Sugar

Brown sugar is refined white sugar to which molasses has been added. It supplies caramel flavor notes, color and moisture to batters and doughs. In baked sweets, it's a particularly welcome ingredient when a soft, tooth-sinking texture is desired (think brownies and chewy chocolate chip cookies). Light brown sugar contains less molasses than dark brown and is therefore milder in flavor. When it makes a difference in a recipe, we specify which to use but, flavor aside, the two are interchangeable. Store brown sugar in a tightly sealed airtight container to prevent drying.

Molasses

Dark, sticky, bittersweet molasses is a by-product of sugar refinery. The syrup lends deep color and bold, smoky notes to baked goods, such as gingerbread and molasses spice cookies. Grandma's and Brer Rabbit are two widely available brands, and both offer mild and dark varieties. For most baking applications, either will work, but do not substitute blackstrap molasses, which is assertively bitter and will easily overwhelm other ingredients.

Honey

Honey comes in numerous varieties with taste profiles that are determined by the flora visited by the honeybees. For use in baking recipes, we recommend choosing relatively mild, neutral clover or wildflower honey, with a light golden hue. Stronger, darker-colored options, such as buckwheat and chestnut, easily overwhelm other ingredients.

Maple Syrup

Smoky-sweet, uniquely delicious maple syrup is available in color classes established by the International Maple Syrup Institute: golden, amber, dark and very dark. The intensity of taste corresponds with the depth of color. For baking—and for drizzling onto waffles and pancakes, too—we recommend seeking out dark or very dark, as the more pronounced maple flavor will hold its own in the presence of other ingredients. After opening, store maple syrup in the refrigerator.

Powdered Sugar

Also known as confectioner's sugar, powdered sugar is finely ground granulated sugar that is blended with a small amount of cornstarch to prevent caking. Its ultra-fine texture allows the sugar to incorporate smoothly and completely dissolve into frostings, icings and glazes. Sifted through a fine-mesh sieve just before serving, powdered sugar dusted on a dessert such as apple strudel lends a snowy finished look.

Turbinado Sugar

Turbinado sugar is a coarse-grained sugar. Minimal refining leaves the granules with a touch of molasses so the sugar has a golden color and notes of earthy caramel. We sometimes use turbinado as a finishing sugar, sprinkling it onto batter and dough before baking for a textural accent and subtle sparkle. Demerara sugar is similar to turbinado sugar but has milder molasses notes; it also tends to be more difficult to source. The two are interchangeable, but do not use either as a direct substitute for white or brown sugar; the coarse granules do not readily dissolve.

White Sugar

White sugar, also known as granulated sugar, or just plain "sugar," is produced from the juices extracted from sugarcane or beets. This kitchen staple has a pure, clean, direct sweetness. The crystal size of white sugar is perfectly structured to create pockets of air when beaten with butter, resulting in light, aerated batters and doughs, yet it is fine enough to dissolve with relative ease in the presence of moisture.

BAKING ESSENTIALS

Baking, more so than savory cooking, requires precision, along with the right equipment to guarantee great results. In this section, we cover tools for measuring ingredients, countertop appliances, bakeware and other implements that bakers often call upon.

MEASURING TOOLS

Measuring with accuracy and precision is essential for success when baking. These are the tools we depend on for measuring ingredients, taking temperatures and gauging dimensions.

Digital Kitchen Scale

A digital scale is an indispensable tool for any kitchen. Measuring ingredients by weight guarantees consistency and accuracy. We also love the ease and efficiency scales provide—you can pour flour, sugar and other ingredients directly from their containers into your mixing bowl, taring (or zeroing out)

the scale before each addition. We suggest seeking out a digital scale that can be easily switched from metric to pounds and ounces. Also be sure the capacity is great enough to suit your needs and has a platform large enough to hold a broad-based bowl (lightweight scales can be small and tippy).

Instant Thermometer

A digital instant thermometer is handy for making sugar syrup that must be cooked to a precise temperature, as well as for checking for the doneness of baked goods such as rich yeasted breads and cheesecakes. Look for a durable model with a clear display that quickly delivers a reading. It's also sometimes helpful if the thermometer can be easily switched between Fahrenheit and Celsius.

Measuring Cups and Spoons

While we strongly encourage baking by weight, measuring cups and spoons are still essential tools for baking. You'll need both dry and liquid measuring cups—the two should not be used interchangeably—as well as measuring spoons. Look for

good-quality stainless steel dry measuring cups and spoons with smooth, even tops for clean sweeping with a straight edge to ensure accurate measurements. Heavyweight cups and spoons typically are dishwasher-safe; plastic can warp in the dishwasher, which affects their accuracy.

Ruler

Baking is an exacting craft and a good ruler is an invaluable helper. It comes in handy when rolling out doughs to specific dimensions, and also when you're unsure about the measurements of the loaf pan, pie plate or baking sheet that you have on hand. Look for a sturdy, washable ruler with easy-to-read measurements in both inches and centimeters.

SMALL APPLIANCES

Although it is possible to make cake batters, pie doughs and yeasted breads by hand, we rely heavily on small countertop appliances—in particular, a stand mixer and a food processor. They make baking easier and more enjoyable, while also ensuring that ingredients are sufficiently mixed or processed.

Stand Mixer

A stand mixer with paddle, whisk and dough hook attachments is a cornerstone of a baker's kitchen for good reason. It offers unmatched speed and convenience, greatly reducing the time and effort required to mix, whip and knead. A mixer with a bowl capacity of 4½ to 5 quarts is sufficient for the recipes in this book that require a mixer. If you're an avid baker, or plan on baking yeasted breads that can tax the appliance, it's worth investing in a mixer with a powerful motor that can handle the load. Hand mixers, which are more compact and affordable, work great for batters, light doughs and whipping cream and egg whites, but they're much less powerful than a stand mixer and can handle only smallish quantities.

Food Processor

A food processor is a versatile tool. It makes quick work of chopping or grinding nuts and it can puree ingredients that are too sticky or dry to be whirred in a blender. It excels at cutting fat, usually cold butter, into dry ingredients when making pie and tart dough, scones and some types of cookies. When pulsed, the metal blade is efficient at reducing chunks of fat into small bits that are evenly distributed. Food processors come in different sizes. One with a bowl capacity of at least 11 cups is sufficient for general use in baking, but make sure the base is heavy so the machine sits stably on the counter.

Electric Spice Grinder

Electric spice grinders are helpful for grinding whole spices and small amounts of nuts or seeds. Blade-style coffee grinders are inexpensive and work perfectly well—just don't use the same grinder that you use for your coffee, which will impart odors. To clean and remove odors, grind a handful of plain rice. A mortar and pestle can work well, though it's hard to pulverize tough spices, such as cloves or allspice, as finely as with a spice grinder.

BAKEWARE

When it comes to bakeware, we tend to stick to the basics: our recipes do not require highly specialized or hard-to-source pans or molds. Different materials are used to make various types of bakeware. For example, square and rectangular pans, loaf pans and pie plates might be made of metal, glass or ceramic, whereas muffin pans and cake pans are available in metal and silicone. For more information about how bakeware made of these different materials compare, see Choose Bakeware with Care (p. 33). This section touches on the pans used frequently in this book. It also covers baking steels and stones that are important for pizza-making and baking some types of breads.

Baking Pans

We tend to select an 8-inch square baking pan for denser cookies and bars, like shortbread, jam-filled cookies and brownies, that will be cut into small portions for serving. For wet doughs and batters—think sheet and coffee cakes or focaccia—as well as rolls and buns that proof and bake in the pan, we favor a 9-by-13-inch baking pan. It's also the ideal size for baked goods that are cut into medium or large portions for serving and anything made with phyllo, which is often sold in 9-by-13-inch sheets. We recommend owning one each of metal and glass variations to accommodate the requirements of different types of recipes.

Baking Sheets

You'll need at least two rimmed 13-by-18-inch baking sheets, often referred to as half sheet pans. Unlike a flat cookie sheet, these have a lip running around the pan's exterior. It serves as an easy-to-grasp handle for moving the sheet in and out of the oven, and provides a convenient buffer so nothing slides off. The heavier the better for even heating—they won't warp at high heat—and durability. At 9-by-13 inches, quarter sheet pans are our go-to for smaller jobs, like toasting nuts and flours.

Baking Steel or Stone

When placed in the oven, a baking steel or baking stone provides a flat, uniformly hot surface on which to bake. It also conducts and retains heat, minimizing fluctuations in oven temperature. For this reason, a steel or stone is essential for baked goods that require intense, even heat for proper browning and crisping, especially on the bottom—think pizza and rustic breads. We prefer a baking steel over a baking stone, as it possesses greater thermal conductivity, but either will work. In particular, we're big fans of the U.S.-made The Baking Steel, which is virtually indestructible and can be used outside on the grill. If you make pizza frequently or do lots of bread baking on a steel or stone, we also recommend owning a metal or wood baking peel for easily transferring items to and from the oven.

Bundt Pan

With a tube-shaped center and fluted sides, a Bundt pan is an easy way to bake a cake that needs little embellishment or adornment to look "finished." We also use one for monkey bread. Bundt pans come in an array of sizes, but our go-to has a capacity of 12 cups. For easy release, be sure to thoroughly spray or butter all the decorative nooks and crannies.

Cake Pans

Round cake pans come in every size imaginable, but a 9-inch one with straight (not sloped) sides is the standard for many of our simple cakes and quick breads. We recommend owning two of the same brand for efficiently preparing layer cakes.

Loaf Pans

Used for everything from hearty German rye bread to buttery pound cake, loaf pans are an essential part of any baker's kitchen. A 9-by-5-inch loaf pan is our most used size, but there are a few occasions in which we recommend 8½-by-4½-inch loaf pans. We recommend owning two.

Springform Pan

Springform pans have removable bottoms and sides. They're almost always used for cheesecake, since you can unmold whatever is baked in them without needing to invert the pan. This makes them incredibly versatile, but keep in mind these pans are not always leakproof. We use a 9-inch springform for some types of tarts, dense cakes and fruit-topped items that wouldn't fare well with flipping.

Tart Pan

A removable bottom is key for quickly and easily releasing a tart without breaking or blemishing the sides. We use 9-inch fluted tart pans, which tend to be easier to find, but straight-sided varieties work just as well. Ceramic tart pans make for a lovely presentation but lack the removable bottom, so serving can be more complicated.

OTHER BAKING ESSENTIALS

Bakers tend to be drawn to specific-use tools and gadgets. With only a couple exceptions, however, the recipes in this book can be made without any special implements or novelty utensils. A handful of essential items is all that's needed.

Bench Scrapers

Both metal and plastic scrapers are professional kitchen staples for a reason. They're perfect for everything from quickly cleaning a work surface to scooping up and transferring piles of prepped produce to dividing and portioning sticky doughs with ease. While a metal scraper, also known as a bench knife, is better at cutting through dough, a flexible plastic bowl scraper is more versatile. It can do everything mentioned above, plus is great for folding and transferring wet doughs and batters.

Kitchen Parchment

Kitchen parchment, also known as parchment paper, is a must-have for baking enthusiasts. It's used to line baking sheets, baking pans and cake pans for easy release of baked goods. Parchment is heat-resistant but not flameproof, so therefore should not be used under the broiler, and should not be confused with waxed paper. Bleached parchment is stark white; unbleached parchment has a natural brown color. It's sold in continuous rolls, in precut flat sheets or in rolls of precut sheets.

Muffin Pan

We use a 12-cup muffin pan for standard muffins and call on one 24-cup or two 12-cup mini muffin pans for bite-sized tarts and cakes. Avoid silicone molds, which conduct heat poorly and result in uneven browning and rising.

Pie Plate

Glass, ceramic and enamel pie plates can be used interchangeably. Standard diameter is 9 inches; standard depth is 1 to 1¼ inches, but towering meringue-topped cream pies necessitate a deeper dish (those are typically 1½ to 2 inches). You'll find one such pie in this book, but the majority of our recipes are suited to a standard-depth pie plate.

Ramekins

A six-ounce capacity is our go-to ramekin size for individual puddings, custards and soufflés. Our recipes typically yield four or six servings, so having six molds is ideal.

Pastry Brushes

Pastry brushes are essential for finishing washes, brushing phyllo and buttering pans and molds. We favor natural hair brushes because silcone has a tendency to spread unevenly. Clean well in hot water and dry well with a kitchen towel before storing to prevent "off" flavors from developing. Ideally, own one each for sweet and savory applications.

Pie Weights

Pie weights are crucial for prebaking pie and tart crusts. While a bag of beans or even granulated sugar will work in a pinch, we recommend heat-conducting ceramic or metal pie weights. Don't skimp—it's worth buying two sets to ensure there's enough to reach all the way up the sides of a 9-inch pie crust or tart shell.

Rolling Pin

We favor wooden French-style tapered rolling pins because their shape allows for even, precision rolling. Go long—at least 18 inches—to ensure you can roll out the largest pie crusts.

Serrated Knife

A long, stiff serrated knife is the most-used kitchen knife for baking. Beyond slicing baked breads and cakes, it is also the right tool for chopping chocolate and nuts (the teeth pierce rather than smash and generate fewer small pieces and crumbs). We prefer designs with a bit of curve to the blade for a natural slicing motion that's easy on the wrist. Suncraft's Seseragi bread knife is a Milk Street favorite for its highly effective and unique tooth pattern and thinness of the blade.

Silicone Spatulas

Durable, heatproof spatulas are essential baking tools. We recommend owning both small and large spatulas and even concave spoonulas, which are excellent for folding delicate batters together. Silicone has a tendency to hold odors, so we advise color coding for savory and sweet applications. Also, detergents tend to cling to silicone, so rinse well in hot water.

Spray Bottle

For frequent bread makers, a water-filled spray bottle is essential for misting a variety of loaves before they go into the oven and during baking.

Wand-style Grater

We favor wand-style graters, which reduce citrus zest to fine, feathery ribbons. They dull with age and we recommend replacing them every year or so for best results. Graters made from steel tend to last longer than alloy models.

Whisks

Whisks come in all shapes and sizes, each intended for different applications. For most baking tasks, a balloon whisk is the best choice because it incorporates air into egg whites or batters most efficiently. In our testing, GIR's Ultimate Whisk, which has uniquely designed staggered tines, proved more effective than other brands and styles. In addition to a large balloon whisk, it's worth having a small one for blending egg washes, small amounts of glaze, etc.

Wire Racks

A pair of large, sturdy metal racks is recommended for cooling baked goods. Our preferred racks fit into a rimmed 13-by-18-inch baking sheet to contain crumbs, or for icing and glazing cakes or cookies.

FLOUR POWER

Want to be a better baker? Toss your measuring cups. And brace for confusion.

"There's no better way to fail than to measure by volume instead of weighing things," says Francisco Migoya, co-author of The Cooking Lab team's recent cookbook, "Modernist Bread."

Except it isn't as simple as it sounds. When it comes to baking weights, there is little consensus. We surveyed the published metric weights of 1 cup of a dozen varieties of flour from 22 sources. We got nearly as many answers.

One cup of all-purpose flour? Weights ranged from 120 grams to 148 grams. Whole-wheat flour went from 113 grams to 156 grams. Which is to say, measuring flour is the Wild West of culinary endeavors. What to do?

To make sense of it all, we wanted to come up with a reasonable average for each flour. We started by throwing out the outliers, the extreme highs and lows, then averaged the remaining weights. We then performed our own series of measurements here at Milk Street to confirm that the numbers were in the ballpark. They were.

A few final adjustments later, and we had average gram weights for 12 types of flour. Of course, we can't account for every variable (different grain varieties, milling techniques, even humidity can change weights).

FLOUR WEIGHT PER CUP

Type of Flour	Grams per cup
All-purpose	130
Cake	120
Bread	137
Rye (stone, dark)	140
Whole-wheat	140
Buckwheat	140
Semolina	170
Cornmeal (fine)	145
Cornmeal (coarse)	160
Corn flour	122
Almond flour	100
Cornstarch	132
Tapioca starch	124
Rice flour	160
Sweet (glutinous) rice flour	156
Potato starch	156
Potato flour	181

A final word about measuring flour by volume. Don't. Buy a $20 digital scale if you want consistent results. But if you do go by volume, here are some tips for using the "dip and sweep" method.

Do not scoop flour from the bag it came in; that can add more than 20 grams per cup. Pour the flour into a storage container or a bowl, then scoop gently through the flour—not down—to avoid compression.

Finally, sweep off the extra flour using a knife or bench scraper held straight. Do not sweep at a 45-degree angle; this will push the flour into the measuring cup.

CRACKING THE EGG CODE

Cracking the code of great baking often means also cracking plenty of eggs. Whether in a dense cheesecake, an airy meringue or a rich pound cake, eggs deliver a critical dose of protein, fat and moisture that plays a key role in the structure, texture and taste of baked goods. All of which means that misjudging the volume of eggs can lead to disappointing results.

Trouble is, eggs come in a wide variety of sizes, which can present a measurement challenge. If a recipe calls for large eggs (as many do), and you only have jumbos or mediums, adjusting can be a guessing game.

We find we get the best and most consistent results by measuring ingredients by weight. So we set out to find a way to apply this approach to eggs, as well. First, we surveyed the weight of cracked eggs (the yolk and white without the shell) for all egg sizes: On average, medium cracked eggs weigh 44 grams; large, 50 grams; extra-large, 56 grams; and jumbo, 63 grams.

From there, we worked out a handy conversion table for different egg sizes. Using our chart, you can see that, for example, a recipe calling for six large eggs will require seven medium eggs or five jumbo eggs. For best results, we found that the most accurate way to portion the eggs is to whisk them first, then weigh them, using only the total liquified amount needed.

EGGS: CONVERSION BY SIZE AND WEIGHT

If your recipe calls for...	You will need at least...			
Large	Medium	X-Large	Jumbo	Grams
2	3	2	2	100
3	4	3	3	150
4	5	4	4	200
5	6	5	4	250
6	7	6	5	300
7	8	7	6	350
8	9	7	7	400

SECRETS TO SWEET SUCCESS

At Milk Street, when we bake, we measure flours by weight rather than volume, to correct for scooping irregularities and air that can otherwise throw off a recipe. We wondered whether sugars would benefit from a similar treatment.

To find out, we weighed seven dry and five liquid sugars 60 times each, scooping and leveling for the dry and pouring for the liquids. We then averaged the weights to arrive at our own. The results surprised us.

SUGAR WEIGHT PER CUP

Type of Sugar	Grams per cup
White sugar	214
Light brown sugar (lightly packed)	218
Dark brown sugar	199
Cane sugar	212
Turbinado sugar	198
Powdered sugar	124
Superfine sugar	202
Honey	334
Corn syrup	327
Molasses	334
Agave syrup	328
Maple syrup	298

We thought we'd get less variation because granulated sugars—unlike flours—trap little air. While that's true, we hadn't accounted for crystal size, which varied widely from brand to brand.

This showed up in our results, where 1 cup of white sugar weighed as much as 236 grams or as little as 208 grams, even when weighed by the same person. Published weights from other sources showed as much variation as our own testing.

Brown sugar—light and dark—also had glaring irregularities. Because of its moisture content, brown sugar traditionally is packed when measured. But we found its weight per cup varied greatly depending on how firmly it was packed, sometimes measuring 160 grams, other times 246 grams.

Liquid sugars didn't vary nearly as much, but weighing them did solve a persistent problem—stickiness. Even when we used a silicone spatula to scrape honey, molasses and similar sweeteners out of measuring cups, we never got it all. This meant not all of what we measured ended up in our recipe.

The simplest solution was to set the bowl directly on the scale, zero it out, then slowly add the sweetener directly to the other ingredients, no measuring cup needed.

SOLVING DAIRY DILEMMAS

Many baked goods depend on dairy for richness, structure and texture. But some dairy products can be tricky to measure by volume; yogurt and sour cream love to cling to the sides of measuring cups.

The best way to measure them is by weight. But this presents challenges, too. For one thing, recipes often fail to specify dairy weights. And consulting a package may not be much help, either. We've found discrepancies between containers' purported weights by volume, and actual weights.

So we weighed 14 common dairy ingredients. Some are liquids, some are semisolids and a few are solids. In the following table, we've listed these items' weights for ½ cup (8 tablespoons) in grams, as we prefer the precision of metric weights when baking.

DAIRY BY WEIGHT

Type	Weight	Volume
Butter	113 grams	½ cup
Buttermilk, lowfat	118 grams	½ cup
Cottage cheese, whole milk	140 grams	½ cup
Crème fraîche	113 grams	½ cup
Heavy cream	115 grams	½ cup
Mascarpone	120 grams	½ cup
Mexican crema	130 grams	½ cup
Milk, low-fat	115 grams	½ cup
Milk, whole	115 grams	½ cup
Ricotta	135 grams	½ cup
Sour cream	120 grams	½ cup
Yogurt, Greek	120 grams	½ cup
Yogurt, low-fat	120 grams	½ cup
Yogurt, whole milk	120 grams	½ cup

A TOUGH NUT TO CRACK

Cooking with nuts can be tricky. Their odd, irregular shapes guarantee that they won't pack neatly into measuring cups, making precise measurement nearly impossible. Our solution: Measuring by weight ensures greater accuracy in baking, and nuts are no exception. Unfortunately, most recipes call for nuts by volume, not weight.

To clear up the guesswork, we've compiled the weights of the most commonly used nuts (as well as seeds, including sesame and pumpkin, and peanuts, which are legumes). In our testing, we weighed ½ cup of each variety three times, then averaged those results to arrive at their final weights.

NUTS BY WEIGHT

Type	Weight	Volume
Almond, slices	47 grams	½ cup
Almonds, slivered	65 grams	½ cup
Almonds, whole	74 grams	½ cup
Cashews, whole	65 grams	½ cup
Hazelnuts, whole	65 grams	½ cup
Macadamia	72 grams	½ cup
Peanuts, whole	68 grams	½ cup
Pecan, halves	57 grams	½ cup
Pecans, chopped	57 grams	½ cup
Pine nuts	70 grams	½ cup
Pistachios, whole	73 grams	½ cup
Pumpkin seeds (pepitas)	70 grams	½ cup
Sesame seeds	80 grams	½ cup
Sunflower seeds	72 grams	½ cup
Walnuts, chopped	55 grams	½ cup
Walnut, halves	55 grams	½ cup
Walnuts, whole	55 grams	½ cup

TAKING THE MEASURE OF WHOLE SPICES

Whenever possible we prefer to buy whole spices rather than ground. Oxidation can cause store-bought ground spices to lose flavor quickly and can also contribute stale, off flavors to a dish. Whole spices stay fresh longer and pack more flavor, whether used whole or ground as needed. And they can remain fresh stored in a cool, dark cabinet for up to two years (ground spices last about six months, at most).

The only trouble is knowing how much to pulverize when a recipe calls for ground. We hate to be wasteful and grind too much, and few recipes do the conversion for us. So we decided to take the mystery out of this kitchen quandary and suss out equivalencies for 10 common whole and ground spices. Some spices yielded larger volumes when ground because of aeration that occurs during grinding.

WHOLE SPICES BY VOLUME

Spice	Whole	Ground
Allspice berries	1 tablespoon	3¼ teaspoons
Aniseed	1 tablespoon	1 tablespoon
Caraway seeds	1 tablespoon	1 tablespoon
Cloves	1 tablespoon	1 tablespoon
Coriander seeds	1 tablespoon	2¾ teaspoons
Fennel seeds	1 tablespoon	2¾ teaspoons
Juniper berries	1 tablespoon	3¼ teaspoons
Nutmeg (grated)	1 piece	6¾ teaspoons
Peppercorns, black	1 tablespoon	3½ teaspoons
Peppercorns, white	1 tablespoon	4 teaspoons

KNOW YOUR OVEN TEMPERATURES

Some people are more successful at kitchen improv than others. But cooking well without recipes isn't so much about innate talent as it is understanding key equipment. And mastering the oven is at the top of the list. Winging it in the kitchen is easier once you familiarize yourself with oven temperature zones.

Once you understand the five basic temperature ranges—and the foods that cook best in them—it's easier to simply toss a chicken in to roast, bake up a quick bread, crank out some roasted carrots or whip up a pizza for dinner.

And since not all of this is intuitive—for example, a low oven is best for delicate custards, but also for braised meats—we've broken down the most common oven recipes into the temperatures ranges where they do best.

LOW (275°F to 325°F)
Baked custards; dried beans; tough, long-cooking roasts; stews and other braises

MODERATE (325°F to 350°F)
Most baked goods (cakes, cookies, muffins, quick breads, etc.)

MEDIUM-HIGH (375°F to 400°F)
Blind-baked pastry, pork loin, well-marbled beef roasts, whole chickens

HOT (425°F to 450°F)
Biscuits and scones, chicken parts, potatoes for roasting, puff pastry

EXTRA-HOT (475°F to 500°F)
Fish fillets, high-moisture yeasted doughs (pizza, flatbreads, etc.), most vegetables for roasting

TEMPING BAKED GOODS

Of the various ways to tell when cooking is complete—visual cues and time are our most common and comfortable choices—we too often overlook the value of temperature.

Internal temperature is less determinative for baking than it is for meat and poultry, but it is yet another useful tool to add to your repertoire.

Bread, for example. Depending on the accuracy of your oven, the interior can overbake before the exterior shows any signs. Cakes face similar problems, in reverse. The high sugar content means the exterior can brown before the interior is cooked.

To arrive at these temperatures, we surveyed other sources, which were scarce and conflicting. So we cooked breads and desserts in our kitchen, then temped them at the moment of perfect doneness.

Enriched American-style breads (such as Parker House rolls)	195°F
Rustic European-style bread (such as crusty French loaves)	210°F
Quick breads and muffins (such as banana bread)	195°F
Biscuits	205°F
Cheesecake (at the center)	150°F
(about 1 inch from the edge)	170°F
Angel food cake	205°F
Chocolate layer cake	210°F
Sponge cake	205°F
Yellow layer cake	190°F

For each item, we cite the temperature to which a dish should be brought, then removed from the oven or taken off the heat.

Our preferred tool is an instant digital thermometer. To test the accuracy of yours, fill a glass with ice water, then temp it. It should read 32°F. Or take the temperature of boiling water, which should read 212°F at sea level.

Where to temp a food matters, too. The tip of the thermometer should be at the center of the baked good, which is the last area to cross the finish line. If you wish to avoid puncturing the top crust and leaving a hole, insert the thermometer near the edge, with the stem angled so the tip reaches the center. For sauces and custards cooked on the stove, tip the pan to pool the liquid and temp at the center without touching the bottom of the pan.

SIZING UP BAKING TIMES

Too often, baking recipes call for specific pan sizes a home cook simply doesn't have. What to do when you want to make mini-loaves out of a recipe intended for a 9-by-5-inch loaf pan? And what about when you want to convert a 9-by-13-inch cake into cupcakes? We wanted some simple guidelines.

So we selected the most popular and basic baked goods—quick bread, pound cake, layer cake and brownies—and baked the same recipe in a variety of appropriate pans. We monitored doneness to calculate variations in timing from pan to pan, and kept our testing focused on times, not oven temperature.

Some conversions were straightforward. A layer cake baked in an 8-inch round rather than the called-for 9-inch required only a minute longer in the oven and resulted in a slightly taller cake. Brownies were also simple. A double batch baked in a 9-by-13-inch pan needed five minutes longer, but didn't display any other discernible differences.

Conversions for quick bread and pound cake proved trickier. The change in size from a 9-by-5-inch loaf pan to an 8-by-4-inch pan was more drastic, affecting bake time as well as appearance. In the smaller of the two pans, quick breads took considerably longer to bake, browned more deeply and were more domed. Pound cakes acted similarly.

Conversions always involve guesswork, but we did extract a few guiding principles. First, baking in a smaller pan means the depth of the batter will be greater and thus will usually take longer to bake. In a larger pan, the batter will be in a thinner layer and bake more quickly.

Second, if you're using a different pan, adjust your expectations. Not only will the timing change, but the browning and appearance may vary, too. Cakes and breads baked in mini-loaf pans finished quickly but didn't brown much (increasing the oven temperature may help).

Finally, a note on pan color and material. In general, dark pans absorb and conduct heat more quickly than light-colored pans, but for these types of basic baked goods, we didn't observe substantial differences in our testing. We did, however, see a pronounced difference in glass versus metal. Quick breads and cakes didn't brown well in glass, and had tacky bottoms and sides. If a recipe calls for a baking pan, we advise against using a glass baking dish.

BAKING TIME ADJUSTMENTS
t=baking time specified for a particular recipe

	9 x 5" Loaf Pan	8 x 4" Loaf Pan	5¾ x 2" Loaf Pans*	Muffin Pan
Quick bread	t	t+7 minutes	t-7 minutes	t-28 minutes
Pound cake	t	t+10 minutes	t-13 minutes	–
	9" Round Cake Pan	**8" Round Cake Pan**	**9 x 13" Baking Pan**	**Muffin Pan**
Layer cake	t	t+1 minute	t-1 minute	t-11 minutes
	8" Square Baking Pan	**9" Square Baking Pan**	**9 x 13" Baking Pan****	
Brownies	t	t-5 minutes	t+5 minutes	

*(using 3 mini-loaf pans)   **(doubling the recipe)

Chapter 2

Quick Breads, Muffins and More

Savory Kale and Two-Cheese Scones

Start to finish: 1¼ hours (40 minutes active), plus cooling

Makes 12 large scones

70 grams (½ cup) dried currants

87 grams (4 cups) stemmed and finely chopped lacinato or curly kale (see headnote)

1 tablespoon lemon juice

455 grams (3½ cups) all-purpose flour, plus more for dusting

54 grams (¼ cup) white sugar

4 teaspoons baking powder

½ teaspoon baking soda

1¼ teaspoons table salt

2 teaspoons ground black pepper

226 grams (16 tablespoons) salted butter, cut into ½-inch pieces and chilled

113 grams (4 ounces) sharp or extra-sharp cheddar cheese, cut into ¼-inch cubes (1 cup)

15 grams (½ ounce) finely grated pecorino Romano cheese (¼ cup)

1½ cups cold buttermilk

1 large egg, beaten

36 grams (¼ cup) raw shelled sunflower seeds

When standard breakfast pastries are too sugary, bake a batch of these flavorful savory scones. This is our adaptation of the hearty kale and cheese scones created by Briana Holt, of Tandem Coffee + Bakery in Portland, Maine. Dried currants and a small amount of sugar complement the minerally, vegetal notes of the kale and counterbalance the saltiness of the cheddar and pecorino, while a good dose of black pepper adds an undercurrent of spice. Either lacinato kale (also called dinosaur or Tuscan kale) or curly kale will work; you will need an average-sized bunch to obtain the amount of chopped stemmed leaves for the recipe.

Don't allow the buttermilk and butter to lose their chill before use. Keeping them cold helps ensure that the dough will remain workable and won't become unmanageably soft during shaping. When rotating the baking sheets halfway through the baking time, work quickly so the oven doesn't lose too much heat.

Heat the oven to 375°F with racks in the upper- and lower-middle positions. Line 2 rimmed baking sheets with kitchen parchment. In a small microwave-safe bowl, stir together the currants and 2 tablespoons water. Microwave uncovered on high until warm and plump, about 30 seconds; set aside. In a medium bowl, toss the kale and lemon juice; set aside. In a large bowl, whisk together the flour, sugar, baking powder, baking soda, salt and pepper.

To a food processor, add about half of the flour mixture and scatter all of the butter over the top. Pulse until the butter is in pieces slightly larger than peas, 10 to 12 pulses. Transfer to the bowl with the remaining flour mixture. Add the currants and any remaining liquid, the cheddar, pecorino and kale. Toss with your hands until well combined. Add about ⅓ of the buttermilk and toss just a few times with your hands, making sure to scrape along the bottom of the bowl, until the liquid is absorbed. Add the remaining buttermilk in 2 more additions, tossing after each. After the final addition of buttermilk, toss until no dry, floury bits remain. The mixture will be quite crumbly and will not form a cohesive dough.

Lightly dust the counter with flour, turn the mixture out onto it, then give it a final toss. Divide it into 2 even piles, gathering each into a mound, then briefly knead each mound; it's fine if the mixture is still somewhat crumbly. Gather each mound into a ball, then press firmly into a cohesive 5-inch disk about 1½ inches thick. Using a chef's knife, cut each disk into 6 wedges. Place 6 wedges on each prepared baking sheet, spaced evenly apart. Brush the tops with the beaten egg, then sprinkle with the sunflower seeds, pressing lightly to adhere.

Bake until the scones are deep golden brown, 30 to 35 minutes, switching and rotating the baking sheets halfway through. Cool on the baking sheets on wire racks for 5 minutes, then transfer directly to a rack and cool for at least another 5 minutes. Serve warm or at room temperature.

WHY PREHEATING MATTERS

Though it is possible to bring foods to the correct internal temperature by starting them in a cold oven, there are various reasons to heat it before food goes inside. For one, an initial blast of heat is needed to jump start many reactions critical to a dish's final texture and flavor. Sugars begin to brown at 338°F, while proteins begin to brown at 284°F. And unlike stovetop cooking, cooking in the oven relies on indirect heat—meaning quite a bit of heat is required to ensure foods reach these temperatures. With baked goods, this immediate heat exposure also is crucial for oven spring, a term used to describe the initial expansion of dough or batter in the oven. And it evaporates moisture in butter, creating a burst of steam that's responsible for the flaky texture of pie crusts, puff pastry and biscuits.

Most recipes are written to take advantage of these effects, but we ran several tests to nail down the reasons. We found that cold-start cookies baked unevenly (and required a lot of monitoring), while puff pastry turned out unpleasantly pasty. So make sure to read the recipe first and ensure that your oven preheats to the required temperature (and the rack is in the right place) before placing your goods in the oven. Most ovens take 20 to 30 minutes to come to temperature; if you add a baking stone or steel, double that time to accommodate the heat it absorbs.

Tomato, Feta and Black Olive Quick Bread

**Start to finish: 1¼ hours
(30 minutes active), plus cooling**

Makes one 9-inch loaf

260 grams (2 cups) all-purpose flour

1 tablespoon baking powder

½ teaspoon baking soda

2 tablespoons finely chopped fresh dill

¼ teaspoon table salt

½ teaspoon ground black pepper

1 ripe medium tomato, stemmed, seeded and chopped

35 grams (¼ cup) pitted Kalamata olives, chopped

113 grams (4 ounces) feta cheese, crumbled (1 cup)

3 large eggs

½ cup extra-virgin olive oil

180 grams (¾ cup) plain whole-milk Greek yogurt

2 tablespoons pine nuts

The idea for this savory quick bread with Mediterranean flavors comes from Milk Street Facebook Community members Stephanie Huddleston and Alin Manukyan. Tomato, olives, feta and fresh dill add bursts of boldness, while olive oil and Greek yogurt keep the bread tender and moist. Store leftovers at room temperature in an airtight container or tightly wrapped for a few days. Toasting or rewarming slices will refresh the flavors.

Don't forget to seed the tomato. This removes excess moisture that otherwise can cause the crumb to be wet and soggy.

Heat the oven to 350°F with a rack in the middle position. Mist a 9-by-5-inch loaf pan with cooking spray, then line it with an 8-by-14-inch piece of kitchen parchment, allowing the excess to overhang the long sides of the pan.

In a large bowl, whisk together the flour, baking powder, baking soda, dill, salt and pepper. Add the tomato, olives and feta; toss until these ingredients are evenly distributed. In a medium bowl, whisk together the eggs, oil and yogurt. Add the egg mixture to the flour mixture; fold with a silicone spatula until just combined.

Scrape the batter into the prepared pan; smooth the top and sprinkle with the pine nuts. Bake until a toothpick inserted at the center of the loaf comes out with a few moist crumbs attached, 55 to 60 minutes.

Cool in the pan on a wire rack for about 15 minutes. Lift the loaf out of the pan using the parchment and set it directly on the rack. Cool completely.

Whole-Wheat and Muesli Soda Bread

Start to finish: 1½ hours
(25 minutes active), plus cooling

Makes one 9-inch loaf

2 cups cold buttermilk, plus
2 tablespoons for brushing

130 grams (1 to 1½ cups) no-sugar-
added muesli (see headnote), plus
2 tablespoons for sprinkling

280 grams (2 cups)
whole-wheat flour

130 grams (1 cup) all-purpose flour

54 grams (¼ cup) packed
brown sugar

1½ teaspoons baking soda

1 teaspoon baking powder

½ teaspoon table salt

141 grams (10 tablespoons)
salted butter, melted and slightly
cooled, divided

To make this hearty quick bread, we lean on a combination of whole-wheat and all-purpose flours, but also include muesli; it's a simple way to include a mix of nuts and other grains. We soak the muesli in buttermilk to hydrate and soften the ingredients. Just about any type of muesli will work, but use one that is not sweetened with added sugar. Bob's Red Mill, Familia and Alpen are brands that are widely available in supermarkets, but each has a different weight per cup, so it's best to weigh the muesli. If weighing is not an option, use 1 cup of Bob's Red Mill, 1¼ cups Familia or 1½ cups Alpen. Baking the loaf in a cast-iron skillet yields a beautifully browned bottom crust, but a parchment-lined baking sheet gets the job done, too, albeit with a slightly lighter crust. The soda bread is best the day it's baked, but leftovers will keep in an airtight container for up to three days.

Don't slice the bread while it's still warm. The texture is best and the loaf is easiest to slice after it has cooled to room temperature.

Heat the oven to 350°F with a rack in the middle position. In a medium bowl, stir together the 2 cups buttermilk and muesli; let stand for 15 minutes to soften. Meanwhile, in a large bowl, whisk together both flours, the sugar, baking soda, baking powder and salt. Brush the bottom and the sides of a 10- or 12-inch cast-iron skillet with 14 grams (1 tablespoon) melted butter.

Whisk 113 grams (8 tablespoons) of the remaining melted butter into the muesli-buttermilk mixture. Add to the dry ingredients. Using a silicone spatula, fold until a rough, shaggy dough forms; it's fine if the dough still shows some dry, floury patches. Using your hands and working directly in the bowl, gently and lightly fold the dough a few times just until cohesive; do not knead it. Shape the dough into a 6-inch round, then transfer it to the prepared skillet.

Using a serrated knife, score an X into the top of the dough, cutting about ½ inch deep. Brush the surface with 2 tablespoons buttermilk, then sprinkle evenly with the remaining 2 tablespoons muesli. Bake until golden brown and a toothpick inserted into the center comes out clean, 55 to 60 minutes.

Set the skillet on a wire rack and immediately brush the loaf with the remaining 14 grams (1 tablespoon) melted butter. Let cool for about 30 minutes, then transfer the bread directly to the rack and cool completely.

STEPS »

HOW TO MAKE WHOLE-WHEAT AND MUESLI SODA BREAD

1. In a medium bowl, stir together the buttermilk and muesli; let stand for 15 minutes to soften.

2. Whisk the melted butter into the muesli mixture, then add to the dry ingredients.

3. Fold until a rough, shaggy dough forms; it's fine if the dough still shows some dry, floury patches.

4. Using your hands, gently and lightly fold the dough a few times just until cohesive; do not knead it.

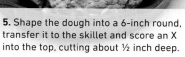

5. Shape the dough into a 6-inch round, transfer it to the skillet and score an X into the top, cutting about ½ inch deep.

6. Brush the surface with buttermilk, then sprinkle with the remaining muesli. Bake for 55 to 60 minutes.

Popovers

Popovers, which are believed to have originated in New England, are related to England's Yorkshire pudding and share an almost-identical ingredient list. In testing, we found using low-fat milk yields crispier, airier popovers. Also, having the batter at room temperature promotes a higher rise, so make sure the eggs are at room temperature and the milk is barely warm before mixing. Finally, poking the popovers with a skewer and baking them for another minute allows steam to escape, which helps prevent the pastries from deflating as they cool. This recipe works in a nonstick 6-cup popover pan or you can use a nonstick muffin pan to make 10 smaller popovers; the baking time will be the same.

Don't open the oven door to check on the popovers' progress as they bake. The heat loss may prevent the proper rise or cause already puffed popovers to deflate.

In a large bowl, whisk the eggs until well combined. Gradually whisk in the milk. Add the flour and salt, then whisk until just combined; do not overmix. Whisk in the melted shortening. (If desired, for easy pouring, transfer the batter to a 1-quart liquid measuring cup.) Cover and let stand at room temperature for at least 30 minutes or up to 2 hours.

About 20 minutes before baking, heat the oven to 400°F with a rack in the middle position. Using shortening, lightly coat a 6-cup nonstick popover pan or the 10 outer cups of a 12-cup nonstick standard muffin pan (leave the center 2 cups uncoated, as they will not be used). Dust the cups with flour, then tap out the excess.

Gently stir the batter to recombine, then divide it evenly among the prepared popover or muffin cups. Bake without opening the oven door until the popovers are well risen and deeply browned, about 45 minutes (the timing is the same for large and small popovers). Working quickly, open the oven door and, using a wooden skewer, poke a hole in each popover. Close the oven door and bake for 1 minute.

Remove the pan from the oven. Using tongs, immediately and gently transfer each popover to a wire rack. Serve warm or at room temperature.

Start to finish: 1 hour 40 minutes (20 minutes active)

Makes 6 large or 10 small popovers

3 large eggs, room temperature

1½ cups low-fat milk, warmed to about 100°F

195 grams (1½ cups) all-purpose flour, plus more for the pan

1½ teaspoons table salt

2 teaspoons vegetable shortening, melted and slightly cooled, plus unmelted shortening for the pan

Bolivian-Style Pepper Jack Cornbread

**Start to finish: 1¼ hours
(20 minutes active)**

Servings: 12

363 grams (2½ cups) fine yellow cornmeal, plus more for the pan

71 grams (⅓ cup) white sugar

2 teaspoons baking powder

¼ teaspoon cayenne pepper

1 tablespoon aniseed

1¼ teaspoons table salt

375 grams (3 cups) corn kernels (cut from 3 to 4 large ears; see headnote)

1 medium red, orange or yellow bell pepper, stemmed, seeded and chopped

1½ cups whole milk

4 large eggs

170 grams (12 tablespoons) salted butter, melted and slightly cooled

227 grams (8 ounces) pepper Jack cheese, cut into ½-inch cubes (2 cups)

Bolivian humintas al horno is not unlike a large, spiced tamale (anise and cinnamon are common) enriched with cheese. Its crumb is moist and dense, and its flavor is savory-sweet. Though traditional recipes might wrap the corn mixture in husks before baking, we opted for the ease of a 9-by-13-inch baking dish. Corn kernels cut from fresh ears work best here. To minimize the mess when cutting, stand the ear in the center of a large bowl. With a long knife, slice downward along the length of the cob, letting the kernels fall into the bowl. If fresh corn isn't in season, thawed frozen kernels are a fine substitute; drain in a colander before using. Refrigerate leftover cornbread for up to two days. To rewarm, wrap in foil and heat in a 300°F oven for 10 to 15 minutes, or melt a little butter in a nonstick skillet, add slices and heat for one to two minutes per side.

Don't use coarse cornmeal; its texture is too gritty. And don't overbake this cornbread or it will be crumbly and dry.

HOW TO MAKE BOLIVIAN-STYLE PEPPER JACK CORNBREAD

1. In a medium bowl, whisk the cornmeal, sugar, baking powder, cayenne, aniseed and salt.

2. In a blender, puree the corn, bell pepper and milk, then transfer to a bowl. Whisk in the eggs and melted butter.

3. Add the cornmeal mixture to the wet ingredients, then whisk until smooth.

4. Pour about half the batter into the prepared pan and spread in an even layer.

5. Scatter the cheese cubes evenly over the batter.

6. Pour the remaining batter evenly over the cheese, then bake at 375°F for 35 to 40 minutes.

Heat the oven to 375°F with a rack in the lower-middle position. Mist a 9-by-13-inch baking pan with cooking spray, dust evenly with cornmeal, then tap out the excess. In a medium bowl, whisk together the cornmeal, sugar, baking powder, cayenne, aniseed and salt. Set aside.

In a blender, combine the corn, bell pepper and milk. Process until very smooth, about 2 minutes, scraping the sides as needed. Transfer to a large bowl and whisk in the eggs and butter. Whisk in the cornmeal mixture until smooth. Pour about half the batter into the prepared pan and spread in an even layer. Sprinkle the cheese on top, then add the remaining batter in an even layer.

Bake until a toothpick inserted at the center comes out clean, 35 to 40 minutes. Cool in the pan on a wire rack for 30 minutes. Serve warm.

Browned Butter Skillet Cornbread

**Start to finish: 30 minutes
(15 minutes active), plus cooling**

Makes one 10-inch cornbread

326 grams (2¼ cups) fine yellow cornmeal, preferably stone-ground

2 teaspoons white sugar

2 teaspoons baking powder

½ teaspoon baking soda

½ teaspoon table salt

2 cups buttermilk

2 large eggs

113 grams (8 tablespoons) salted butter, cut into 6 to 8 pieces

This cornbread is made with only cornmeal—no wheat flour—and just 2 teaspoons sugar, so it's closer in flavor and texture to Southern cornbread than to sweet, cakey-crumbed Northern style. We brown the butter for the batter and for coating the skillet, which brings rich, nutty notes to complement the flavor of the corn. For best flavor, opt for stone-ground fine cornmeal, but standard cornmeal works, too. A cast-iron skillet, 10 inches in diameter, produces a fantastic, deeply browned, crisp bottom crust and nice, straight sides. A conventional skillet (not nonstick) with an oven-safe handle is fine, too, but the bottom of the bread will be lighter in color and not quite as crisp, and the sides will be rounded because of the skillet's sloped shape. We like to invert the cornbread out of the pan for serving, but if you prefer you can cut wedges right in the skillet, though the bottom will soften slightly as it cools.

OVER THE TOP

Chipotle-Honey Butter

**Start to finish: 10 minutes
Makes about ½ cup**

In a medium bowl, combine **113 grams (8 tablespoons) salted butter** (room temperature), **2 tablespoons honey, 1 table-spoon minced chipotle chili in adobo sauce plus 2 teaspoons adobo sauce** and a **pinch of kosher salt.** Whip with a hand mixer on medium-high speed, scraping the bowl as needed, until light and fluffy, about 2 minutes. Serve at room temperature.

Don't pour the batter into the pan until the skillet has heated a couple of minutes, and be sure to warm the batter until bubbling at the edges before sliding the skillet into the oven. This quickly sets the bottom surface and jumpstarts the baking, which aids with browning and prevents the bread from sticking to the pan come time to serve.

Heat the oven to 450°F with a rack in the middle position. In a large bowl, whisk together the cornmeal, sugar, baking powder, baking soda and salt. In a 1-quart liquid measuring cup or medium bowl, whisk together the buttermilk and eggs.

In a 10-inch cast-iron skillet over medium, heat the butter, stirring, until it begins to smell nutty, about 4 minutes. Pour 6 tablespoons of the butter into the dry ingredients, leaving about 2 tablespoons in the pan; set the skillet off the heat. Whisk the buttermilk-egg mixture into the dry ingredients until smooth.

Return the skillet to medium and cook the remaining butter, stirring, until the milk solids are toasted and browned, about 2 minutes. Coat the sides of the skillet with butter by either swirling the pan or with a brush. Pour in the batter and cook, without stirring, until bubbling at the edges, about 1 minute. Transfer to the oven and bake until light golden brown and a toothpick inserted at the center comes out with few crumbs attached, 15 to 18 minutes.

Transfer the skillet to a wire rack (the handle will be hot). Cool for about 5 minutes, then invert the cornbread onto the rack, removing the pan. Serve warm or at room temperature.

OVER THE TOP

Jalapeño-Scallion Butter

Start to finish: 15 minutes
Makes about ½ cup

In a medium bowl, combine **113 grams** (**8 tablespoons**) **salted butter** (room temperature), **2 scallions** (thinly sliced), **1 small jalapeño chili** (stemmed, seeded and minced), **1 teaspoon grated lime zest plus 1 teaspoon lime juice**, **¼ teaspoon ground black pepper** and a pinch of **kosher salt**. Whip with a hand mixer on medium-high speed, scraping the bowl as needed, until light and fluffy, about 2 minutes. Serve at room temperature.

BAKING BASIC

CHOOSE BAKEWARE WITH CARE

Not all bakeware is created equal. Indeed, the material a pan is made of affects how the foods in it cook. Metal is a far better conductor of heat than glass, and that means metal pans cook more quickly. Additionally, the color of your pans plays a role, too. Dark-colored metal pans absorb and distribute heat more quickly than light-colored pans. To find out what this means for our baking, we prepared pound cakes using loaf pans made from glass, light-colored aluminum and dark nonstick-coated aluminum. In each case, we used the same recipe, baked it at the same temperature and for the same amount of time. As expected, the cake baked in the glass pan had the lightest crust, with relatively little browning. The dark nonstick pan had the darkest crust, even to the point of overbaking at the edges. The lighter aluminum pan fell somewhere in the middle. Our takeaway: Glass pans run less risk of overbaking, but also make it harder to achieve a rich, dark, flavorfully browned crust. By the same token, when baking with dark nonstick pans—unless you are using a recipe that was specifically designed for this type of bakeware—it's a good idea to reduce either the temperature or baking time (or both) to prevent tough, overbaked crusts.

Neapolitan Salami-Provolone Buns

**Start to finish: 2 hours
(35 minutes active), plus cooling**

Makes twelve 3-inch buns

170 grams (6 ounces) thinly sliced salami, roughly chopped

113 grams (4 ounces) thinly sliced prosciutto, roughly chopped

488 grams (3¾ cups) all-purpose flour, plus more for dusting

1 tablespoon instant yeast

2 teaspoons ground black pepper

170 grams (12 tablespoons) cold salted butter, cut into ½-inch cubes

227 grams (8 ounces) provolone cheese, preferably aged provolone, cut into ¼-inch cubes

1¼ cups warm water (100°F to 110°F)

At the tiny Salumeria Pio in Naples, Pio di Benedetto bakes and sells his much-simplified version of a regional favorite, panini napoletani. The richly flavored buns typically are made from yeasted dough layered with meat and cheese, then rolled, sliced and baked. Di Benedetto mixes the meat and cheese right into the dough. Instead of lard, we opt for butter, though you can substitute an equal amount of lard for 4 tablespoons of the butter. In Naples, di Benedetto sells his buns as a breakfast item, but they're also great served with braised beans or hearty greens. Leftovers keep and reheat well. Store in an airtight container in the refrigerator for up to two days; rewarm on a baking sheet tented with foil in a 350°F oven for 15 to 20 minutes.

Don't finely chop the cured meats. Chop them only roughly so they have presence in the baked breads. After microwaving, be sure to cool the meats to room temperature. If they have any warmth, they will cause the butter to soften, making the dough sticky and difficult to handle.

In a large microwave-safe bowl, combine the salami and prosciutto. Microwave on high, uncovered, until the meats just begin to crisp, about 1 minute, stirring once halfway through. Pour off and discard any fat in the bowl; cool to room temperature.

Line 2 rimmed baking sheets with kitchen parchment. In a food processor, combine the flour, yeast and pepper; pulse until well combined, about 12 pulses. Scatter in the butter, then pulse until the mixture resembles coarse sand, 10 to 12 pulses. Empty the mixture into the large bowl containing the meats, then add the provolone. Using a silicone spatula, fold until the ingredients are evenly distributed. Drizzle the water over the mixture, then fold with the spatula until the mixture comes together in a cohesive, evenly moistened dough.

Using a ½-cup dry measuring cup, scoop the dough into 12 even portions, lightly packing the dough into the cup and placing 6 on each prepared baking sheet, evenly spaced; the dough should easily invert out of the cup in a puck-like shape. Cover each baking sheet with a kitchen towel and let rise at room temperature for 1 hour.

Meanwhile, heat the oven to 425°F with a rack in the middle position. Uncover 1 baking sheet and bake until the buns are golden brown, 25 to 27 minutes. Remove from the oven and, using a wide metal spatula, transfer the buns to a wire rack. Bake the second batch in the same way. Cool to room temperature.

Colombian Cheese Buns

**Start to finish: 1½ hours
(30 minutes active), plus cooling**

Makes 20 buns

16-ounce container low-fat
small-curd cottage cheese

1 large egg

248 grams (2 cups) tapioca starch
(see headnote)

137 grams (1 cup) bread flour

37 grams (¼ cup) white or yellow
masarepa (see headnote)

39 grams (3 tablespoons) white
sugar

2 teaspoons baking powder

¾ teaspoon table salt

227 grams (8 ounces) queso Oaxaca
cheese, shredded (2 cups)

227 grams (8 ounces) cotija cheese,
crumbled (2 cups)

Savory but lightly sweetened and with a moist, chewy crumb,
almojábanas are cheesy, bun-shaped breads that we first tasted in
Ubaté—Colombia's center of dairy production. The region boasts an
abundance of locally made cheeses, such as cuajada and campesino,
two types often used in the making of almojábanas. Cuajada and
campesino are high in moisture and low in fat, so despite the impressive amounts we saw mixed into almojábana dough, the baked
buns were always soft and airy, never greasy or heavy. To replicate
that texture using ingredients readily available in the U.S., we turned
to a combination of low-fat cottage cheese, salty cotija and Oaxacan
cheese. Cotija is dry and crumbly, whereas queso Oaxaca is creamy
and mozzarella-like; both are Mexican cheeses that can be found in
Latin American grocery stores, as well as most well-stocked supermarkets. In addition to bread flour, masarepa—the precooked,
fine-ground cornmeal used to make arepas—is a key ingredient in
many traditional recipes. Though it may look similar to products like
masa or masa harina, they are not interchangeable, as they are made
from nixtamalized corn, meaning the grain has been treated with an
alkali. Corn flour or cornmeal, which are dried and ground but not
precooked, won't do the trick, either. Finally, many cooks also add
tapioca starch, also called tapioca flour, which gives the buns their
characteristic chewiness; look for it alongside the cornstarch or
alternative flours. Store extra buns in an airtight container at room
temperature for up to two days; reheat in a 400°F oven for about five
minutes before serving.

Don't use full-fat cottage cheese; it will cause the buns to spread far too much. Be
sure to select the small-curd, low-fat variety with either one or two percent milkfat.

Heat the oven to 375°F with a rack in the middle position. Mist 2 rimmed baking
sheets with cooking spray. In a small bowl, whisk together the cottage cheese and
egg. In a stand mixer, combine the tapioca starch, bread flour, masarepa, sugar,
baking powder and salt; mix with the paddle attachment on low until well combined, about 10 seconds.

Add the cottage cheese mixture, Oaxacan cheese and cotija; mix on low, scraping
the bowl and pushing the dough off the attachment as needed, until the dough is
curdy and evenly moistened, about 4 minutes. If the dough tries to climb out of the
bowl, stop the mixer, push it back down and continue mixing.

Divide the dough into 18 portions (about 80 grams or ¼ cup each), placing them on
an unfloured counter. Roll each portion between your hands, forming it into a

smooth ball. Arrange 9 dough balls, evenly spaced, on each baking sheet, then lightly press with your hand to slightly flatten.

One baking sheet at a time, bake until golden brown, 25 to 27 minutes. Cool on the baking sheet on a wire rack for about 5 minutes. Transfer directly to the rack and serve barely warm or at room temperature.

Brazilian Cheese Puffs

Start to finish: 40 minutes

Makes 24 puffs

186 grams (1½ cups) tapioca starch

⅔ cup whole milk

⅓ cup grapeseed or other neutral oil

1 large egg

½ teaspoon table salt

½ teaspoon dry mustard

85 grams (3 ounces) Asiago cheese, shredded (1¼ cups)

These savory puffs—called pão de queijo—are similar to popovers, with two important differences. Tapioca starch (also called tapioca flour) gives them a unique chewiness, while a generous dose of cheese makes them particularly savory. In Brazil, the cheese of choice is queijo minas curado. We found that more widely available Asiago had just the right balance of salty-sharp flavor to make delicious puffs. Pão de queijo are best eaten within a couple hours of baking, but the puffs can be frozen and reheated in a 350°F oven for five to 10 minutes (do not thaw before reheating). You will need a nonstick 24-cup mini muffin pan for this recipe.

Don't forget to stop the blender and scrape the jar as needed when processing the batter. This ensures the tapioca starch that clings to the sides of the jar will be fully incorporated. Don't worry about over blending. There's no wheat flour in the batter, so there's no risk of developing gluten that can toughen the puffs.

Heat the oven to 400°F with a rack in the middle position. Mist a nonstick 24-cup mini muffin pan with cooking spray. In a blender, combine all ingredients. Blend until smooth, about 1 minute, scraping the sides of the blender jar as needed.

Divide the batter among the cups of the prepared muffin pan. Bake until the puffs are well risen and deep golden brown, 20 to 25 minutes. Immediately transfer the puffs from the pan to a wire rack by lifting them out one at a time. Serve warm or room temperature.

> **VARIATION**
>
> ## Brazilian Cheese Puffs with Gruyère and Chives
>
> Substitute an equal amount of **Gruyère cheese** for the Asiago. After blending, stir in **2 tablespoons finely chopped fresh chives**.

Herbed Irish Ale Bread with Caraway

This quick, easy beer bread is savory with caraway, dill, chives, black pepper and a full bottle of Irish red ale, which lends the loaf yeasty notes and hints of butterscotch. Smithwick's and Killian's are commonly available brands in the U.S. If you like the coffee-like bittersweetness of stout, Guinness also works wonderfully. An electric spice grinder is the best way to coarsely grind the caraway; pulse the seeds a few times, but don't pulverize them to a fine powder. If the butter for brushing the just-baked loaf solidifies upon standing, simply re-melt it a few minutes before removing the bread from the oven. Serve slices with corned beef and cabbage or slathered with softened butter.

Don't whisk vigorously after adding the beer. Gentle mixing prevents excessive foaming as well as gluten development that toughens the bread. Don't slice the bread while warm. Like all quick breads, this loaf slices more easily and cleanly after it has cooled to room temperature.

Heat the oven to 375°F with a rack in the middle position. Mist a 9-by-5-inch loaf pan with cooking spray. In a large bowl, whisk together both flours, the baking powder, baking soda, caraway, salt and pepper. Add the dill and chives, then toss until evenly distributed. In a small bowl, combine the honey and 57 grams (4 tablespoons) melted butter; whisk until well combined. Drizzle the mixture into the dry ingredients, then add the beer and, if using an 11.2-ounce bottle, add 1½ tablespoons water. Whisk gently just until evenly moistened; do not overmix. The batter will be thick.

Scrape the batter into the prepared pan and smooth the surface. Brush the top with 14 grams (1 tablespoon) of the remaining melted butter. Bake until golden brown and a toothpick inserted at the center comes out clean, 40 to 45 minutes.

Remove from the oven and immediately brush the top with the remaining 14 grams (1 tablespoon) melted butter. Cool in the pan for about 5 minutes, then invert onto a wire rack. Turn the loaf right side up and cool to room temperature, about 1½ hours.

**Start to finish: 1 hour
(20 minutes active), plus cooling**

Makes one 9-inch loaf

260 grams (2 cups) all-purpose flour

60 grams (½ cup) cake flour

1 tablespoon baking powder

½ teaspoon baking soda

2 tablespoons caraway seeds, coarsely ground (see headnote)

½ teaspoon table salt

1 teaspoon ground black pepper

¼ cup finely chopped fresh dill

¼ cup finely chopped fresh chives

1 tablespoon honey

85 grams (6 tablespoons) salted butter, melted, divided

11.2- or 12-ounce bottle Irish red ale, such as Smithwick's or Killian's (see headnote)

Orange-Cranberry Soda Bread with White Chocolate Chunks

**Start to finish: 1¼ hours
(25 minutes active), plus cooling**

Makes one 7½-inch loaf

210 grams (1½ cups) dried cranberries, roughly chopped

1 tablespoon grated orange zest, plus 2 tablespoons orange juice

1¾ cups cold buttermilk

325 grams (2½ cups) all-purpose flour, plus more for dusting

105 grams (¾ cup) whole-wheat flour

1 teaspoon baking soda

1 teaspoon table salt

113 grams (4 ounces) white chocolate, chopped into ½-inch chunks

This is not your traditional Irish soda bread. The crumb is fragrant with orange zest and studded with tangy dried cranberries plus bits of creamy white chocolate that add the perfect amount of sweetness. We adapted the recipe from "Rising Hope" by Rachel Stonehouse and Kaila H. Johnson, both members of the team at London's Luminary Bakery, a social enterprise that supports disadvantaged women by teaching them baking skills. The bread is the creation of Aine, the former head baker at Luminary Bakery. The rustic loaf is special enough for a holiday breakfast or brunch, but it comes together so quickly and easily that it's great at any time of year.

Don't chop the white chocolate into tiny bits. Keep the pieces chunky—roughly ½ inch—otherwise they will simply disappear into the crumb. Also, don't knead the dough as if it was a yeasted dough. Handle it gently, as if making biscuits or scones. A light, gentle touch helps ensure a tender crumb.

Heat the oven to 400°F with a rack in the middle position. Line a rimmed baking sheet with kitchen parchment. In a medium microwave-safe bowl, stir together the cranberries and orange juice. Microwave, uncovered, on high for 1 minute, stirring once halfway through. Stir again, then set aside until cooled to room temperature. In a liquid measuring cup, stir together the orange zest and buttermilk.

In a large bowl, whisk together both flours, the baking soda and salt. Add the cooled cranberries and the white chocolate; toss until the ingredients are evenly distributed. Make a well in the middle of the mixture and pour in the buttermilk. Using a silicone spatula, fold the buttermilk into the flour mixture until a rough, shaggy dough forms; it's fine if the dough still shows some dry, floury patches.

Lightly flour the counter and turn the dough out onto it. Using your hands and a metal bench scraper, gently and lightly fold the dough a few times just until cohesive; do not knead it. Shape the dough into a ball and, using the bench scraper to loosen it from the counter, transfer it to the prepared baking sheet. Lightly dust the top with flour. Using a serrated knife, score an X into the top of the dough, cutting about ¾ inch deep.

Bake until the bread is deep golden brown, 35 to 40 minutes; if turned upside down and tapped on the bottom, the loaf should sound hollow. Cool for about 10 minutes on the baking sheet on a wire rack, then transfer the loaf to the rack and cool for at least 1 hour before slicing.

French Spice Bread (Pain d'Epices)

Start to finish: 1 hour 25 minutes (10 minutes active), plus cooling

Makes one 9-inch loaf

133 grams (8 tablespoons) salted butter, melted, plus more for the pan

228 grams (1¾ cups) all-purpose flour, plus more for the pan

100 grams (1 cup) almond flour

1½ teaspoons ground cinnamon

1 teaspoon baking soda

1 teaspoon ground ginger

½ teaspoon ground mace

¼ teaspoon table salt

½ teaspoon ground black pepper

334 grams (1 cup) honey

½ cup whole milk

2 large eggs

2 tablespoons minced crystallized ginger

1 tablespoon finely grated fresh ginger

2 teaspoons grated orange zest

Honey-based spice breads and cakes have been produced in one form or another throughout Europe since the Middle Ages. For good reason: The hygroscopic honey retains moisture, ensuring the breads remain moist during storage. Its antibacterial properties also act as a preservative. Meanwhile, the spices—and therefore the flavor—only improve with time. We wanted a lighter, less sweet alternative to the more common gingerbread, something that tastes as good straight up as it does toasted and topped with butter and marmalade for a quick breakfast or afternoon-coffee accompaniment. This French version is just that. For a fruitier version, add 1 cup golden raisins, chopped dates, figs or dried apricots. Melting the butter in a liquid measuring cup in the microwave, then using the same cup for the honey, made it easy to measure out and add the honey; it slid right out. For maximum spice flavor, we used pepper and three kinds of ginger. If you can't find crystallized (candied) ginger, just skip it; the cake still will be delicious. And if you can't find ground mace, substitute ¼ teaspoon each of ground nutmeg and allspice.

Don't use baking spray in place of butter. While it's fine in many situations, butter helps create the dark crust that sets pain d'épices apart from other quick breads. Use melted butter and a pastry brush to coat it liberally over the inside of the pan.

Heat the oven to 325°F with a rack in the upper-middle position. Coat the bottom and sides of a 9-by-5-inch loaf pan with butter. Dust evenly with all-purpose flour, then tap out the excess.

In a medium bowl, whisk together both flours, the cinnamon, baking soda, ground ginger, mace, salt and pepper. In a large bowl, whisk together the butter and honey until smooth. Add the milk, eggs, crystallized ginger, fresh ginger and orange zest; whisk until thoroughly combined.

Add the flour mixture to the wet ingredients and fold only until no dry flour remains. Transfer the batter into the prepared pan, then bake until firm to the touch and a toothpick inserted at the center comes out with a few moist crumbs, 65 to 70 minutes. Let cool in the pan on a wire rack for 10 minutes. Remove from the pan and let cool completely, about 2 hours.

HOW TO GET OUT OF STICKY SITUATIONS

When you need to measure peanut butter, molasses or honey—or any sticky ingredient—don't settle for losing half of the volume to the measuring cup, and half of your cooking time attempting to scrape it out. Instead, coat the measuring cup with cooking spray first. The ingredient will slide out of the cup easily. With this trick, cleanup becomes a breeze, and you lose no time swiping your spatula around the measuring cup to save any drops of your honey or syrup.

Rice Flour Drop Biscuits

Start to finish: 50 minutes
(15 minutes active)

Makes eight biscuits

195 grams (1½ cups)
all-purpose flour

80 grams (½ cup) rice flour
(see headnote)

2 teaspoons white sugar

2½ teaspoons baking powder

½ teaspoon baking soda

½ teaspoon table salt

85 grams (6 tablespoons) cold
salted butter in a single chunk, plus
28 grams (2 tablespoons) salted
butter, melted

1 cup cold buttermilk

VARIATION

Rice Flour Drop Biscuits with Bacon, Cheddar and Dill

Omit the salt and toss **8 ounces bacon** (cooked and chopped), **4 ounces (1 cup) shredded extra-sharp cheddar cheese** and **2 tablespoons finely chopped fresh dill** into the flour mixture before grating in the butter.

Drop biscuits are a breeze to make because the dough is simply scooped and dropped onto a baking sheet—no rolling or cutting required. Thanks to a combination of all-purpose flour and rice flour—the latter does not contain gluten that can toughen—our biscuits have a superbly light, tender crumb to contrast the crisp exteriors. We especially like them made with brown rice flour, as it lends a subtly nutty flavor, but white rice flour works equally well. Bob's Red Mill and Arrowhead Mills are two brands widely available in supermarkets. Keeping the ingredients cold also helps produce tender biscuits and prevents the dough from becoming unmanageably sticky.

Don't use sweet (also called glutinous) rice flour, which is flour made by milling a type of rice that is especially high in starch. It won't work in this recipe.

In a large bowl, whisk together both flours, the sugar, baking powder, baking soda and salt. Refrigerate the flour mixture while the oven heats. Heat the oven to 450°F with a rack in the middle position. Line a rimmed baking sheet with kitchen parchment.

Remove the flour mixture from the refrigerator. Set a box grater in the bowl and grate the 85 grams (6 tablespoons) cold butter on the large holes. Using your hands and working quickly, toss the butter into the dry ingredients until evenly distributed. Add the buttermilk and, using a silicone spatula, fold it into the flour-butter mixture until evenly moistened and no dry patches remain; the dough will be sticky, with a curdy appearance.

Using a ⅓-cup dry measuring cup, scoop the dough into 8 mounds onto the prepared baking sheet, spacing them evenly; if needed, use a small spatula or spoon to pull the dough out of the cup. Brush the mounds with the melted butter.

Bake until golden brown, 15 to 18 minutes. Cool on the baking sheet on a wire rack for at least 10 minutes, then transfer directly to the rack. Serve warm or at room temperature.

Toasted Oat and Maple Scones

**Start to finish: 1¼ hours
(45 minutes active)**

Makes 8 scones

FOR THE SCONES:

150 grams (1½ cups) old-fashioned rolled oats

½ cup maple syrup (see headnote), divided

½ cup cold buttermilk

1 large egg

260 grams (2 cups) all-purpose flour, plus more for dusting

71 grams (⅓ cup) white sugar

1 tablespoon baking powder

½ teaspoon baking soda

½ teaspoon table salt

½ teaspoon freshly grated nutmeg

198 grams (14 tablespoons) cold salted butter, cut into 1-tablespoon pieces

FOR THE GLAZE:

28 grams (2 tablespoons) salted butter, melted

124 grams (1 cup) powdered sugar

2 tablespoons maple syrup

1 tablespoon buttermilk, plus more if needed

¼ teaspoon freshly grated nutmeg

These hearty scones get deep, sweet flavor by coating rolled oats in maple syrup before toasting them, resulting in amplified nuttiness and crunch. Processing a portion of the oat mixture with the other dry ingredients distributes the flavor and texture through every bite, while freshly grated nutmeg adds warmth and spice. To balance maple's sweeter notes, tangy buttermilk moistens and binds the dough and helps thin the simple powdered-sugar glaze. The darker the maple syrup, the better the scones will taste. We recommend seeking out either "dark" or "very dark" syrup for the boldest, richest flavor. If you need to pack or transport the scones, wait for 30 minutes or so to allow the glaze to fully set. These are best the day they're baked, but stored in an airtight container, extras will keep for up to two days.

Don't bake immediately after cutting the dough into wedges. The scones need at least 15 minutes of chilling first, otherwise they tend to spread and lose their shape in the oven.

Heat the oven to 400°F with a rack in the middle position. Line a rimmed baking sheet with kitchen parchment. In a large bowl, toss the oats with ¼ cup maple syrup until evenly coated. Distribute in an even layer on the baking sheet; reserve the bowl. Bake until golden brown, 7 to 8 minutes, stirring once halfway through. Cool on a wire rack for 10 minutes, then transfer to a small bowl; reserve the baking sheet and parchment. Increase the oven to 450°F.

In a small bowl or 2-cup liquid measuring cup, whisk together the buttermilk, egg and the ¼ cup remaining maple syrup; set aside. In a food processor, combine ½ cup of the toasted oats, the flour, white sugar, baking powder, baking soda, salt and nutmeg. Process until the oats are as fine as the flour, about 15 seconds.

Scatter the butter over the flour mixture, then pulse until the pieces are no larger than about ¼ inch, about 15 pulses. Transfer to the reserved bowl. Add ¾ cup of the remaining toasted oats to the flour-butter mixture; toss. Pour in the buttermilk mixture, then fold with a silicone spatula just until a shaggy dough forms; it's OK if some dry pockets remain.

Lightly dust the counter with flour, then turn the dough out onto it. Using your hands and working quickly, gently knead the dough just until cohesive, about 5 turns; do not overwork the dough. Gather the dough and press it into a 6-inch disk about 1½ inches thick. Using a chef's knife, cut the disk in half, then cut each half into 4 wedges. Place the wedges on the reserved baking sheet, spaced evenly apart; refrigerate uncovered for at least 15 minutes or up to 1 hour.

Bake the scones until golden brown, 13 to 15 minutes. Cool on the baking sheet on a wire rack for 5 minutes. Transfer directly to the rack and cool for another 5 minutes; reserve the baking sheet.

To make the glaze, in a medium bowl, whisk the melted butter, powdered sugar, maple syrup, buttermilk and nutmeg until smooth. The glaze should have the consistency of pourable yogurt; if it's too thick, thin it by stirring in additional buttermilk 1 teaspoon at a time. Set the rack with the scones in the reserved baking sheet. Using a spoon, drizzle the glaze onto the scones (it's fine if they're still slightly warm), then sprinkle with the remaining toasted oats. Let the glaze dry for at least 10 minutes.

Lemon-Raspberry Olive Oil Muffins

Start to finish: 45 minutes (20 minutes active), plus cooling

Makes 12 muffins

½ cup extra-virgin olive oil, plus more for the pan

358 grams (2¾ cups) all-purpose flour

48 grams (⅓ cup) fine cornmeal

2 teaspoons baking powder

½ teaspoon baking soda

¼ teaspoon table salt

214 grams (1 cup) white sugar

2 teaspoons grated lemon zest, plus 3 tablespoons lemon juice

2 large eggs

240 grams (1 cup) plain whole-milk yogurt

6-ounce container raspberries (about 1¼ cups)

160 grams (½ cup) raspberry jam

Turbinado sugar, for sprinkling (see headnote)

A combination of olive oil and yogurt makes for moist muffins with just the right richness and a hearty, rustic crumb. Cornmeal adds texture as well as earthy sweetness—a perfect complement to the fresh raspberries and raspberry jam folded into the batter. For added crunch and a sparkling exterior, we sprinkle turbinado sugar over the muffins before baking. Turbinado is a less refined sugar with large, golden crystals and notes of molasses. If you can't find it, simply sprinkle an additional teaspoon of white sugar over each muffin.

Don't substitute vegetable or another neutral oil for the olive oil. The flavor of the muffins depends on olive oil. Opt for a good quality, fruity extra-virgin olive oil.

Heat the oven to 400°F with a rack in the upper-middle position. Brush the cups and surface of a standard 12-cup muffin pan with oil. In a medium bowl, whisk together the flour, cornmeal, baking powder, baking soda and salt; set aside.

In a large bowl, combine the white sugar and lemon zest; rub together with your fingers until fragrant and beginning to clump. Whisk in the ½ cup oil and eggs until well combined and slightly thickened, about 30 seconds. Whisk in the yogurt and lemon juice. Add the flour mixture and fold with a silicone spatula until just shy of incorporated. Scatter the raspberries over the batter and fold a few times. Add the jam and fold gently until the batter has a marbled appearance.

Scoop the batter into the cups of the prepared muffin pan, dividing it evenly. Sprinkle each with a scant ¼ teaspoon turbinado sugar. Bake until the muffins are golden brown and a skewer inserted into the centers comes out clean, 25 to 28 minutes, rotating the pan halfway through. Cool in the pan on a wire rack for 15 minutes. Lift the muffins out of the pan and set directly on the rack. Serve warm or at room temperature.

BAKING BASIC

OLIVE OIL VS. BUTTER

Whether it's for flavor or health reasons, some sources online suggest substituting olive oil for butter in baked goods. But though oil and butter often are interchangeable in savory cooking, the swap isn't as simple when baking. For biscuits, scones and pie pastry, in which cold, solid butter is cut into dry ingredients until reduced to pebbly bits, oil is not an appropriate substitute—it would be absorbed by the dry ingredients and the dough would be sodden and unworkable. Cakes, quick breads, brownies and some types of cookies have a bit more wiggle room. The butter in these baked goods usually is either creamed or melted. Creaming involves beating softened butter with sugar, incorporating air into the mixture that helps the batter or dough rise during baking. If the butter is melted, however, it often simply is whisked with the sugar and/or eggs; no air is incorporated, and rise is usually provided in large part by either baking powder, baking soda, beaten egg whites or a combination. In recipes in which the butter is creamed, oil is not an appropriate substitute because it cannot trap and hold air the way softened butter can.

However, in baked goods made with melted butter, oil is a reasonable substitute. Cakes, in particular, stand to benefit from using oil because unlike butter, oil remains fluid at room temperature, which contributes to a moist mouthfeel and softer crumb (take, for instance, carrot cake and chiffon cake). If you're considering extra-virgin olive oil, keep in mind that its flavor is assertive. We found that it was not a good match for a plain vanilla cake—milder-tasting regular or light olive oil are better choices. But we did find that extra-virgin's fruity, peppery notes work well with spices, citrus and chocolate. In some cases, we found that baked goods made with olive oil did not brown as well as those made with butter. Also bear in mind that butter has a water content of about 16 percent, so if you're substituting oil—which contains no water—you may want to scale back a bit to prevent greasiness. As a guide, 8 tablespoons of butter (1 stick) contain approximately ¼ ounce, or 1½ teaspoons, of water.

Zucchini Bread with Orange Zest and Chocolate Chunks

Unlike basic (and often boring) zucchini bread, this quick bread is saturated with citrusy orange flavor thanks to a simple step of rubbing orange zest into the sugar. This draws out the zest's essential oils and evenly distributes them throughout the loaf, which also is studded with chunks of bittersweet chocolate. Ample zucchini shreds dot the crumb with flecks of green and keep it amazingly moist, but the summer squash flavor disappears into the background. We also sprinkle the bread, inspired by a recipe from "Tartine" by Elisabeth M. Prueitt and Chad Robertson, with turbinado sugar, a coarse, golden raw sugar, to add a crystalline crunch and sparkle. If you can't find turbinado, use an equal amount of white sugar. Tightly wrapped and refrigerated, the loaf will keep for up to five days; bring to room temperature to serve.

Don't skip the step of rubbing the orange zest into the sugar. This draws out the zest's essential oils and distributes them for bright citrus flavor throughout the loaf.

Heat the oven to 350°F with a rack in the middle position. Mist a 9-by-5-inch loaf pan with cooking spray, dust evenly with flour, then tap out the excess. In a medium bowl, whisk together the flour, baking powder, baking soda and salt.

In a large bowl, combine the white sugar and orange zest. Use your fingers to rub them together until fragrant and the sugar clumps. Whisk in the eggs, oil and orange juice. Stir in the zucchini, then the flour mixture; stir until almost completely incorporated. Stir in the chocolate.

Scrape the batter into the prepared pan and smooth the top. Sprinkle evenly with the turbinado sugar. Bake until well browned and a toothpick inserted at the center comes out with a few moist crumbs attached, 65 to 70 minutes.

Cool in the pan on a wire rack for about 10 minutes. Turn out the loaf and cool completely before serving.

Start to finish: 1½ hours (30 minutes active), plus cooling

Makes one 9-inch loaf

260 grams (2 cups) all-purpose flour, plus more for the pan

½ teaspoon baking powder

½ teaspoon baking soda

½ teaspoon table salt

161 grams (¾ cup) white sugar

1 tablespoon grated orange zest, plus ¼ cup orange juice

2 large eggs

⅓ cup grapeseed or other neutral oil

340 grams (12 ounces) zucchini, shredded on the large holes of a box grater (about 3 cups)

113 grams (4 ounces) bittersweet chocolate, roughly chopped, or 113 grams (¾ cup) bittersweet chocolate chunks

1 tablespoon turbinado or white sugar (see headnote)

Browned Butter–Cardamom Banana Bread

Start to finish: 1¼ hours (25 minutes active), plus cooling

Makes one 9-inch loaf

113 grams (8 tablespoons) salted butter, plus more for the pan

260 grams cups (2 cups) all-purpose flour, plus more for the pan

1 teaspoon baking powder

1 teaspoon baking soda

½ teaspoon table salt

1¼ teaspoons ground cardamom

533 grams (2 cups) mashed ripe bananas (from 4 or 5 large bananas)

149 grams (¾ cup) packed dark brown sugar

2 teaspoons vanilla extract

2 large eggs

1 tablespoon white sugar (optional)

For a more flavorful banana bread without more effort, we paired one of banana's most complementary spices, cardamom, with nutty browned butter. Blooming the spice in hot butter intensified the flavor. For just the right texture, we found we needed two leaveners. Baking powder gave the bread lift; baking soda resulted in a well-browned top and a pleasantly dense crumb. While we preferred the deeper flavor of dark brown sugar, light brown works just as well. Sprinkling granulated sugar over the top of the loaf just before baking created a crisp, brown crust that we loved.

Don't forget to remove the saucepan from the heat before adding the cardamom and mashed bananas. This ensures the butter and pan will cool sufficiently so the eggs won't curdle when whisked in.

Heat the oven to 350°F with a rack in the upper-middle position. Lightly coat a 9-by-5-inch loaf pan with butter. Dust evenly with flour, then tap out the excess. In a large bowl, whisk together the flour, baking powder, baking soda and salt.

In a medium saucepan over medium, melt the butter. Once melted, cook, swirling the pan often, until the butter is fragrant and deep brown, 2 to 5 minutes. Remove the pan from the heat and immediately whisk in the cardamom. Carefully whisk in the mashed bananas (the butter will sizzle and bubble up). Whisk in the brown sugar and vanilla. Add the eggs and whisk until well combined. Add the butter-banana mixture to the flour mixture and, using a silicone spatula, fold until just combined and no dry flour remains.

Transfer the batter to the prepared pan and sprinkle evenly with the white sugar (if using). Bake until well browned, the top is cracked and a toothpick inserted at the center comes out clean, 50 to 55 minutes, rotating the pan halfway through. Cool in the pan on a wire rack for 15 minutes, then turn out the loaf and cool completely before serving. Cooled bread can be wrapped tightly and stored at room temperature for up to 4 days or refrigerated for up to 1 week.

Triple Ginger Scones with Chocolate Chunks

**Start to finish: 1¼ hours
(40 minutes active)**

Makes 12 scones

455 grams (3½ cups) all-purpose flour, plus more for dusting

71 grams (⅓ cup)
white sugar

4 teaspoons baking powder

½ teaspoon baking soda

2 tablespoons ground ginger

1½ teaspoons grated nutmeg

1¼ teaspoons table salt

1½ teaspoons ground black pepper

1¼ cups cold buttermilk

2 tablespoons finely grated
fresh ginger

1 tablespoon grated orange zest

254 grams (18 tablespoons) salted butter, cut into ½-inch pieces and chilled

142 grams (5 ounces) roughly chopped bittersweet chocolate

136 grams (1 cup) finely chopped crystallized ginger

1 large egg, beaten

These rich, flavor-packed oversized scones are the creation of Briana Holt of Tandem Coffee + Bakery in Portland, Maine. Ginger in three different forms—ground, fresh and crystallized—gives these breakfast pastries plenty of kick, as does black pepper. Keep both the butter and buttermilk in the refrigerator until you're ready to use them so they stay as cold as possible, which makes the dough easier to handle. Holt recommends serving the scones after they've cooled to room temperature, but we also loved them warm, while the chocolate is soft and melty.

Don't worry if the flour-butter mixture doesn't form a cohesive dough immediately after all the buttermilk has been added. In fact, it will be very crumbly, but a brief kneading and the act of shaping and pressing the mixture into disks will bring it together. When kneading, though, take care not to overwork the dough, which will result in tough, not tender, scones.

Heat the oven to 375°F with racks in the upper- and lower-middle positions. Line 2 rimmed baking sheets with kitchen parchment. In a large bowl, whisk together the flour, sugar, baking powder, baking soda, ground ginger, nutmeg, salt and pepper. In a 2-cup liquid measuring cup or a small bowl, stir together the buttermilk, grated ginger and orange zest.

To a food processor, add about ⅓ of the flour mixture and scatter the butter over the top. Pulse until the butter is in large pea-sized pieces, 10 to 12 pulses. Transfer to the bowl with the remaining flour mixture. Add the chocolate and crystallized ginger, then toss with your hands until evenly combined. Pour in about ⅓ of the buttermilk mixture and toss just a few times with your hands, making sure to scrape along the bottom of the bowl, until the liquid is absorbed. Add the remaining buttermilk in 2 more additions, tossing after each. After the final addition of buttermilk, toss until no dry, floury bits remain. The mixture will be quite crumbly and will not form a cohesive dough.

Lightly dust the counter with flour, turn the mixture out onto it, then give it a final toss. Divide it into 2 even piles, gathering each into a mound, then very briefly knead each mound; it's fine if the mixture is still somewhat crumbly. Gather each mound into a ball, then press firmly into a cohesive 5-inch disk about 1½ inches thick. Brush the tops of each disk lightly with beaten egg. Using a chef's knife, cut each disk in half, then cut each half into 3 wedges. Place 6 wedges on each prepared baking sheet, spaced evenly apart.

Bake until the scones are deep golden brown, 27 to 30 minutes, switching and rotating the baking sheets halfway through. Cool on the baking sheets on wire racks for 5 minutes, then transfer directly to a rack and cool for at least another 5 minutes. Serve warm or at room temperature.

Carrot-Tahini Quick Bread with Candied Ginger and Pistachios

Start to finish: 1 hour 20 minutes (30 minutes active), plus cooling

Makes one 9-inch loaf

260 grams (2 cups) all-purpose flour

1 tablespoon baking powder

½ teaspoon baking soda

½ teaspoon table salt

73 grams (½ cup) plus 1 tablespoon pistachios, finely chopped

34 grams (¼ cup) finely chopped crystallized ginger

2 large eggs

285 grams carrots (2 large), peeled and grated on the large holes of a box grater (about 2 cups)

109 grams (½ cup) packed light brown sugar

½ cup buttermilk

⅓ cup grapeseed or other neutral oil

80 grams (⅓ cup) plus 2 tablespoons tahini, divided

3 teaspoons grated orange zest, divided, plus 3 tablespoons orange juice

124 grams (1 cup) powdered sugar

This delicious quick-bread version of moist, tender carrot cake was suggested by Milk Street Facebook Community member Michelle Downs Matlack. Pistachios and tahini lend the bread loads of nutty notes, and crystallized ginger and orange bring bright, bracing flavor. Serve slices for breakfast or as an afternoon pick-me-up alongside a cup of coffee or tea.

Don't forget to zest the orange before halving and juicing it. The zest is easiest to grate when the fruit is whole.

Heat the oven to 350°F with a rack in the middle position. Mist a 9-by-5-inch loaf pan with cooking spray, then line it with an 8-by-14-inch piece of kitchen parchment, allowing the excess to overhang the long sides of the pan.

In a medium bowl, whisk together the flour, baking powder, baking soda and salt. Add the ½ cup pistachios and crystallized ginger; toss to combine.

In a large bowl, whisk the eggs. Add the carrots, brown sugar, buttermilk, oil, 80 grams (⅓ cup) of the tahini and 2 teaspoons orange zest, then stir with a silicone spatula until well combined. Add the flour mixture and mix just until evenly moistened. Scrape the batter into the prepared pan and smooth the top. Bake until a toothpick inserted at the center of the loaf comes out clean, 50 to 55 minutes.

Cool in the pan on a wire rack for about 15 minutes. Lift the loaf out of the pan using the parchment and set it directly on the rack. Let cool completely.

Remove the parchment liner under the loaf. In a medium bowl, combine the powdered sugar, the remaining 2 tablespoons tahini, the remaining 1 teaspoon orange zest and the orange juice. Whisk until smooth. Pour the glaze onto the loaf and smooth with a spatula, then sprinkle with the 1 tablespoon pistachios. Let stand for about 15 minutes before slicing.

Cardamom-Spiced Pistachio and Apricot Muffins

Start to finish: 45 minutes (15 minutes active), plus cooling

Makes 12 muffins

FOR THE MUFFINS:

166 grams (1 cup) dried apricots, finely chopped

6 tablespoons orange juice, divided, plus 2 teaspoons grated orange zest

109 grams (¾ cup) unsalted raw or roasted pistachios

358 grams (2¾ cups) all-purpose flour

1¼ teaspoons ground cardamom

2 teaspoons baking powder

½ teaspoon baking soda

½ teaspoon table salt

2 large eggs

8-ounce container (1 cup) sour cream

161 grams (¾ cup) white sugar

85 grams (6 tablespoons) salted butter, melted and slightly cooled

FOR THE GLAZE:

124 grams (1 cup) powdered sugar

1 teaspoon grated orange zest, plus 2 tablespoons orange juice, plus more as needed

Pistachio flour—which we make by grinding nuts into all-purpose flour—along with sour cream give these muffins a tender, flavorful crumb. Dried apricots plumped in orange juice bring floral, fruity notes, and cardamom contributes warm, sweet spice. A drizzle of orange glaze and a final sprinkling of chopped apricots and pistachios give the muffins a bakery-style finish. If you prefer to skip the glaze, simply scatter the apricots and pistachios reserved for garnish onto the batter before baking. We tested both raw and roasted pistachios in this recipe. Either works well; just be sure they are unsalted.

Don't forget to remove the zest from the oranges before juicing them. The zest is easier to grate when the fruits are whole. Also, it's fine if there are still some small pieces of pistachio in the flour after grinding; these bits add texture and color to the finished muffins.

To make the muffins, heat the oven to 350°F with a rack in the middle position. Generously mist a standard 12-cup muffin pan with cooking spray. In a small microwave-safe bowl, combine the apricots and 3 tablespoons orange juice. Microwave on high until the apricots absorb the juice, about 45 seconds. Reserve ¼ cup apricots for garnish; set the remainder aside.

In a food processor, process the pistachios until finely chopped, 15 to 20 seconds. Measure out ¼ cup and set aside. To the pistachios in the food processor, add ½ cup of the flour; process until finely ground, 30 to 45 seconds. Add the remaining flour, the cardamon, baking powder, baking soda and salt. Pulse 5 to 10 times to combine. In a large bowl, whisk together the eggs, sour cream, white sugar, butter, the remaining 3 tablespoons orange juice and the orange zest. Add the flour-nut mixture and the remaining apricots. Fold with a silicone spatula until just combined.

Scoop the batter into the cups of the prepared muffin pan. Bake until the muffins have risen above the pan and a skewer inserted into the centers comes out clean, 23 to 25 minutes, rotating the pan halfway through. Cool in the pan on a wire rack for 10 minutes. Lift the muffins out of the pan, set them directly on the rack and set the rack on a baking sheet; cool for another 10 minutes.

To make the glaze, in a small bowl, whisk together the powdered sugar and orange juice; the glaze should be smooth, with the consistency of regular yogurt. If it is too thick, whisk in additional juice ½ teaspoon at a time to achieve the proper consistency. Whisk in the orange zest. Using a spoon, drizzle glaze onto each muffin, then sprinkle with the reserved apricots and pistachios. Let the glaze set for a few minutes before serving.

Banana-Hazelnut Bread

**Start to finish: 1½ hours
(30 minutes active), plus cooling**

Makes one 9-inch loaf

98 grams (¾ cup) hazelnuts

210 grams (1¾ cups) cake flour

2 teaspoons ground cinnamon

2 teaspoons baking powder

1 teaspoon baking soda

½ teaspoon table salt

400 grams (1½ cups) mashed ripe bananas (from 3 to 4 large bananas)

161 grams (¾ cup) white sugar

⅓ cup grapeseed or other neutral oil

2 teaspoons vanilla extract

1 tablespoon turbinado sugar or white sugar

At the now-closed ultra-modern Black Isle Bakery in Berlin, owner Ruth Barry baked a small array of simple but well-crafted treats—homey, inviting goodies such as loaf cakes, cookies, buns and tarts. We thought her banana hazelnut loaf was especially delicious, the nut and fruit flavors in perfect balance and the crumb extremely moist and tender. It also happens to be dairy- and egg-free. Once cooled, the bread will keep in an airtight container at room temperature for up to three days; after that, it can be refrigerated for a couple days longer, but bring to room temperature before serving.

Don't use underripe bananas. For best flavor and texture, the unpeeled bananas should be darkly speckled on the outside and very soft on the inside. Don't over-toast the hazelnuts. Aim for lightly golden so the nuts that are chopped and sprinkled on top of the loaf don't become too dark during baking.

Heat the oven to 350°F with a rack in the middle position. Put the hazelnuts in a 9-by-5-inch loaf pan and toast in the oven until lightly browned, 8 to 10 minutes, stirring once halfway through. Cool to room temperature. If the nuts are skin-on, rub them in a clean kitchen towel to remove as much of the skins as possible (it's fine if some of the skins remain). Roughly chop 33 grams (¼ cup) of the hazelnuts and set aside.

Mist the loaf pan with cooking spray, then line it with an 8-by-14-inch piece of kitchen parchment, allowing the excess to overhang the long sides of the pan. Mist the parchment with cooking spray.

In a food processor, combine the flour, cinnamon, baking powder, baking soda, salt and remaining 65 grams (½ cup) hazelnuts. Process until the nuts are finely ground, 30 to 45 seconds. Transfer the mixture to a large bowl, then return the food processor bowl and blade to the base.

To the processor, add the bananas, white sugar, oil and vanilla. Process until smooth, creamy and aerated, about 30 seconds. Add the banana mixture to the dry ingredients and fold with a silicone spatula until just combined. Transfer to the prepared pan and smooth the top. Sprinkle evenly with the turbinado sugar and chopped hazelnuts. Bake until golden brown and a toothpick inserted at the center comes out clean, 50 to 55 minutes.

Cool in the pan on a wire rack for 10 minutes, then lift the loaf out of the pan using the parchment. Set the bread directly on the rack and cool completely. Peel off and discard the parchment before slicing.

Chapter 3

Sweet and Savory Breads

Poppy Seed Bread

**Start to finish: 5 hours
(1 hour active)**

Makes one 1¾-pound loaf

1¼ cups whole milk

111 grams (⅓ cup) honey

2 tablespoons grated lemon zest,
plus 4 teaspoons lemon juice

1 large egg

1½ teaspoons instant yeast

1 teaspoon vanilla extract

325 grams (2½ cups) all-purpose
flour, plus more as needed

85 grams (6 tablespoons) salted
butter, cut into 6 pieces, room
temperature

½ teaspoon plus ⅛ teaspoon
table salt, divided

130 grams (1 cup) poppy seeds

71 grams (⅓ cup) white sugar

83 grams (⅔ cup) powdered sugar

This bread, with its inner swirl of poppy seed filling, has a touch of richness from milk and butter and a subtle sweetness from honey. It's great sliced and served for breakfast or brunch. You will need a full cup of poppy seeds; instead of purchasing multiple jars from the supermarket, check the bulk section of natural foods stores, spice shops or markets that specialize in Eastern European foods. Be sure to use room-temperature butter; if it's cold and firm, it won't incorporate properly into the dough. The bread can be baked a day in advance. If that's your plan, hold off on making and applying the glaze. Wrap the cooled, unglazed loaf tightly in plastic and store at room temperature. About 30 minutes before serving, make the glaze and drizzle it on.

Don't try to grind the poppy seeds in a food processor, as the seeds won't break down. An electric coffee grinder dedicated to spice grinding is the best tool for the task. Don't use a serrated knife to slash the loaf before baking, as the blade will tug at the dough and make ragged cuts; a sharp paring or carving knife is a better choice.

In a medium saucepan, combine the milk, honey and lemon zest. Warm over medium, whisking, until the honey dissolves and the mixture is just warm to the touch, about 2 minutes; do not simmer. Off heat, measure ¾ cup of the mixture into the bowl of a stand mixer; leave the remainder in the saucepan and set aside.

To the mixer bowl, add the egg, yeast and vanilla; whisk to combine. Add the flour and the ½ teaspoon salt. Mix with the dough hook on low until an evenly moistened dough forms, about 2 minutes; the dough should be sticky to the touch but should not cling to the sides of the bowl. If the dough feels too wet, knead in more flour 1 tablespoon at a time. Increase to medium and add the butter 1 piece at a time, mixing until fully incorporated after each; if the butter clings to the bowl, scrape down the sides. After all the butter has been added, continue mixing until the dough is smooth and silky, about 2 minutes. Using a silicone spatula, scrape the sides of the bowl and gather the dough in the center. Cover with plastic wrap and let rise at room temperature until doubled, 1½ to 2 hours.

Meanwhile, using an electric spice grinder, process the poppy seeds in 3 batches, grinding until fine and powdery, about 15 seconds; add each batch to the remaining milk mixture in the saucepan. Add the white sugar and the remaining ⅛ teaspoon salt, then set the pan over medium and cook, stirring occasionally with a silicone spatula, until simmering and thick enough that the spatula leaves a clear trail when drawn through the center, 3 to 5 minutes. Transfer to a medium bowl and cool to room temperature; the mixture will continue to thicken as it cools.

STEPS »

HOW TO MAKE POPPY SEED BREAD

1. After adding all of the butter one piece at a time, knead the dough until smooth and silky.

2. Cook the filling until a spatula leaves a clear trail when drawn through the mixture, 3 to 5 minutes.

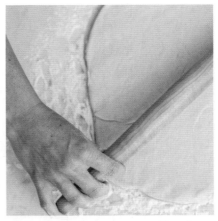

3. On a floured counter, use a rolling pin to roll the risen dough into a 12-inch square about ⅜ inch thick.

4. Spread the cooled filling in an even layer on the dough, leaving a ½-inch border along all edges.

5. Roll the dough into a tight cylinder. Pinch the seal to seam, then transfer seam side down to the prepared sheet.

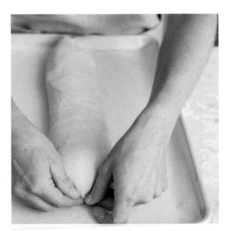

6. Pinch the open ends to seal, then tuck them under. Cover and let rise until just shy of doubled, about 30 minutes.

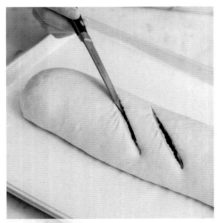

7. Using a sharp paring knife and starting at the center, make 5 shallow, evenly spaced diagonal cuts in the top of the loaf.

8. Bake at 325°F until deep golden brown, 35 to 45 minutes; the center of the bread should reach 200°F.

9. Once the bread has cooled, make the glaze, then drizzle over the top. Let dry for about 30 minutes.

When the dough has doubled in size, heat the oven to 325°F with the rack in the middle position. Line a baking sheet with kitchen parchment.

Generously dust the counter with flour and scrape the dough out onto it. Use a rolling pin to roll the dough to a 12-inch square about ⅜ inch thick. Spread the poppy seed filling in an even layer on the dough, leaving a ½-inch border along all edges. Starting with the side closest to you, roll the dough into a tight cylinder; pinch the seam to seal. Transfer seam side down to the prepared baking sheet. Pinch the open ends to seal, then tuck the pinched seams under. Loosely cover with plastic wrap and let rise at room temperature until almost doubled, about 30 minutes.

Using a sharp paring knife, and starting in the center of the loaf, make a shallow diagonal cut, about 4 inches long; cut through the outermost layer of dough to reveal the poppy seed filling just underneath. Make 2 more evenly spaced cuts on each side of the center one, for a total of 5 cuts. Bake until the bread is deep golden brown, 35 to 45 minutes; if you have an instant thermometer, the center of the loaf should reach 200°F. Cool completely on the baking sheet on a wire rack, at least 1 hour.

In a small bowl, whisk together the powdered sugar and lemon juice. Drizzle the glaze onto the loaf. Let dry for about 30 minutes.

BAKING BASIC

DO-AHEAD BREAD

The allure of freshly baked bread too often is tamed by the time it takes to make it. So we tried prepping the dough in advance, then experimented with freezing it at several stages for baking later to determine the best way—and whether it really saves any time. We tested three kinds of dough: traditional bread dough, dinner roll dough and pizza dough. We froze each variety at two different stages—some immediately after mixing and kneading, and some after the dough had been allowed to rise. To bake, we let each batch thaw overnight in the refrigerator, then brought the dough to room temperature before baking.

For comparison, we also baked fresh versions of each dough that had never been frozen. In all cases, we found that the frozen doughs baked just as well as the freshly made doughs, with little difference in taste or texture. Despite the delicious results, we did not find freezing to be much of a shortcut when dealing with large amounts of dough, as in loaves of bread and pizza dough. In addition to overnight thawing, it took another three hours for the doughs to come to room temperature. Freezing was a shortcut for smaller pieces of dough, such as dinner rolls, which came to room temperature in just 90 minutes.

German-Style
Winter Squash Bread

This inviting, impressive, braided loaf gets its warm, golden hue from roasted butternut squash. The squash also gives the crumb a moistness, and the milk, eggs and butter lend a brioche-like richness. The German bread called Kürbisbrot (pumpkin bread, literally translated), in particular Luisa Weiss' recipe from her book "Classic German Baking," was our starting point for this autumnal loaf. Kürbisbrot is commonly shaped as a simple round loaf, but we took Weiss' suggestion and made a special-occasion bread by forming the dough into a braid. We also added a touch of allspice for a warm, subtle fragrance and a sprinkle of pumpkin seeds just before baking. The dough is soft and sticky but also strong and elastic; it requires a sturdy stand mixer to develop a solid gluten structure that would be difficult to make by hand. When you turn the dough out of the mixer bowl, it may seem too wet and batter-like to be shapeable, but with rising and refrigerating, it becomes workable. Store leftover bread at room temperature in an airtight container or zip-close bag for up to three days. It makes great toast once it begins to stale.

Don't be tempted to use canned squash instead of roasted fresh squash. Its flavor is more muted and its water content alters the moistness of the dough. Also, don't forget to bring the butter to room temperature before starting the recipe, as it needs to be very soft in order to incorporate properly into the batter-like dough. Finally, don't add too much more flour during kneading, before the butter is mixed in. If the dough pulls away cleanly from the sides of the bowl, it contains enough flour.

Heat the oven to 425°F with a rack in the middle position. Mist a rimmed baking sheet with cooking spray. Place the squash halves cut side down on the prepared baking sheet and roast until a skewer inserted through the neck of the squash meets no resistance, 35 to 40 minutes. Remove from the oven, turn the squash halves cut side up and set aside until cool enough to handle.

Scoop the flesh out of the skins into a large bowl; discard the skins. Using a silicone spatula, mash the flesh until smooth. If the squash is still warm, let cool completely. Measure 230 grams (1 cup) of the squash into a medium bowl; reserve the remainder for another use. To the squash, add the milk, honey and 2 eggs. Whisk until homogeneous; set aside. Mist a large bowl with cooking spray.

In a stand mixer with the dough hook, mix the flour, yeast, allspice and salt on low until combined, about 20 seconds. With the mixer running, gradually pour in the squash mixture, then continue mixing until a wet, slightly lumpy dough forms, about 2 minutes, scraping the bowl once. Increase to medium and knead the

**Start to finish: 6 hours
(45 minutes active), plus cooling**

Makes one 1¾-pound loaf

1½- to 2-pound butternut squash, halved lengthwise and seeded

¼ cup whole milk

2 tablespoons honey

3 large eggs, divided

406 grams (3 cups plus 2 tablespoons) all-purpose flour, plus more as needed and for dusting

1 teaspoon instant yeast

¾ teaspoon ground allspice

1 teaspoon table salt

57 grams (4 tablespoons) salted butter, cut into 4 pieces, room temperature

26 grams (3 tablespoons) pumpkin seeds, roughly chopped

mixture, scraping the bowl once or twice, until it pulls away cleanly from the sides, 5 to 6 minutes. If it sticks to the bowl, add 2 tablespoons flour and knead for about 2 minutes before assessing if even more flour is needed.

Add the butter one piece at a time and mix until it is almost fully incorporated, about 30 seconds, before adding another piece. After all the butter has been added, mix on medium until the dough is smooth and elastic and pulls away from the sides of the bowl, 7 to 9 minutes. Detach the bowl and hook from the mixer, then lift out the hook with dough clinging to it; the dough should fall from the hook and stretch into a translucent "pane." If it breaks before forming a pane, continue kneading on medium for another 1 to 2 minutes, then test again. The dough will resemble a stretchy, webby batter.

Using a plastic dough scraper or silicone spatula, scrape the dough into the prepared bowl, cover tightly with plastic wrap and let rise at room temperature until bubbles form on the surface, about 1 hour. Refrigerate for at least 4 hours or up to 24 hours.

Line a rimmed baking sheet with kitchen parchment. Lightly flour the counter. Turn the dough out onto the counter and divide it into 3 even portions. Lightly flour your hands and roll each portion into an 18-inch rope. Position the ropes perpendicular to the counter's edge but parallel to each other; flour the counter as needed. Firmly pinch together the far ends of the ropes. Flour your fingers, then lift the right rope, cross it over the middle rope and lay it between the 2; adjust the spacing of the ropes as you go. Now cross the left rope over the new middle rope and lay it between the 2. Repeat the braiding until you reach the ends of the ropes. Firmly pinch together the ends. Tuck the 2 pinched ends under the loaf.

Transfer the loaf to the prepared baking sheet; gently reshape, if needed. Mist a large sheet of plastic wrap with cooking spray and drape it, greased side down, over the loaf. Lay a kitchen towel on top. Let rise at room temperature until doubled in size and the dough springs back slowly when lightly pressed with a fingertip, about 1½ hours. Meanwhile, heat the oven to 350°F with a rack in the middle position.

In a small bowl, beat the remaining egg. Lightly brush the dough with the beaten egg, then sprinkle evenly with the pumpkin seeds. Bake until golden brown and the center of the loaf reaches 190°F to 200°F, 30 to 35 minutes. Let the loaf cool on the baking sheet on a wire rack for about 10 minutes. Transfer the bread, still on the parchment, directly to the rack. Cool for at least 1 hour before slicing.

HOW TO MAKE GERMAN-STYLE WINTER SQUASH BREAD

1. After adding the squash mixture to the dry ingredients, knead on low until a wet, lumpy dough forms.

2. After incorporating the butter, knead the dough until it forms a translucent "pane" as it falls from the dough hook.

3. To braid the dough after rising, on a lightly floured counter, divide into thirds. Roll each piece into an 18-inch rope.

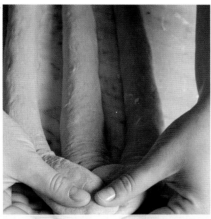

4. Place the ropes parallel to each other and firmly pinch together the ends that are farthest from you.

5. Lift the right rope, cross it over the middle rope and lay it between the two; adjust the spacing of the ropes as you go.

6. Cross the left rope over the new middle rope and lay it between the other two. Flour the counter to prevent sticking.

7. Repeat the process, without stretching the ropes, until you reach the ends nearest you, forming a tight braid.

8. Pinch the ends to seal, then tuck each end under the loaf. Transfer to the prepared baking sheet, cover and let rise.

9. Brush the risen loaf with beaten egg, sprinkle with chopped pumpkin seeds and bake at 350°F for 30 to 35 minutes.

Portuguese Cornbread

**Start to finish: 4½ hours
(15 minutes active)**

Makes 1 loaf

204 grams (1⅔ cups) corn flour
(see headnote)

2 tablespoons honey

1 cup boiling water, plus ¼ cup
water at room temperature

137 grams (1 cup) bread flour,
plus more for dusting

70 grams (½ cup) rye flour

2 teaspoons instant yeast

1 teaspoon table salt

Known as broa, Portuguese cornbread shares little but its name
with the cakey, honeyed version familiar to Americans. Beneath a
crackling, creviced crust, the heart of broa is dense, moist and deeply
flavored. At Padaria Amadina & Neto, a two-centuries-old broa
baker in Avintes, Portugal, we learned that traditionally, the bread is
made with corn flour, which is dried corn that is ground finer than
cornmeal. If you can't find corn flour, you can use finely ground
cornmeal, but the bread will have some granularity in the crumb.
This hearty loaf is delicious sliced and spread with salted butter.
Stored in an airtight container or zip-close bag, leftover broa will
keep for up to three days at room temperature; the flavor and texture
are best if the bread is toasted before serving.

Don't let the loaf rise for longer than indicated, as the bread may bake up with an
unpleasantly boozy, slightly sour flavor. Unlike most bread doughs that double in
bulk during rising, this one increases only by about 50 percent.

Line a rimmed baking sheet with kitchen parchment. In a stand mixer fitted with
the paddle attachment, mix the corn flour, honey and boiling water on low until
evenly moistened and a thick mash forms, 30 to 60 seconds. Turn off the mixer and
let stand until just warm to the touch, about 30 minutes.

Add the room-temperature water, bread and rye flours, yeast and salt. Using the
dough hook attachment, mix on low, scraping down the bowl as needed, until a
cohesive dough forms, about 5 minutes; the dough should clear the sides of the bowl
and feel tacky but not excessively sticky.

Turn the dough out onto the counter and use your hands to shape the dough into a
ball about 5 inches in diameter. Set on the prepared baking sheet, dust the top with
flour and cover with a kitchen towel. Let rise in a warm, draft-free spot until the
volume increases by about half, 1 to 1½ hours. Meanwhile, heat the oven to 500°F
with a rack in the middle position.

Bake the bread for 15 minutes. Reduce the oven to 300°F and continue to bake
until deep golden brown, another 30 to 35 minutes. Transfer the bread from the
baking sheet to a wire rack and let cool completely, about 2 hours.

KNEAD TO KNOW

Kneading develops the gluten and structure required for bread dough to stretch, rise and support itself with the captured carbon dioxide gases produced during fermentation. It can be hard to tell when a yeasted bread dough is adequately kneaded, or needs a bit more kneading to develop the proper amount of gluten. Time on the dough hook isn't always indicative of doneness because stand mixers vary in effectiveness—some brands might work the dough more effectively and with greater speed than others.

That's why we favor visual and tactile cues over time and typically include all three in our recipe instructions. Underkneaded dough, which looks rough, lumpy or shaggy, produces dense and gummy bread because the dough lacks the strength to capture and support the gasses. Overkneaded dough is dense, intractable, prone to ripping and tough because the dough is worked beyond elasticity.

A smooth appearance and supple, elastic feel is typically indicative that a dough is fully kneaded and primed for a successful rise. For dense breads or doughs enriched with sugars, fats or other ingredients that can disrupt the dough structure—like the cooked mashed squash in our German-Style Winter Squash Bread (p. 71)—it's best to double check the gluten development by gently stretching a portion of the dough with your fingers. If it can be stretched without ripping until thin enough to be transparent—a stage called "windowpane"—the dough is sufficiently kneaded. If it tears, knead for another couple of minutes before testing again. Note that windowpane isn't applicable to high-hydration doughs (like pizza or focaccia doughs), which typically are developed via folding, or gently stretching the dough up and over itself.

Japanese Milk Bread

**Start to finish: 4 hours
(50 minutes active), plus cooling**

Makes two 1½-pound loaves

FOR THE WATER ROUX:

¼ cup plus 2 tablespoons whole milk

34 grams (¼ cup) bread flour

FOR THE DOUGH:

3 large eggs, divided

1 cup whole milk, room temperature

639 grams (4⅔ cups) bread flour,
plus more for dusting

70 grams (½ cup) rye flour

80 grams (¼ cup plus 2 tablespoons)
white sugar

27 grams (¼ cup) nonfat or low-fat
dry milk powder

1½ tablespoons instant yeast

1¾ teaspoons table salt

113 grams (8 tablespoons) salted
butter, cut into 1-tablespoon pieces,
room temperature, plus melted
butter for brushing the pans

Japanese milk bread is a fluffy, slightly sweet, fine-textured loaf. It stays moister and softer longer than standard sandwich bread thanks in part to the Asian technique of incorporating tangzhong into the dough. Tangzhong is a mixture of flour and liquid cooked to a gel; it's often referred to as "water roux," though it does not contain any butter or oil and serves a different purpose than a classic roux. The gelatinized starch in tangzhong can hold onto more water than uncooked flour, thereby offering several benefits. The dough is easy to handle despite the high hydration level; the loaf attains a high rise and a light, airy crumb; and the baked bread keeps well. Sonoko Sakai, author of "Japanese Home Cooking," makes her milk bread with a small amount of non-wheat flour combined with bread flour. When adapting her formula, we opted to use rye flour for its nutty flavor. This recipe makes two loaves, so you will need two 8½-by-4½-inch loaf pans; metal works better than glass for heat conduction and browning. The baked and cooled bread keeps well at room temperature in an airtight container or plastic bag for several days. It can be stored in the refrigerator for slightly longer, but then is best rewarmed or toasted. Or the bread can be frozen, unsliced and wrapped in plastic then foil, for up to one month.

Don't be tempted to add more flour to the dough as it is kneaded. It will be sticky and gluey, but after rising, it will be workable. When shaping the dough, use minimal flour so the dough remains as moist as possible. Lastly, when inverting the loaves from the pan and turning them upright to cool, handle them gently; they are delicate and easily separate at the seam.

To make the water roux, in a medium saucepan, whisk ½ cup water, the milk and flour until lump-free. Set over medium and cook, whisking, until the mixture thickens (a silicone spatula drawn through the mixture leaves a trail) and bubbles slowly, 2 to 4 minutes. Scrape into a medium bowl, press a sheet of plastic wrap directly onto the surface and cool to room temperature.

To make the dough, add 2 eggs to the cooled roux and whisk well. Add the whole milk and whisk until homogeneous and smooth. In the bowl of a stand mixer, whisk together the bread and rye flours, sugar, milk powder, yeast and salt. Attach the bowl and dough hook to the mixer and, with the machine running on low, slowly add the roux-egg mixture.

THE TANGZHONG TECHNIQUE

Japanese milk bread—which is made with milk, eggs and plenty of butter—boasts a hallmark fluffy texture often attributed to the addition of tangzhong, sometimes called a "water roux." This roux is made by cooking a small amount of flour, water and sometimes milk (usually in a ratio of 1 part flour to 5 parts liquid) until the mixture becomes a thick slurry. This process gelatinizes the flour's starch and traps moisture. When added to the bread dough, the trapped moisture in the gel increases the liquid in the recipe but doesn't interact with the gluten in the flour. That means less gluten development, which creates a lighter, softer crumb.

Some sources claim you can adapt any bread recipe to work with the tangzhong method to give it a lighter texture akin to milk bread. The process is complex and involves calculating the hydration level of the recipe's ingredients and using a certain percentage of those ingredients to create the roux. We tested this numerous times with multiple bread recipes, but the results were disappointing. Not only were the loaves not noticeably lighter or fluffier, some actually were denser. The most significant advantage we found was that these tangzhong-adapted loaves did stay moister longer and had an overall better shelf life. This led us to conclude that Japanese milk bread's trademark airy texture isn't due to the tangzhong method alone. Rather, the dairy and eggs play a role, too.

With the mixer still running, add the butter 1 tablespoon at a time. Increase speed to medium-low and knead until the dough is very strong and elastic, 10 to 12 minutes; it will stick to the sides of the bowl. Using a silicone spatula, scrape the bowl and gather the dough in the center. Cover with plastic wrap and let rise at room temperature until doubled, about 1½ hours. Meanwhile, brush 2 metal 8½-by-4½-inch loaf pans with melted butter.

Lightly flour the counter. Gently punch down the dough, then turn it out onto the prepared counter. Using a chef's knife or bench scraper, divide the dough into 4 portions, each about 355 grams (about 12½ ounces). Shape each into a smooth ball. Using your hands, pat one ball into a 7-by-4-inch rectangle, then fold the dough into thirds like a business

Milk Bread Dinner Rolls

Make the dough and let it rise as directed. While the dough is rising, brush 2 metal 9-inch cake pans with melted butter. After turning the dough out onto the lightly floured counter, use a chef's knife or bench scraper to divide it into 24 portions, each about 57 grams (2 ounces). Form each portion into a taut ball by rolling it against the counter in a circular motion under a cupped hand, then pinch the seam on the bottom. Place 12 dough balls in each prepared pan (3 in the center and 9 around the perimeter), then drape a kitchen towel over the pans. Let rise at room temperature until doubled, about 45 minutes.

Meanwhile, heat the oven to 350°F with a rack in the middle position. In a small bowl, whisk the remaining egg until well combined. When the rolls have doubled, gently brush the tops with the beaten egg. Bake until well risen and golden brown, about 30 minutes. Cool in the pans on a wire rack for 10 minutes. Invert the rolls out of the pans onto the rack, then turn them upright. Serve warm or at room temperature. Makes 2 dozen rolls.

letter. Pinch the seam to seal. Turn the dough seam side down and place on one side of one of the prepared loaf pans so the seam is perpendicular to the length of the pan. Shape a second portion of dough, then place it in the pan alongside the first portion, positioning it the same way; there should be just a small amount of space between the 2 pieces of dough. Cover the pan with a clean kitchen towel.

Repeat the process with the remaining portions of dough, then place under the towel alongside the first pan. Let rise at room temperature until the dough domes 1 to 1½ inches over the rim of the pan, about 1 hour. Meanwhile, heat the oven to 350°F with a rack in the middle position. In a small bowl, whisk the remaining egg until well combined; set aside.

When the dough is properly risen, gently brush the tops with the beaten egg. Bake until the loaves are well risen and golden brown, 30 to 35 minutes. Cool in the pans on a wire rack for 15 minutes. Gently invert the bread out of the pans, stand them upright on the rack and cool for at least 1 hour before slicing.

HOW TO MAKE JAPANESE MILK BREAD

1. To make the roux, in a saucepan, cook the water, milk and bread flour, whisking, until thickened. Scrape into a bowl, press plastic wrap against the surface; let cool.

2. Whisk 2 eggs into the cooled roux, followed by the room-temperature milk. In the bowl of a stand mixer, whisk together the remaining dry ingredients.

3. Using the dough hook with the mixer running on low, add the roux, followed by the butter, 1 tablespoon at a time. Knead on medium-low until the dough is elastic.

4. Scrape the dough into a large buttered bowl; brush the surface with melted butter. Cover with plastic wrap and let rise until doubled, about 1½ hours.

5. Punch down the dough, then turn it out onto a floured counter. Divide the dough into 4 portions and shape each portion into a smooth ball.

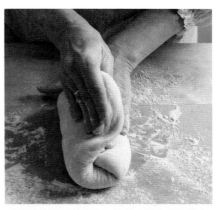

6. Pat one ball into a 7-by-4-inch rectangle, then fold into thirds. Pinch the seam. Place, seam side down, on one side of a buttered loaf pan. Shape a second ball and place in the pan next to the first portion, then cover.

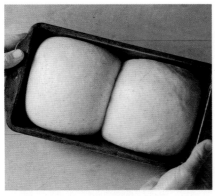

7. Repeat with the remaining dough. Place the second pan under the towel. Let rise until the dough domes 1 to 1½ inches over the rim of the pan, about 1 hour.

8. Brush the risen dough with beaten egg. Bake until the loaves are golden brown, 30 to 35 minutes. Cool in the pans for 15 minutes, then invert onto a wire rack, turn upright and cool completely.

Chinese Sesame-Scallion Bread

**Start to finish: 2 hours
(30 minutes active)**

Makes one 10-inch round

217 grams (1⅔ cups) all-purpose flour, plus more if needed

39 grams (¼ cup) sweet (glutinous) rice flour (see headnote)

1 teaspoon instant yeast

¾ teaspoon table salt, divided

¾ cup warm (100°F) water

1 tablespoon honey

4 teaspoons toasted sesame oil, divided

1 bunch scallions, finely chopped (about 1 cup)

40 grams (4 tablespoons) sesame seeds, divided

2 tablespoons grapeseed or other neutral oil

This bread, known as zhima dabing—which translates as "sesame big pancake"—is similar to Chinese scallion pancakes (cong you bing), but is much larger and thicker and has a lighter, fluffier crumb. The addition of sweet rice flour (also called glutinous) gives the crust a unique crispness and the interior a satisfying chew. If you're unable to find sweet rice flour with the baking ingredients, check the Asian aisle for a white box labeled "mochiko" (the Japanese term for the flour). Chop the scallions by thinly slicing them first, then running the knife over them a few times to further break them down. To make sure the scallions stay fresh, prep them toward the end of the dough's one-hour rising time.

Don't use regular rice flour in place of the sweet rice flour, as it won't produce the same texture. Don't use pretoasted sesame seeds, as the seeds brown deeply as the bread cooks; already toasted seeds may end up scorched and bitter. Don't worry if some scallions are exposed on the surface of the dough as you flatten it into a round; this is normal.

In a stand mixer fitted with the dough hook, mix both flours, the yeast and ½ teaspoon of salt on low until combined, about 30 seconds. In a liquid measuring cup or small bowl, whisk the water and honey until dissolved. With the mixer on low, slowly pour the honey water into the flour mixture. Continue mixing on low until an evenly moistened dough forms, about 1 minute. Stop the mixer and check the dough; if it feels wet or very sticky, add an additional 1 to 3 tablespoons all-purpose flour. Continue mixing on low until smooth, about 4 minutes. The dough should feel tacky but not stick to your fingers.

Coat a medium bowl with 1 teaspoon of the sesame oil. Place the dough in the bowl and turn to coat. Cover with plastic wrap and let rise in a warm, draft-free spot until the dough has doubled in size, about 1 hour.

Coat a rimmed baking sheet with 1 teaspoon of the remaining sesame oil. Turn the dough out onto the baking sheet and use your hands to press into a 12-by-9-inch rectangle. In a small bowl, toss the scallions with the remaining 2 teaspoons sesame oil, then distribute evenly over the dough. Sprinkle with the remaining ¼ teaspoon salt. Starting from a long side, roll the dough into a cylinder and pinch the seam to seal. Roll the cylinder seam side down, then coil it into a tight spiral and tuck the end under. Using your hands, press the coil to slightly flatten, sprinkle with 20 grams (2 tablespoons) of sesame seeds and press to adhere. Flip the coil and sprinkle the second side with the remaining 2 tablespoons sesame seeds. Press and flatten into an even 10-inch round.

Add the grapeseed oil to a 12-inch nonstick skillet and swirl to evenly coat the bottom. Carefully transfer the dough to the skillet; reshape into a 10-inch round, if needed. Cover with a lid and let rise until about doubled in size, about 30 minutes.

Place the covered skillet over medium and cook until the bottom of the bread is deep golden brown, 5 to 6 minutes. Uncover and, using tongs and a wide metal spatula, carefully flip the bread. Cook until golden on the second side, about 3 minutes. Slide the bread onto a wire rack and let cool for at least 10 minutes. Cut into quarters to serve.

Turkish Pide Breads

**Start to finish: 2¼ hours
(30 minutes active)**

Makes two 10-inch breads

2 cups warm water (110°F), divided

2¼ teaspoons instant yeast

2 teaspoons honey

137 grams (1 cup) plus 411 grams
(3 cups) bread flour, plus more for
dusting

5 tablespoons extra-virgin
olive oil, divided

1½ teaspoons table salt

1 large egg, well beaten

1 tablespoon nigella seeds
(see headnote), sesame seeds
or a combination

The Turkish name for this bread is pide ekmeği, which translates as "pita bread." But these are not the thin, pocketed flatbreads familiar to most Americans. Pide ekmeği are roughly the size of a small pizza, with an airy, open crumb and a tender, almost pillowy quality. Sometimes a sprinkling of seeds adds texture and flavor. We encountered pide ekmeği served alongside tepsi kebab, or "tray kebab," during a visit to Türkiye. We tried basic bread-making formulas, but ultimately found that starting with a sponge—a mixture of yeast, flour and water that becomes bubbly after standing for 30 minutes—produced breads not only with the lightness we were after, but also a more complex flavor. For dusting the breads just before baking, we use nigella seeds, which have an earthy, slightly bitter flavor with notes of allium. Sesame seeds are good, too—or use a combination. The bread is best served warm or at room temperature the day of baking, but foil-wrapped leftovers reheat well in a 400°F oven in about 10 minutes.

Don't be tempted to add more flour to the dough during mixing. The dough's relatively high hydration is key to the bread's light, airy crumb.

In the bowl of a stand mixer, whisk together 1 cup warm water, the yeast, honey and 137 grams flour. Cover and let stand at room temperature for 30 minutes; the mixture, called a "sponge," will rise slightly and become bubbly.

To the sponge, add the remaining 411 grams flour, the remaining 1 cup warm water and 3 tablespoons of the oil. Using the dough hook, mix on medium for 5 minutes, scraping the bowl as needed. Add the salt and knead on medium until a sticky, batter-like dough forms (it will not clear the sides of the bowl), about another 5 minutes, scraping the bowl as needed. Detach the bowl from the mixer. Scrape the sides of the bowl. Cover the bowl with a kitchen towel and let rise at room temperature until doubled, 1 to 1½ hours. Meanwhile, drizzle the remaining 2 tablespoons oil onto a rimmed baking sheet, then brush to coat evenly.

When the dough has doubled, generously dust the counter with flour, then turn the dough out onto it; divide in half. Shape each portion into a smooth ball, flouring your hands as needed. Set a dough ball on each side of the prepared baking sheet, cover with a towel and let rest 15 minutes. Meanwhile, heat the oven to 475°F with a rack in the middle position.

Using your hands, gently pat and flatten each portion into a 10-by-7-inch oval, taking care not to press out all of the air. Re-cover with the towel and let rest for 20 minutes; it's fine if the ovals end up touching.

STEPS »

HOW TO MAKE TURKISH PIDE BREADS

1. In the bowl of a stand mixer, whisk together 1 cup of warm water, the yeast, honey and 137 grams flour.

2. To the sponge, add the remaining 411 grams flour, the remaining 1 cup warm water and 3 tablespoons of oil.

3. Knead on medium until a sticky, batter-like dough forms (it will not clear the sides of the bowl).

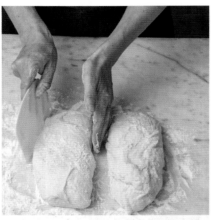

4. Generously dust the counter with flour, turn the dough out onto it, and divide in half.

5. Shape each portion into a smooth ball, flouring your hands as needed. Set a dough ball on each side of the baking sheet.

6. Using your hands, gently pat and flatten each portion into a 10-by-7-inch oval, taking care not to press out all of the air.

7. Imprint a series of dimples, spaced about 1 inch apart, into the oval by firmly pressing your fingertips straight down into the dough.

8. Now imprint another series of dimples, also spaced about 1 inch apart, perpendicular to the first set, creating a grid pattern of dimpled troughs in the dough.

9. Sprinkle the ovals with the nigella seeds. Bake until golden brown and well risen, 16 to 18 minutes.

Gently brush one portion of dough with egg. Imprint a series of dimples, spaced about 1 inch apart, into the oval by firmly pressing your fingertips straight down into the dough. Again using your fingertips, imprint another series of dimples, also spaced about 1 inch apart, perpendicular to the first set, creating a rough grid pattern in the dough. Brush the second dough portion with egg and dimple it the same way as the first.

Sprinkle the ovals with the nigella seeds. Bake until light golden brown and well risen, 16 to 18 minutes. Cool for about 5 minutes on the baking sheet, then transfer to a wire rack. Serve warm or at room temperature.

BAKING BASIC

BREAD ON THE DOUBLE

Recipes for yeasted doughs typically involve two rises. The first one is the fermentation stage, also known as bulk fermentation or first rise, which occurs just after the initial mixing and kneading. During this stage, the yeast is fueled by the starch's sugars to create carbon dioxide and alcohol (fermentation), creating gasses that inflate the dough and prompt gluten strength—a crucial step for building structure. The second rise, or proofing, occurs after the dough is collapsed (sometimes referred to as punched down) and shaped; which releases and redistributes accumulated gasses. During the second rise, further fermentation reinflates the dough, developing chewiness, a more uniform texture and a complex flavor in the process. Without that second rise, the excess gas buildup can cause loaves to crack or blow out. Also, the loaf will likely taste boozy from alcohol buildup during the fermentation.

Moroccan Seeded Breads with Semolina

**Start to finish: 2 hours
(20 minutes active), plus cooling**

Makes two 7-inch loaves

40 grams (¼ cup) sesame seeds

1⅔ cups warm water (100°F)

2 tablespoons extra-virgin olive oil, plus more for the baking sheet

1 tablespoon honey

390 grams (3 cups) all-purpose flour, divided, plus more as needed and for dusting

170 grams (1 cup) semolina flour

53 grams (⅓ cup) flax seeds

20 grams (⅓ cup) wheat bran

1 tablespoon fennel seeds, lightly crushed

2¼ teaspoons instant yeast

¾ teaspoon table salt

Khobz is a Moroccan yeasted bread that's flat but not thin and pliable like a typical flatbread. It's a low, small, pleasantly dense round loaf present at almost every meal and, being the daily bread, typically is quite plain in flavor. But the bread that home cook Houda Mehdi showed us how to make in her kitchen in Fes, Morocco, was fantastically flavored with sesame, flax and fennel seeds, as well as semolina and wheat bran. We adapted her recipe, adding a small measure of olive oil for a slightly more tender crumb and to lend a little richness. Leftovers will keep in an airtight container for up to two days; to reheat, wrap the bread in foil and warm in a 400°F oven for about 10 minutes.

Don't add all of the all-purpose flour at the outset. Only 260 grams (2 cups) is c ombined with the semolina, wheat bran, seeds and yeast; the remainder is added only after the dough has rested for 20 minutes. This allows the semolina and wheat bran to hydrate, which results in a more manageable dough and better-textured baked crumb.

In a 10-inch skillet over medium, toast the sesame seeds, stirring, until fragrant and lightly browned, about 3 minutes. Transfer to the bowl of a stand mixer and cool. In a 2-cup liquid measuring cup or small bowl, stir the water, oil and honey.

To the cooled sesame, add 260 grams (2 cups) all-purpose flour, the semolina, flax seeds, wheat bran, fennel seeds and yeast. Mix with the dough hook on low until well combined, about 1 minute. With the mixer running, slowly add the water mixture. Mix on low until the dough comes together, about 5 minutes, scraping the bowl once or twice. Cover and let the dough rest for 20 minutes.

With the mixer running on low, add the remaining 130 grams (1 cup) all-purpose flour and the salt. Knead until the dough is smooth and pulls away from the sides of the bowl, about 7 minutes; if the dough is sticky and clings to the sides of the bowl, knead in additional flour 1 tablespoon at a time until it reaches the proper consistency.

Lightly brush a rimmed baking sheet with oil. Dust the counter with flour and turn the dough out onto it, then divide the dough in half. Using your hands cupped around the dough, form each piece into a taut ball on an unfloured area of the counter. Press each ball into a 7-inch round about ¾ inch high, then place on the prepared baking sheet. Cover with a kitchen towel and let rise at room temperature until nearly doubled, 45 to 60 minutes; it's fine if the rounds end up touching each other. Meanwhile, heat the oven to 475°F with a rack in the middle position.

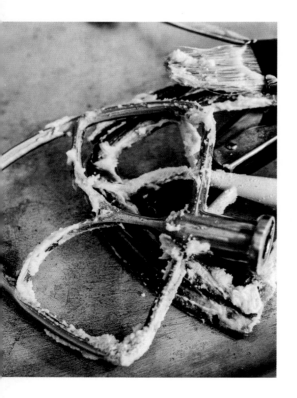

When the breads are properly risen, use a sharp knife to score a slit about
3 inches long and ¼ inch deep into the surface of each round. Bake until the breads
are well browned, 18 to 20 minutes. Cool on the baking sheet for about 5 minutes,
then transfer to a wire rack and cool completely.

German-Style Seeded Rye Bread

Start to finish: 15¾ hours
(20 minutes active), plus cooling

Makes one 9-inch loaf

**FOR THE PREFERMENT
AND SOAKER:**

65 grams (½ cup) all-purpose flour

½ cup buttermilk

½ teaspoon instant yeast

100 grams (½ cup) pearled farro

½ cup beer, preferably Hefeweizen
(see headnote)

FOR THE DOUGH:

350 grams (2½ cups) rye flour (see
headnote)

65 grams (½ cup) all-purpose flour

2 tablespoons flax seeds, divided

2 tablespoons sesame seeds,
divided

2 tablespoons pumpkin seeds,
divided

1½ teaspoons table salt

½ teaspoon instant yeast

1 cup warm water (100°F)

This recipe takes inspiration from German Vollkornbrot, a dense, hearty loaf with an earthy, tangy flavor. It gets its distinctive dark hue from whole-grain rye flour and usually is packed with seeds and rough-cut rye berries, called rye chops. In the U.S., rye chops can be challenging to source; we instead opt for pantry-friendly pearled farro, which provides a similar texture. Soaking the farro in beer softens it while infusing the grains with ferment-y flavor. We like the maltiness of German Hefeweizen, but feel free to experiment; opting for a bolder brew is a simple way to tweak the bread's flavor. Sourdough starter and multi-day fermentation make traditional Vollkornbrot notably tart. To capture this quality in a fraction of the time, we mix a portion of the dough's flour with buttermilk. Either dark rye flour (sometimes called whole rye flour) or medium rye flour works well. The former contains the entire ground rye kernel with nothing sifted out, bringing more assertive earthy and nutty notes. This loaf takes some time to make but is surprisingly easy— no stand mixer required—and it delivers bold, satisfying flavor and hearty texture. To serve, slice thinly and dress with any number of toppings—from a thick layer of butter or jam to slices of cheese or smoked fish. Well wrapped, the bread will keep at room temperature for up to a week.

Don't slice the bread until it has cooled completely. With such a high quantity of rye flour, Vollkornbrot often is rested for 24 to 48 hours after baking. Because our recipe includes some all-purpose flour, you don't have to wait that long. But hold off until the bread is at least room temperature, otherwise it will be gummy.

To make the preferment and soaker, in a large bowl, stir the flour, buttermilk and yeast; this is the preferment. In a small bowl, combine the farro and beer; this is the soaker. Cover both with plastic wrap and refrigerate at least 12 hours or up to 24.

To make the dough, to the bowl with the preferment, add the soaker, both flours, 1 tablespoon each flax seeds, sesame seeds and pumpkin seeds, the salt, yeast and water. Using a silicone spatula, mix until no dry, floury bits remain; the dough will be thick and dense; do not overmix. Cover and let rise at room temperature until just shy of doubled, 1½ to 1¾ hours.

Mist a 9-by-5-inch loaf pan with cooking spray. Using a silicone spatula, scrape the dough into the pan. With a dampened hand, gently flatten the dough into an even

layer, pushing it to the edges and into the corners. Sprinkle evenly with the remaining flax, sesame and pumpkin seeds. Using a dry hand, gently press them into the dough so they adhere. Cover with plastic wrap and let rise at room temperature until the dough rises slightly (it will not double) and has a slightly domed surface, about 40 minutes. Meanwhile, heat the oven to 400°F with a rack in the middle position.

Bake until the bread is deeply browned, pulls away from the sides of the pan and the center reaches 200°F, 60 to 70 minutes. Immediately invert the loaf out of the pan onto a wire rack, then turn it upright. Cool completely before slicing.

Georgian Cheese Bread

**Start to finish: 2 hours
(20 minutes active)**

**Makes one 12-inch
boat-shaped bread**

FOR THE DOUGH:

260 grams (2 cups) all-purpose
flour, plus more for dusting

1 teaspoon instant yeast

1 teaspoon white sugar

⅔ cup warm water (100°F),
plus more if needed

1 tablespoon plus 3 teaspoons
extra-virgin olive oil

¾ teaspoon table salt

FOR THE FILLING:

170 grams (1½ cups) shredded
whole-milk mozzarella cheese

85 grams (¾ cup) crumbled feta
cheese

113 grams (4 ounces) cream cheese,
cut into 1-inch cubes

½ teaspoon ground black pepper

1 large egg yolk, room temperature

1 tablespoon salted butter, room
temperature

1 tablespoon chopped fresh chives
(optional)

Georgia's staple snack, khachapuri, comes in many regional forms, but all are versions of savory cheese-filled bread. Adjaruli khachapuri, from the southwestern area of Adjara, is the best-known variety outside of Georgia, and it's easily recognizable by its boat-like shape. Near the end of baking, an egg is cracked into the cheesy center and a pat of butter finishes the still-hot khachapuri. For our version, we make the dough in a food processor, which also makes quick work of mixing the cheeses for the filling. Rather than top the bread with a whole egg, we add only a yolk, as we found it tricky to time the perfect cooking of the white. Adjaruli khachapuri is best eaten hot, fresh from the oven—tear off the edges of the bread and dip them into the cheese filling.

Don't wait to add the egg yolk and butter to the khachapuri. Do so as soon as the bread comes out of the oven and stir to combine. The heat from the cheese mixture will both cook the yolk and melt the butter, creating a delicious sauce for dipping.

To make the dough, in a food processor, combine the flour, yeast and sugar; pulse until combined, about 5 pulses. Add the water and 1 tablespoon oil, then process until a smooth, slightly sticky ball forms, about 30 seconds. If the mixture is dry, mix in additional water, 1 teaspoon at a time (up to 1 tablespoon total). Let rest in the food processor for 5 minutes. Meanwhile, coat a medium bowl with 1 teaspoon of the oil.

Sprinkle the salt over the dough and process until the dough is smooth and pliable, about 1 minute. Transfer the dough to the prepared bowl and turn to coat; return the food processor bowl and blade to the base. Cover the dough with plastic wrap and let rise at room temperature until doubled, about 45 minutes.

Meanwhile, make the filling. In the now-empty processor, combine all three cheeses and the pepper. Process until the mixture is creamy and well combined, about 1 minute, scraping the bowl about halfway through. Set aside, covered, at room temperature until ready to use. Heat the oven to 475°F with a rack in the middle position.

When the dough has doubled, line a rimmed baking sheet with kitchen parchment. Dust the counter with flour and turn the dough out onto it. Working from the center outward, gently dimple the dough with your fingers, forming an 8-inch round with thicker edges. Transfer the dough to the baking sheet, then stretch it into a 12-inch-by-6-inch oval.

Mound the filling on the dough and spread it in an even layer, leaving a 1½-inch border around the edges. Fold the unfilled sides onto the filling, then twist each end

STEPS »

1. For the filling, combine all 3 cheeses and the pepper. Process until creamy and well combined. Set aside, covered.

2. Turn the dough onto a counter lightly dusted with flour. Working from the center outward, gently dimple the dough with your fingers, forming an 8-inch round with thicker edges.

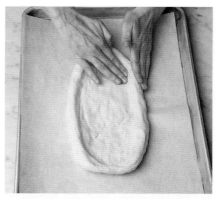

3. Transfer the dough to the parchment-lined baking sheet, then stretch it into a 12-by-6-inch oval.

4. Mound the filling on the dough and spread in an even layer, leaving a 1½-inch border around the edges.

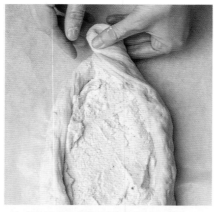

5. Fold the unfilled sides onto the filling, then twist each end 3 or 4 times, forming a boat shape.

6. Transfer the baked bread to a cutting board. Add the egg yolk, butter and chives (if using). Using a fork, swirl until well combined.

3 or 4 times to form a boat shape. Brush the edges with the remaining 2 teaspoons oil. Let rise at room temperature until slightly puffy, about 20 minutes.

Bake until the edges of the khachapuri are golden brown and the filling is bubbling and spotty brown, about 15 minutes. Using a wide metal spatula and working quickly, transfer the khachapuri to a cutting board. Immediately add the egg yolk, butter and chives (if using) to the center of the filling. Using a fork, swirl until well combined. Serve right away.

Georgian Cheese Bread with Fresh Herbs

Follow the recipe to make the dough. While the dough is rising, in the now-empty food processor, combine **1 bunch scallions** (roughly chopped), **1 cup lightly packed fresh flat-leaf parsley** and **½ cup lightly packed fresh dill.** Pulse until roughly chopped, about 10 pulses. Add **113 grams (1 cup) shredded whole-milk mozzarella cheese, 57 grams (½ cup) crumbled feta cheese, 60 grams (2 ounces) cream cheese** (cut into 1-inch cubes) and **½ teaspoon ground black pepper.** Process until the mixture is creamy, smooth and well combined, about 1 minute, scraping the bowl about halfway through. Set the filling aside, covered, at room temperature until ready to use. Continue with the recipe to shape, fill and bake the dough and add the egg yolk and butter after baking as directed.

DOUGH LINGO

Preferment is a broad category of dough starters that provide leavening, structure and a tangy, complex flavor to breads and doughs. They are all a combination of flour (typically white, rye or semolina), water and yeast (either commercial or wild) that given time creates the ideal conditions for the yeast and lactic acid bacteria to feast on the flour's carbohydrates. Preferments go by varying names according to country of origin, particular usage, ingredients and consistency. Most preferments—biga, chef, poolish or sponge—have a roughly 24-hour lifespan; the yeast dies off after consuming all the sugars in the starch. Sourdough starter and French levain are different in that they can be maintained for years and must be continually "fed" by adding new flour to keep the yeasts alive and maintain acidity levels (the "sour" in sourdough). Pate fermentee, or old dough, is another type of starter that starts fresh dough with a reserved portion of an earlier batch.

To avoid confusing terminology, we refer to all dough starters in this book as a preferment, regardless of flour, moisture content or ratios.

Olive Oil Challah with Golden Raisins

**Start to finish: 3½ hours
(1¼ hours active), plus cooling**

Makes two 1¼-pound loaves

43 grams (⅓ cup), plus 607 grams (4⅔ cups) all-purpose flour, plus more for dusting

155 grams (1 cup) golden raisins

¼ cup orange juice

3 large eggs, room temperature, plus 1 large egg, for brushing

½ cup extra-virgin olive oil, plus more for the pans

63 grams (3 tablespoons) honey

2 teaspoons table salt

2¼ teaspoons instant yeast

For our challah, we borrowed the water roux (also called tangzhong) technique that's used to make tender, fluffy Japanese milk bread (p. 76). A water roux is a mixture of water and starch cooked to a gel-like paste. It's a way to increase the hydration level in a bread dough but keep the mixture workable (instead of turning it wet) while also extending the shelf-life of the baked loaf. In our challah, the water roux also helped produce a better-structured crumb, with the light, feathery quality characteristic of the bread. Oil is the fat of choice in traditional challah. For more complex, nuanced flavor, we chose extra-virgin olive oil over a flavorless neutral oil. And to complement the fruity, peppery notes of olive oil, we mix golden raisins plumped in orange juice into the dough at the end of kneading. Though we love the look of challah formed into an intricate six-strand braid or an impressively mounded crown, for ease, we make two simple braids and bake them in loaf pans. Well wrapped, the loaves will keep at room temperature for two or three days. For longer storage, wrap in foil and freeze for up to a month. To refresh, thaw the still-wrapped loaf at room temperature (about 30 minutes), then completely unwrap, place on a baking sheet and warm in a 300°F oven for about 15 minutes.

Don't forget to drain the raisins before adding them to the dough. Also, don't cut into the challah while it's still warm. With such a light, tender crumb, the bread slices more easily and has a better texture after cooling to room temperature.

In a small saucepan, whisk together 1 cup water and the 43 grams (⅓ cup) flour until smooth. Over medium, cook, whisking constantly, until it thickens (a silicone spatula drawn through the mixture leaves a trail) and bubbles slowly, 2 to 4 minutes; this is a "water roux." Scrape the mixture into a stand mixer bowl, press a sheet of plastic wrap directly against the surface and cool until barely warm, at least 30 minutes.

Meanwhile, in a small saucepan, combine the raisins and orange juice; bring to a simmer over medium, stirring, then remove from the heat. (Alternatively, in a small microwave-safe bowl, combine the raisins and juice; microwave on high until simmering, about 1 minute.) Cool to room temperature, stirring occasionally.

To the cooled water roux, whisk in the 3 eggs. Whisk in the oil and honey. Add the remaining 607 grams (4⅔ cups) flour, the salt and yeast, then attach the bowl and dough hook to the mixer. Mix on low until a sticky, slightly elastic dough forms,

STEPS »

about 5 minutes. Scrape the bowl and push the dough off the hook. Drain the raisins in a fine-mesh strainer, pressing on them with a spoon to remove excess liquid. Add the raisins to the dough and mix on medium-low, scraping the bowl as needed, until the raisins are evenly distributed and the dough is tacky but not wet, about another 5 minutes. Detach the bowl from the mixer and use the spatula to scrape the bowl and gather the dough at the center. Cover with plastic wrap and let rise at room temperature until doubled, about 1½ hours. Meanwhile, brush two 9-by-5-inch loaf pans with oil, then line each with an 8-by-14-inch piece of kitchen parchment, allowing the excess to overhang the long sides of the pan.

Lightly flour the counter and turn the dough out onto it. Using a bench scraper or chef's knife, divide the dough in half; each piece should weigh about 650 grams (23 ounces). Now divide each half into 3 equal pieces, for a total of 6 pieces; cover with a kitchen towel. Roll each portion back and forth against the counter to form a 12-inch rope; as you work, keep the previously formed ropes covered.

Position 3 ropes perpendicular to the counter's edge but parallel to each other. Firmly pinch together the far ends of the ropes. Flour your fingers, then lift the right rope, cross it over the middle rope and lay it between the other 2; adjust the spacing of the ropes as you go. Now cross the left rope over the new middle rope and lay it between the 2. Repeat the braiding until you reach the ends of the ropes. Firmly pinch together the ends. Tuck the ends under the loaf and transfer the braid to a prepared loaf pan, compacting it as needed to fit. Cover with a kitchen towel. Shape the second loaf in the same way and cover. Let rise at room temperature until the loaves have increased by half and the dough feels puffy but slowly springs back when gently poked with a finger, 1¼ to 1½ hours.

About 45 minutes into rising, heat the oven to 350°F with a rack in the lower-middle position. In a small bowl, whisk the remaining egg. When the loaves have risen by 50 percent, brush the tops with beaten egg. Place the pans in the oven, spaced several inches apart, and immediately reduce the temperature to 325°F. Bake until the loaves are golden brown and the centers reach about 185°F to 190°F, 45 to 50 minutes.

Transfer the pans to a wire rack and cool for 30 minutes. Using the parchment slings, lift the loaves from their pans, peel off the parchment and set them directly on the rack. Cool for at least 1 hour before slicing.

HOW TO MAKE OLIVE OIL CHALLAH

1. To the cooled water roux, add the eggs and whisk until incorporated. Add the oil and honey; whisk until homogeneous.

2. Add flour, salt and yeast, mix until a sticky, elastic dough forms. Knead on low with the dough hook for about 5 minutes.

3. Add the drained raisins and knead on medium-low until the raisins are evenly distributed, about 5 minutes.

4. Turn the dough out onto a lightly floured counter. Divide the dough in half, then divide each half into 3 pieces.

5. Roll each portion back and forth against the counter to form a 12-inch rope.

6. Place 3 ropes perpendicular to the counter and parallel to each other. Firmly pinch together the far ends of the ropes.

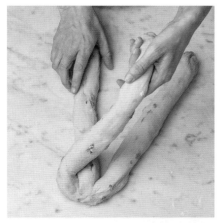

7. Lift the right rope, cross it over the middle rope, lay it between the two, adjust the spacing of the ropes as you go.

8. Now cross the left rope over the new middle rope and lay it between the two.

9. Continue braiding until you reach the ends of the ropes. Firmly pinch together the ends.

Sweet and Savory Breads

Ciabatta

**Start to finish: 18 hours
(1 hour active), plus cooling**

Makes two 11-ounce loaves

480 grams (3½ cups) bread flour,
plus more for dusting

1½ teaspoons instant yeast

1½ teaspoons table salt

Ciabatta means "slipper" in Italian, a reference to its low, wide shape. The bread's characteristic thin crust and open, airy crumb are products of high hydration, meaning the dough contains a high ratio of water to flour. The resulting mixture is wet and requires a different approach to gluten development than stiffer, more conventional bread doughs. Time is a key ingredient: it allows the flour to slowly absorb water while yeast works in tandem, creating CO_2 that begins inflating and strengthening gluten networks. Simultaneously, the dough's flavor improves via fermentation. We perform a series of stretches and folds on the dough, which slowly and gently builds gluten in a way that an electric mixer cannot. With each stretch and fold, you'll feel the dough develop strength and tension while becoming more cohesive. Another factor that's essential for ciabatta's crisp crust is steam. You'll need a spray bottle filled with water to spritz the bread before it goes into the oven, as well as after five minutes of baking. This keeps its surface moist, discouraging crust formation and letting the loaf expand. It won't begin forming a crust until later, ensuring the crust is thin and crackly, not thick or tough. You'll also need a rectangular steel or stone on which to bake the ciabatta. They're extremely efficient at conducting high heat evenly, ensuring that the loaf gets good oven spring, as well as a crisp crust. And a pizza peel is the easiest way to shuttle the loaves in and out of the oven.

Don't hesitate to liberally flour your work surface and dough as you divide and shape the ciabatta. Also, don't worry if the loaves aren't perfect rectangles. An irregular shape is part of the breads' rustic charm. The dough inevitably will lose some of its airiness during shaping, but take care to deflate it as little as possible. Lastly, avoid dripping or misting water onto the oven door when spritzing the loaves five minutes into baking. Though oven windows are made of tempered glass, it's still a good idea to make sure water doesn't make contact with the glass when it's scorchingly hot.

In a large bowl, combine the flour, yeast, salt and 1⅔ cups water. Mix by hand until a wet, tacky dough forms; it will be dry and shaggy to start but will come together after a few minutes. Cover with plastic wrap and let rise at room temperature for 2 hours (the mixture may not double during this time), then refrigerate for 8 hours or up to 12 hours.

Remove the dough from the refrigerator and let stand until room temperature, up to 4 hours. Place the bowl directly in front of you. Dampen your dominant hand with water, then slide it down the inside of the bowl at the side farthest from you, all

STEPS »

HOW TO MAKE CIABATTA

1. Dampen your hand with water and slide it down the far side of the bowl. Scoop a portion of dough, stretch it up, then tuck it down against the side of the bowl closest to you.

2. Rotate the bowl 90 degrees and repeat, remoistening your hand as needed. Repeat 4 more times for a total of 6 folds. Re-cover the dough and let rest 1 hour.

3. Repeat the set of 6 folds. Re-cover the dough and let rest again 1 hour. Heat the oven to 450°F with a baking steel or stone on the lower middle rack. Cut two 8-by-14-inch sheets of kitchen parchment.

4. Dust the counter with flour and gently turn the dough out onto it. Liberally flour the dough. Divide the dough in half.

5. Sprinkle the cut sides of the dough portions with flour. Gently roll one half onto its cut side.

6. Stretch the dough until it is 10 inches long. Transfer to a parchment sheet, then stretch into a 5-by-11-inch rectangle. Repeat with the second portion. Cover and let rise.

7. Uncover the loaves and liberally spritz each all over with water.

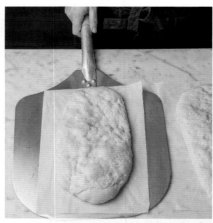

8. Using a pizza peel, slide the loaves one at a time with their parchment onto the steel or stone, placing side by side.

9. Bake for 5 minutes; spritz the loaves again. Bake until the loaves are golden brown and the centers register 200°F.

the way to the bottom. Scoop the dough at the bottom and stretch it upward, then fold it over the dough in the bowl, tucking it down toward the side of the dough that is closest to you. Rotate the bowl 90 degrees and repeat, remoistening your hand as needed. Repeat 4 more times for a total of 6 folds. Re-cover the dough and let rest at room temperature 1 hour.

Repeat the set of 6 folds. Re-cover the dough and let rest again at room temperature for 1 hour. Meanwhile, heat the oven to 450°F with a baking steel or stone on the lower-middle rack. Cut 2 sheets of kitchen parchment, each measuring about 8 by 12 to 14 inches.

Generously dust the counter with flour and gently turn the dough out onto it; try not to deflate it. Liberally flour the top of the dough. Using a dough scraper or bench knife, divide the dough in half, again trying to preserve its airiness. Sprinkle the cut sides with flour, then gently roll one half onto its cut side. Holding the short ends, gently pull the dough, stretching it from the center until it is roughly 10 inches long. Transfer to the center of one of the parchment sheets. Using your hands, gently dimple and stretch the dough, working outward from the center, to form a rough 5-by-11-inch rectangle of relatively even thickness. Repeat with the second portion of dough, placing it on the second parchment sheet. Drape a kitchen towel over each loaf and let rise until slightly puffy with a few bubbles across the surface, about 30 minutes. Have ready a spray bottle filled with water.

Uncover the loaves and liberally spritz each all over with water. Using a pizza peel, slide the loaves one at a time with their parchment onto the steel or stone, placing them side by side. Bake for 5 minutes, then spritz the loaves again; work quickly to avoid letting too much heat escape the oven and avoid spraying or dripping water onto the oven-door window. Bake until the loaves are golden brown and the centers register 200°F, 15 to 18 minutes.

Using the pizza peel, transfer the loaves with their parchment to a wire rack. Cool for about 5 minutes. Remove and discard the parchment, then cool completely.

KNOW WHEN TO FOLD

Most bread recipes a few decades old (or older) generally call for kneading, while many contemporary recipes often call for dough to be folded. The change—if there really has been a change—comes down to baking trends. But first, we should define our terms. Kneading dough involves working it with a repeated push-pull motion to generate gluten formation. Folding is a more gentle technique; the dough is pulled upward and outward to stretch the elastic dough, then folded over on itself periodically during the rise. Generally, the moisture content of the dough determines which method is best. The wetter the dough, the more difficult it is to knead, so folding often is better for doughs such as pizza, focaccia, ciabatta and high-hydration sourdoughs. The final texture of the bread also is a consideration: Folding allows for an irregular crumb and larger air pockets.

Kneading, meanwhile, deflates air pockets, creating a tighter, denser crumb more suitable for loaves of sliceable sandwich bread. To compare the two techniques directly, we made both a kneaded and a folded version of whole-wheat levain bread. Made with a sourdough-like natural starter, this bread features a dough firm enough to knead, but with enough hydration that it also can be folded. After baking and cooling, the folded dough did indeed have larger air pockets and a chewier, looser crumb than the kneaded loaf.

Limpa (Swedish Rye Bread)

**Start to finish: 5 hours
(30 minutes active), plus cooling**

Makes a 1½-pound loaf

1 teaspoon aniseed

1 teaspoon fennel seeds

1 teaspoon coriander seeds

140 grams (1 cup) rye flour
(see headnote)

3 tablespoons packed dark
brown sugar

1 cup buttermilk, room temperature

57 grams (4 tablespoons) salted
butter, melted and slightly cooled

206 grams (1½ cups) bread flour

1 teaspoon instant yeast

1 teaspoon table salt

The Swedish rye bread called limpa tends to be a plain-looking loaf, but its flavor is anything but. A mix of spices gives the crumb a warm, heady aroma while orange zest or oil is commonly added for citrusy brightness. Limpa is a classic on the Swedish holiday table, but we think it's a great bread to bake at any time. Subtly sweet and hearty, it pairs well with cheeses and smoked or cured meats and fish. It's also delicious toasted and smeared with salted butter. We use a trio of seeds in our loaf—aniseed, fennel and coriander—and instead of the more typical whole milk or water, we use buttermilk. We like the pleasant tang and subtle richness it provides; it also yields an especially tender, moist crumb. Rye flour of any type—light, medium or dark—works well. But rye is very low in gluten, so the crumb's structure is supplied by bread flour, which is high in protein. Make sure to allow the loaf to cool completely before slicing.

Don't use pre-ground spices. Whole seeds that are toasted then coarsely ground impart much more flavor and character than pre-ground spices. And don't forget to lower the oven temperature 15 minutes into baking. This allows the loaf to rise before the crust has a chance to fully set.

In an 8-inch skillet over medium, toast all of the seeds, stirring, until fragrant and beginning to pop, about 2 minutes. Transfer to a spice grinder and cool. Pulse until coarsely ground. Measure 1 teaspoon of the spice mix and set aside for sprinkling; transfer the remainder to the bowl of a stand mixer.

To the spices in the mixer bowl, add the rye flour, brown sugar, buttermilk and melted butter. Stir with a silicone spatula until well combined, then let stand at room temperature for 10 minutes; the mixture will thicken.

Add the bread flour, yeast and salt. Attach the bowl and dough hook to the mixer; mix on low until a smooth dough forms, about 5 minutes; it will be tacky but not wet. Transfer the dough to the counter and knead a few times by hand. Shape it into a ball and return it to the bowl, seam-side down. Cover with plastic wrap and let rise at room temperature until almost doubled, about 1½ hours.

Line a rimmed baking sheet with kitchen parchment. Lightly flour the counter and turn the dough out onto it. Using your hands, roll the dough back and forth on the counter to form it into a 10-inch log about 2½ inches wide with tapered ends. Transfer to the baking sheet, smoothest side up. Cover with a kitchen towel and let rise at room temperature for 1 hour; the loaf will expand, but will not double. About 30 minutes into rising, heat the oven to 375°F with the rack in the lower-middle position.

Lightly brush the surface of the loaf with water, then sprinkle evenly with the reserved spice mix. Using a paring knife, cut 3 diagonal slashes, each about 3 inches long and ¼ inch deep, into the loaf, spacing them evenly. Bake for 15 minutes, then lower the oven to 325°F. Bake until the loaf is golden brown and the center reaches 190°F, 35 to 40 minutes.

Cool on the baking sheet on a wire rack for 10 minutes. Transfer the loaf directly to the rack and cool completely.

Greek Olive Bread
with Rosemary and Oregano

**Start to finish: 3¼ hours
(45 minutes active), plus cooling**

Makes a 1½-pound loaf

1 cup warm water (100°F), plus
more if needed

1½ tablespoons extra-virgin olive
oil, plus more for brushing

4 teaspoons honey, divided

260 grams (2 cups) all-purpose
flour, plus more for dusting

70 grams (½ cup) whole-wheat flour

1¾ teaspoons instant yeast

¾ teaspoon dried oregano

¼ teaspoon ground black pepper

¾ teaspoon table salt

138 grams (1 cup) pitted Kalamata
olives, roughly chopped

1 small garlic clove, minced

1½ teaspoons minced fresh
rosemary

1 teaspoon chopped fresh oregano

This hearty loaf is our take on eliopsomo, a traditional Greek olive bread. Bolstered by whole-wheat flour and honey, the dough is soft and subtly sweet—a nice contrast to the savoriness of Kalamata olives. Kneading chopped olives directly into the dough interferes with gluten development, resulting in a weaker crumb structure, so instead we flatten the dough into a rectangle, sprinkle on a filling of chopped Kalamatas mixed with rosemary and garlic, then roll it up into a log. After baking, slicing the loaf reveals a salty, herbaceous spiral that runs through it. For making this dough, we also employ a brief autolyse, or resting time after combining the flours and liquids. This allows the whole-wheat flour to hydrate and jumpstarts gluten development.

Don't be tempted to add extra flour when mixing the dough; it may look quite sticky, but will firm up as it rises. Unlike many bread doughs, this one will be wet enough to cling to the bowl—it will not clear the sides—when kneading is complete.

In a liquid measuring cup or small bowl, stir together the water, oil and 2 teaspoons honey. In the bowl of a stand mixer with the dough hook, mix both flours, the yeast, dried oregano and pepper on low until combined, about 5 seconds. With the mixer running, add the water mixture and mix until a soft, slightly lumpy dough forms, about 3 minutes, scraping the bowl once or twice. Feel the dough; it should be sticky. If not, add water 1 teaspoon at a time, mixing after each addition, until the dough feels sticky but not wet. Let rest in the mixer bowl for 5 minutes.

Add the salt and knead on medium until the dough is smooth and forms a mass around the hook, but still adheres to the sides of the bowl, about 5 minutes. Scrape the sides of the bowl and gather the dough in the center. Cover with plastic wrap and let rise at room temperature until doubled, 1 to 1½ hours. Meanwhile, in a small bowl, stir together the olives, garlic, rosemary and fresh oregano; set aside.

Line a rimmed baking sheet with kitchen parchment. Lightly flour the counter. Turn the dough out onto the counter and, using your hands, gently press and stretch it into a 10-by-7-inch rectangle with a short side facing you. Distribute the olive mixture in an even layer over the dough, spreading it to the edges. Starting from the side nearest you, roll the dough into a tight log. Pinch the seam to seal and transfer seam side down to the prepared baking sheet. Pinch the open ends to seal, then tuck the pinched seams under; the loaf should measure about 10 inches long by 3½ inches wide. Loosely cover with plastic wrap and let rise at room temperature until doubled, about 1 hour.

STEPS >>

HOW TO MAKE GREEK OLIVE BREAD

1. Knead the dough on medium until it is smooth and forms a mass around the hook, but still adheres to the bowl's sides.

2. In a small bowl, stir together the olives, garlic, rosemary and fresh oregano; set aside.

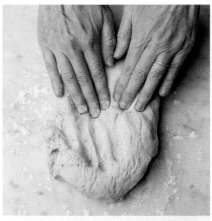

3. Turn the dough onto the counter. Using your hands, gently press and stretch into a 10-by-7-inch rectangle.

4. Distribute the olive mixture in an even layer over the dough, spreading it to the edges.

5. Starting from the side nearest you, roll the dough into a tight log.

6. Pinch the seam to seal and transfer seam-side down to the prepared baking sheet.

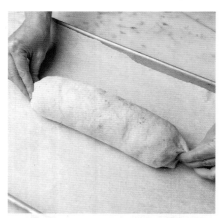

7. Pinch the open ends to seal, then tuck the pinched seams under; the loaf should measure about 10 inches long and 3½ inches wide.

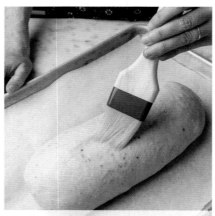

8. When the loaf has doubled, about 1 hour, brush it with the honey-water mixture.

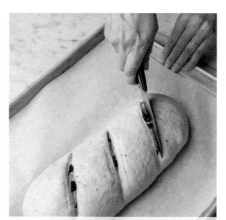

9. Using a paring knife, make 3 diagonal slashes, each about 3 inches long, in the loaf, cutting through to reveal the filling.

About 40 minutes into rising, heat the oven to 375°F with a rack in the lower-middle position. In a small bowl, whisk together 2 tablespoons water and the remaining 2 teaspoons honey.

When the loaf has doubled, brush it with the honey-water mixture (you may not use it all). Using a paring knife, make 3 diagonal slashes, each about 3 inches long, in the loaf, spacing them evenly along the length of the loaf; the slashes should cut through the outermost layer of dough to reveal the olive filling just underneath. Bake until the loaf is golden brown and the center reaches 200°F, 40 to 45 minutes.

Cool on the baking sheet on a wire rack for about 10 minutes. Transfer the loaf directly to the rack and cool completely, about 2 hours.

Three-Seed Beer Pretzels

**Start to finish: 11½ hours
(1½ hours active), plus cooling**

Makes ten 4½-inch pretzels

548 grams (4 cups) bread flour,
plus more as needed

2¼ teaspoons instant yeast

2¼ teaspoons table salt

¾ cup amber ale or lager

28 grams (2 tablespoons) salted
butter, cut into ½-inch cubes, room
temperature

36 grams (1½ tablespoons) barley
malt syrup (see headnote) or
molasses

85 grams (⅓ cup) baking soda

35 grams (¼ cup) raw pumpkin
seeds

36 grams (¼ cup) raw shelled
sunflower seeds

10 grams (2 tablespoons) caraway
seeds

1 large egg white, beaten

2 teaspoons flaky salt

These soft pretzels offer a chewy, salty crust and soft, slightly sweet interior. Dark, sticky barley malt syrup supplies earthy sweetness and contains enzymes that help the pretzels develop a rich, golden hue. Look for it where you'd find molasses, which is a great substitute, if needed. To hydrate the dough, we've opted for beer, which provides a complex, slightly funky flavor. Any variety works, but we especially like the grassiness of hefeweizen and the caramel notes of amber ale. Traditional Bavarian pretzels get their snappy texture and mahogany tone from lye. While the flavor it yields is unparalleled, lye is tricky to work with, so instead, we gently heat baking soda to make it more alkaline, then dissolve it in water that we briefly boil the pretzels in. This gives them characteristics akin to the classic Bavarian pretzels. A sprinkle of flaky salt and a savory seed mix add flavorful crunch. Enjoy slightly warm or at room temperature and with any variety of mustard.

Don't flour the counter when working with the dough. An unfloured surface provides traction for easier shaping. Also, make sure the pot of alkalized water is simmering by the time the shaped pretzels have almost doubled. If the pretzels have to wait for the water to heat, the yeast may lose some of its oomph. Finally, don't leave the pretzels in the water for longer than 30 seconds or they may not rise well in the oven.

In the bowl of a stand mixer, stir the flour, yeast and table salt. Add the beer, ⅔ cup water, butter and barley malt syrup; mix with the dough hook on low until a shaggy dough forms, about 2 minutes. Increase to medium and mix until the dough is smooth, shiny, elastic and pulls away from the sides of the bowl, 6 to 7 minutes; if the dough climbs up the hook, stop and push it off. The dough should feel tacky but should not stick and cling to your fingers. If it does, knead in up to 2 tablespoons more flour. Cover the bowl with plastic wrap and refrigerate at least 8 hours or up to 24 hours.

Meanwhile, heat the oven to 275°F with a rack in the middle position. Line a rimmed baking sheet with kitchen parchment. Spread the baking soda in an even layer on it and bake without stirring for 1 hour; it will not change in appearance. Cool, then transfer to a small airtight container; set aside. (The baked baking soda can be stored at room temperature for up to 1 month.) Reserve the parchment-lined baking sheet.

When ready to shape the dough, remove it from the refrigerator and gently punch it down. Let stand, covered, until doubled in bulk, about 2 hours. Meanwhile, line

RISING TO THE CHALLENGE

Yeast doughs are notoriously persnickety about achieving a proper rise. Several factors are at play, but among the most common are the temperature and humidity of the room. Warmth and humidity speed up yeast activity; lower temps make them more sluggish. The ideal ambient temperature for dough fermentation typically is between 70°F and 80°F, with a relative humidity of 75 to 85 percent. But average room temperature often is between 68°F and 73°F, with a relative humidity of no more than 55 percent. Add changing seasons, and achieving optimal proofing conditions can be tough. This is why professional bakers often use proofing boxes, enclosed devices designed to regulate temperature and humidity.

Since most home bakers don't have these, we wanted to determine the best way to mimic those conditions. Some people set a steaming cup of water in an oven or microwave, but these have drawbacks. Most microwaves are too small for large bowls of dough, and using the oven to proof means you can't heat it in advance. A large (100-quart) cooler worked well. It was large enough to accommodate both two cups of boiling water and a large bowl of dough. The water increased the temperature inside the cooler by 20°F and held it near there for close to two hours. For the second rise, adding a fresh cup of boiling water was plenty. But we preferred a large clear plastic storage bin. Because they are not insulated, bins required three cups of water to hold the appropriate temperature. But this is offset by the convenience of being able to see the dough without lifting the lid (and releasing heat and humidity).

another rimmed baking sheet with kitchen parchment, then mist it and the reserved one with cooking spray. In a small bowl, stir together the pumpkin, sunflower and caraway seeds; set aside.

Heat the oven to 450°F with racks in the upper- and lower-middle positions. In a large Dutch oven over medium-low, whisk 3 quarts water and the baking soda; cover the pot. Turn the dough out onto an unfloured counter. Using a chef's knife or bench scraper, divide it into 10 pieces, each about 95 grams (3¼ ounces). Roll each into a log roughly 6 inches long; keep the logs covered.

Place 1 dough log in the center of your work surface. Using your hands and applying only light pressure to start, roll the

HOW TO MAKE THREE-SEED BEER PRETZELS

1. Using a chef's knife or bench scraper, divide the dough into 10 pieces, each about 95 grams (3¼ ounces).

2. Roll each piece into a log 6 inches long; keep the logs covered. Place 1 log in the center of your work surface.

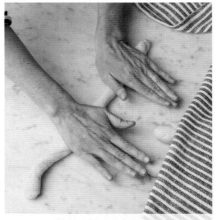

3. Using your hands, applying only light pressure to start, roll the dough back and forth to stretch it to a 26- to 28-inch rope.

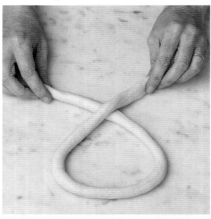

4. Cross the arms of the rope, forming an X about 3 inches in from each end.

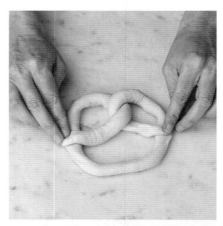

5. Twist the arms around each other and attach the ends to the "belly" at 4 o'clock and 8 o'clock. Press firmly to seal.

6. Transfer to the baking sheet and shape the pretzel so it measures about 4½ inches wide.

7. Carefully transfer 2 or 3 pretzels to the simmering alkalized water, taking care not to crowd the pot.

8. Using a small knife, score a horizontal slash along the belly of each boiled and drained pretzel.

9. Sprinkle the egg white-washed, unbaked, pretzels with the seed mixture, followed by flaky salt.

dough back and forth against the counter to stretch it to a 26- to 28-inch rope. If the dough springs back when rolled, let it rest, covered, for 10 to 15 minutes; begin rolling additional pieces while the previous ones rest. If the dough has air pockets that resist rolling, apply forceful pressure as your hands pass over the bubble in order to get the dough to stretch.

Cross the arms of the rope, forming an X about 3 inches in from each end, then twist the arms around each other and attach the ends to the "belly" at the 4 o'clock and 8 o'clock positions; press firmly to seal. Transfer the pretzel to a prepared baking sheet and shape it so it measures about 4½ inches wide. Shape the remaining portions in the same way, placing 5 pretzels, evenly spaced, on each baking sheet. Cover with kitchen towels and let rise at room temperature until puffy but not doubled in bulk, 15 to 20 minutes. Meanwhile, bring the water to a simmer, covered, over medium-high, whisking occasionally to ensure the soda dissolves.

Carefully transfer 2 or 3 pretzels to the simmering water, taking care not to crowd the pot; the pretzels will expand as they simmer. Cook, gently ladling water over the pretzels, for 30 seconds. Using a slotted spoon, return the pretzels to the baking sheet; repeat with the remaining pretzels.

Brush the surface of each pretzel with egg white. Using a small, sharp knife, score a horizontal slash, about ¼ inch deep and 3 inches long, along the belly of each pretzel. Sprinkle the pretzels with the seed mixture, followed by flaky salt. Bake until deeply browned, 14 to 16 minutes, switching and rotating the baking sheets halfway through. Cool on the baking sheets for 5 minutes, then transfer the pretzels to a wire rack. Serve warm or at room temperature.

VARIATION

Cheesy Soft Pretzels

Follow the recipe, omitting the pumpkin, sunflower and caraway seeds. After brushing the boiled pretzels with egg white, score as directed and sprinkle them with flaky salt, followed by **2 ounces (½ cup) shredded cheddar or Gruyère cheese**. Bake and cool as directed.

VARIATION

Pretzel Rolls

Follow the recipe to make and divide the dough, omitting the pumpkin, sunflower and caraway seeds. After dividing the dough into 10 portions, form each portion into a ball, creating a smooth, taut surface and pinching any seams on the bottom to seal them. Place 5 rolls, evenly spaced, on each baking sheet, then cover with kitchen towels and let rise at room temperature until puffy but not quite doubled in bulk, about 1 hour. About 30 minutes into rising, heat the oven to 450°F with racks in the upper- and lower-middle positions. Continue with the recipe to boil the rolls and return them to the baking sheets. Brush them with the egg white, then use a small, sharp knife to score an X, about ½ inch deep and 2 inches long, in the top of each roll. Sprinkle with flaky salt, then bake and cool as directed. Makes ten 4½-inch rolls.

Turkish-Style Sesame Rings

**Start to finish: 4½ hours
(2 hours active)**

Makes eight 5-inch simits

455 grams (3½ cups)
all-purpose flour

1½ teaspoons instant yeast

1½ teaspoons table salt

1 cup plus 2 tablespoons
warm water (100°F to 110°F)

107 grams (⅔ cup) white
sesame seeds

20 grams (2 tablespoons)
black sesame seeds, or additional
white sesame seeds

42 grams (2 tablespoons) honey

21 grams (1 tablespoon) molasses

A simit is a Turkish sesame-coated bread ring that resembles a slender bagel formed from twisted dough. It's a street-food favorite that's typically eaten at breakfast, but we think it's also great with dips and spreads or alongside soups and stews. True simits are dipped in a mixture of water and pekmez (grape molasses) before they're dredged in sesame seeds and baked. The result is a golden, lightly crunchy exterior that contrasts a pleasantly chewy crumb, with a subtle sweetness and the earthy, nutty flavor of sesame. Instead of pekmez, we use a combination of honey and molasses, which lends sweetness and helps with browning. We like the speckled look of a couple tablespoons of black sesame seeds mixed into white sesame, but it's fine to use only white. The rings are best eaten within a few hours of baking, but they will keep in an airtight container for a couple days. To rewarm, lay the rings on a baking sheet and place in a 375°F oven for about eight minutes.

Don't flour your work surface when rolling the dough ropes and forming the rings. The tackiness of the dough against an unfloured counter creates the resistance needed for shaping. If during rolling the dough springs back, cover it and allow the gluten to relax for a few minutes while you work on another piece.

HOW TO MAKE TURKISH-STYLE SESAME RINGS

1. Using a chef's knife or bench scraper, divide the dough into 8 pieces, each about 3 ounces; cover with a kitchen towel.

2. Using your hands, roll each piece back and forth against the counter into a rope roughly 18 inches long.

3. Roll each rope to a length of 30 inches, about ⅜ inch thick. Fold the rope in half and press the ends together to seal.

4. Twist the ends of the doubled rope in opposite directions while gently stretching it to create a tight spiral about 14 inches long.

5. Place outstretched fingers through the center of the ring with the seam under your palm. Roll on the counter to create a secure seal.

6. Gently transfer 1 ring to the honey-water mixture, turn to coat. Then place in the sesame seeds and turn to coat.

In a stand mixer with the dough hook, mix the flour, yeast and salt on low until combined, about 1 minute. With the mixer running, gradually add the water; mix until a dough forms that clears the sides of the bowl, 1 to 2 minutes. Increase to medium-low and knead until elastic, slightly stiff and clears the sides of the bowl, about 5 minutes. Detach the bowl from the mixer and lift out the hook. Use a silicone spatula to scrape the bowl and gather the dough in the center. Cover with plastic wrap and let rise at room temperature until doubled, 1½ to 2 hours.

About 1 hour into rising, heat the oven to 375°F with racks in the upper- and lower-middle positions. Line 2 rimmed baking sheets with kitchen parchment. Distribute both white and black sesame seeds in an even layer on 1 prepared baking sheet. Toast on the upper rack until golden brown, 2 to 4 minutes, stirring once halfway through. Transfer the seeds to a wide, shallow bowl or pie plate, reserving the parchment-lined baking sheet; set the seeds aside. Increase the oven to 400°F.

When the dough has doubled, turn it out onto an unfloured counter. Using a chef's knife or bench scraper, divide it into 8 pieces, each about 88 grams (3 ounces); cover the pieces with a kitchen towel. Using your hands, roll each piece back and forth against the counter into a rope roughly 18 inches long; keep the others covered while you work. If the dough springs back when rolled, let it rest, covered, for about 10 minutes; roll other pieces while the previous ones rest.

Place 1 rope in the center of your work surface. Roll it into a 30-inch-long rope about ⅜ inch thick. Fold the rope in half and firmly press together the open ends to seal. Twist the ends of the doubled rope in opposite directions while gently stretching it to create a tight spiral about 14 inches long. Draw the ends together to create a ring and firmly press the joined ends to seal. Place your outstretched fingers through the center of the ring and position the seam under your palm. Roll the seam back and forth against the counter to create a secure seal. Place the ring on one of the prepared baking sheets. Shape the remaining portions in the same way, placing 4 rings on each baking sheet and draping a kitchen towel over each baking sheet once full. Let rest for about 10 minutes.

Meanwhile, in another wide, shallow bowl or pie plate, whisk together the honey, molasses and ¼ cup water. Gently transfer 1 ring to the honey-water mixture and turn to coat, then place in the sesame seeds and turn to coat. Return the ring to the baking sheet, gently reshaping it to a 5-inch diameter. Repeat with the remaining rings. Let rest, uncovered, for 15 minutes; the rings will rise slightly, but not double. If any of the seams come undone, firmly press them together to reseal.

Bake the rings until golden brown, 22 to 27 minutes, rotating the baking sheets and switching their positions halfway through. Cool on the baking sheets for about 5 minutes, then use a wide metal spatula to transfer to a wire rack. Serve warm or at room temperature.

Sicilian Semolina and Sesame Bread

Our version of pane siciliano, or Sicilian sesame bread, has a soft, fine quality and a rustic, satisfying chew. The crumb's golden hue comes from semolina. Milled from durum wheat and commonly used to make pasta, semolina is relatively high in protein and has a slightly more granular texture than fine cornmeal. Bob's Red Mill, a brand widely available in supermarkets, works well, but pass on semolina labeled "coarse," as it will give the bread an unpleasant grittiness. Sesame seeds, on the interior and exterior of the loaf, bring earthy flavor that enhances the nutty nuances of the semolina. Baking the S-shaped coiled loaf in a steamy oven allows it to rise properly before the exterior sets and helps create a crispier crust because it facilitates starch gelatinization. The dough also makes terrific buns (see the instructions p. 117). Store leftovers in a zip-close bag at room temperature for up to four days. To refresh the loaf, wrap it in foil and warm in a 325°F oven for 15 minutes.

Start to finish: 2¾ hours (35 minutes active), plus cooling

Makes a 1¾-pound loaf

40 grams (4 tablespoons) sesame seeds, divided

1¼ cups plus 3 tablespoons warm water (100°F), divided

3 tablespoons extra-virgin olive oil

1 tablespoon plus 1 teaspoon honey, divided

340 grams (2 cups) semolina flour (see headnote), plus more for dusting

137 grams (1 cup) bread flour

2¼ teaspoons instant yeast

1½ teaspoons table salt

Don't flour the counter before turning the dough out onto it for shaping. The dough needs to stick slightly so it can be rolled into a log; on a floured surface it will slide around. Don't use a glass baking dish for the water in the oven; it can shatter. Finally, don't allow the shaped loaf to fully double in size before baking. We found that slightly underproofing this bread results in a better-textured crumb.

In an 8-inch skillet over medium, toast 30 grams (3 tablespoons) of sesame seeds, stirring, until fragrant and lightly browned, about 3 minutes. Transfer to a spice grinder and cool completely, then pulse until coarsely ground, about 6 pulses.

In a 2-cup liquid measuring cup, stir together 1¼ cups warm water, the oil and 1 tablespoon honey. In the bowl of a stand mixer, whisk together the ground sesame, both flours, the yeast and salt. Attach the bowl and dough hook to the mixer. With the mixer on low, gradually add the water mixture. Increase to medium and knead until a smooth dough forms and clears the sides of the bowl, about 10 minutes. Using your hands, form the dough into a ball in the bowl, cover with plastic wrap and let rise at room temperature until doubled, 1 to 1½ hours. Meanwhile, line a rimmed baking sheet with kitchen parchment and dust it with semolina.

Turn the dough out onto a dry counter (not floured). Form the dough into a thick log about 12 inches long. Using your hands, roll the log back and forth against the counter while applying light pressure, stretching the dough into an evenly thick rope about 30 inches long. Starting at one end, tightly coil the rope, stopping at the rope's midpoint. Coil the other end of the rope in the opposite direction from the first, forming an S shape.

HOW TO MAKE SICILIAN SEMOLINA AND SESAME BREAD

1. Form the dough into a thick log. Roll it against the counter, stretching it into an evenly thick rope about 30 inches long.

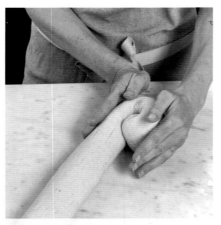

2. Starting at one end of the dough rope, use your hands to tightly coil the dough, stopping at the midpoint of the rope.

3. Repeat with the other end, only this time coil the dough in the opposite direction from the first coil, forming an S.

4. When the dough has almost doubled, brush it with a mixture of honey and water.

5. Sprinkle the dough with the remaining sesame seeds.

Place the shaped dough on the prepared baking sheet; reshape if needed. Drape a kitchen towel over the loaf and let rise at room temperature until just shy of doubled, 45 to 60 minutes. About 20 minutes into rising, position racks in the middle and lower-middle of the oven. Place a 9-by-13-inch metal baking pan on the lower rack and heat the oven to 375°F. In a small bowl, stir together the remaining 3 tablespoons warm water and the remaining 1 teaspoon honey. Have ready 3 cups hot tap water to pour into the baking pan to create steam for baking the bread.

When the dough has almost doubled, brush it with the honey-water mixture (you will not use it all), then sprinkle evenly with the remaining 1 tablespoon sesame seeds. Place the baking sheet in the oven, carefully pour the hot tap water into the baking pan and quickly close the oven door. Bake until golden brown and the center reaches 200°F, 35 to 40 minutes.

Cool the loaf on the baking sheet on a wire rack for about 5 minutes. Transfer directly to the rack and cool completely.

VARIATION

Semolina and Sesame Buns

Start to finish: 2½ hours (40 minutes active), plus cooling
Makes six 4½-inch buns

After mixing and allowing the dough to double, divide it into 6 equal portions, each about 145 grams (5 ounces). Form each portion into a taut ball by rolling it against the counter in a circular motion under a cupped hand; place seam-side down and evenly spaced on the prepared baking sheet. Using your hand, flatten each ball to a 1-inch thickness (if you wish to make taller, rounder rolls, do not flatten the portions). Drape a kitchen towel over the buns and let rise at room temperature until doubled, 30 to 45 minutes. Meanwhile, position racks in the middle and lower-middle of the oven. Place a 9-by-13-inch metal baking pan on the lower rack and heat the oven to 375°F. In a small bowl, stir together the remaining 3 tablespoons warm water and the remaining 1 teaspoon honey. Have ready 3 cups hot tap water to pour into the baking pan to create steam for baking the bread. When the buns have doubled, brush them with the honey-water mixture (you will not use it all), then sprinkle evenly with the remaining 1 tablespoon sesame seeds. Place the baking sheet in the oven, carefully pour the hot tap water into the baking pan and quickly close the oven door. Bake until golden brown and the centers reach 200°F, 30 to 35 minutes. Cool on the baking sheet on a wire rack for about 5 minutes. Transfer directly to the rack and cool completely.

Pumpkin Seed Rolls

**Start to finish: 3½ hours
(1 hour active), plus cooling**

Makes 15 rolls

FOR THE SPONGE:

70 grams (½ cup) rye flour

½ cup warm water (100°F)

1 tablespoon honey

2 teaspoons instant yeast

FOR THE DOUGH:

140 grams (1 cup) pumpkin seeds

80 grams (½ cup) sesame seeds

57 grams (4 tablespoons) salted
butter, cut into 4 pieces and chilled

343 grams (2½ cups) bread flour,
plus more for dusting

1 cup room temperature water
(70°F)

1¼ teaspoons table salt

FOR FINISHING:

1 large egg, lightly beaten

Flaky salt, for sprinkling

Rye flour brings texture and earthy flavor to these pumpkin seed rolls that are based on a classic Bavarian bread, Kürbiskern Brötchen. We added toasted pumpkin seeds, as is traditional, and threw in some sesame seeds, as well. Then we processed the seeds with chilled butter in a food processor to create a nut butter, which we added to the sponge before kneading for a tender, moist and flavorful crumb. These rolls are best served the day they are baked. For ease they can be made in the morning, then reheated in a 350°F oven for 10 minutes just before serving. The seed-butter mixture can be prepared up to three days ahead and refrigerated. Just be sure to pull it out an hour before using to bring it to room temperature.

Don't be tempted to add extra flour when mixing the dough; it will look quite sticky but will firm up as it rises. Otherwise, the rolls won't have enough chew.

To make the sponge, in the bowl of a stand mixer, whisk together the rye flour, warm water, honey and yeast. Cover and let stand at room temperature until doubled and bubbly, about 1 hour.

Meanwhile, in a 12-inch skillet over medium, combine the pumpkin seeds and sesame seeds and toast, stirring, until the sesame seeds are golden (some pumpkin seeds will pop), 5 to 8 minutes. Measure out 80 grams (½ cup) of the mixture and set aside. Transfer the rest to a food processor and process until finely ground, about 1 minute. Add the butter and process until just melted and combined, about another 20 seconds.

When the sponge is ready, add the bread flour, water and seed-butter mixture. Mix with the dough hook on low until just combined, about 1 minute. Let stand for 5 minutes. Add the salt, then mix on low until the dough forms a mass around the hook, but still adheres to the sides, about 5 minutes. The dough should look and feel sticky but not wet. Cover the bowl and let rise until tripled in size, about 1 hour.

Heat the oven to 450°F with a rack in the middle position. Line a baking sheet with kitchen parchment. Turn the dough out onto a well-floured surface, being careful not to deflate it. Lightly flour the top of the dough and gently press it into a 10-by-6-inch rectangle. To create 15 equal portions of dough (about 2 ounces each), cut the rectangle into thirds lengthwise, then into fifths crosswise.

Gently round each portion into a ball, creating a smooth, taut surface and pinching together any seams on the bottom. Arrange the rolls evenly on the baking sheet. Brush the tops generously with the beaten egg and sprinkle the reserved seed mixture over them, pressing gently to adhere. Top each with a small sprinkle of flaky salt. Cover and let rise until nearly doubled in size, 30 to 35 minutes.

Bake until the rolls are deep golden brown, 20 to 25 minutes, rotating the baking sheet once halfway through. Using tongs, immediately transfer the rolls to a wire rack. Let cool for at least 30 minutes before serving.

THE WETTER THE CRUST, THE CRISPER THE CRUNCH

While it may feel counterintuitive, a moist oven environment during baking generates a crisper crust, enhanced rise and better browning for some styles of breads, including lean, high-hydration doughs like ciabatta (recipe p. 98) or Italian semolina loaf (recipe p. 115). The moisture condenses on the loaf's surface, which lowers the dough's surface temperature to allow for greater oven spring by slowing the rate at which the crust firms. The crust stays softer and more elastic for longer, allowing it to expand with the dough's growth. Once the dough sets after the oven spring is exhausted, the moisture on the surface gelatinizes sugars in the surface starches, which intensifies browning.

There are three common methods for adding moisture to the oven (while steam injection is standard in commercial ovens, it's only recently becoming common to home ovens—and is expensive). A roasting pan or cast-iron skillet of hot water can be placed on a lower rack, which will then evaporate in the heat to maintain a high humidity level. Instead of water, ice cubes also work, which can be a little easier to manouver in and out of the oven, as they won't splash. Lastly, the bread can be spritzed before and during baking with a spray bottle filled with water. A word of caution: Don't let water touch the oven's glass door; cold water can lead to thermal shock and cracking if it makes contact with the tempered glass on the oven door. It's best to pour the water into the pan, then put into the oven.

Portuguese-Style Sweet Potato Rolls

**Start to finish: 3 hours
(45 minutes active), plus cooling**

Makes eight 5-inch rolls

12 ounces orange-flesh sweet
potatoes, peeled and cut into
1-inch chunks

43 grams (3 tablespoons) salted
butter, cut into 3 pieces

1 tablespoon honey

¾ teaspoon table salt

411 grams (3 cups) bread flour,
plus more for dusting

2 teaspoons instant yeast

The Portuguese sweet potato bread known as bolo de caco is a griddled bread that resembles an English muffin or thick pita bread round. For our version, we use widely available orange-fleshed sweet potatoes rather than the white variety that's more traditional; the potatoes give the bread a saffron hue and a rich, moist crumb. The traditional way to cook bolos de caco is on a stone slab; we use a skillet set on the stovetop to brown the rounds, then finish baking them in the oven. The flatbreads typically are split while warm, spread with Garlic-Chive Butter (recipe below) and served as part of a meal, but you also could toast the halves and have them for breakfast or use them to make a sandwich.

Don't begin mixing the cooked sweet potato mixture until it has cooled for 30 minutes. Otherwise, the heat from the potatoes may kill the yeast. Don't worry if you don't own an instant thermometer for testing the breads. Simply bake them for the full 14 minutes. The sweet potato in the dough makes this a forgiving recipe, so even if slightly overbaked, the crumb still will be moist and tender.

In a medium saucepan over medium-high, combine the potatoes, butter, honey, salt and ⅔ cup water. Bring to a boil, stirring to melt the butter, then reduce to low, cover and cook until a skewer inserted into the potatoes meets no resistance, 15 to 20 minutes. Transfer the potatoes and any liquid to the bowl of a stand mixer. Cool until just warm to the touch, about 30 minutes. Meanwhile, mist a medium bowl with cooking spray.

Using the paddle attachment, beat the mixture on low until smooth, about 1 minute. Switch to the dough hook and add the flour and yeast. Mix on low until a smooth dough forms, about 5 minutes. Increase to medium-high and knead for 1 minute to strengthen the dough. Transfer to the prepared bowl, cover with plastic wrap and let rise in a warm, draft-free spot until the dough is doubled in size, about 1 hour.

Heat the oven to 350°F with a rack in the middle position. Line a rimmed baking sheet with kitchen parchment. Turn the dough out onto a lightly floured counter, then divide into 8 pieces. Form each piece into a taut ball by rolling it against the counter in a circular motion under a cupped hand; place seam-side down on the prepared baking sheet. Using your hand, press and flatten each ball until it measures about 4 inches wide and ¼ inch thick. Cover with plastic wrap and let rise until doubled in size, about 30 minutes.

Heat a 12-inch skillet over medium until water flicked onto the surface immediately sizzles. Place 4 dough rounds seam-side up in the pan and cook until deep golden brown, 1 to 2 minutes. Using a wide metal spatula, flip and cook the second sides until golden brown, about 1 minute. Return to the baking sheet, then repeat with the remaining rounds, returning them to the baking sheet.

Bake the flatbreads in the oven until the centers reach 200°F, 12 to 14 minutes. Immediately transfer directly to a wire rack and cool for at least 15 minutes.

STEPS »

Sweet and Savory Breads

HOW TO MAKE PORTUGUESE-STYLE SWEET POTATO ROLLS

1. Combine the sweet potatoes, butter, honey, salt and water in a medium saucepan over medium-high. Bring to a boil.

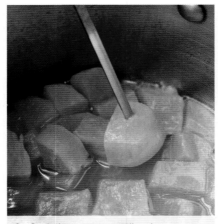

2. Cook the potatoes until a skewer inserted into the potatoes meets no resistance, 15 to 20 minutes.

3. Transfer the potatoes to the bowl of a stand mixer. Cool, then beat with the paddle attachment until smooth.

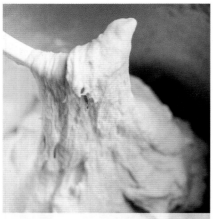

4. Add the flour and yeast. Mix on low with the dough hook until smooth. Knead on medium-high for 1 minute.

5. Let the dough rise in an oiled, covered bowl in a warm, draft-free spot until doubled in size, about 1 hour.

6. While the oven heats, turn the dough out on a lightly floured counter, then divide into 8 pieces.

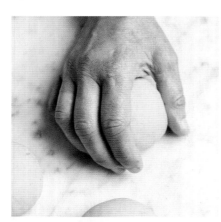

7. Roll each piece against the counter in a circular motion under a cupped hand to form a taut ball.

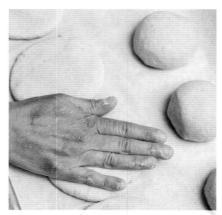

8. Place the dough balls onto the parchment-lined baking sheet. Flatten each ball into a disk 4 inches wide and ¼ inch thick.

9. Place 4 dough rounds seam side up in the skillet and cook; flip when browned. Cook the second sides. Repeat with the remaining rounds, then bake.

Orange–Olive Oil Sweet Breads

French gibassiers (pronounced zhe-bah-see-ay) take a couple different forms. In certain areas of Provence, the baked good is a cookie made with olive oil. But the better-known version is a sweet yeasted bread rich with butter, olive oil and eggs and flavored with orange blossom water, candied orange and aniseed. Typically offered at breakfast, the bread, shaped like a leaf or fleur-de-lys, features lots of crevices that are perfect for catching the butter and sugar embellishments added after baking. We've made individually sized breads that will impress guests. Candied orange can be difficult to source, so it's optional; instead, we rely on grated orange zest for citrusy brightness. But we recommend seeking out orange blossom water, as its floral aroma is key. Look for it in supermarkets alongside the vanilla extract or in the international aisle. Middle Eastern grocery stores also stock it. These breads are best the day of baking, but leftovers will keep for a couple days in an airtight container; reheat in a 350°F oven for five to six minutes.

Don't bake both baking sheets of gibassiers at the same time; the breads rise and brown better if baked one trayful at a time. But be sure to bake the first six that are shaped, so they don't overproof. Finally, don't butter all the breads before sugaring them; butter and sugar each one at a time. If all 12 are first buttered before sugaring, the butter will set and the sugar will not adhere.

In a 2-cup liquid measuring cup or small bowl, whisk the milk, oil, whole egg and egg yolk, orange zest and orange blossom water. In a stand mixer with the dough hook, mix the flour, 71 grams (⅓ cup) sugar, the yeast and salt on low until combined, about 10 seconds. With the mixer running, slowly pour in the egg mixture, then mix until a shaggy dough forms, about 1 minute. Increase to medium and mix until the dough is evenly moistened and starts to pull away from the bottom of the bowl, 6 to 7 minutes.

With the mixer running, add the room-temperature butter 1 piece at a time, mixing until fully incorporated after each; scrape the bowl as needed. Knead on medium, scraping the bowl once or twice, until the dough is smooth, shiny and elastic, 8 to 10 minutes. Lift out the hook with dough clinging to it; the dough should fall from the hook in a thick, shiny rope that will not stick to your fingers when lightly pressed. With the mixer running on low, sprinkle in the aniseed followed by the candied orange (if using); mix until evenly distributed throughout the dough, about 2 minutes. Using a silicone spatula, scrape the sides of the bowl and gather the dough in the center. Cover with plastic wrap and let rise at room

**Start to finish: 12 hours
(1 hour active)**

Makes twelve 5-inch breads

¾ cup whole milk, room temperature

¼ cup extra-virgin olive oil

1 large egg, plus 1 large egg yolk, room temperature

1 tablespoon grated orange zest

2 teaspoons orange blossom water

342 grams (2½ cups) bread flour, plus more for dusting

143 grams (⅔ cup) white sugar, divided

2¼ teaspoons instant yeast

½ teaspoon table salt

57 grams (4 tablespoons) salted butter, cut into ½-inch pieces, room temperature, plus 57 grams (4 tablespoons) salted butter, melted

4 teaspoons aniseed, lightly crushed

41 grams (¼ cup) finely chopped candied orange (optional)

STEPS »

temperature until just shy of doubled, about 45 minutes, then refrigerate for at least 8 hours or up to 24 hours.

When you are ready to shape the dough, remove it from the refrigerator. Line 2 rimmed baking sheets with kitchen parchment. Dust the counter with flour and scrape the chilled dough onto it. Form the dough into a log about 3½ inches in diameter, then, using a metal bench scraper or chef's knife, cut crosswise into 12 portions; each piece should be a stubby sausage shape 3½ to 4 inches long.

Dust a cutting board with flour and set 1 dough portion on top, parallel with the counter's edge. With your hand, slightly flatten the dough into an oval about 4 inches long and 2 inches wide. Using a sharp paring knife misted with cooking spray, cut a 1-inch crosswise slit in the center of the oval, then cut a slit on each side, spaced ¾ inch from the center slit. Now, using the tip of the knife, notch four ¾ to 1-inch cuts along the edge of the dough nearest you; stagger the cuts with the internal slits, pulling the knife toward you to ensure a clean, complete cut.

Form a bear claw-like shape by drawing together the ends of the dough into a semicircle with the notches on the outside; the notches will fan apart. Place on a prepared baking sheet and cover with a kitchen towel. Shape the remaining dough portions in the same way, placing 6 on each baking sheet. Let rise at room temperature until doubled and the dough slowly springs back when lightly pressed, 1 to 1½ hours. Meanwhile, heat the oven to 350°F with a rack in the middle position. Place the remaining 71 grams (⅓ cup) sugar in a medium bowl for sugaring the gibassiers.

Bake the first 6 breads that were shaped until golden brown, 15 to 18 minutes. Remove from the oven and set the baking sheet on a wire rack. Bake the remaining breads the same way. While the second batch bakes, let the first batch cool for a few minutes, then brush the top of one bread with butter, dunk the buttered side into the sugar and return it to the baking sheet sugared side up. Butter and sugar the remaining 5 breads in the same way.

When the second batch is done, set the baking sheet on a wire rack and cool for a few minutes, then butter and sugar the breads in the same way as the first batch. Serve warm or at room temperature.

HOW TO MAKE ORANGE–OLIVE OIL SWEET BREADS

1. Dust the counter with flour and scrape the chilled dough onto it.

5. Using a paring knife misted with cooking spray, cut a 1-inch crosswise slit in the center, then cut a slit on each side, spacing them ¾ inch from the center cut.

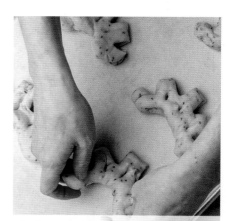

7. Form a bear claw-like shape by drawing the ends of the dough into a semicircle with the notches on the outside; the notches will fan apart.

2. Form the dough into a log about 3½ inches in diameter.

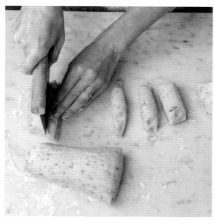

3. Using a metal bench scraper or chef's knife, cut crosswise into 12 portions, each piece should be 3½ to 4 inches long.

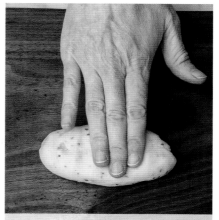

4. Place a portion on a cutting board. Slightly flatten it into an oval about 4 inches long and 2 inches wide..

6. Using the knife tip, notch four ¾- to 1-inch cuts along the edge of the dough nearest you; stagger the cuts with the internal slits.

8. To finish, brush the top of a cooled baked bread with butter, dunk the buttered side into the sugar and return to the baking sheet sugar side up.

Sweet and Savory Breads

Palestinian-Style Turmeric Bread

**Start to finish: 2¼ hours
(30 minutes active), plus cooling**

Makes four 7-inch rounds

618 grams (4¾ cups) all-purpose flour, plus more as needed and for dusting

80 grams (½ cup) white or black sesame seeds, or a combination, toasted and cooled

107 grams (½ cup) white sugar

1 tablespoon instant yeast

3 tablespoons aniseed, coarsely ground

3 tablespoons nigella seeds (see headnote), coarsely ground

1 teaspoon ground turmeric

1 teaspoon table salt

1⅔ cups warm water (100°F to 110°F)

½ cup extra-virgin olive oil, plus more for greasing and brushing

¼ teaspoon almond extract

We first tasted ka'ak asfar, which translates as "yellow bread," at a Palestinian bakery. The warm, golden glow of the round, flattish loaves came from turmeric, and sesame seeds and fragrant spices flavored the subtly sweet, almost cake-like crumb. Hoping to replicate ka'ak asfar at home, we turned to Reem Kassis, author of "The Palestinian Table," who explained that the bread is a holiday food, sometimes closely associated with Easter, though it's common to find it year-round. We adapted her recipe, swapping the difficult-to-source mahleb, a spice ground from a type of cherry pit and a common flavoring in Middle Eastern baking, for a small measure of almond extract. In addition to sesame seeds, the recipe calls for nigella seeds, which are teardrop-shaped and black; their flavor is unique, with slightly herbal, onion-y notes. Look for them in Middle Eastern markets, spice shops or well-stocked supermarkets. If you can't find them, the bread still is delicious without them. To grind the aniseed and nigella seeds, crush them in a mortar with a pestle or pulse them in an electric spice grinder.

Don't add the toasted sesame seeds to the dry ingredients while still hot. Allow them to cool so they don't damage the yeast. Be sure to let the breads cool completely before slicing so the knife blade doesn't compress or tear the crumb.

In a stand mixer with the dough hook, mix the flour, sesame seeds, sugar, yeast, aniseed, nigella seeds, turmeric and salt on medium until well combined, about 1 minute. In a 1-quart liquid measuring cup or medium bowl, combine the water, oil and almond extract. With the mixer running on low, slowly pour the liquid ingredients into the flour mixture. Knead on medium-low until the mixture forms a smooth, elastic ball and clears the sides of the bowl, 7 to 10 minutes, occasionally scraping the bottom and sides of the bowl; if needed, knead in up to 2 tablespoons additional flour. Lightly oil a large bowl and transfer the dough to it. Brush the dough with oil, cover with plastic wrap and let rise at room temperature until doubled in bulk, about 1 hour.

Heat the oven to 400°F with a rack in the middle position. Line a rimmed baking sheet with kitchen parchment and brush it with oil. Dust the counter with flour, turn the dough out onto it and divide it into fourths. Using your hands, form each piece into a smooth, taut ball, then press it into a 5-inch round about ¾ inch thick. Dimple the rounds with your fingertips, then transfer to the prepared baking sheet, staggering them to give them as much space as possible. Loosely cover with plastic

wrap and let rise at room temperature until nearly doubled in bulk, about 30 minutes; it's fine if the risen rounds touch slightly.

Uncover and bake until the breads are golden brown, 12 to 15 minutes. Set the baking sheet on a wire rack and cool for about 10 minutes, then transfer the loaves directly to the rack. Cool to room temperature.

Sweet and Savory Breads

Chocolate and Tahini Babka

**Start to finish: 10 hours
(2½ hours active), plus cooling**

Makes two 9-inch loaves

FOR THE DOUGH:

2 large eggs plus 2 large
egg yolks, room temperature

1 cup whole milk, room temperature

2¼ teaspoons instant yeast

2 teaspoons vanilla extract

536 grams (4 cups plus 2 tablespoons) all-purpose flour, plus
more if needed and for dusting

71 grams (⅓ cup) white sugar

1 teaspoon table salt

113 grams (8 tablespoons) salted
butter, room temperature, cut into
1-tablespoon pieces, plus more
for the pans

FOR THE FILLING:

57 grams (4 tablespoons) salted
butter, cut into 3 or 4 pieces

¼ cup whole milk

124 grams (1 cup) powdered sugar

21 grams (¼ cup) unsweetened
cocoa powder

2 teaspoons instant espresso
powder

½ teaspoon table salt

90 grams (¼ cup plus
2 tablespoons) tahini

1 teaspoon vanilla extract

4 ounces bittersweet chocolate,
finely chopped

FOR THE SYRUP:

71 grams (⅓ cup) white sugar

1 teaspoon instant espresso powder

Jewish-style babkas originated as a way to utilize leftover challah dough. To keep the pastry kosher, no dairy was allowed, so both the dough and filling typically were oil-based. These days, bakeries across the globe have reinvented the classic, crafting buttery babkas with creative fillings and toppings. We set out to make a babka in this style: rich, plush and complete with two flavor variations. The first features dark chocolate and nutty tahini, which complement each other beautifully. For the second, we combine cinnamon, brown sugar and walnuts with a hint of orange. Both babkas are brushed with flavored syrup, which gives them a shiny, sweet crust and locks moisture in the loaves, keeping them fresh for up to three days. Once fully cooled, you also can wrap the babka tightly in plastic wrap, then enclose it in foil and freeze for up to a month. To refresh, thaw the still-wrapped loaf at room temperature (this takes about 30 minutes), then completely unwrap, place on a baking sheet and warm in a 300°F oven for about 15 minutes.

Don't forget to return the dough half that's waiting to be shaped to the refrigerator so it remains chilled while you shape the first. When baking the loaves, be sure to set the pans on a baking sheet to catch any drips that otherwise would end up on the oven floor. Space the loaf pans a few inches apart to allow air circulation for more even baking.

To make the dough, in a 1-quart liquid measuring cup or medium bowl, whisk the eggs plus yolks, milk, yeast and vanilla. In a stand mixer with the dough hook, mix the flour, sugar and salt on low until combined, about 30 seconds. With the mixer running, slowly add the egg mixture, then knead on medium until a wet, slightly lumpy dough forms, about 2 minutes, scraping the bowl once or twice.

With the mixer running on medium, add the butter 2 pieces at a time, mixing for about 30 seconds after each addition. When all the butter has been added, scrape the bowl and mix on medium until the dough is smooth, elastic and pulls away from the sides of the bowl, 7 to 9 minutes. If the dough is too sticky to clear the sides of the bowl, mix in up to 2 tablespoons flour, kneading for about 2 minutes after each addition. Scrape the sides of the bowl and gather the dough in the center. Cover with plastic wrap and let rise at room temperature until just shy of doubled, 30 to 45 minutes, then refrigerate for at least 6 hours or up to 24 hours.

When you are ready to shape the dough, make the filling. In a small saucepan, combine the butter and milk. Bring to a simmer over medium, stirring; when the butter is melted, remove from the heat and cool for a few minutes. In a medium bowl, whisk the sugar, cocoa, espresso powder and salt. Whisk in the milk-butter

mixture until almost smooth; it's OK if tiny lumps remain. Add the tahini and whisk until smooth, then whisk in the vanilla; set aside.

Butter two 9-by-5-inch loaf pans, then line each with an 8-by-14-inch piece of kitchen parchment, allowing the excess to overhang the long sides of the pan; set aside.

Remove the dough from the refrigerator. Lightly flour the counter and turn the dough out onto it. Using a chef's knife or bench scraper, divide it in half; each piece should weigh about 540 grams (19 ounces). Return 1 piece to the bowl; re-cover and refrigerate. Using your hands, form the remaining piece into a rough 6-by-8-inch rectangle. Using a rolling pin, roll it into a 12-by-18-inch rectangle with a long side nearest you (it's OK if the rectangle does not have perfectly squared corners); lightly dust with flour as needed to prevent sticking.

STEPS »

Sweet and Savory Breads

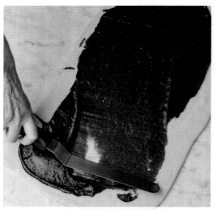

1. Spread half of the chocolate filling on the rolled-out dough, leaving a 1-inch border on the long side farthest from you.

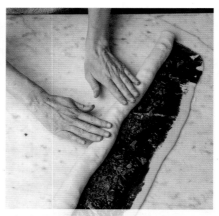

2. Sprinkle with half of the chopped chocolate. Starting with the side closest to you, roll the dough into a tight cylinder.

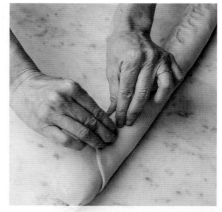

3. Pinch the seam. Roll the cylinder onto the seam, then roll it against the counter until about 18 inches long. Cover and repeat with the second portion.

4. Place the first cylinder seam side down. Cut the cylinder in half lengthwise into two rope-like pieces with cut sides that expose the layers.

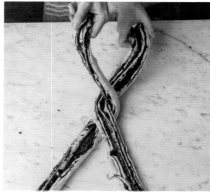

5. With the cut sides facing up, cross the ropes at their midpoints, forming an X. Starting at the center of the X, form a twist by passing one rope under the other, keeping the cut sides up.

6. Continue passing one rope under the other until you reach the ends; you should get in 3 to 5 twists. Pinch the ends. Repeat with the ropes on the other side.

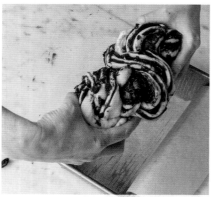

7. Shorten and compact the loaf by gently squishing both short ends together until the loaf measures about 9 inches.

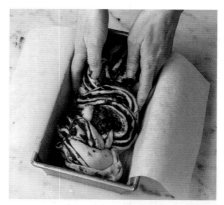

8. Transfer to a prepared pan and cover with a towel. Form the second loaf in the same way. Let rise until doubled, 1 to 1½ hours.

9. After baking, brush the top of each loaf with syrup. Cool, remove the loaves from their pans and set them on the rack. Peel back the parchment and brush all sides with the remaining syrup.

Using an offset icing spatula, spread half of the chocolate filling in an even layer over the dough, leaving a 1-inch border on the long side farthest from you. Sprinkle the filling evenly with half of the chopped chocolate. Starting with the side closest to you, roll the dough into a tight cylinder; pinch the seam to seal. Roll the cylinder onto its seam and, using your hands, gently roll it back and forth against the counter to extend its length to about 18 inches; if any sections are thicker than others, apply more pressure to those areas when rolling to even them out. Cover the cylinder with a kitchen towel. Remove the second portion of dough from the refrigerator; roll it out, spread on the remaining filling, sprinkle with the remaining chopped chocolate and form the dough into an even cylinder as you did the first portion; cover with another towel.

Place the first cylinder seam side down. Using a chef's knife and starting at one end, cut the cylinder in half lengthwise; slice straight down and use firm, even pressure (do not use a sawing motion). You will have two rope-like pieces with cut sides that expose the layers of filling and dough. With ropes positioned perpendicular to the counter's edge and the cut sides facing up, cross them at their midpoints, forming an X. Starting at the center of the X, where the ropes meet, form the sections of the ropes closest to you into a twist by passing one under the other, always keeping the cut sides up; you should get in 3 to 5 twists. Pinch the ends together to seal. Repeat with the ropes on the other side of the X. Using your hands, shorten and compact the loaf by gently and simultaneously squishing both short ends together until the loaf measures about 9 inches. Transfer to a prepared pan and cover loosely with a towel. Shape the second cylinder in the same way and cover. Let rise at room temperature until doubled, 1 to 1½ hours.

Meanwhile, make the syrup. In a small saucepan, combine the sugar, espresso powder and ¼ cup water. Bring to a simmer over medium, stirring occasionally to dissolve the sugar. Remove from the heat and set aside. Heat the oven to 350°F with a rack in the middle position. Cut two 9-by-12-inch pieces of foil.

Uncover the loaf pans and place them, spaced about 3 inches apart, on a rimmed baking sheet. Place the baking sheet in the oven and bake until golden brown, about 30 minutes. Working quickly, rotate the baking sheet 180 degrees and lay a piece of foil over each loaf. Continue to bake until the centers reach 190°F to 200°F, about another 10 minutes.

Set the baking sheet with the loaf pans on a wire rack. Brush the top of each warm babka with 1 to 2 tablespoons syrup. Cool for 30 minutes, then, using the parchment slings, lift the babkas from their pans and set them directly on the wire rack. Peel back the parchment on the sides and brush all sides with the remaining syrup. Cool completely, then remove and discard the parchment.

Cinnamon-Walnut Babka

Follow the recipe to make the dough and prepare the pans. When you are ready to shape the dough, make the filling: In a medium bowl, whisk together **199 grams (1 cup) packed brown sugar, 1 tablespoon ground cinnamon, 1 tablespoon grated orange zest** and **¼ teaspoon table salt.** Add **57 grams (4 tablespoons) salted butter** (cut into 3 or 4 pieces, room temperature) and rub the butter into the spiced sugar until the mixture resembles wet sand. Cover and set aside at room temperature. Have ready **110 grams (1 cup) walnuts** (toasted and finely chopped). Follow the recipe to divide the dough, then roll out and fill each portion, sprinkling half of the butter-sugar mixture on each rectangle, then evenly sprinkling half of the walnuts onto the butter-sugar layer. Form the dough into cylinders of even thickness, cut the cylinders and shape the loaves as directed, then cover and let rise. While the loaves rise, make the syrup: In a small saucepan, combine **71 grams (⅓ cup) white sugar, ¼ cup water** and **three 3-inch strips orange zest.** Bring to a simmer over medium, stirring to dissolve the sugar; remove from the heat and set aside. Follow the recipe to bake the babkas and brush with syrup, discarding the orange zest from the syrup before use.

Buttermilk Monkey Bread

**Start to finish: 9½ hours
(50 minutes active), plus cooling**

Servings: 10 to 12

FOR THE DOUGH:

3 large eggs, room temperature

1 cup buttermilk, room temperature

2¼ teaspoons instant yeast

423 grams (3¼ cups) all-purpose flour, plus more for dusting

140 grams (1 cup) whole-wheat flour

54 grams (¼ cup) white sugar

1 teaspoon table salt

85 grams (6 tablespoons) salted butter, cut into 1-tablespoon pieces, room temperature

**FOR THE BUTTER
AND SUGAR COATINGS:**

141 grams (10 tablespoons) salted butter, cut into 6 to 8 pieces

2 teaspoons ground cinnamon

1 teaspoon freshly grated nutmeg

1 teaspoon vanilla extract

214 grams (1 cup) white sugar

FOR THE GLAZE (OPTIONAL):

93 grams (¾ cup) powdered sugar

3 tablespoons buttermilk

1 teaspoon vanilla extract

¼ teaspoon ground cinnamon

Monkey bread gets an update that makes the pull-apart loaf even better thanks to buttermilk, a little whole-wheat flour and a lighter hand with sugar. The result is more tender and nuanced—and less sweet—than the versions many of us grew up with. Browned butter infused with vanilla and warm spices coats the nuggets of dough before they're rolled in sugar and piled into the pan. We like the combination of cinnamon and nutmeg because they call to mind freshly fried doughnuts, but feel free to try other sweet spices, such as cardamom, allspice or cloves. Assembly takes a little time but is well worth it. The recipe is designed so the dough can be made in advance, then shaped and baked the day of serving. However, if you want to make the bread start to finish in a single go, after mixing, allow the dough to rise at room temperature until doubled, about two hours, and prepare the butter for coating during this time. Made this way, the dough will not be cold for shaping, so you may need to use more flour when cutting it into pieces. The optional brush-on glaze gives the monkey bread a lustrous finish and a crackly coating—like a glazed doughnut—but feel free to skip it.

Don't add extra flour to the dough after the butter is mixed in. The dough will be sticky but will become workable after rising, once the flour has hydrated. When coating the dough bits, be sure to allow excess butter to drip off the pieces before dropping them into the sugar. If butter gets into the sugar, the granules will clump, resulting in a too-thick sugar cloak.

To make the dough, in the bowl of a stand mixer, whisk the eggs, buttermilk and yeast. Add both flours, the white sugar and salt; attach the dough hook and mix on low until a slightly sticky dough forms, about 5 minutes, scraping the bowl and pushing the dough off the hook once or twice. With the mixer running on medium-low, add the butter 1 piece at a time, mixing for 30 to 60 seconds before adding the next piece.

After all the butter has been added, mix on medium-low until the dough is smooth and elastic and begins to slap the sides of the bowl, 4 to 5 minutes; it will be sticky, slightly webby and cling to the bottom of the bowl. Detach the bowl from the mixer and use a spatula to scrape and gather the dough at the center. Cover with plastic wrap and let rise at room temperature for 1 hour (the dough will not double), then refrigerate for at least 8 hours or up to 24 hours.

When you are ready to shape the dough, remove the dough from the refrigerator and make the coating. In a small saucepan over medium, cook the butter, swirling the pan, until the milk solids at the bottom are deeply browned and the butter has

STEPS »

a rich, nutty aroma, 4 to 6 minutes. Immediately transfer to a small microwave-safe bowl, then stir in the cinnamon and nutmeg; cool for a few minutes, then stir in the vanilla. Place the white sugar in another small bowl. Mist a 12-cup Bundt pan with cooking spray.

Lightly flour the counter and scrape the dough out onto it. Lightly flour the dough and pat it into an 8-inch square. Using a metal bench scraper or a chef's knife, cut the dough into quadrants and cover with a kitchen towel. Place one portion on the counter and, using your hands, roll it back and forth against the counter to stretch the dough into a 16-inch rope. Using the bench scraper or knife, cut the rope into 16 pieces; it's fine if the pieces are slightly uneven in size. Place the pieces under the towel. Roll and cut the remaining dough portions in the same way. You will have 64 pieces of dough.

Stir the butter mixture to remix the spices. Drop 3 or 4 pieces of dough into it. Using a fork, toss the pieces to coat, then lift them out, allowing excess butter to drip back into the bowl; drop the pieces into the sugar. Using a spoon, toss in the sugar to coat, then place in the prepared Bundt pan. Butter and sugar the remaining dough in the same way, piling the pieces evenly in the pan. (If the butter mixture cools and thickens as you work, microwave it on high for a few seconds.) Cover with the kitchen towel and let rise at room temperature until the pieces are puffy, fill the pan about three-fourths and slowly spring back when poked, 45 to 50 minutes. Meanwhile, heat the oven to 350°F with a rack in the lower-middle position.

Bake until the bread is well-risen and golden brown, 30 to 35 minutes; a thermometer inserted about 2 inches from the edge into the center of the bread should register 190°F to 195°F. Cool in the pan on a wire rack for 10 minutes. Invert the bread onto a platter and lift off the pan. Cool for at least 30 minutes; if glazing, cool until barely warm to the touch.

To make the glaze (if using), in a small bowl, whisk the powdered sugar, buttermilk, vanilla and cinnamon. Using a pastry brush, evenly brush the glaze onto the bread. Let dry for at least 30 minutes before serving.

HOW TO MAKE BUTTERMILK MONKEY BREAD

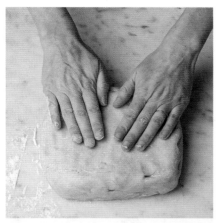

1. Lightly flour the counter and scrape the dough out onto it. Lightly flour the dough and pat it into an 8-inch square.

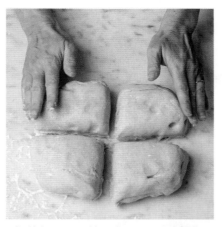

2. Using a metal bench scraper or chef's knife, cut the dough into quadrants and cover with a kitchen towel.

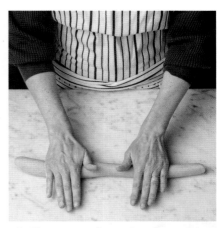

3. Place one portion on the counter and roll it back and forth against the counter to stretch the dough into a 16-inch rope.

4. Cut the rope into 16 pieces; it's fine if they are slightly uneven. Place the pieces under the towel. Roll and cut the remaining dough portions in the same way. You will have 64 pieces of dough.

5. Drop 3 or 4 pieces of dough into the butter mixture. Using a fork, toss the pieces to coat, then lift them out, allowing excess butter to drip back into the bowl.

6. Drop the pieces into the sugar. Using a spoon, toss in the sugar to coat.

7. Place in the prepared pan. Butter and sugar the remaining dough in the same way, piling the pieces evenly in the pan.

8. Cover and let rise until the pieces are puffy, fill the pan about three-fourths and slowly spring back when poked, 45 to 50 minutes.

9. If finishing with the optional glaze, brush it onto the warm bread after inverting and allowing it to cool about 30 minutes. Let dry for at least 30 minutes before serving.

Sweet and Savory Breads

Hot Cross Buns

Made with orange zest, bourbon (for plumping the currants and in a finishing glaze) and buttermilk instead of regular milk, our hot cross buns are deliciously light and tender, with just the right buttery sweetness. Lyle's Golden Syrup is an amber-hued sweetener common to the U.K. We like the butterscotch notes it adds, but honey works, too. The work is spread over a couple days so the buns can be baked and served for breakfast or brunch. If you wish to bake the buns the same day, after shaping them, let them rise at room temperature until just shy of doubled, about an hour. Halfway into rising, heat the oven and prepare the egg wash and piping mixture. Once doubled, brush the buns with egg wash and pipe on the crosses, then bake and glaze as directed. Store extra buns in an airtight container up to three days; rewarm wrapped in foil in a 300°F oven for 10 to 15 minutes.

Don't heat the buttermilk to bring it to room temperature. Buttermilk curdles easily; it's best to let it stand at room temperature. Don't forget to pat the currants dry after draining their soaking liquid. Additional moisture can make the rather sticky dough difficult to handle when shaping. Finally, be sure to reserve the bourbon that remains after draining the currants. It's used later to make the glaze.

To make the dough, in a small microwave-safe bowl, stir the currants and bourbon. Microwave, uncovered, on high until warm, about 30 seconds, stirring once. Stir again, then set aside until plump, about 15 minutes. Drain in a fine-mesh strainer set over a small bowl; reserve the liquid. Turn the currants onto a paper towel–lined plate and pat dry; set aside.

In a 2-cup liquid measuring cup or small bowl, whisk the buttermilk, whole egg, egg yolk, golden syrup and orange zest. In a stand mixer with the dough hook, mix the flour, yeast, salt, cinnamon, allspice and nutmeg on low until combined, about 20 seconds. With the mixer running, add the buttermilk mixture; mix until a shaggy dough forms, about 45 seconds. Increase to medium-low and knead until sticky and elastic, 8 to 10 minutes; if the dough climbs up the hook, occasionally push it off.

With the mixer running on medium-low, add the butter 1 piece at a time, mixing until almost fully incorporated, about 30 seconds; scrape the bowl as needed. Knead on medium-low until shiny and once again elastic, 3 to 5 minutes. Scrape the dough off the hook. With the mixer running on medium-low, add the currants in 2 batches. Knead until distributed throughout the dough, 1 to 2 minutes. Detach the bowl from the mixer and use a silicone spatula to scrape the bowl and gather the dough at the center. Cover with plastic wrap and let rise at room temperature until doubled, 1 to 1½ hours.

Start to finish: 13 hours (1¼ hours active), plus cooling

Makes 12 buns

FOR THE DOUGH:

93 grams (⅔ cup) dried currants

⅓ cup bourbon

1 cup buttermilk, room temperature

1 large egg, plus 1 large egg yolk

63 grams (3 tablespoons) Lyle's Golden Syrup (see headnote) or honey

1 tablespoon grated orange zest

411 grams (3 cups) bread flour, plus more for dusting

2¼ teaspoons instant yeast

¾ teaspoon table salt

½ teaspoon ground cinnamon

¼ teaspoon ground allspice

¼ teaspoon freshly grated nutmeg

57 grams (4 tablespoons) salted butter, cut into 4 pieces, room temperature

FOR THE EGG WASH AND PIPING MIXTURE:

1 large egg

34 grams (¼ cup) bread flour

FOR THE GLAZE:

Bourbon, as needed

2 tablespoons Lyle's Golden Syrup or honey

STEPS »

1. Turn the dough out onto a lightly floured counter and divide into 12 portions.

2. Form the portions into taut balls by rolling each against the counter in a circular motion under a cupped hand.

3. To make the piping mixture, combine the flour and water. The mixture should be thick and fall slowly from the whisk.

4. When the buns have doubled, brush them with egg wash.

5. Pipe a continous line across the center of each row of buns, then pipe a continuous line down the center of each column.

6. When the buns are done, set the pan on a wire rack and immediately brush with the glaze.

Meanwhile, mist a 9-by-13-inch baking pan or baking dish with cooking spray. Line the pan with a 12-by-16-inch piece of parchment positioned so the excess overhangs the pan's long sides. Mist the parchment with cooking spray; set aside.

When the dough has doubled, lightly flour the counter and turn the dough out onto it. Divide into 12 portions, each about 77 grams (2½ ounces). Form each into a taut ball by rolling it against the counter in a circular motion under a cupped hand. Place seam-side down in the prepared pan, arranging them in 3 rows of 4. Mist a sheet of plastic wrap with cooking spray and drape over the pan, then cover loosely with a kitchen towel. Refrigerate for at least 8 hours or up to 24 hours.

About 2 hours before you are ready to bake, remove the buns from the refrigerator. Let stand at room temperature, covered, until almost doubled, 1½ to 2 hours.

About 1 hour into rising, in a small bowl, beat the egg for the wash until well combined; set aside. In another small bowl, combine the flour and 2½ tablespoons water; whisk until smooth. The mixture should form a thick paste that falls slowly from the whisk and mounds on itself in the bowl; if too thick, whisk in more water a few drops at a time. Transfer to a quart-size, zip-close bag. Press out the air and push the mixture to one corner; twist the bag to keep the batter contained in the corner; set aside. Heat the oven to 350°F with a rack in the middle position.

When the buns have doubled, brush them with egg wash (you will not need to use all of the egg). With the piping mixture still pushed to the corner of the bag, use scissors to snip off ⅛ to ¼ inch from the tip of the bag. Pipe a continuous line across the center of each row of buns, then pipe a continuous line down the center of each column of buns, creating a cross on the center of each bun. Bake until the buns are deep golden brown, 30 to 35 minutes.

Meanwhile, make the glaze. Measure the bourbon reserved from soaking the currants, then supplement with additional bourbon to total 3 tablespoons. In a small saucepan, combine the bourbon and syrup. Simmer over medium, stirring, until lightly syrupy and reduced to about 3 tablespoons, about 2 minutes; set aside off heat.

When the buns are done, set the pan on a wire rack and immediately brush with the glaze. Cool for 10 minutes. Using the parchment sling, lift the buns from the pan and set directly on the rack. Serve warm or at room temperature.

EGG WASH EXPLAINER

An egg wash—applied to pastries just before baking—promotes beautiful, lustrous browning thanks to proteins that undergo the Maillard reaction in the heat of the oven. It produces a shiny, golden finish and develops deeper flavor, while also helping seeds and other toppings adhere. Some recipes call for whole egg, others just yolks or whites, and the kind of wash you use largely depends on the desired visual effect. A yolk-only wash produces a glossy golden-yellow hue, while egg whites offer the most shine, with more subdued coloration. A wash with a whole egg falls somewhere between the two.

Regardless of the type, most egg washes are thinned with a liquid such as water or milk, which keeps the glaze from turning gloppy. In our testing, we found that egg washes used on doughs with chemical leaveners—such as baking soda—tend to brown better; the alkalinity of the leaveners can enhance browning. For example, an egg-washed biscuit dough browned better than an egg-washed bread dough (which relies on yeast rather than baking soda for leavening). That said, when it comes to sweet pastry, one of our favorite washes involves no eggs at all. Rather, we simply brush the pastry with water, then sprinkle it with sugar, which lightly browns and caramelizes, adding sweetness, crunch and a bit of sparkle. We like this for its simplicity and thriftiness, but if high gloss or a deep, mahogany crust is desired, an egg is best.

Swedish Cardamom Buns

Swedish kardemummabullar are soft, rich yeasted buns with an aromatic butter, sugar and cardamom filling. This recipe does require a bit of time and willingness to roll, measure, cut and shape the buns. We think it's worth it. Despite being rich with butter, milk and an egg yolk, the dough is remarkably easy to handle. It's essential to use cardamom that you have ground yourself. Preground cardamom doesn't come close to having the same flavor, aroma or visual appeal. Be sure to purchase decorticated cardamom seeds—seeds that have been removed from the thick, fibrous pods—and grind them in a mortar with a pestle or pulse them in an electric spice grinder to a mix of powder and tiny flecks. For the dough's first rise (the bulk fermentation), we use a 9-by-13-inch baking dish as the container. This allows the dough to cool more quickly once it's in the refrigerator. It also makes the dough easy to roll into a rectangle for filling because it takes on the shape of the baking dish. If you wish to make the buns over the course of two days, the ideal stopping point is after putting the dough in the refrigerator; it can remain there for up to 24 hours before rolling, filling, shaping and baking. Leftover baked buns will keep for up to three days in an airtight container; they reheat well in a 350°F oven for 5 to 8 minutes.

Don't overheat the milk, and be sure the butter has cooled after melting. The 20-minute kneading time in the mixer warms the dough, so making sure the milk and butter are not too hot will prevent the dough from overheating, which can adversely affect the yeast.

To make the dough, in a stand mixer with the dough hook, mix both flours, the sugar, yeast, cardamom and salt on low until combined, about 30 seconds. In a liquid measuring cup or small bowl, combine the milk and butter. With the mixer running on low, gradually add the milk mixture to the dry ingredients, followed by the egg yolk. Mix on low until the ingredients form a rough, sticky dough, 2 to 3 minutes.

Increase to medium-low and knead until the dough is smooth and elastic and pulls away cleanly from the sides of the bowl, about 20 minutes. The dough should be supple and soft to the touch; it also will feel warm.

Mist a 9-by-13-inch baking dish with cooking spray. Scrape the dough into the baking dish and press it with your hands to flatten it into an even layer that is as thin as possible. Cover with plastic wrap and let rise at room temperature until just shy of doubled in size, about 1 hour. Transfer to the refrigerator and chill for at least 2 hours or up to 24 hours.

Start to finish: 6 hours (1 hour active)

Makes 16 buns

FOR THE DOUGH:

390 grams (3 cups) all-purpose flour, plus more for dusting

103 grams (¾ cup) bread flour

80 grams (6 tablespoons) white sugar

1 tablespoon instant yeast

1 teaspoon cardamom seeds, ground (see headnote)

¾ teaspoon table salt

1¼ cups whole milk, warmed to 100°F

113 grams (8 tablespoons) salted butter, melted and cooled

1 large egg, separated, white refrigerated in an airtight container and reserved for brushing

FOR THE FILLING:

170 grams (12 tablespoons) salted butter, room temperature

163 grams (¾ cup) packed light brown sugar

2 teaspoons cardamom seeds, ground

2 tablespoons white sugar

STEPS »

HOW TO MAKE SWEDISH CARDAMOM BUNS

1. On a floured counter, roll the dough into a 12-by-16-inch rectangle, occasionally flipping the dough to prevent sticking.

2. Spread the filling (a mixture of butter, sugar and cardamom) in an even layer on the dough, all the way to the edges.

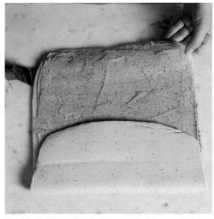

3. Once the filling has been spread evenly, fold the top third of the dough down over itself, then fold the bottom third up.

5. Rotate the dough so a long side is nearest you, trim the short sides, then cut the dough into 16 even strips.

6. Pick up one strip by the ends and "bounce" it against the counter while gently stretching it to about 16 inches.

7. Twist the ends of the strip in opposing directions while gently stretching it to create a loose spiral about 16 inches long.

9. Fully wrap the strip around your index, middle and ring fingers without untwisting the spiral.

10. Tuck the end under and up into the center to create a knot. Pinch the center of the bottom to seal.

11. Arrange 8 buns on each baking sheet, placing them in 2 outer rows of 3 and an inner row of 2.

4. Rotate the folded dough so a short end is nearest you and roll it once again into a 12-by-16-inch rectangle.

8. Holding it in place between your thumb and index, middle and ring fingers, wrap the strip around your fingers.

12. When the buns are nearly doubled in size, lightly brush each one with egg white, then sprinkle with white sugar.

When you are ready to fill, shape and bake the buns, make the filling. In a medium bowl, mash together the butter, brown sugar and cardamom until well combined; set aside. Line 2 rimmed baking sheets with kitchen parchment.

Lightly flour the counter and turn the chilled dough out onto it with a short end nearest you; try to maintain the rectangular shape. Lightly dust the dough with flour and roll it into a 12-by-16-inch rectangle of even thickness, occasionally flipping the dough to ensure it is not sticking. Spread the filling in an even layer on the dough, all the way to the edges. Fold the top third of the dough down over itself, then fold the bottom third up. Rotate the dough so a short side is nearest you and roll the dough once again into a 12-by-16-inch rectangle of even thickness.

Rotate the rectangle so a long side is parallel with the counter's edge. Using a metal bench scraper or pizza wheel, trim the short sides to create straight lines; discard the scraps. Cut the dough crosswise into 16 even strips.

Pick up one strip by the ends and gently stretch it to about 16 inches by gently "bouncing" it against the counter while very gently pulling on the ends. Twist the ends of the strip in opposing directions while gently stretching it to create a loose spiral about 16 inches long. With one end of the strip held in place by your thumb against your index, middle and ring fingers, wrap the strip around your 3 fingers without untwisting the spiral, then tuck the end under and up into the center while sliding out your fingers to create a knot. Pinch the center of the bottom of the bun to seal so the coil does not unwind during baking. Place on one of the prepared baking sheets.

Shape the remaining dough strips in the same way, arranging 8 buns on each baking sheet, placing them in 2 outer rows of 3 and an inner row of 2, for staggered spacing. Drape a kitchen towel over each baking sheet or cover lightly with plastic wrap and let rise until the buns are nearly doubled in size, 45 minutes to 1½ hours (timing depends on the temperature of the dough as well as the ambient temperature in the room).

While the buns are rising, heat the oven to 400°F with a rack in the middle position. In a small bowl, use a fork to beat the reserved egg white with 1 tablespoon water.

When the buns are nearly doubled in size, lightly brush each on the first baking sheet with egg white, then sprinkle with half of the white sugar. Bake until the buns are deep golden brown, 15 to 18 minutes; it is normal for some filling to seep out and caramelize on the baking sheet. Meanwhile, brush the remaining buns with egg white and sprinkle with the remaining white sugar.

When the buns are done, cool on the baking sheet on a wire rack. Bake the buns on the second baking sheet in the same manner. Serve slightly warm or at room temperature.

Kolaches

A kolache (pronounced koh-LAH-chee) is a rich, tender yeasted bun with a center hollow that traditionally is filled with sweet cheese and fruit before baking. Czech in origin, kolaches were brought to the U.S. by immigrants from Central Europe who settled in the Great Plains during the 1800s. We fill the buns with spoonfuls of lemon-scented sweetened cream cheese plus jam, then finish them with a dusting of crumb topping (you can skip the topping; the buns still will be delicious). Use one or multiple varieties of jam (blueberry and apricot were our favorites). So the kolaches can be served freshly baked for breakfast or brunch, we developed this recipe to be made over the course of a couple days; plan accordingly. First, make the dough, let it rise until almost doubled, then refrigerate it (for up to 24 hours) to slow down the yeast's activity. The next morning, shape the chilled dough, let it rise for 1 to 1½ hours, then fill and bake the buns. The kolaches are best the day of baking but will keep overnight, covered and stored at room temperature.

Don't add more flour to the dough during mixing; the dough should feel sticky. When portioning and shaping it, it's fine to dust the counter and your hands to make the dough workable, but use only as much flour as is needed. And be sure to keep the cream cheese filling and jam refrigerated until needed. Cold fillings stay in place better during baking.

To make the dough, in a small bowl or a 2-cup liquid measuring cup, whisk together the whole eggs and egg yolks, the melted butter, milk and lemon zest. In a stand mixer with the dough hook, mix the flour, white sugar, yeast and salt on low until combined, about 20 seconds. With the mixer running, gradually add the milk-egg mixture; mix, scraping the bowl once or twice, until a slightly lumpy dough forms, about 2 minutes. Increase to medium-high and mix until the dough is smooth, shiny and elastic and pulls away from the sides of the bowl, 8 to 10 minutes.

Detach the bowl from the mixer and lift out the hook with dough clinging to it; the dough will be sticky and fall from the hook in a thick rope into the bowl. Using a silicone spatula, scrape the sides of the bowl and gather the dough in the center. Cover with plastic wrap and let rise at room temperature until just shy of doubled, about 45 minutes, then refrigerate for at least 8 hours or up to 24 hours.

When you are ready to shape the dough, remove it from the refrigerator. Line a rimmed baking sheet with kitchen parchment. Dust the counter with flour and scrape the chilled dough out onto it. Divide into 12 portions, each about 70 grams (2½ ounces). Flour your hands, then form each piece into a taut ball by rolling it against an unfloured surface in a circular motion under a cupped hand. Place the balls seam down on the prepared baking sheet in 3 rows of 4, spaced 1½ to 2 inches

FOR THE DOUGH:

2 large eggs plus 3 large egg yolks, room temperature

85 grams (6 tablespoons) salted butter, melted and cooled

⅔ cup whole milk, warm (110°F)

1 tablespoon grated lemon zest

390 grams (3 cups) all-purpose flour, plus more for dusting

85 grams (⅓ cup plus 1 tablespoon) white sugar

2¼ teaspoons instant yeast

½ teaspoon table salt

FOR FILLING AND FINISHING:

8 ounces cream cheese, cut into chunks, room temperature

23 grams (3 tablespoons) powdered sugar

2 teaspoons grated lemon zest, plus 1 teaspoon lemon juice

1 large egg

160 grams (½ cup) fruit jam, such as blueberry, raspberry, strawberry, cherry or apricot, well chilled (see headnote)

FOR THE CRUMB TOPPING (OPTIONAL):

2 tablespoons all-purpose flour

1 tablespoon white sugar

1 tablespoon salted butter, cut into ½-inch cubes, room temperature

STEPS »

1. Using the dough hook, knead the dough until elastic. Detach the bowl and lift out the hook; the dough should fall in a thick rope into the bowl.

2. Let the dough rise, then chill for up to 24 hours. Divide into 12 portions. Form each into a taut ball by rolling it under a cupped hand.

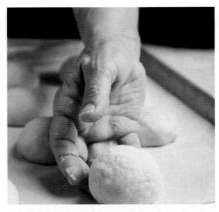

3. Once shaped, place the dough portions seam down on the parchment-lined baking sheet in 3 rows of 4, spaced 1½ to 2 inches apart.

4. Leaving the dough balls on the baking sheet, use your fingers to create a 2-inch wide hollow in each about as deep as the ball itself.

5. Fill each hollow with 1 tablespoon of cream cheese filling. Use the back of a spoon to create indentations in the filling.

6. Into each indentation, spoon 2 teaspoons jam. If using crumb topping, sprinkle it onto the edges of the buns.

7. Bake until the buns are golden brown and spring back when gently pressed, 20 to 22 minutes.

apart. Mist a sheet of plastic wrap with cooking spray and drape it over the baking sheet, then cover loosely with a kitchen towel. Let rise until the balls have expanded slightly and hold an indentation when lightly pressed, 1 to 1½ hours.

Meanwhile, make the cream cheese filling and crumb topping (if using). In a medium bowl, combine the cream cheese, powdered sugar and lemon zest and juice; mix with a silicone spatula until smooth. Cover and refrigerate until needed. In a small bowl, whisk the egg with 1 teaspoon water; set aside for brushing the shaped dough. To make the crumb topping, in a small bowl, stir together the flour and white sugar. Add the butter and toss, then use your fingers to rub it into the flour mixture until it is in pea-sized pieces; cover and refrigerate until needed. Heat the oven to 350°F with a rack in the middle position.

Leaving the dough balls in place on the baking sheet, use your fingers to create a 2-inch-wide hollow in each that is about as deep as the ball itself; it's fine if this causes the portions to touch. Brush the buns with the egg wash. Remove the cream cheese filling and jam from the refrigerator. Fill each hollow with 1 slightly mounded tablespoon cream cheese filling. Use the back of a small spoon to create an indentation in each portion of cream cheese filling, then spoon 2 teaspoons jam into each. If using the crumb topping, sprinkle it onto the edges of the buns.

Bake until the buns are golden brown and spring back when gently pressed, 20 to 22 minutes. Cool on the baking sheet on a wire rack for at least 10 minutes. Serve warm or at room temperature.

Babas au Rhum

**Start to finish: 2¾ hours
(40 minutes active)**

Servings: 8

Four 4-inch strips orange zest,
plus 3 tablespoons orange juice

214 grams (1 cup) plus 40 grams
(3 tablespoons) white sugar, divided

⅓ cup dark rum

2 large eggs, plus 2 large egg yolks,
room temperature

244 grams (1¾ cups plus
2 tablespoons) all-purpose flour

2 teaspoons instant yeast

¼ teaspoon table salt

57 grams (4 tablespoons) salted
butter, cut into 1-tablespoon pieces,
plus 28 grams (2 tablespoons) salted
butter, room temperature,
for greasing the pan

1 cup cold heavy cream

A classic French dessert with Eastern European roots, babas au rhum traditionally consists of yeasted, mildly sweet, bread-like individual cakes heavily soaked in a boozy, rum-spiked syrup. At Restaurant Astier in Paris, we tried a lighter, fresher iteration. They skip the syrup bath and serve the cakes with a side of rum for drizzling. For our version, we opted for an orange-infused rum syrup—the sweet, fruity notes of citrus juice balance the alcohol's bite. Cooking strips of orange peel in the mix softens and sweetens them, creating quick-candied citrus that we use to flavor the butter-rich dough. The final touch is a dollop of lightly sweetened whipped cream that ties everything together. If you don't plan to serve all eight babas, still brush them all with syrup; the extras can be stored overnight in an airtight container at room temperature (the syrup also can be stored at room temperature). To serve, wrap the babas in foil and warm at 350°F for eight to 10 minutes, then halve and serve as directed. (If refrigerated overnight, the whipped cream will slightly deflate; re-whisk before using.)

Don't be alarmed by the dough's elasticity when you transfer it to the muffin pan. This is what gives the cakes their light, fluffy texture. Be sure to generously grease the muffin pan; 2 tablespoons of softened butter for 8 cups will seem like a lot, but it ensures that the babas can be lifted out with ease.

In a small saucepan over medium, combine the orange zest and juice, 214 grams (1 cup) sugar and ½ cup water. Bring to a simmer over medium and cook, stirring once or twice, until the sugar has dissolved and the syrup thickens, 3 to 5 minutes; you should have about 1 cup. Transfer the orange zest to a cutting board and finely chop; set aside. Stir the rum into the syrup. Cool to room temperature, then cover and set aside.

In a liquid measuring cup or small bowl, whisk together the whole eggs, yolks and ¼ cup water. In a stand mixer with the dough hook, mix the flour, yeast, remaining 40 grams (3 tablespoons) sugar and salt on low until combined. With the mixer running, slowly add the egg mixture. Knead on medium until a wet, slightly lumpy dough forms, about 2 minutes, scraping the bowl once or twice.

Add the 57 grams (4 tablespoons) butter and knead on medium, scraping the bowl once or twice, until the dough is smooth, elastic and forms a mass around the hook that mostly pulls away from the sides of the bowl, 7 to 9 minutes. Detach the bowl and hook, then lift out the hook with dough clinging to it; the dough should fall in a thick, shiny, sticky rope; if it does not, knead for a couple more minutes and retest. Add the chopped orange zest and mix on medium to combine, about 1 minute. Scrape the sides of the bowl and gather the dough in

the center. Cover tightly with plastic wrap and let rise at room temperature until doubled, 1 to 1½ hours.

Meanwhile, using a pastry brush, liberally coat the insides of the 8 outer cups of a standard 12-cup muffin pan with the remaining 28 grams (2 tablespoons) butter, leaving the cups in the center row empty.

When the dough has doubled, use lightly oiled hands and a large spoon to scoop dough into the prepared cups until each is about two-thirds full; the dough will be stretchy and sticky, so you may need to "cut" the dough with the edge of the spoon. Mist a large sheet of plastic wrap with cooking spray, then lay it over the pan, greased side down. Let rise at room temperature until doubled, 30 to 40 minutes. Meanwhile, heat the oven to 350°F with the rack in the middle position.

Uncover the pan and bake until the babas are golden brown and a toothpick inserted at the centers comes out clean, 16 to 18 minutes. Meanwhile, in a stand mixer with the whisk attachment, beat the cream and 2 tablespoons rum syrup on medium-high until the mixture holds soft peaks, 2 to 3 minutes. Cover and refrigerate until ready to use.

When the babas are done, cool in the pan for 5 minutes. Gently lift each out and set on a wire rack. Cool for another 5 minutes, then brush the outsides of the warm babas with about ½ cup rum syrup. The babas can be served right away or kept on the rack at room temperature for up to 2 hours.

To serve, halve each baba lengthwise and place 2 halves, cut sides up, on each serving plate. Drizzle the cut side of each half with about 1 tablespoon of the remaining rum syrup. If needed, re-whisk the whipped cream to soft peaks, then dollop onto the babas. Serve right away.

German Blueberry Streusel Cake

Classic German Streuselkuchen is a lush, fine-crumbed, yeasted cake topped with a remarkably hefty amount of buttery-crisp streusel. We've added a layer of fresh blueberries to the mix. Not only do the berries add color, but their fruity tartness is a perfect foil for the richness of the cake and streusel. Brown sugar is not used in the streusel for true German Streuselkuchen, but we included a little to give the topping a touch of golden color and subtle notes of molasses. This coffee cake is perfect for breakfast or brunch or as a casual dessert. We found that a slow, cold rise resulted in a crumb that's especially moist, tender and flavorful; this also makes it easier to bake the cake the morning of serving. However, if you wish to start and finish in a single go, after patting the dough into the pan, cover and let it rise at room temperature for 20 to 30 minutes instead of chilling it; at this time, also remove the streusel from the refrigerator. Top the dough with the berries and streusel, then bake as indicated. Leftovers will keep at room temperature for a couple of days; the topping will soften slightly, but the flavors are still great.

Don't forget to bring the butter to room temperature for both the streusel and the cake. Softened butter incorporates more easily with the other ingredients. Be sure to allow the Streuselkuchen to cool completely before serving. Its texture is best at room temperature.

To make the streusel, in a stand mixer with the paddle attachment, mix the flour, both sugars and salt on medium-low until well combined and any lumps of brown sugar have broken apart, 1 to 2 minutes. With the mixer on low, add the butter 1 piece at a time, then mix on medium-low until fully incorporated and the mixture resembles damp sand, 1 to 2 minutes. Transfer the streusel to a medium bowl, cover and refrigerate. Wipe the mixer bowl and the paddle attachment.

To make the dough, in a 2-cup liquid measuring cup or small bowl, whisk the milk, whole egg and yolk, lemon zest and yeast. In the mixer bowl using the paddle attachment, mix the flour, sugar, salt and cinnamon on medium-low until combined, about 30 seconds. With the mixer running, slowly add the milk-egg mixture; mix until the dry ingredients are evenly moistened, about 30 seconds. Increase to medium and beat until a sticky, webby mixture forms, about 3 minutes.

Scrape the bowl. With the mixer running on medium-low, add the butter 1 piece at a time, mixing for about 15 seconds before adding the next. When all the butter has been added, scrape the bowl and mix on medium until a very sticky, elastic, batter-like dough forms, 2 to 3 minutes. Remove the paddle attachment and scrape

**Start to finish: 3¼ hours
(45 minutes active), plus cooling**

Makes a 9-by-13-inch cake

FOR THE STREUSEL:

195 grams (1½ cups) all-purpose flour

107 grams (½ cup) white sugar

50 grams (¼ cup) packed dark brown sugar

½ teaspoon table salt

141 grams (10 tablespoons) salted butter, cut into 1-tablespoon pieces, room temperature

FOR THE DOUGH AND BERRIES:

⅔ cup whole milk, room temperature

1 large egg, plus 1 large egg yolk, room temperature

2 teaspoons grated lemon zest

1½ teaspoons instant yeast

325 grams (2½ cups) all-purpose flour, plus more for dusting

71 grams (⅓ cup) white sugar

½ teaspoon table salt

½ teaspoon ground cinnamon

70 grams (5 tablespoons) salted butter, cut into 1-tablespoon pieces, room temperature, plus more for the pan

290 grams (2 cups) blueberries

off the dough that clings, allowing it to fall back into the bowl. Scrape the sides of the bowl and gather the dough in the center. Cover and let rise at room temperature for 1½ hours; the dough will not double.

Meanwhile, butter a 9-by-13-inch baking pan or glass baking dish, then line it with a 16-inch sheet of foil so the ends overhang the long sides of the pan. Butter the foil.

After the dough has risen for 1½ hours, scrape the dough into the center of the prepared pan. Lightly dust the top of the dough with flour and flour your hands. Starting from the center and using outstretched hands, firmly press the dough into an even layer to the edges and into the corners of the pan. Re-flour your hands as needed and press the dough firmly to remove as many air bubbles as possible. Do not pull or stretch the dough, which may cause it to tear, and make sure the edges are not thicker than the center. Cover with plastic wrap, drape a kitchen towel over the pan and refrigerate for 8 to 24 hours.

When you are ready to bake, remove the dough and streusel from the refrigerator and let stand at room temperature for about 45 minutes; the dough will rise only slightly. About 30 minutes into rising, heat the oven to 350°F with a rack in the lower-middle position.

Uncover the pan. Scatter the blueberries on the dough in a single layer. Scoop up a big handful of streusel, firmly squeeze in your hand it until it forms a cohesive clump, then crumble and break the clump into bits no larger than the size of a shelled peanut, scattering them onto the berry-topped dough; aim for a mix of fine crumbles and larger pebbly pieces. Continue adding the remaining streusel in this way, evenly covering the surface.

Bake until the streusel is light golden brown, 30 to 35 minutes. Cool in the pan on a wire rack for about 30 minutes. Run a thin-bladed knife between the cake and pan along the short edges of the pan. Using the foil overhang as handles, lift the cake out of the pan and set it on the rack. Cool completely before serving.

German Cherry Streusel Cake

Follow the recipe to make the streusel and dough, allow the dough to rise, pat it into the prepared baking pan and refrigerate as directed. After removing the dough from the refrigerator, cut **225 grams (1½ cups) pitted fresh or thawed frozen cherries** in half if medium in size or into quarters if large, then pat dry to wick away excess moisture, especially if using frozen.Continue with the recipe to heat the oven and top the dough, using the cherries in place of the blueberries. Bake and remove from the pan as directed.

Chapter 4

Flatbreads

Seeded Crackers with Smoked Paprika and Olive Oil

Start to finish: 45 minutes, plus resting and cooling

Makes about two dozen 1½- to 2-inch crackers

195 grams (1½ cups) all-purpose flour, plus more for dusting

85 grams (½ cup) semolina flour or 70 grams (½ cup) dark rye flour

1¼ teaspoons table salt

1 teaspoon baking powder

½ teaspoon smoked paprika

¼ teaspoon ground black pepper

3 tablespoons white sesame seeds

1 tablespoon fennel seeds or caraway seeds or both, crushed

1 tablespoon poppy seeds or nigella seeds or both

¼ cup extra-virgin olive oil, plus more for brushing

¼ cup grapeseed or other neutral oil

Flaky salt (optional)

Packed with pops of texture and flavor, these crackers are easy to make and customize. Semolina adds crispness and crunch, but we also love the earthy notes and tenderness lent by rye flour. The combination of olive oil and neutral oil gives the crackers a snappy bite and rich flavor. As for the seeds, there's room to experiment with whatever you have, though we've included guidelines informed by what we enjoyed most. Rather than try and cut thin, fragile dough into neat rounds or rectangles, we break the crackers into uneven shapes and shards after baking. The crackers are great with cheese, offered with dips or spreads, or served with soup or salad. They keep well in an airtight container for a few days.

Don't try to knead the dough into a smooth ball. Knead just enough to ensure the flour is hydrated—overworking causes the crackers to become tough. Also, keep a close eye on them as they bake and pull them just as the edges begin to brown. The semolina can develop bitter notes if allowed to get too dark.

In a large bowl, whisk together both flours, the salt, baking powder, paprika and pepper. Add the sesame, fennel and poppy seeds; toss well. Add both oils and ½ cup water. Using a silicone spatula, stir until a shaggy dough forms; it's fine if some dry pockets remain.

Lightly dust the counter with all-purpose flour and turn the mixture out onto it. Knead by hand just until the dough is pliable, evenly moistened and only slightly sticky; it will not form a smooth ball. Do not overknead. Divide the dough in half and shape each portion into a 1-inch-thick disk. Wrap each in plastic and refrigerate for at least 1 hour or up to 24 hours.

About 20 minutes before you are ready to bake, remove the dough disks from the refrigerator. Heat the oven to 350°F with racks in the upper- and lower-middle positions. Have ready 2 baking sheets and two 12-by-16-inch sheets of kitchen parchment.

Place 1 parchment sheet on the counter and lightly dust with all-purpose flour. Unwrap 1 dough disk and place it on the parchment. Using a lightly floured rolling pin, roll the dough to an even ⅛-inch thickness; it's fine if the dough is oddly shaped. If the dough tears or resists rolling, it's too cold; cover and let stand a few minutes before continuing. Transfer the parchment with the rolled dough to a baking sheet. Lightly brush all over with olive oil.

Using the second parchment sheet, roll out the remaining dough disk in the same way and brush with olive oil. Use a fork to poke holes every 1 to 2 inches across the surface of the dough sheets, then sprinkle with flaky salt (if using).

Bake until the cracker sheets are crisp and beginning to brown, 25 to 35 minutes, rotating the baking sheets and switching their positions about halfway through. Cool completely on the baking sheets on wire racks. Break the cracker sheets into 1½- to 2-inch pieces or shards.

MASTERING OVEN HOT SPOTS

Oven temperature can vary widely depending on rack height, heat source, even placement front to back. This creates hot spots, often the real culprit in unevenly cooked or burned food. While oven thermometers can help manage this, it's best to invest a little time familiarizing yourself with your oven's nuances. In general, gas ovens have the greatest disparities because the heating cycle of the flame is less consistent than an electric coil, which also distributes heat more evenly. In gas ovens, the top and back tend to be hotter than the bottom and front, sometimes varying by more than 20 percent. In electric ovens, the difference usually is between 5 to 15 percent. To test what this meant for cooking, we baked sugar cookies—12 cookies per baking sheet to create a grid to indicate hot spots—one at a time on each rack of the ovens at Milk Street. The cookies baked on the top suffered from the worst hot spots, browning too much too quickly. Cookies baked on the bottom were unevenly cooked, some browning too much, others needing more time. Those in the middle cooked most evenly, though even they suffered from some hot spots. To manage this in your own oven, first do a few test batches of cookies to identify hot spots. Second, keeping those spots in mind, always rotate food during baking front to back and top to bottom (if cooking on multiple racks) to even out the effects. Third, always heat the oven for at least 20 minutes for as even heating as possible. Finally, never trust baking times; they never will be perfectly accurate for your oven. Check early and often.

Lahmajoun

Start to finish: 2¼ hours
(1 hour active)

Makes twelve 5-inch lahmajoun

FOR THE DOUGH:

293 grams (2¼ cups) all-purpose flour, plus more for dusting

2¼ teaspoons instant yeast

1 teaspoon white sugar

¾ teaspoon table salt

1 cup warm water (100°F to 110°F)

1 tablespoon extra-virgin olive oil, plus more to grease the bowl and baking sheets

FOR THE TOPPING:

1 ripe large tomato, halved and seeded

1 medium red bell pepper

½ medium red onion

4 medium garlic cloves

½ cup lightly packed fresh flat-leaf parsley

1 pound ground lamb or ground beef

3 tablespoons tomato paste

1 tablespoon Aleppo pepper

1 tablespoon dried oregano

1 tablespoon ground cumin

2 teaspoons ground sumac

Kosher salt

FOR SERVING:

Lemon wedges

Roughly chopped fresh flat-leaf parsley

An aficionado of the food and cooking of the Mediterranean, Ana Sortun, cookbook author and award-winning chef at Boston restaurants Oleana, Sarma and Sofra, has a deep knowledge of Turkish cuisine. She taught us her way of making lahmajoun, a Turkish flatbread topped with ground meat (typically lamb, though beef works, too) seasoned with tomatoes, bell pepper and spices. Though lahmajoun often are very thin, hers are thicker and more substantial, with a soft yet chewy crust. Sortun prefers to hand-chop the ingredients for the topping, combining them on the cutting board and running a knife over them until they're well integrated; this method yields a rustic texture. If, however, you favor speed, the topping can be made in a food processor; see the instructions p. 160. The common way to eat lahmajoun is to squeeze on some juice from a lemon wedge and roll up the flatbread. This recipe makes smallish lahmajoun with thicker-than-typical crusts, so feel free to cut them for serving or simply fold them in half for easier eating, but be sure to offer lemon wedges on the side.

Don't compact the topping into a patty when flattening the dough. Keep the meat mixture loose and distribute it as evenly as possible on the round. When dimpling the rounds with your fingers, don't be afraid to push some of the topping into the dough so the meat mixture fuses with the bread during baking.

To make the dough, in a stand mixer with the dough hook, mix the flour, yeast, sugar and table salt on medium until well combined, about 15 seconds. With the mixer on low, gradually add the water and oil; mix until a sticky, slightly curdy dough forms, about 3 minutes. Increase to medium and continue kneading, scraping the bowl once or twice, until the dough is smooth, supple, elastic and clears the sides of the bowl, about 10 minutes; if needed, knead in up to 2 tablespoons additional flour. The finished dough should feel slightly tacky but not unworkable. Meanwhile, oil a large bowl.

Lightly dust the counter with flour and turn the dough out onto it. Shape the dough into a ball and place it in the prepared bowl, then turn the ball so all sides are oiled. Cover with a kitchen towel and let rise at room temperature until doubled in bulk, 45 to 60 minutes.

Meanwhile, to make the topping, grate the tomato halves against the large holes of a box grater (start with the cut sides against the grater) into a medium bowl; stop when you reach the skin and discard it. On a large cutting board, stem, seed and finely chop the bell pepper; peel and finely chop the onion and finely chop the garlic and parsley. Push the ingredients to one side of the board as they are done. When they are all prepped, gather them on the board, then add the ground meat, tomato

paste, Aleppo pepper, oregano, cumin, sumac and 1½ teaspoons kosher salt. Using a chef's knife, chop the ingredients until well integrated. Add the tomato pulp to the mixture (reserve the bowl) and chop it in until well combined. Transfer the filling to the reserved bowl; cover and refrigerate until ready to use.

Heat the oven to 450°F with a rack in the middle position. Line 2 rimmed baking sheets with kitchen parchment, then brush the parchment with oil.

When the dough is properly risen, dust the counter with flour and turn the dough out onto it. Divide the dough evenly into 12 portions (about 45 grams each) and form each into a taut ball. Arrange 6 dough balls on each prepared baking sheet, spaced evenly apart and staggered to give the portions as much room as possible. Cover each baking sheet with a kitchen towel and let the dough rest for about 30 minutes.

Using your hands, flatten each portion of dough into a round 4 to 5 inches in diameter. Evenly divide the topping among the rounds (about ⅓ cup each). Use your fingers to press each portion on one baking sheet into a round about 6 inches in diameter while dimpling the surface and evenly distributing the topping; press the topping into the dough but do not compact it into a patty. It's fine if the dough rounds touch slightly.

Slide the baking sheet into the oven and bake until the crust is light golden brown and the topping is sizzling at the edges, 14 to 17 minutes. Meanwhile, shape the second batch. When the first batch is done, use a wide metal spatula to transfer the lahmajoun directly to a wire rack. Bake the second batch in the same way as the first.

Sprinkle the lahmajoun with parsley and serve with lemon wedges. To eat, squeeze lemon juice onto the lahmajoun and fold it half.

VARIATION

To make the topping in a food processor:

Grate the tomato halves as directed. Stem, seed and cut the bell pepper into chunks. Peel and cut the onion into chunks. In a food processor, combine the bell pepper, onion, garlic and parsley; pulse until the vegetables are chopped, about 10 pulses; scrape the bowl once or twice. Add the ground meat, tomato paste, Aleppo pepper, oregano, cumin, sumac and 1½ teaspoons kosher salt. Pulse until the mixture is well combined, about 5 pulses; do not overprocess. Add the grated tomato (reserve the bowl) and pulse a few times to combine; transfer to the reserved bowl. Cover and refrigerate until ready to use.

Greek Yogurt and Olive Oil Flatbreads

These soft, plush flatbreads from chef Marianna Leivaditaki are simple to make. Yogurt and olive oil give them rich flavor and a little semolina flour adds a pleasing texture. The breads are cooked one at a time in a skillet on the stovetop (cast-iron works best for browning, but nonstick does a decent job, too) and hot out of the pan, they're brushed with olive oil seasoned with za'atar, sumac and dried oregano. Serve them warm for making sandwich or kebab wraps, as an accompaniment to stews or braises, or for dipping into hummus and other spreads. The flatbreads are best when freshly made, of course, but extra can be stored in a zip-close bag at room temperature for up to three days; to rewarm, wrap the breads in foil and pop them into a 350°F oven for a few minutes.

Don't be afraid to add more all-purpose flour when rolling out the dough. The dough is quite sticky, so additional flour is needed to prevent it from sticking to the counter.

Start to finish: 1 hour

Makes eight 7-inch flatbreads

1 cup warm water (110°F)

60 grams (¼ cup) whole-milk Greek yogurt, room temperature

½ cup extra-virgin olive oil, divided, plus more for the bowl

293 grams (2¼ cups) all-purpose flour, plus more for dusting

85 grams (½ cup) semolina flour

1 tablespoon instant yeast

1 teaspoon table salt, divided

1 teaspoon za'atar

½ teaspoon ground sumac

½ teaspoon dried oregano

In a small bowl, whisk together the water, yogurt and ¼ cup oil. In a large bowl, whisk together both flours, the yeast and ¾ teaspoon salt. Make a well in the center and pour the liquids into the well. Using a silicone spatula, gradually incorporate the dry ingredients into the wet; once combined, the mixture should form a shaggy dough.

Dust the counter with all-purpose flour and turn the dough out onto it; reserve the bowl. Knead the dough until smooth and elastic, about 2 minutes, adding flour as needed to prevent sticking. Lightly coat the same bowl with oil, then return the dough to it. Cover with a clean kitchen towel and let rise at room temperature until the dough has doubled in bulk, 30 to 60 minutes.

Meanwhile, cut eight 9-inch squares of kitchen parchment; set aside. In a small bowl, stir together the remaining ¼ cup oil, the za'atar, sumac, oregano and the remaining ¼ teaspoon salt; set aside.

When the dough is ready, dust the counter with flour, then turn the dough onto the surface. Using a dough scraper or bench knife, divide the dough into 8 pieces, each about 87 grams (3 ounces). Form each portion into a taut ball, keeping the formed balls covered with the kitchen towel as you shape the rest. Set 1 ball on a lightly floured surface and, using a rolling pin, roll it into an 8-inch round about ⅛ inch thick, dusting with flour as needed. Lightly flour a parchment square and set the round on top. Repeat with the remaining dough balls, stacking the rounds on top of each other, with a parchment square between the layers.

Heat a 10- to 12-inch cast-iron skillet over medium until water flicked onto the surface immediately sizzles and evaporates. Pick up a dough round by its parchment liner, invert it into the pan and peel off and discard the parchment. Cook until large bubbles form and the bottom is spottily browned, 1 to 2 minutes. Using tongs, flip the bread and cook until the second side is golden brown, about 1 minute. Transfer to a wire rack and brush the surface with the za'atar oil. Cook the remaining dough rounds in the same way and brush them with za'atar oil. Wipe out the pan if excess flour begins to build up and smoke, and adjust the heat as needed. Serve warm or room temperature.

Turkish-Style Flaky Flatbreads

We tried katmer, a flaky, unleavened flatbread sometimes sweetened with sugar, tahini and/or nuts, in Türkiye. The bread's thin profile, tender texture and golden-brown spots were reminiscent of lavash, but it boasted buttery-rich layers that lightened it considerably and made it especially delicious. A series of rolls and folds, with butter and oil brushed in between, create the dough's signature flakiness. When the katmer hits a hot griddle or skillet, its layers steam apart. The folded dough packets can be made up to 24 hours in advance, then covered and refrigerated; there's no need to let them come to room temperature before the final roll. Serve the finished breads warm or at room temperature with meze or as a part of a meal. The sweet version, see recipe p. 165, is great for breakfast or as an accompaniment to coffee or tea.

Don't shortcut the resting times for the dough. Without sufficient resting between steps, it will be difficult to roll the dough thinly without it springing back. Make sure to get the cast-iron skillet very hot before adding each flatbread, otherwise it won't puff up.

Start to finish: 1 hour, plus resting and refrigeration

Makes eight 10-inch flatbreads

650 grams (5 cups) all-purpose flour, plus more if needed and for dusting

1 teaspoon table salt

85 grams (6 tablespoons) salted butter, melted and slightly cooled

¼ cup plus 2 tablespoons extra-virgin olive oil

STEPS >>

HOW TO MAKE TURKISH-STYLE FLAKY FLATBREADS

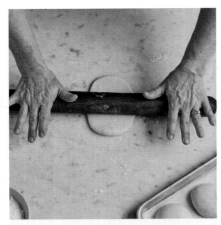

1. Set 1 dough ball on a lightly floured surface and roll it into a rough 11-inch square, dusting with flour as needed.

2. After rolling, lightly brush the surface of the dough with about 4 teaspoons of the butter-oil mixture.

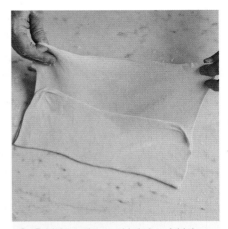

3. Fold down the top third, then fold the bottom up over it; press gently to seal and brush with more butter-oil mixture.

4. Fold it into thirds, forming a square packet, then dust with flour. Repeat the process with the remaining dough balls.

5. When ready to cook, set 1 packet on a lightly floured surface and roll into a 10-inch square; dust with flour as needed.

6. Flour a square of kitchen parchment and place a dough packet on top.

7. Repeat for all packets, stacking them on top of each other, separated by parchment.

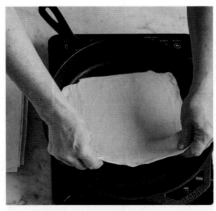

8. Pick up a dough square by two corners, peel it off the parchment and lay it in the skillet, taking care not to let the dough fold over itself.

9. Cook until bubbles form and the bottom is spottily browned, 1 to 2 minutes. Using tongs, flip and cook until the second side is golden brown.

In a stand mixer with the dough hook, mix the flour and salt on low to combine, about 5 seconds. With the mixer on low, slowly add 1¾ cups water. Knead until the dough is smooth and clears the sides of the bowl, about 5 minutes. If the dough sticks to the bowl after 5 minutes, knead in up to 2 tablespoons more flour, 1 tablespoon at a time, until it clears the sides.

Lightly flour the counter and turn the dough out onto it. Using a bench knife, divide the dough into 8 even pieces. Form each into a taut ball by rolling it against the counter in a circular motion under a cupped hand. Space the balls about 1 inch apart on a lightly floured surface, then cover with a kitchen towel; let rest for 30 minutes. Meanwhile, in a medium bowl, stir together the butter and oil.

Set 1 dough ball on a lightly floured surface and, using a rolling pin, roll it into a rough 11-inch square of even thickness, dusting with flour as needed. Lightly brush the surface of the dough with about 4 teaspoons of the butter-oil mixture. Fold the top third of the dough down over itself, then fold the bottom third up; press gently to seal. Lightly brush the surface with about 1 teaspoon of the butter-oil mixture. Fold the strip into thirds, forming a small, squarish packet; press gently to seal. Dust the surface of the packet with flour, then transfer it to a large plate; repeat with the remaining dough balls, keeping the packets in a single layer. Cover with plastic wrap and refrigerate for at least 30 minutes or up to 24 hours. Meanwhile, cut eight 12-inch squares of kitchen parchment; set aside.

When ready to cook, lightly flour the counter. Set 1 packet on the lightly floured surface and, using a rolling pin, roll it into a 10-inch square of even thickness, dusting with flour as needed. Lightly flour a parchment square and set the dough square on top. Repeat with the remaining dough packets, stacking the dough squares on top of each other, separated by parchment.

Heat a 12-inch cast-iron skillet over medium-high until water flicked onto the surface immediately sizzles. Pick up a dough square by 2 corners, peel it off the parchment and lay it in the skillet, taking care not to let the dough fold over itself. Cook until bubbles form and the bottom is spottily browned, 1 to 2 minutes. Using tongs, flip and cook until the second side is golden brown, 1 to 2 minutes. Cook for about another minute, flipping as needed, until lightly puffed and browned all over. Transfer to a wire rack and cover with a kitchen towel. Cook the remaining dough in the same way. Wipe out the pan if excess flour begins to build up and smoke, and adjust the heat as needed. Serve warm or at room temperature.

VARIATION

Turkish-Style Flaky Flatbreads with Sweet Spiced Tahini

Follow the recipe to make and divide the dough. While the dough balls rest, in a medium bowl, whisk together **90 grams (6 tablespoons) tahini, 85 grams (6 tablespoons) salted butter** (melted and slightly cooled), **80 grams (6 tablespoons) white sugar, 2 teaspoons ground coriander** and **1 teaspoon ground cinnamon.** Continue with the recipe, using the tahini mixture in place of the butter-oil mixture.

Italian Flatbreads

Start to finish: 30 minutes

Makes four 10-inch flatbreads

60 grams (¼ cup) plain whole-milk yogurt

274 grams (2 cups) bread flour

1 teaspoon table salt

1½ teaspoons baking powder

75 grams (⅓ cup) lard, room temperature

One of our favorite flatbreads originates in Romagna, in northern Italy. Flour, salt, water or milk, and lard or olive oil are thrown together to make a quick dough. After a short rest, the flatbread—a piadina—is cooked on a griddle or skillet, then is stuffed with a sweet or savory filling and folded in half to make a sandwich. We started by finding the right fat for our dough. Butter was wrong. Olive oil gave us a pleasant texture and flavor, but something was missing. So we gave lard a shot. And what a difference. The piadine were tender and flavorful, with just the right chew. (Vegetable shortening works as a substitute for lard, though the breads won't be as tasty.) Still, we wanted more suppleness in the crumb and found our answer in naan, a flatbread from India that adds a scoop of yogurt to the dough. Just ¼ cup plain yogurt improved the texture of the piadine and also imparted more complex flavor. For a simple finish, brush the warm cooked piadine with spicy garlic oil, or for a heartier topping, see our prosciutto and ricotta topping (recipes facing page).

In a liquid measuring cup, whisk together ¼ cup water and the yogurt. In a food processor, combine the flour, salt and baking powder; process for 5 seconds. Add the lard and process until combined, about 10 seconds. With the processor running, add the yogurt mixture. With the processor still running, add another ¼ cup water 1 tablespoon at a time until the dough forms a smooth, moist ball, about 1 minute. (If the dough does not form a ball in the food processor, transfer to a counter and knead by hand until it does.)

Divide the dough into 4 pieces. Form each into a ball, then cover with plastic wrap. Let rest for 15 minutes. Using a rolling pin, roll each ball into a 10-inch round of even thickness. If the dough springs back when rolled, let it rest, covered, for 10 to 15 minutes; begin rolling additional pieces while the previous ones rest. Using a fork, prick holes all over each dough round.

Heat a 12-inch cast-iron skillet over medium-high until water flicked onto the surface immediately sizzles. Place 1 dough round in the heated skillet and cook until the bottom is charred in spots, 1 to 2 minutes. Using tongs, flip and cook the second side until spotty brown, about 30 seconds. Transfer to a plate and tent with foil. Serve warm.

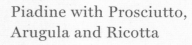

Piadine with Prosciutto, Arugula and Ricotta

After dividing the dough, while it rests, in a medium bowl, stir together **¾ cup whole-milk ricotta cheese** and **½ teaspoon grated lemon zest;** taste and season with **kosher salt and ground black pepper,** then set aside. Roll out the dough and cook as directed. Divide the ricotta mixture among the warm piadine, spreading it over half of one side, then top the breads with **8 slices prosciutto,** dividing it evenly. In a medium bowl, toss **4 cups lightly packed baby arugula** with **2 tablespoons lemon juice** and a pinch of kosher salt. Divide the arugula among the piadine, mounding it on top of the prosciutto. Drizzle with **extra-virgin olive oil** and fold in half to enclose the filling.

VARIATION

Piadine with Spicy Garlic and Herb Oil

After dividing the dough, while it rests, in a food processor, combine **⅔ cup extra-virgin olive oil, 2 cups lightly packed fresh flat-leaf parsley, ½ cup roughly chopped fresh chives, ¼ cup roughly chopped fresh dill, 1 table-spoon red pepper flakes, 1 large garlic clove** (smashed and peeled) and **½ teaspoon each kosher salt and ground black pepper.** Process until smooth, about 20 seconds, scraping the bowl as needed. Transfer to a small bowl or jar. Roll out the dough and cook as directed. Brush the warm piadine with oil. (Extra oil can be served on the side or saved for drizzling onto soups, pasta dishes, bean dishes, cooked polenta or fried eggs or used to make vinaigrettes.)

Turkish Flatbreads

**Start to finish: 1¾ hours
(45 minutes active)**

Makes six 8- to 9-inch flatbreads

260 grams (2 cups) all-purpose flour, plus more for dusting

½ teaspoon table salt

2 tablespoons plus ½ teaspoon extra-virgin olive oil, divided

The Turkish flatbread called yufka is fast and easy to make largely because it's unleavened (that is, yeast free). As chef Ana Sortun, whose recipe from "Soframiz" we adapted, explains, yufka is more slender than a flour tortilla but more substantial than phyllo. The flatbreads can be used to make sandwich wraps or for scooping up dips and spreads. Or fill, fold and toast them to make savory, sandwich-like gozleme. This dough comes together quickly, requires only an hour of rest, is a breeze to roll out and each bread cooks in just a couple minutes on the stovetop. A cast-iron skillet works best for getting nice brown spots on the flatbreads, but nonstick works, too. As the breads come out of the skillet, we slip them into a plastic bag to keep them soft and pliable. Once all the breads have been cooked, cool to room temperature, then seal the bag and store at room temperature for up to a day (the breads are best used within 24 hours of making).

Don't cook the flatbreads on both sides or they will become too crisp and cracker-like for folding and wrapping. Browned on only one side, the breads will be fully cooked and ready to eat but will remain soft and pliable.

In a medium bowl, whisk together the flour and salt. In a liquid measuring cup, combine ⅔ cup water and the 2 tablespoons oil. Make a well in the center of the flour and pour in the water mixture. Using a spatula, incorporate the dry ingredients from the outside in toward the center, stirring until the liquid is incorporated and a shaggy dough forms, 1½ to 2 minutes.

Lightly flour the counter and turn the dough out onto it; reserve the bowl. Knead by hand until the dough is smooth and elastic, about 4 minutes. Wipe out the reserved bowl and coat it with the remaining ½ teaspoon oil. Place the dough in the bowl and turn to coat with oil; cover with plastic wrap and let rest at room temperature for about 1 hour. Meanwhile, cut six 9-inch squares of kitchen parchment; set aside.

Transfer the dough to the counter. Using a dough scraper or bench knife, divide the dough into 6 pieces, each about 70 grams (2½ ounces), then form each portion into a taut ball. Dust the dough balls lightly with flour and cover with a clean kitchen towel. Lightly flour the counter, set 1 ball on top and, using a rolling pin, roll it into an 8- to 9-inch round about ⅛ inch thick. Place the round on a parchment square. Repeat with the remaining dough balls and stack the rounds on top of each other, placing a square of parchment between the layers.

Heat a 12-inch cast-iron skillet over medium-high until water flicked onto the surface immediately sizzles and evaporates. Place 1 dough round in the pan and

Gozleme with Butternut Squash and Feta

Follow the recipe to make the yufka. In a food processor, pulse
12 ounces peeled and seeded butternut squash (cut into rough
1-inch cubes), **1 medium yellow onion** (roughly chopped) and
¼ teaspoon each table salt and **ground black pepper** until finely
chopped (about the size of rice grains), 15 to 20 pulses. In a 12-inch
cast-iron or nonstick skillet over medium-high, melt **2 tablespoons
salted butter.** Add the squash mixture; cook, stirring occasionally,
until beginning to brown, 7 to 9 minutes. Add 1 tablespoon tomato
paste and **1 medium garlic clove** (finely chopped); cook, stirring,
until fragrant, 1 to 2 minutes. Transfer to a medium bowl and cool
for about 5 minutes. Meanwhile, wash and dry the skillet. Into the
squash mixture, stir **113 grams (1 cup) crumbled feta cheese,**
1½ teaspoons Aleppo pepper (or ½ teaspoon red pepper flakes),
¾ teaspoon ground cumin and **½ teaspoon ground cinnamon.**
Taste and season with salt and black pepper. Divide the squash
mixture evenly among the flatbreads, spreading it over the center
third of the unbrowned sides, and fold the sides over the filling like
a business letter. In the same skillet over medium, heat **1 tablespoon extra-virgin olive oil** until shimmering. Add 3 of the filled
flatbreads and cook until golden brown on both sides, about 3
minutes per side, then transfer to individual plates. Using another
1 tablespoon extra-virgin olive oil, cook the remaining filled
flatbreads in the same way. Makes 6 gozleme.

VARIATION

Beef, Spinach and Feta Gozleme

Follow the recipe to make the yufka. In a 12-inch cast-iron or nonstick skillet over medium, combine **12 ounces 90 percent lean ground beef, 3 tablespoons tomato paste, 2½ teaspoons ground cumin, ¼ teaspoon table salt, ½ teaspoon pepper** and **½ cup water;** cook, breaking the beef into small bits, until the meat is no longer pink, 5 to 6 minutes. Add a **5-ounce container baby spinach** (roughly chopped); cook, stirring, until the pan is dry, about 3 minutes. Transfer to a bowl; cool for about 10 minutes, then stir in **113 grams (1 cup) crumbled feta cheese** and **4 scallions** (thinly sliced). Wash and dry the skillet. Divide the beef mixture evenly among the flatbreads, spreading it over the center third of the unbrowned sides; fold each like a business letter. In the skillet over medium, heat **1 tablespoon extra-virgin olive oil** until shimmering. Add 3 of the filled flatbreads and cook until golden on both sides, about 3 minutes per side, then transfer to plates. Using another **1 tablespoon extra-virgin olive oil,** cook the remaining filled flatbreads in the same way. Makes 6 gozleme.

cook until slightly puffed and the bottom is spotty brown, 1 to 1½ minutes. Using tongs, transfer the flatbread browned side down to a 1-gallon zip-close bag (this keeps the breads soft and pliable). Cook the remaining rounds in the same way, stacking them in the bag. Wipe out the pan if excess flour begins to build up and smoke, and adjust the heat as needed. Use immediately or cool, seal the bag and store at room temperature for up to 1 day.

FANCY FATS

Lard is rendered pig fat and, though it fell from favor years ago, it long was the choice fat for many traditional pie crust and biscuit recipes, as well as for Mexican beans and frying chicken. It has made a comeback in recent years, with high-end options first showing up at farmers markets and premium supermarkets, then spreading more widely. To test whether they are worth the price, we tested two widely available options—the conventional Goya Manteca Refined Lard and its gourmet-grade competitor Epic Rendered Pork Fat. We tried both in pie crust. The differences were stark. The Epic lard produced an especially delicate, shatteringly crisp crust—but with surprisingly gamey notes. The Goya pie crust was slightly less flaky, but with a more desirably neutral flavor. Though we liked the texture of the Epic lard pie crust, we wouldn't recommend it for a typical sweet pie. However, it would be stellar in a savory meat pie or a quiche. Ultimately, if you're looking for a fat that adds more savory complexity and richness, premium lard is worth it. But if you mainly use lard for sweet pastries, skip the pricey stuff.

Quick Flatbreads with Yogurt and Whole Wheat

Start to finish: 40 minutes

Makes 6 flatbreads

206 grams (1½ cups) bread flour (see headnote), plus more for dusting

35 grams (¼ cup) whole-wheat flour

1 teaspoon table salt

1 teaspoon baking powder

180 grams (¾ cup) plain whole-milk yogurt

2 teaspoons honey

43 grams (3 tablespoons) salted butter, melted, or flavored butter (see recipes facing page)

Made throughout the Middle East, non-yeasted flatbreads are the definition of quick bread, taking little time to prepare. We added yogurt to a simple whole wheat–enriched dough for its tangy bite and tenderizing qualities. Bread flour makes up the bulk of the dough and gives these flatbreads pleasant chew, but you can substitute an equal amount of all-purpose flour. If you do use all-purpose, you will likely have to add a couple extra tablespoons of flour during kneading because the dough will be slightly wetter. To cook the flatbreads, you'll need a 12-inch cast-iron skillet; a 10-inch cast-iron skillet will work, too, but there will be a little less room for maneuvering the rounds when flipping them. Brush the breads hot out of the skillet with melted plain butter or with one of our Flavored Butters.

Don't leave any floury bits in the bowl during mixing. All the flour must be incorporated so that the dough isn't too sticky to work with. Don't overflour the counter when rolling out the rounds; excess flour will scorch in the skillet.

In a large bowl, stir together both flours, the salt and baking powder. Add the yogurt and honey, then stir until a shaggy dough forms. Using your hands, knead the dough in the bowl until it forms a cohesive ball, incorporating any dry bits; the dough will be slightly sticky.

Turn the dough out onto a counter dusted with bread flour and knead until just tacky instead of sticky, about 1 minute. The finished dough may appear slightly lumpy; this is fine. Divide into 6 pieces and shape each into a ball. Loosely cover with plastic wrap and let rest for 10 minutes.

Heat a 12-inch cast-iron skillet over medium-high until water flicked onto the surface immediately sizzles. Meanwhile, on a lightly floured counter, roll each ball to an 8-inch circle. Place 1 dough round in the heated skillet and cook until the bottom is dark spotty brown, 1 to 1½ minutes. Using tongs, flip and cook the second side until dark spotty brown, about 1 minute. Transfer to a wire rack, then brush the surface with melted butter. Repeat with the remaining dough rounds. Serve warm.

Flavored Butters

Garlic-Herb Butter

In a small saucepan over medium, combine **43 grams (3 table-spoons) salted butter** and **1 medium garlic clove** (finely grated). Cook, stirring, until the garlic is fragrant and lightly sizzling, about 30 seconds. Off heat, stir in a **pinch of salt** and **2 tablespoons finely chopped fresh flat-leaf parsley, 1 table-spoon finely chopped fresh dill**, and **1 tablespoon finely chopped fresh cilantro, tarragon** or **basil.**

Za'atar Butter

In a small saucepan over medium, combine **43 grams (3 table-spoons) salted butter** and **1 tablespoon za'atar.** Cook, stirring, until the butter is bubbling, about 30 seconds.

Harissa Butter

In a small bowl, stir together **43 grams (3 tablespoons) salted butter**, melted, and **1 tablespoon harissa paste.**

Lebanese Flatbreads with Tomatoes, Za'atar and Sumac

**Start to finish: 2 hours
(1 hour active)**

Makes twelve 5-inch flatbreads

FOR THE DOUGH:

120 grams (½ cup) plain
whole-milk yogurt

⅓ cup plus 4 tablespoons
extra-virgin olive oil, divided

260 grams (2 cups) all-purpose
flour, plus more if needed and
for dusting

2 teaspoons instant yeast

1 teaspoon table salt

FOR THE TOPPING:

1 pound ripe tomatoes, cored,
seeded and chopped

Kosher salt and ground black pepper

¾ cup extra-virgin olive oil

3 tablespoons za'atar

1 tablespoon ground sumac

Pomegranate molasses, to serve
(optional)

These savory flatbreads are Middle Eastern in origin, but we learned about them in São Paulo, Brazil, where they're called esfihas (sometimes spelled esfirras). The breads were introduced to Brazil by Arab immigrants, particularly from Lebanon and Syria, in the late 19th century. Esfihas might be formed into dumpling-like buns that fully enclose a filling, but the ones we favored were open-face like pizzas and about the size of a saucer. At São Paulo's Restaurante & Rotisserie Halim, Yasmin Sultan showed us how to make those pizza-style esfihas. We adapted the recipe, adding some yogurt to the dough for a richer, more tender crumb that complements a simple topping of chopped tomatoes and olive oil mixed with za'atar and sumac. Za'atar is an herb, seed and spice blend; sumac is the ground dried berries of the sumac plant. Look for both in well-stocked grocery stores, spice shops and Middle Eastern markets. If you have leftover esfihas, wrap them well and refrigerate for up to two days. Rewarm in a 425°F oven on a wire rack set in a baking sheet for five to eight minutes.

Don't skip the step of salting and draining the tomatoes. Removing the excess moisture is important for preventing the crusts from becoming soggy.

To make the dough, in a 2-cup liquid measuring cup or small bowl, whisk together the yogurt, the ⅓ cup of the oil and ⅓ cup water. In a stand mixer with the dough hook, mix the flour, yeast and table salt on medium until well combined, about 15 seconds. With the mixer on low, drizzle in the yogurt mixture. Increase to medium and knead until the mixture forms a smooth, elastic dough that clears the sides of the bowl, 7 to 10 minutes; if the dough sticks to the bowl, knead in additional flour, 1 tablespoon at a time. Meanwhile, coat 2 rimmed baking sheets with 2 tablespoons oil each.

Generously dust the counter with flour and turn the dough out onto it. Divide the dough into 12 portions, each about 45 grams (1½ ounces). Form into smooth balls, then place 6 on each prepared baking sheet, evenly spaced. Cover with kitchen towels and let rise until doubled in bulk, 45 minutes to 1 hour.

To make the topping, in a colander or fine-mesh sieve set in or over a bowl, toss the tomatoes with 1 teaspoon kosher salt; set aside. In a medium bowl, stir together the oil, za'atar, sumac and 1 teaspoon each kosher salt and pepper; set aside.

To shape, top and bake the flatbreads, heat the oven to 500°F with a rack in the middle position. Using your fingers, press each dough ball into a 5-inch round

directly on the baking sheet; start at the center of the dough and work outward, leaving the edge slightly thicker. Spoon the oil mixture onto the rounds, dividing it evenly and making sure to include the solids that settle at the bottom. Shake the colander of tomatoes to drain as much moisture as possible. Divide the tomatoes evenly among the rounds, leaving a ½-inch edge, and lightly press them into the dough. Let rise, uncovered, until the edges of the dough are puffy, 20 to 30 minutes.

Bake the flatbreads one baking sheet at a time until the edges are golden brown, 8 to 10 minutes. Cool on the baking sheet on a wire rack, then use a wide metal spatula to transfer the flatbreads directly to the wire rack. Cool for a few minutes. Serve warm, drizzled with pomegranate molasses (if using).

Umbrian Flatbreads with Mushrooms, Rosemary and Fontina

Start to finish: 1 hour,
plus resting time for the dough

Servings: 4

FLATBREADS:

260 grams (2 cups) all-purpose flour, plus more for dusting

2 teaspoons baking powder

1 teaspoon table salt

¼ cup extra-virgin olive oil

FILLING:

1 tablespoon extra-virgin olive oil

1 medium garlic clove, chopped

½ teaspoon red pepper flakes

12 ounces cremini mushrooms, trimmed, halved and thinly sliced

1 tablespoon finely chopped fresh rosemary

Kosher salt and ground black pepper

½ cup jarred roasted red peppers, patted dry and chopped

1 tablespoon balsamic vinegar

113 grams (1 cup) shredded fontina cheese, shredded

2 cups lightly packed baby arugula

Torta al testo is a simple Umbrian flatbread often served with soups or stews. But Perugia home cook Silvia Buitoni taught us that the breads also can be split and filled to make fantastic sandwiches. Though some versions are leavened with yeast, Buitoni used baking powder for a quick-and-easy dough that can be shaped and skillet-cooked after just a brief rest. We added a small measure of olive oil to her formula to give the bread a little suppleness and richness. This recipe calls for a 12-inch cast-iron skillet; the steady heat of cast iron excels at even browning and cooking the flatbreads. After the breads are done, we use the same pan to cook a savory mushroom and fontina filling that's piled into the split breads to make hearty sandwiches. We've also included a sausage, broccoli rabe and provolone version.

Don't knead this dough as you would a yeasted bread dough or the flatbreads will be tough. Knead it just enough to bring it together into a smooth, cohesive mass; this should take less than a minute.

To make the flatbreads, in a large bowl, whisk together the flour, baking powder and table salt. In a 2-cup liquid measuring cup, combine the oil and ½ cup water. Stir while slowly pouring the oil-water mixture into the dry ingredients. Stir until a shaggy dough forms, adding 1 to 3 tablespoons more water, as needed, if the mixture is too dry. Dust the counter with flour, then turn the dough out onto it. Knead until the dough is smooth and cohesive, about 30 seconds. Divide it in half, shape each piece into a smooth ball and set on a lightly floured surface. Cover with a kitchen towel and let rest for at least 15 minutes or up to 1 hour.

Using your hands, press each dough ball into a 5½-inch round. Heat a 12-inch cast-iron skillet over medium-low until water flicked onto the surface immediately sizzles. Add 1 round to the skillet and cook until well browned in spots, 5 to 6 minutes. Using a wide metal spatula, flip the round and cook until the second side is spotty brown, another 4 minutes. Transfer to a wire rack. Cook the second round in the same way. Wrap the breads in a kitchen towel and set aside while you make the filling.

To make the filling, in the same skillet over medium, heat the oil until shimmering. Add the garlic and pepper flakes, then cook, stirring, until fragrant, about 30 seconds. Add the mushrooms, rosemary and ½ teaspoon kosher salt and black pepper; cook, stirring occasionally, until the liquid released by the mushrooms

has evaporated, 10 to 12 minutes. Add the roasted peppers and cook, stirring, until heated through, about 1 minute. Stir in the vinegar; season and taste with salt and pepper. Push the mushrooms into a rough 8-inch round at the center of the skillet, then sprinkle the cheese on top. Cover the pan and remove from the heat.

To assemble the sandwiches, cut both flatbreads in half to create 4 half moons. Using a serrated knife, split each piece in half horizontally; you will have 8 half moons. Divide the mushroom mixture evenly over 4 pieces by sliding a wide metal spatula under a portion and then sliding it onto the bread. Top with the arugula, dividing it evenly. Cover with the untopped flatbread halves and press firmly.

VARIATION

Umbrian Flatbreads with Sausage, Broccoli Rabe and Provolone

Follow the recipe to make the flatbreads. While they cool, in the same skillet, heat **1 tablespoon extra-virgin olive oil** over medium until shimmering. Add **1 pound sweet Italian sausages;** cover and cook, turning occasionally, until the centers reach 160°F, about 8 to 10 minutes. Transfer to a plate and tent with foil. To the fat remaining in the skillet, add **1 medium garlic clove** (chopped) and **¼ teaspoon red pepper flakes;** cook, stirring, until fragrant, about 30 seconds. Add **1 pound broccoli rabe or Broccolini** (trimmed and cut into ¼-inch pieces) and **½ teaspoon salt;** cook, stirring, until just starting to soften, about 1 minute. Add **¼ cup water,** cover and cook, stirring occasionally, until the stem pieces are tender and only a little liquid remains, 4 to 5 minutes. Stir in **2 teaspoons grated lemon zest,** then taste and season with **salt and ground black pepper.** Push the rabe into a rough 8-inch round at the center of the skillet, then lay **113 grams (4 ounces) sliced provolone cheese** on top. Cover and remove from the heat. Cut the sausages on the diagonal into ½-inch slices. Cut both flatbreads in half to create 4 half moons, then, using a serrated knife, slice each piece in half horizontally; you will have 8 half moons. Divide the rabe evenly among 4 pieces by sliding a wide metal spatula under a portion and then sliding it onto the bread, then top with the sausage. Cover with the untopped flatbread halves and press firmly.

Potato-Stuffed Naan

At Pappa Gee Happy Bhai Food Corner in Lahore, Pakistan, Jawaid Ahmed taught us to make aloo naan, a fluffy flatbread filled with chili- and herb-spiked potatoes and cabbage. The resulting bread is tender yet chewy, spottily browned and studded with pockets of spicy, fragrant filling. To recreate it back at Milk Street, there were a few obstacles. First was developing an easy-to-handle dough that was sturdy enough to withstand filling and rolling but baked up light and fluffy. The second was imitating the hot, fast bake of a tandoor oven. For the dough, we looked to yogurt, an ingredient often used in naan. Its calcium content makes for tender bread, so even with the rigors of rolling and stuffing, the naan stayed pleasantly soft. As for cooking, we tried countless oven and broiler settings, but found a hot cast-iron skillet worked best. The naan are hearty enough to be a light meal on their own or with chutney, but also pair wonderfully with a simple curry. Leftovers reheat nicely in a cast-iron skillet over medium; warm each for two to three minutes per side.

Don't be tempted to adjust the water or flour quantities while kneading, as the dough will go through stages. At first, it may seem too dry. After a few minutes of kneading, it may feel too wet. With continued kneading, it will become supple, slightly tacky and workable. Don't melt the ghee before brushing it onto the naan; we found that melted ghee made the breads heavy and greasy. Room-temperature ghee brushed onto the hot bread melts into a light, non-oily coating.

To make the dough, in a small bowl or liquid measuring cup, whisk together the yogurt and ¾ cup plus 2 tablespoons water. In a large bowl, whisk together the flour, yeast and salt. Make a well in the center and pour in the yogurt mixture. Using a silicone spatula, gradually mix the ingredients; once combined, the mixture should form a shaggy dough.

Using your hands, gather the dough and knead in the bowl until no dry, floury bits remain. Turn the dough out onto the counter; reserve the bowl. Knead until mostly smooth and the dough springs back when gently pressed, about 6 minutes. Wipe out the bowl and lightly coat it with oil. Place the dough in it and turn to coat. Cover and let rise at room temperature until doubled, 45 minutes to 1 hour.

Meanwhile, make the filling. In a large microwave-safe bowl, toss the potatoes, ghee, cumin seeds, chili powder, salt and 2 tablespoons water. Cover and microwave on high until a skewer inserted into the potatoes meets no resistance, 10 to 13 minutes, shaking the bowl once about halfway through (do not uncover). Remove from the microwave and carefully uncover. Using a potato masher or the back of a large spoon, mix and mash until broken down but still chunky. Stir in the cabbage, mint, cilantro and chilies; set aside.

**Start to finish: 3 hours
(1½ hours active)**

Makes six 6-inch naan

FOR THE DOUGH:

80 grams (⅓ cup) plain, whole-milk yogurt

455 grams (3½ cups) all-purpose flour

2¼ teaspoons instant yeast

1 teaspoon table salt

Grapeseed or other neutral oil, for greasing the bowl and baking sheets

FOR THE FILLING:

1½ pounds russet potatoes, peeled and cut into ½-inch chunks

1½ tablespoons ghee or salted butter, room temperature

1½ teaspoons cumin seeds

1 teaspoon Kashmiri chili powder or ¾ teaspoon sweet paprika plus ¼ teaspoon cayenne pepper

1 teaspoon table salt

3 ounces (1 cup) finely shredded napa cabbage

2 tablespoons finely chopped fresh mint

2 tablespoons finely chopped fresh cilantro

2 serrano chilies, stemmed, seeded and minced

FOR BRUSHING AND SPRINKLING:

Ghee or salted butter, room temperature

Sesame seeds

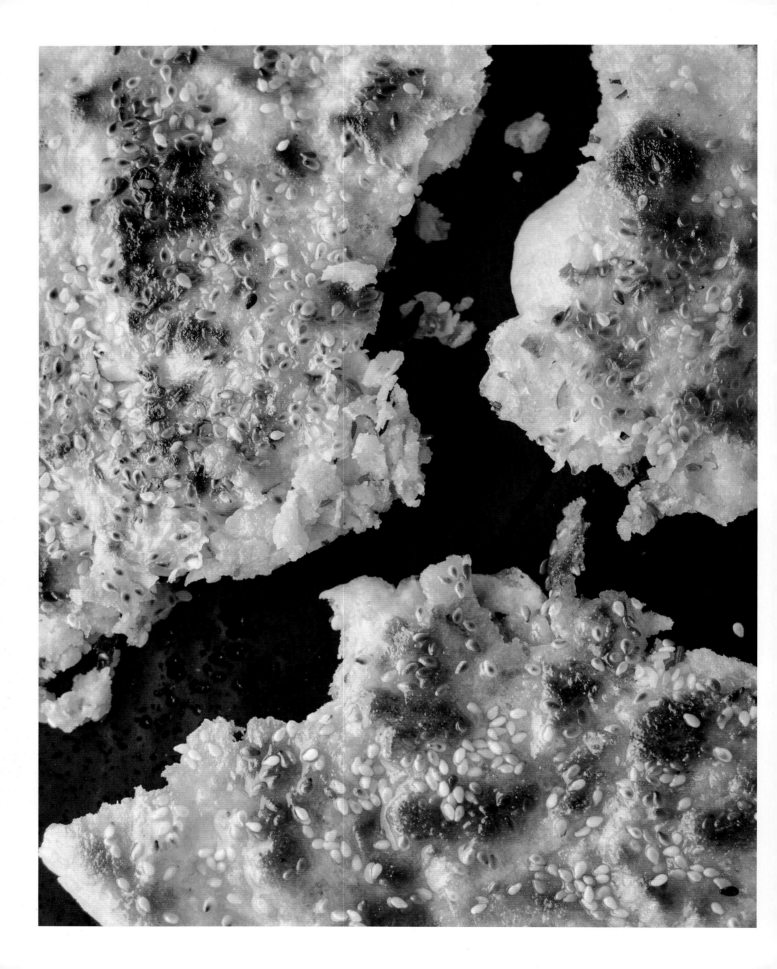

When the dough has doubled, coat 2 rimmed baking sheets with 1 tablespoon oil each. Turn the dough out onto an unfloured counter and divide into 6 portions. Form each into a taut ball by rolling it against the counter in a circular motion under a cupped hand. Place the balls on one of the baking sheets, evenly spaced, and turn each one to coat with oil. Cover and let rise until puffy but not doubled, 25 to 30 minutes.

On an unfloured counter and working 1 at a time, use a rolling pin to roll out the dough balls to 7-inch rounds about ⅜ inch thick; place 3 rounds on each baking sheet and cover with plastic wrap to prevent drying. Evenly divide the filling among the rounds, mounding it in the centers. Working with 1 round, gather the edges of the dough up and around the filling, enclosing it; pinch the seam to seal. Transfer the ball to an unfloured counter, turning it seam side down. Using your fingers, gently pat it into an even disk, then gently roll into a 6-inch round about ½ inch thick; it's OK if there are small tears in the surface. (If large tears begin to form, set the disk aside to rest for a few minutes before continuing.) Return the round to the baking sheet; re-cover with plastic wrap. Repeat with the remaining dough balls.

Heat a 10- or 12-inch cast-iron skillet over medium-high until water flicked onto the surface sizzles and evaporates within seconds, 4 to 6 minutes. Lightly brush the first filled and rolled round on both sides with ghee, then lightly sprinkle the seam-free side with sesame seeds. Dimple the seeded side of the round by firmly pressing your fingertips straight down into the dough. Place in the skillet and cook until spottily charred on the bottom, 2 to 2½ minutes. Using a metal spatula, flip and cook until spottily charred on the second side, another 1½ to 2 minutes. Transfer to a large plate and lightly brush both sides with ghee. Repeat with the remaining naan, stacking them on the plate; reduce the heat as needed if the skillet builds up too much heat and cooks the naan too quickly. Serve warm

VARIATION

Garlic Naan with Green Chili and Cilantro

Follow the recipe to make the dough; omit the filling and the ghee and sesame seeds for brushing and sprinkling. While the dough rises, in a small bowl, stir together **3 tablespoons salted butter** (room temperature), **2 tablespoons finely chopped fresh cilantro, 2 medium garlic cloves** (finely grated) and **1 serrano chili** (stemmed, seeded and minced); set aside. Divide, shape and roll the dough into 7-inch rounds (this naan is unfilled) as directed. Follow the recipe to dimple and cook the rounds, lightly brushing each on both sides with the butter mixture after transferring to a plate.

VARIATION

Naan with Spiced Raisins and Nuts (Peshawari Naan)

Follow the recipe to make the dough; omit the filling and the ghee and sesame seeds for brushing and sprinkling. While the dough rises, in a medium bowl, stir together **78 grams (½ cup) golden raisins (chopped), 45 grams (½ cup) unsweetened shredded coconut, 33 grams (¼ cup) slivered almonds** (toasted and chopped), **57 grams (4 tablespoons) salted butter** (melted), **27 grams (2 tablespoons) white sugar, ½ teaspoon ground cinnamon and ½ teaspoon ground cardamom;** set aside. Divide, shape, roll and fill the dough as directed, using the raisin mixture in place of the potato filling; be extra gentle when handling the filled dough. Follow the recipe to dimple and cook the rounds, lightly brushing each on both sides with salted butter (room temperature) after transferring to a plate.

Orange-Fennel Spanish Olive Oil Tortas

**Start to finish: 2 hours
(15 minutes active), plus cooling**

Makes ten 5½-inch tortas

240 grams (2 cups) cake flour

1 tablespoon fennel seeds

1 teaspoon grated orange zest

½ teaspoon table salt

2¼ teaspoons instant yeast

½ cup warm water (100°F)

⅓ cup extra-virgin olive oil

White sugar, for sprinkling

1 large egg white, well beaten

These thin, crisp, cracker-like Spanish breads, called tortas de aceite, are subtly sweet from a sprinkle of sugar that forms a frosty coating. But the star is extra-virgin olive oil. The fruity, peppery flavor of olive oil is complemented by fragrant orange zest and fennel seeds. Serve with coffee, tea or dessert wine; include them on a cheese board; or tuck a shard into a bowl of ice cream. You can enjoy them as soon as they've cooled completely, but we found their flavor and texture improve after an overnight rest. In an airtight container, they'll keep for several days.

Don't use all-purpose flour. The lower protein content of cake flour means less gluten development in the dough so these tortas bake up with a shorter, flakier, more delicate texture than the typical flatbread.

In the bowl of a stand mixer, whisk the flour, fennel seeds, orange zest, salt and yeast. Attach the bowl and dough hook to the mixer and, with the machine running on low, slowly add the water, then the oil. Mix on medium just until the dough comes together and no dry flour remains, 3 to 5 minutes; the dough will be shiny but will not be smooth. Using a silicone spatula, scrape the sides of the bowl and gather the dough in the center, forming a ball. Cover with plastic wrap and let rise at room temperature until doubled, about 45 minutes. Meanwhile, line 2 rimmed baking sheets with kitchen parchment.

Turn the dough out onto an unfloured counter, then divide it into 10 portions, each about 45 grams (1½ ounces). Form each into a smooth ball by rolling it against the counter in a circular motion under a cupped hand.

Sprinkle 1 teaspoon sugar onto the counter, covering an area about 4 inches in diameter, then set 1 dough ball on the sugar. With your hand, flatten the ball slightly, then use a rolling pin to roll the dough into a round about 5½ inches in diameter; flip the dough a few times so both sides are sugared. Transfer to a prepared baking sheet, leaving space for 4 additional rounds. Roll out the remaining dough balls in the same way, using 1 teaspoon sugar for each and placing 5 rounds on each baking sheet. Cover with kitchen towels and let rise for 30 minutes. Meanwhile, heat the oven to 400°F with racks in the upper- and lower-middle positions.

Brush the surface of each torta lightly with egg white, then prick with a fork about every ¼ inch. Bake until deep golden brown, 18 to 21 minutes, rotating the baking sheets and switching their positions about halfway through. Using a wide spatula, transfer the tortas to wire racks. Cool completely.

VARIATION

Spanish Olive Oil Tortas with Cinnamon and Sesame

Follow the recipe, substituting **1 tablespoon sesame seeds** for the fennel seeds and **½ teaspoon ground cinnamon** for the orange zest.

Pita Bread

**Start to finish: 4 hours
(40 minutes active)**

Servings: Ten 5½ inch pita rounds

4 tablespoons grapeseed or other
neutral oil, divided

171 grams (1¼ cups) bread flour,
plus extra for dusting

175 grams (1¼ cups)
whole-wheat flour

2¼ teaspoons instant yeast

2 teaspoons white sugar

¾ cup warm water (100°F to 110°F),
plus more if needed

60 grams (¼ cup) plain
whole-milk yogurt

1¼ teaspoons table salt

Pita bread is a yeast-leavened flatbread from the Mediterranean and Middle East. We make ours with whole-wheat flour and whole-milk yogurt for full flavor and a pleasant chew. Yogurt is common in some flatbreads but is generally not used in pita. We, however, found it helped produce a soft, elastic dough and a tender, but slightly chewy baked bread. To ensure the breads puff nicely and form pockets, they're baked two at a time on a heated baking steel or stone. We preferred a stand mixer for making the dough, but a food processor worked, too. To make the dough in a processor, combine the flours, yeast and sugar in the work bowl and pulse until combined. Add the water, yogurt and 2 tablespoons of oil and process until a smooth, slightly sticky ball forms, about 1 minute. Add additional water, 1½ teaspoons at a time (up to 2 tablespoons total), if the dough feels too dry. Let the dough rest in the processor for five minutes, then add the salt and process until smooth and pliable, about one minute. Knead by hand on a lightly floured counter for one minute, then

transfer to an oiled medium bowl and turn to coat. Cover with plastic wrap and let rise in a warm, draft-free spot until not quite doubled in bulk. Continue with the recipe from the third step to shape and bake. It's not unusual if one or two of the rounds don't puff during baking—the bread will still taste great. The ones that do puff will not deflate as they cool. Store leftover pita in a zip-close bag for up to a day. To warm, wrap the pitas in foil and heat for four minutes at 300°F.

Don't forget to heat the baking steel or stone for a full hour before baking. And do cover the pita breads with a towel when they come out of the oven to keep them soft.

Coat a medium bowl with 1 teaspoon of the oil; set aside. In the bowl of a stand mixer fitted with the dough hook, add both flours, the yeast and sugar. Mix on low until combined, about 5 seconds. Add the water, yogurt and 2 tablespoons of oil. Mix on low until a smooth ball forms, about 3 minutes. Feel the dough; it should be slightly sticky. If not, add water 1½ teaspoons at a time (no more than 2 tablespoons total), mixing after each addition, until slightly sticky. Let rest in the mixer bowl for 5 minutes.

Add the salt and knead on low until smooth and pliable, 10 minutes. Transfer to the prepared bowl, forming it into a ball and turning to coat with oil. Cover with plastic wrap and let rise in a warm, draft-free area until well risen but not quite doubled in volume, 1 to 1½ hours.

Dust a rimmed baking sheet evenly with bread flour. Transfer the dough to the counter. Using a dough scraper or bench knife, divide the dough into 10 pieces (about 2 ounces each). Form each into a tight ball and place on the prepared baking sheet. Brush each ball with ½ teaspoon of the remaining oil, then cover with a damp kitchen towel. Let rise in a warm, draft-free area until well risen but not quite doubled, 30 to 60 minutes. Meanwhile, heat the oven to 500°F with a baking steel or stone on the upper-middle rack.

Lightly dust two rimmed baking sheets with bread flour and lightly dust the counter. Place a dough ball on the counter; use a lightly floured rolling pin to roll the ball into a round ⅛ inch thick and 5½ inches in diameter. Set on one of the prepared baking sheets. Repeat with the remaining dough

HOW TO MAKE PITA BREAD

1. To form pieces of dough into balls, press down the dough then gather the edges toward the center to make a seam.

2. After forming the dough balls, place them seam side down on the floured baking sheet and brush each with oil.

3. Cover with a damp kitchen towel and let rise until not quite doubled.

4. On a lightly floured counter, using a lightly floured rolling pin, roll each dough round to ⅛ inch thick and 5½ inches wide.

5. Place 5 dough rounds on each of 2 floured baking sheets. Cover with a damp kitchen towel and let rest for 10 minutes.

6. Using a peel, transfer 2 dough rounds to the oven. When the rounds are puffed and light golden brown, about 3 minutes, use the peel to remove them.

balls, placing them in a single layer on the baking sheets. Cover with a damp kitchen towel and let rest for 10 minutes.

Lightly dust a peel with bread flour, then place 2 dough rounds on the peel without flipping them. Working quickly, open the oven and slide the rounds onto the baking steel. Immediately close the door. Bake until the breads have puffed and are light golden brown, about 3 minutes. Using the peel, remove the breads from the oven. Transfer to a wire rack and cover with a dry kitchen towel. Repeat with the remaining dough rounds. Serve warm or room temperature.

Roman Cloud Bread

We learned about this unique Italian bread from Angelo Arrigoni of Panificio Arrigoni, a bakery that for decades operated just outside the Vatican. The crisp yet pleasantly chewy, cracker-thin flatbreads are known as nuvola or "cloud" bread, a nod to their airy texture and puffy shape. Once cooled, the rounds are cracked open, creating a delicious bowl for a bitter greens salad, often accented by resinous pine nuts and Parmesan cheese (see our recipe p. 189). The breads can behave somewhat unpredictably in the oven. Occasionally even within the same batch, three will puff impressively while the fourth... not so much. If you end up with a bread or two that puffs less, rather than crack it open and try to fill it, simply break it in half or quarters and serve the pieces alongside soup, salad, dips or spreads. For make-ahead convenience, the baked breads will keep at room temperature for a few hours.

Don't worry if you don't have a baking steel or stone. An overturned baking sheet works well as a flat surface for baking the breads. A hot oven is important for proper puffing, so after slipping a dough round into the oven to bake, quickly close the oven door to prevent excessive heat loss.

In a medium bowl, combine the flour, yeast and salt; stir with a wooden spoon. Add the water and stir, scraping the sides of the bowl, until a shaggy, slightly floury dough forms. Turn the dough out onto the counter and knead by hand until well developed and elastic, about 8 minutes. The dough will be quite sticky to start but will become less so with kneading; do not add more flour. Shape the dough into a ball; the surface will not be perfectly smooth. Wash and dry the bowl, then lightly coat it with oil. Return the dough to the bowl, turning to coat with the oil. Cover with plastic wrap and let rise at room temperature until doubled in bulk, 1 to 1½ hours.

About 30 minutes into rising, position an oven rack about 6 inches from the element. Place a baking steel or stone or an inverted baking sheet on the rack and heat the oven to 450°F.

When the dough has doubled in bulk, lightly dust the counter with flour and turn the dough out onto it. Using a knife, divide the dough into 4 pieces. Form each into a loose ball, then cover the balls with a kitchen towel; let rest for 15 minutes.

Lightly flour the counter and set 1 ball on top; keep the remaining portions covered. Using a rolling pin, roll the ball into a thin round about 8 inches in diameter, dusting with flour as needed; it's fine if the dough does not form a perfect circle. Lightly dust a pizza peel with flour, then transfer the dough to the peel; reshape the round if needed. Slide the round onto the baking steel and quickly

Start to finish: 2 hours (45 minutes active)

Servings: 4

274 grams (2 cups) bread flour, plus more for dusting

1 teaspoon instant yeast

1 teaspoon table salt

¾ cup plus 1 tablespoon warm water (100°F to 110°F)

Extra-virgin olive oil

close the oven door. Bake until the bread is puffed and deep golden brown in spots, 8 to 10 minutes.

Using tongs, gently grip the bread and transfer to a wire rack. Shape and bake the 3 remaining dough balls in the same way. (The breads will hold well at room temperature for a few hours.) If desired, lightly brush the breads with oil.

Mixed Greens and Fennel Salad

In a large bowl, combine **2 small garlic cloves** (finely grated), **2 or 3 oil-packed anchovy fillets** and **1 teaspoon kosher salt.** Using a fork, mash to a paste. Whisk in **⅓ cup extra-virgin olive oil, 3 tablespoons lemon juice** and **½ teaspoon black pepper.** Add **1 romaine heart** (cut crosswise into ½-inch pieces); **4 cups lightly packed baby arugula or radicchio** (cut into bite-size pieces) or a combination; **1 small fennel bulb** (trimmed, halved and thinly sliced); **⅓ cup toasted pine nuts** and **1 ounce Parmesan cheese** (½ cup, finely grated). Toss well, then taste and season with **kosher salt and pepper.** Place 4 Roman cloud breads on individual serving plates. Using the blunt side of the blade of a chef's knife, crack open each bread. Fill each bread with a quarter of the salad, allowing it to spill onto the plates. Sprinkle with additional **Parmesan cheese** and serve right away.

Coconut Milk–Flour Tortillas

**Start to finish: 1 hour 10 minutes
(35 minutes active)**

Makes 8 tortillas

390 grams (3 cups) all-purpose
flour, plus more for dusting

2 teaspoons packed light or
dark brown sugar

½ teaspoon table salt

1 teaspoon baking powder

42 grams (3 tablespoons) salted
butter, cut into ½-inch cubes,
room temperature

1 cup coconut milk

These flatbread-like tortillas were inspired by actress and cookbook author Isha Sumner's durudia, or Honduran tortillas. The soft, chewy rounds are rich in flavor thanks to a little butter and a healthy dose of coconut milk; the latter also makes the dough extremely easy to roll out. The tortillas taste best when freshly made, but leftovers can be cooled, stacked, wrapped in foil and stored at room temperature for up to two days. To reheat, place the foil-wrapped stack in a 350°F oven for 10 to 15 minutes.

Don't use light coconut milk. The fat content of regular coconut milk is necessary for tender tortillas. Make sure to vigorously shake the can or thoroughly mix the coconut milk before measuring to distribute the fat that rises to the top upon standing.

In a stand mixer with the dough hook, mix the flour, sugar, salt and baking powder on medium-low until combined, about 30 seconds. Add the butter and mix until the mixture is crumbly, about 1 minute. With the mixer running, gradually add the coconut milk, then continue mixing until a smooth dough forms, about 5 minutes.

Transfer to the counter, then use your hands to roll the dough into a 14-inch log about 2 inches in diameter. Cut into 8 even pieces, then form each piece into a ball. Place on a large plate, cover with plastic wrap and refrigerate for 30 minutes or up to 24 hours.

Using a rolling pin, roll each ball on a lightly floured counter to an 8-inch round, stacking the rounds as they are done between pieces of kitchen parchment.

Heat a 10- or 12-inch skillet over medium until water flicked onto the surface immediately sizzles. Place a dough round in the skillet and cook until bubbles begin to form, then gently shake the pan. Continue to cook until the bottom is light spotty brown, then, using tongs, flip and cook until the second side is spotty brown; the total cooking time should be about 3 minutes. Transfer to a kitchen towel and wrap loosely. Cook the remaining tortillas in the same way. Serve warm.

HOW TO MAKE COCONUT MILK TORTILLAS

1. After incorporating the butter and with the mixer running on medium-low, gradually pour the coconut milk into the dough mixture.

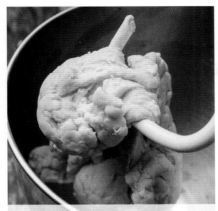

2. Continue kneading, incorporating the liquid, until the dough is smooth, about 5 minutes.

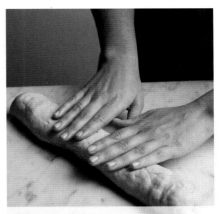

3. Transfer to the counter, then use your hands to shape the dough into a 14-inch cylinder about 2 inches in diameter.

4. Using a bench scraper or chef's knife, divide the dough into 8 pieces. Shape each piece into a loose ball.

5. Roll each ball against the counter to tighten. Don't flour the counter so the dough grips it, making it easier to shape.

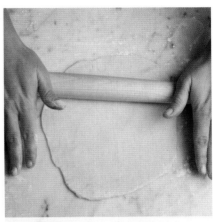

6. Using a rolling pin, roll each ball into an 8-inch round, stacking the rounds between pieces of parchment.

7. Place a round in the hot skillet. Cook until bubbles form; shake the pan to loosen the tortilla, ensuring it does not stick.

8. Continue to cook until the bottom is spotty brown. Using tongs, flip and cook until the second side is spotty brown.

Homemade Corn Tortillas

Start to finish: 1 hour

Makes twelve 6-inch tortillas

240 grams (2 cups) masa harina

¼ teaspoon table salt

1½ cups warm water (about 110°F), plus more as needed

In Mexico City, we learned that fresh, homemade corn tortillas, warm and perfumed with the lingering sweetness of corn, are key to a great taco. Making your own corn tortillas using masa harina (flour ground from nixtamalized corn) is not difficult, but it does require a few pieces of equipment. You will need a tortilla press, a 10- or 12-inch nonstick skillet, a 10- to 12-inch cast-iron griddle or skillet, and a spray bottle filled with water. When pressing the tortillas, rounds cut from a clean plastic grocery bag (or a gallon-size zip-close cut into two 8-inch squares) ensure the dough won't stick to the press. For cooking the tortillas, we use a two-stage method. During the second stage, we lightly drag a metal spatula across the tortilla, which often triggers a puffing action. Though a puffed tortilla deflates when removed from the pan, its texture is lighter and airier than one that hasn't risen. But don't worry if your tortillas don't puff—they still will be better than store-bought. If you need more than a dozen tortillas, this recipe can be scaled up.

Don't confuse masa harina with cornmeal or corn flour. Though all are made from corn, they are different products. In most supermarkets, masa harina is sold alongside the regular flour, or check the aisle where Latin American groceries are stocked.

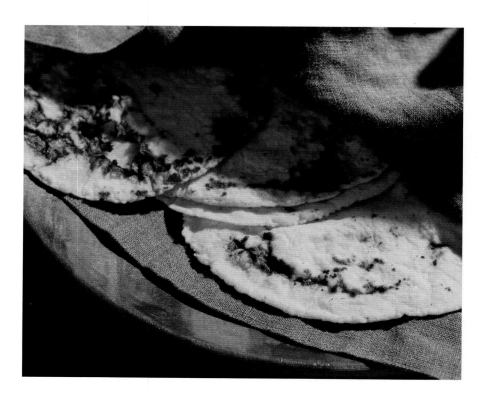

HOW TO MAKE CORN TORTILLAS

1. Pinch off a small piece of dough, roll it into a ball and flatten it. If the edges crack, knead in more water, 1 tablespoon at a time.

2. Set 1 masa ball on the plastic-lined tortilla press and flatten it slightly with your hands. Cover with the second plastic round. Close the press, open it, rotate the masa and press again. The tortilla should be 6 inches in diameter.

3. Peel off the top plastic round. Using the plastic on the bottom, flip the tortilla onto your hand and peel away the plastic. Place the tortilla in the nonstick skillet and cook until the tortilla releases from the pan.

4. Transfer the tortilla without flipping it to the cast-iron pan. Lightly drag the spatula across the tortilla 2 or 3 times; the tortilla should begin to puff. Cook until the edges begin to brown on the bottom.

5. Flip the tortilla and cook, pressing lightly on the edges, until lightly charred on the second side, about 30 seconds.

6. Transfer the tortilla to the prepared plate (it will deflate) and enclose in the towel. Continue until all of the dough has been pressed and cooked, stacking the tortillas as they are done.

Flatbreads

In a large bowl, stir together the masa harina and salt. While stirring with a silicone spatula, gradually add the water, then stir until the masa is evenly moistened. Transfer the masa to the counter and knead until smooth and putty-like, about 1 minute. Pinch off a small piece, roll it into a ball and flatten it; if the edges crack, knead in more water, 1 tablespoon at a time, then test again.

Transfer the masa to a large sheet of plastic wrap and wrap it tightly. Let rest at room temperature for at least 15 minutes or up to 1 hour to allow the masa to hydrate. Meanwhile, cut out two 8-inch rounds from a clean plastic grocery bag (alternatively, cut a gallon-size zip-close plastic bag into two 8-inch squares).

Divide the masa into 12 portions (each about 40 grams). Using your hands, roll each into a smooth ball and set on a plate. Lightly spritz with water and cover with a kitchen towel. Set a 10- or 12-inch nonstick skillet over medium-low and a 10- to 12-inch cast-iron skillet or griddle over high. Heat both until the cast-iron pan is very hot, about 10 minutes.

While the pans are heating, line a large plate with another kitchen towel and spritz the towel with water a few times to dampen. Open the tortilla press and lay one of the plastic rounds on the plate. Set 1 masa ball in the center and flatten it slightly with your hand. Cover with the second plastic round. Close the press and press down firmly on the handle. Open the press, rotate the masa in the plastic 180 degrees and press firmly again; the tortilla should be about 6 inches in diameter. If the pans are not yet fully heated, leave the tortilla in the plastic until they are.

Peel off the top plastic round. Using the plastic on the bottom, flip the tortilla onto the palm of your hand and slowly peel away the plastic. Using both hands, carefully place the tortilla in the nonstick skillet and cook until the edges begin to dry and the tortilla releases easily from the pan, about 20 seconds. While the tortilla is cooking, press another ball of masa; set aside.

Using a wide metal spatula, flip the tortilla and cook until it releases easily from the pan, about 30 seconds. Now transfer the tortilla without flipping it to the cast-iron pan. Immediately, quickly and lightly drag the metal spatula across the tortilla 2 or 3 times; the tortilla should begin to puff. Cook until the edges begin to brown on the bottom, 15 to 20 seconds, then flip the tortilla and cook, pressing lightly on the edges, until lightly charred on the second side, about 30 seconds.

Transfer the tortilla to the prepared plate (it will deflate) and enclose in the towel. Cook the second tortilla in the same way and press another; stack the tortillas as they are done and keep them wrapped in the towel (make sure the towel remains lightly moistened with water). Continue until all of the dough has been pressed and cooked. If the masa balls begin to dry out as they sit, lightly spritz them with water. Serve warm.

Homemade Flour Tortillas

Soft, supple and with a satisfying chew, homemade flour tortillas taste far better than store-bought brands and don't take a lot of effort or time to make. Lard is traditional in flour tortillas; many supermarkets sell non-hydrogenated lard, packed in glass jars, in the aisle near the coconut and olive oils. If you prefer, butter also makes fantastic tortillas. A mixture of milk and water as the liquid is unconventional; we got the idea from Mexican chef Enrique Olvera. Milk not only adds a subtle sweetness, it also helps the tortillas remain soft and pliable for longer. If you prefer to skip the milk, feel free to use only water. This recipe makes eight 10-inch tortillas; to make smaller ones, simply cut the dough log into 10 pieces and roll each into an 8-inch round. A well-seasoned cast-iron skillet or griddle is essential for cooking the tortillas, as it heats evenly and holds its temperature. Its surface also is stick-resistant. The tortillas are best freshly made, but leftovers can be cooled, stacked, wrapped in foil and stored at room temperature for up to two days. To reheat, place the foil-wrapped stack in a 350°F oven for 10 to 15 minutes.

Start to finish: 1 hour 10 minutes (40 minutes active)

Makes eight 10-inch tortillas

520 grams (4 cups) all-purpose flour, plus more for dusting

½ teaspoon table salt

113 grams (8 tablespoons) lard, in 1-tablespoon portions, or salted butter, cut into ½-inch cubes, cool room temperature

½ cup whole milk (see headnote)

STEPS »

Don't skip the step of heating the milk-water mixture. Warm liquid softens the lard that has been cut into the flour so the fat incorporates more easily. Also, don't worry if the tortillas aren't rolled into neat, perfect circles; it's more important that they're of an even thickness.

In a medium bowl, stir together the flour and salt. Add the lard and, using your fingertips, rub it into the flour until the mixture resembles coarse sand.

In a liquid measuring cup, combine the milk and ¾ cup water. Microwave on high until the mixture reaches about 110°F, about 30 seconds. Pour into the flour mixture in 3 or 4 additions, stirring a few times with a silicone spatula after each. Once all the liquid has been incorporated, stir, scraping the bottom of the bowl, until the mixture forms a shaggy dough.

Lightly flour the counter and turn the dough out onto it. Knead 5 or 6 times to form a smooth ball, then form into an even 14-inch log. Cut into 8 pieces. Shape each into a taut ball by rolling it under a cupped hand in a circular motion against the counter. Place the balls on a large plate, cover with a kitchen towel and let rest for 30 minutes.

On a lightly floured counter, use a rolling pin to roll 1 ball into a 10-inch round, then transfer to another large plate or a baking sheet and cover with a kitchen towel. Repeat with the remaining balls, stacking the rounds as they are done; keep the stack covered. Line the plate used to hold the dough balls with the kitchen towel used to cover them; set near the stove.

HOW TO MAKE FLOUR TORTILLAS

1. Stir together the flour and salt. Add the lard and, using your fingertips, rub it into the flour until the mixture resembles coarse sand.

2. Pour in the warm milk-water mixture in 3 or 4 additions, stirring a few times after each. After all the liquid has been added, stir until the mixture forms a shaggy dough.

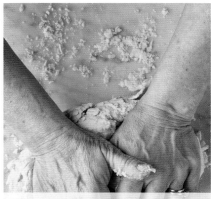

3. On a lightly floured counter, knead the dough 5 or 6 times to form a smooth ball.

4. Form the dough into a 14-inch log of even thickness by rolling it back and forth against the counter.

5. Using a metal bench knife, cut the log into 8 even pieces.

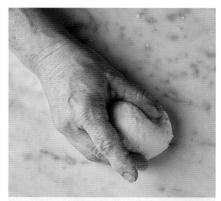

6. Shape the pieces into taut balls by rolling them under a cupped hand in a circular motion against the counter. Place the balls on a plate, cover with a towel and let rest for 30 minutes.

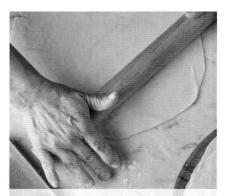

7. On a lightly floured counter, roll 1 ball into a 10-inch round, then transfer to another large plate or a baking sheet. Cover with a towel. Repeat with the remaining balls, stacking the rounds; keep the stack covered.

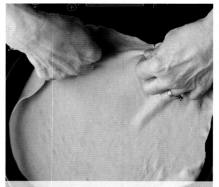

8. Heat a 10- or 12-inch cast-iron skillet over medium. Place a dough round in the pan and cook until bubbles begin to form, then shake the pan to ensure the tortilla is not sticking. Cook until the bottom is spotty brown.

9. Using tongs, flip the tortilla. Cook until the second side is spotty brown. Transfer to the prepared plate, then fold the towel over it. Cook the remaining tortillas in the same way, stacking them as they are done.

Heat a 10- or 12-inch cast-iron skillet over medium until water flicked onto the surface sizzles and evaporates within seconds, 4 to 6 minutes. When the skillet is hot, place a dough round in the pan. Cook until bubbles begin to form, then gently shake the pan to ensure the tortilla is not sticking. Cook until the bottom is light spotty brown, 2 to 3 minutes. Using tongs, flip the tortilla. Cook until the second side is spotty brown, 1 to 2 minutes. Transfer to the prepared plate, then fold the towel over it. Cook the remaining tortillas in the same way, stacking them as they are done. Serve warm.

Chapter 5

Pizza Plus

Tomato-Olive Focaccia

**Start to finish: 7¼ hours
(40 minutes active), plus cooling**

Servings: 12

502 grams (3⅔ cups) bread flour

5 teaspoons instant yeast

1 teaspoon white sugar

2 cups water, cool room temperature

8 tablespoons extra-virgin
olive oil, divided

1¾ teaspoons table salt, divided

130 grams (1 cup) cherry tomatoes,
halved

138 grams (1 cup) Castelvetrano
olives, pitted and halved (see
headnote)

1 teaspoon dried oregano

¾ teaspoon ground black pepper

This recipe recreates the light, open-crumbed focaccia we ate at Panificio Fiore in Bari, Italy. To achieve that texture, the dough must be wet—so wet, in fact, it verges on a thick, yet pourable batter. Resist the temptation to add more flour than is called for. Shaping such a sticky, high-hydration dough by hand is impossible. Instead, the dough is gently poured and scraped into the oiled baking pan; gravity settles it into an even layer. If you have trouble finding Castelvetrano olives, substitute any large, meaty green olive. To slice the baked focaccia for serving, use a serrated knife and a sawing motion to cut through the crust and crumb without compressing it. If desired, serve with extra-virgin olive oil for dipping. For convenience, the dough can be prepared and transferred to the baking pan a day in advance. After it has settled in the pan, cover tightly with plastic wrap and refrigerate. The next day, prepare the toppings. Uncover, top the dough with the olives and tomatoes and let stand at room temperature for 45 minutes, then finish and bake as directed.

Don't disturb the dough during its rise. And when transferring the dough to the baking pan, handle it gently. The goal is to retain as much gas in the dough as possible so the focaccia bakes up with an airy texture. Don't use a baking dish made of glass or ceramic; neither will produce a crisp, browned exterior, and glass is not safe to use in a 500°F oven.

In a stand mixer with the dough hook, mix the flour, yeast and sugar on medium until combined, about 30 seconds. With the mixer on low, drizzle in the water, then increase to medium and mix until the ingredients form a very wet, smooth dough, about 5 minutes. Turn off the mixer, cover the bowl and let stand for 10 minutes. Meanwhile, coat the bottom and sides of a large bowl with 2 tablespoons of oil; set aside.

Sprinkle 1 teaspoon of salt over the dough, then knead on medium until smooth and elastic, about 5 minutes; the dough will be wet enough to cling to the sides of the bowl. Using a silicone spatula, scrape the dough into the oiled bowl. Dip your fingers into the oil pooled at the sides of the bowl and dab the surface of the dough until completely coated with oil. Cover tightly with plastic wrap and let stand at room temperature for 5½ to 6 hours; during this time, the dough will double in volume, deflate, then rise again (but will not double in volume again).

After the dough has risen for about 4½ hours, heat the oven to 500°F with a baking steel or stone on the middle rack. Mist a 9-by-13-inch metal baking pan with cooking spray, then pour 2 tablespoons of the remaining oil in the center of the pan; set aside.

STEPS »

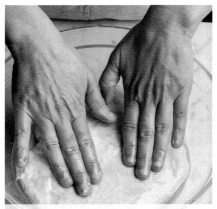

1. Scrape the dough into a bowl greased with 2 tablespoons oil. Dab the surface of the dough with the oil until well coated.

2. Cover the bowl with plastic wrap; let rise at room temperature for 5½ to 6 hours.

3. During this time, the dough will double in volume, deflate then rise again (but not double).

4. Gently pour the dough into the prepared pan, scraping the bowl with a silicone spatula.

5. Scatter olives evenly over the dough, then do the same with the tomatoes (without juices). Let stand, uncovered, at room temperature for 20 minutes. Drizzle the dough with 4 tablespoons olive oil.

6. Sprinkle with dried oregano, kosher salt and black pepper. Bake for 20 to 22 minutes.

When the dough is ready, gently pour it into the prepared pan, scraping the sides of the bowl with a silicone spatula to loosen; try to retain as much air in the dough as possible. The dough will eventually settle into an even layer in the pan; do not spread the dough with a spatula, as this will cause it to deflate. Set aside while you prepare the tomatoes.

In a medium bowl, use a potato masher to lightly crush the tomatoes. Scatter the olives evenly over the dough, then do the same with the tomatoes, leaving the juice and seeds in the bowl. If the dough has not fully filled the corners of the pan, use your hands to lightly press the toppings to push the dough into the corners. Let stand uncovered at room temperature for 20 minutes.

Drizzle the dough with the remaining 4 tablespoons oil, making sure each tomato is coated. Sprinkle evenly with the oregano, remaining ¾ teaspoon salt and the pepper. Place the pan on the baking steel or stone and bake until golden brown and the sides of the focaccia have pulled away from the pan, 20 to 22 minutes. Cool in the pan on a wire rack for 5 minutes. Using a wide metal spatula, lift the focaccia from the pan and slide it onto the rack. Cool for at least 30 minutes before serving.

BAKING BASIC

DOUGH HYDRATION

Hydration refers to a dough's moisture content, and often is expressed as a quantity of liquid in relation to flour, called a baker's percentage. Hydration levels—which can vary widely by bread variety—help determine a dough's workability and rise, as well as the texture of the finished loaf.

Low-hydration doughs, which generally have 60 percent or less hydration, are stiff and elastic, making them easy to handle, and have a tight crumb and chewy texture, like pretzels and bagels. Medium hydration doughs, which fall in the 60 percent to 75 percent range, are sturdy enough to hold their shape, yet supple enough to expand significantly. Their crumbs are soft and closed, as in hearth-style loaves, sandwich breads and challah.

High hydration doughs, such as ciabatta, focaccia and most sourdoughs, have 75 percent or greater hydration and tend to be sticky and slack. To develop structure, these doughs often require a series of folds or turns over time; they're too wet to build gluten strength via conventional kneading. They tend to bake up with a thin, crisp crust and airy, irregular crumb.

To calculate hydration, divide the combined weight of all liquid ingredients in a recipe by the total flour weight. For example: a dough made with 650 grams water and 1,000 grams flour has 65 percent hydration. Keep in mind that whole grains have a higher capacity for absorption, so a whole-wheat dough hydrated at 70 percent will feel firmer than a dough made with the same ratio with all-purpose flour.

Potato-and-Herb Focaccia

**Start to finish: 3½ hours
(30 minutes active)**

Makes one 9-by-13-inch loaf

8 ounces Yukon Gold potatoes, unpeeled, cut into ¾-inch chunks

6 sprigs plus ¼ cup chopped fresh rosemary, thyme or a combination

3 medium garlic cloves, smashed and peeled

1¾ teaspoons table salt, divided

411 grams (3 cups) bread flour

4 tablespoons extra-virgin olive oil, divided, plus more for oiling your hands

2 teaspoons instant yeast

2 teaspoons white sugar

69 grams (½ cup) pitted Kalamata olives, slivered (optional)

1½ ounces Parmesan cheese, finely grated (¾ cup; optional)

Ground black pepper, for sprinkling

Common to the Puglia region of Italy, potato focaccia is a particularly moist version of the classic Italian bread. We embedded ours with deep herbal flavors by seasoning the cooking water for the potatoes with rosemary or thyme, as well as garlic. Then we made the starchy, herb-infused cooking liquid do double duty, using it in the dough, too. Yukon Gold potatoes give the focaccia color and texture, and don't require peeling (the soft skins disappear into the dough). For our herbs, we like a combination of rosemary and thyme, but oregano and bay leaves work, too. After the dough comes together, you may need to add more cooking liquid (up to ¼ cup) to achieve the proper texture; the dough should be soft and sticky, and just barely clear the sides of the bowl. The focaccia is delicious with a sprinkling of herbs and black pepper, but Kalamata olives and Parmesan cheese are welcome additions. Flaky sea salt, such as Maldon, is a nice touch, as well.

Don't use a glass baking dish. The bread won't brown and crisp properly. If you don't have a metal baking pan, stretch the focaccia into a rough 9-by-13-inch rectangle and bake on a rimmed baking sheet.

In a medium saucepan, combine the potatoes, herb sprigs, garlic, 1 teaspoon salt and 3 cups water. Cover and bring to a boil over high. Uncover, reduce to medium and simmer until a skewer inserted into the potatoes meets no resistance, 12 to 14 minutes. Drain, reserving the cooking liquid; let the liquid cool until just barely warm, 20 to 30 minutes (it should be no hotter than 115°F). Meanwhile, discard the herb sprigs, then return the potatoes, garlic and any loose herb leaves to the saucepan. Using a potato masher or fork, mash until smooth and creamy. Transfer the potatoes to the bowl of a stand mixer fitted with the dough hook.

To the mixer bowl, add the flour, 2 tablespoons oil, the yeast, sugar and remaining ¾ teaspoon salt. Add 1¼ cups of the cooled reserved cooking water, then mix on low until the ingredients form a dough, about 1 minute. Increase to medium-high and mix until the dough clears the sides of the bowl but sticks to the bottom, 3 to 5 minutes, adding more cooking liquid 1 tablespoon at a time as needed (the dough should be very soft and sticky and just clear the sides of the bowl). Using a silicone spatula, scrape the sides of the bowl and gather the dough in the center. Cover with plastic wrap and let rise at room temperature until not quite doubled, 30 to 60 minutes. Meanwhile, coat the bottom and sides of a 9-by-13-inch metal baking pan with the remaining 2 tablespoons oil.

Transfer the dough to the prepared pan and, using oiled fingers, press and spread it into an even layer, all the way into the corners. Cover and let rise at room temperature until puffed, 30 to 60 minutes. Meanwhile, heat the oven to 400°F with a rack in the middle position.

When the dough is risen, use a chopstick to poke the dough all over, then sprinkle with the chopped herbs, olives (if using), Parmesan (if using) and a few grinds of black pepper. Bake until the edges are browned and crisp and the top is golden brown, 35 to 40 minutes. Cool in the pan on a wire rack for 10 minutes, then transfer the focaccia directly to the rack. Serve warm or at room temperature.

Pour-in-the-Pan Pizza
with Tomatoes and Mozzarella

The crust for this pizza borrows from the Milk Street recipe for a light, open-crumbed focaccia, our re-creation of the focaccia we encountered in Bari, Italy. The pizza dough is unusual in a couple ways: It uses so much water that it verges on a batter and it rises for at least four hours on the counter (be sure to place the bowl in a warm spot). After rising, the dough is poured out onto a greased 13-by-18-inch rimmed baking sheet (also known as a half sheet pan) to rest for 20 minutes before being nudged with oiled fingers to the edges of the pan. Instead of making a single large pizza, you could make two 12-inch pies using low-lipped, disk-shaped pizza pans, like the ones used in American-style pizzerias; see directions p. 208.

Don't forget to mist the baking sheet with cooking spray. The olive oil alone isn't enough to prevent sticking; a coating of cooking spray is important to ensure the pizza releases easily. Don't use fresh mozzarella; it contains too much moisture and will make the surface of the pizza soggy. Likewise, be sure to drain the juices from the tomatoes.

In a stand mixer with the dough hook, mix the flour, sugar and yeast on medium until combined, about 30 seconds. With the mixer running, add the water and mix on medium until a sticky dough forms, about 5 minutes; scrape the bowl and dough hook once during mixing. Turn off the mixer and let rest 10 minutes. Add 2 teaspoons salt and mix on medium for another 5 minutes. The dough will be shiny, wet and elastic.

Coat a large bowl with 1 tablespoon of the oil. Mist a silicone spatula with cooking spray and use it to scrape the dough into the bowl. Flip the dough with the spatula to oil all sides. Cover tightly with plastic wrap and let rise in a warm spot for 4 to 5 hours.

When the dough is ready, generously mist a 13-by-18-inch rimmed baking sheet with cooking spray, then pour 1 tablespoon of the remaining oil onto the center of the baking sheet. Gently scrape the dough onto the center of the sheet and let rest, uncovered, for 20 minutes.

Meanwhile, heat the oven to 500°F with a rack in the lowest position. If using Campari tomatoes, cut them into quarters; if using cherry tomatoes, cut them in half. Place the tomatoes in a large bowl and mash gently with a potato masher. Transfer to a fine-mesh strainer set over a bowl and set aside to drain until ready to use.

**Start to finish: 6 hours
(35 minutes active)**

Servings: 4 to 6

398 grams (2¾ cups plus 2½ tablespoons) bread flour

2 teaspoons white sugar

Two ¼-ounce packets instant yeast (4½ teaspoons)

1½ cups water, 100°F to 110°F

Table salt and ground black pepper

3 tablespoons extra-virgin olive oil, divided, plus more for oiling your hands

1 pound Campari or cherry tomatoes

170 grams whole-milk mozzarella cheese, shredded (1½ cups)

1 teaspoon dried oregano

Kosher or flaky sea salt, for sprinkling (optional)

After the dough has rested, oil your hands, and, working from the center, gently push it into an even layer to the edges and into the corners of the baking sheet; be careful not to press out all of the air. It's fine if the dough does not completely fill the pan, but it should come close.

Drizzle the tomatoes with the remaining 1 tablespoon oil, then toss. Scatter over the dough, leaving a narrow border. Let rest for another 30 minutes. Scatter the cheese over the dough, then sprinkle with the oregano, pepper and kosher or flaky salt (if using). Bake until the surface of the pizza is golden brown and the bottom is crisped and well browned, 18 to 20 minutes. Slide the pizza from the pan onto a wire rack and cool for a few minutes before slicing.

VARIATION

To Top It Off

Because pour-in-the-pan pizza dough is extremely wet, it's important to use toppings that are dry, or the pie will bake up with a soggy surface. The following are some of our favorite toppings; we suggest using no more than two in addition to the tomatoes and mozzarella. Scatter the ingredient(s) onto the tomato-topped dough just before adding the cheese. If you are using high-sodium toppings, such as olives or capers, you may wish to skip the salt that's sprinkled on before baking.

- Sliced pepperoni or salami
- Black or green olives, pitted and halved
- Roasted red peppers, patted dry and cut into strips
- Marinated artichoke hearts, patted dry and cut into chunks
- Capers, drained and patted dry

VARIATION

How to Make Two 12-Inch Round Pizzas

Follow the recipe to make and rise the dough. When the dough is ready, generously mist two 12-inch round pizza pans with cooking spray, then pour 1 tablespoon oil onto the center of each. Scrape half the dough onto the center of each pan. Continue with the recipe, allowing the dough to rest for 20 minutes before pushing it to the edges of the pans and adding toppings. Bake one at a time, reducing the baking time to 12 to 15 minutes.

Pizza Dough

This pizza dough is a wet, high-hydration dough (about 76 percent hydration). It also starts with a preferment—which, in this case, is a mixture of bread and semolina flours, a little sugar, yeast, salt and water that's left to stand for an hour at room temperature, during which time it becomes active and bubbly. The preferment then is mixed with more bread flour, olive oil, salt and water, then the dough rises for about 1½ hours. The end result is a pizza crust with a rustic, open crumb; a chewy-crisp texture; and bubbles that char in the oven, forming the spotting that's characteristic of high-end pizzeria pies. The flavor is wheaty and complex yet clean, not yeasty and boozy like drier doughs made with an abundance of yeast. For make-ahead and storage convenience, there are a couple good stopping points in this recipe. After 30 minutes of room-temperature rising, the dough can be refrigerated for up to 24 hours. Or, after dividing into four portions, the dough can be allowed to rise at room temperature for 30 minutes, then refrigerated for up to 48 hours. For topping and baking instructions, refer to specific pizza recipes, but keep in mind you will need a peel for shuttling the pies into and out of the oven and a baking stone or steel. Before baking, we heat the oven and steel (or stone) for an hour at 500°F or 550°F to build up heat, but prior to shaping and topping pies, we switch the oven to broil. The upper heating element browns and chars the surface of the pizza while the hot steel crisps the bottom crust.

Don't be shy about flouring the counter as you portion and shape the dough. This dough is wet—almost pourable—but as long as it and the work surface are floured, it's very workable. It's much more compliant than lower-hydration doughs and does not snap back with the same vigor, so it's easy to shape into rounds.

To make the preferment, in the bowl of a stand mixer, stir together both flours, the sugar, yeast, salt and 1 cup water. Cover and let stand at room temperature for 1 hour; the mixture will resemble a thick, bubbly batter.

To make the dough, to the preferment, add the flour, oil, salt and 1 cup water; stir to roughly combine. Attach the bowl and dough hook to the mixer. Mix on low until well combined, about 2 minutes, then increase to medium-low and mix until an elastic, webby dough forms, 8 to 10 minutes; scrape the sides of the bowl and push the dough off the hook a few times during mixing. Scrape the sides of the bowl and gather the dough in the center of the bowl. Cover and let rise at room temperature until doubled, about 1½ hours. (If making ahead, let rise for about 30 minutes, then refrigerate for up to 24 hours.)

**Start to finish: 4¼ hours
(40 minutes active)**

**Makes about 2½ pounds dough
(enough for four 10-inch pizzas)**

FOR THE PREFERMENT:

137 grams (1 cup) bread flour

85 grams (½ cup) semolina flour

2 teaspoons white sugar

¾ teaspoon instant yeast

¼ teaspoon table salt

FOR THE DOUGH:

411 grams (3 cups) bread flour, plus more for dusting

1½ tablespoons extra-virgin olive oil

1½ teaspoons table salt

Generously flour the counter and a rimmed baking sheet. Using floured hands and a bowl scraper or silicone spatula, scrape the dough out onto the counter; if the dough was refrigerated, it's fine to work with it while it is cold. The dough will be very sticky. Dust with flour, then use a floured metal bench scraper or chef's knife to divide the dough into 4 portions. Flour the cut sides of each piece of dough.

Form each portion into a taut ball by cupping your hands around the base of the dough, slightly cradling it. Rotate and drag the dough along the counter, allowing the base to catch on the surface to create tension that pulls the dough into a tighter round. Repeat a few more times, until the dough forms a relatively uniform ball. Transfer to the baking sheet, spacing the portions evenly. Dust the dough balls with flour, then cover with a kitchen towel. Let rise at room temperature until doubled, 1 to 1½ hours if the dough was room temperature before portioning, or about 2 hours if it was refrigerated. (If you intend to save any portions for baking in the next day or two, let rise for only 30 minutes, then transfer to a 3- to 4-cup plastic container with a tight-fitting lid and refrigerate for up to 48 hours). The dough now is ready to shape and bake.

Fig, Blue Cheese and Prosciutto Pizza

This pizza features a trio of contrasting flavors—sweet, savory and tangy—provided by a classic combination of fresh figs, prosciutto, blue cheese and balsamic vinegar. In the intensely hot oven, the prosciutto crisps and adds a welcome textural contrast. For drizzling onto the pizza after baking, look for balsamic syrup sold alongside the regular balsamic vinegar in the grocery store. Or, pull out the stops and go with a high-quality, aged balsamic vinegar from Modena, Italy.

Don't forget to heat the baking steel (or stone) for at least an hour before baking, and be sure to turn the oven to broil before shaping the dough.

At least 1 hour before baking, heat the oven to 500°F (or 550°F if that's your oven's maximum temperature), with a baking steel or stone on the middle rack.

When you are ready to shape the dough, heat the oven to broil (use the low setting if your oven offers multiple broiler settings). Generously dust the counter with all-purpose flour and set one portion of dough on top. With your hands, slightly flatten the dough, then with your fingertips gently press it into an 8-inch round of relatively even thickness. Flip the dough over and press into a 10-inch round, working from the center outward and leaving a ½-inch border around the perimeter; occasionally flip the dough to ensure the bottom is not sticking to the counter.

Dust a baking peel with semolina, then transfer the round to the peel and, if needed, reshape into a 10-inch round; gently shake the peel to ensure the round slides freely. Brush the round with 1 tablespoon oil. Arrange half the fig slices on the dough, then sprinkle with half the blue cheese. Arrange half of the prosciutto between the figs.

Slide the pizza onto the baking steel and bake until the crust is spottily browned and the prosciutto is crisp, 6 to 9 minutes. Using the peel, transfer the pizza to a cutting board. Dust any residual semolina off the peel.

Shape, top and bake the second portion of dough in the same way. While the second pizza is baking, drizzle the first one with ½ teaspoon of the balsamic syrup, then sprinkle with half of the scallions and black pepper.

When the second pizza is done, remove it from the oven and finish it with the remaining balsamic syrup, the remaining scallions and black pepper. Cut into slices and serve.

Start to finish: 45 minutes

Makes two 10-inch pizzas

All-purpose flour, for dusting the counter

Two portions pizza dough (recipe p. 209)

Semolina flour, for dusting the pizza peel

2 tablespoons extra-virgin olive oil

6 ounces fresh figs, stemmed and sliced into ¼-inch rounds

3 ounces blue cheese, crumbled (¾ cup)

2 ounces prosciutto (about 4 slices), cut crosswise into 2-inch ribbons

1 teaspoon balsamic syrup or aged balsamic vinegar (see headnote)

2 scallions, thinly sliced on the diagonal

Ground black pepper, to serve

Pizza with Pepperoni, Mozzarella and Hot Honey

Start to finish: 45 minutes

Makes two 10-inch pizzas

All-purpose flour, for dusting the counter

Two portions pizza dough (recipe p. 209)

Semolina flour, for dusting the pizza peel

Simple tomato sauce for pizza (recipe facing page)

8 ounces fresh mozzarella cheese, sliced ¼ inch thick and patted dry

4 ounces thinly sliced pepperoni or other spicy salami (see headnote)

¼ cup drained pickled peppers, such as peperoncini or cherry peppers, thinly sliced if whole, patted dry

⅓ cup lightly packed fresh basil, torn

Hot honey (see headnote), to serve

Finely grated Parmesan cheese, to serve (optional)

These pizzas feature a combination of salty, spicy, tangy and sweet flavors. Pepperoni is the type of chili-spiked salumi that's easiest to find, but if you can get hot capicola or hot soppressata, they're also fantastic. Pickled peppers bring vinegary brightness and a drizzle of hot honey after baking layers on more spiciness along with a sweetness that works with the other flavors. Hot honey is sold at most supermarkets, but if it's not available, finish the pies with a drizzle of regular honey and a sprinkling of red pepper flakes.

Don't forget to pat the mozzarella dry after slicing. Removing the excess moisture from fresh mozzarella will help prevent the crust from turning soggy after baking.

At least 1 hour before baking, heat the oven to 500°F (or 550°F if that's your oven's maximum temperature), with a baking steel or stone on the middle rack.

When you are ready to shape the dough, heat the oven to broil (use the low setting if your oven offers multiple broiler settings). Generously dust the counter with all-purpose flour and set one portion of dough on top. With your hands, slightly flatten the dough, then with your fingertips, gently press it into an 8-inch round of relatively even thickness. Flip the dough over and press into a 10-inch round, working from the center outward and leaving a ½-inch border around the perimeter; occasionally flip the dough to ensure the bottom is not sticking to the counter.

Dust a baking peel with semolina, then transfer the round to the peel and, if needed, reshape into a 10-inch round; gently shake the peel to ensure the round slides freely. Spread half of the tomato sauce (about 1 cup) evenly on the dough, leaving a ½-inch border. Top with half of the mozzarella, followed by half the pepperoni, then half of the pickled peppers.

Slide the pizza onto the baking steel and bake until the crust is spottily browned and the pepperoni is beginning to crisp, 6 to 9 minutes. Using the peel, transfer the pizza to a cutting board. Dust any residual semolina off the peel.

Shape, top and bake the second portion of dough in the same way. While the second pizza is baking, top the first one with half of the basil, then drizzle with honey. If desired, sprinkle with Parmesan. Cut into slices and serve.

When the second pizza is done, remove it from the oven and finish it with the remaining basil and honey; if desired, sprinkle with Parmesan. Cut into slices and serve.

MASTERING MOZZARELLA

Fresh mozzarella's high moisture content makes it leak water onto the pizza as it bakes, leaving unappealing pools of milky liquid. It's the reason we rarely recommend using it on homemade pizzas (the intensely high heat of professional pizza ovens evaporates the moisture before it pools).

However, if you do want to give it a whirl, we've found a simple solution. Thinly slice the cheese, then press it with paper towels to extract as much liquid as possible. The easiest way to do this is to freeze the cheese for 15 to 20 minutes (to make it easier to slice), then cut it with a thin slicing or serrated knife. The slices then can be placed between paper towels and pressed under a heavy pan or weighted baking sheet.

OVER THE TOP

Simple Tomato Sauce for Pizza

Start to finish: 15 minutes
Makes about 2 cups (enough for two 10-inch pizzas)

In a medium bowl, stir together a **14½-ounce can crushed tomatoes, 2 table-spoons finely grated Parmesan cheese, 2 tablespoons extra-virgin olive oil, 2 medium garlic cloves** (finely grated), **1 teaspoon white sugar, ½ teaspoon dried oregano, ¼ to ½ teaspoon red pepper flakes** and **¼ teaspoon each salt and ground black pepper.**

Upside-Down Pizza with Onions, Potatoes and Thyme

**Start to finish: 2½ hours
(30 minutes active)**

Servings: 6

FOR THE DOUGH:

445 grams (3¼ cups) bread flour,
plus more for dusting

1 teaspoon white sugar

1¼ teaspoons table salt

1 teaspoon instant yeast

2 tablespoons extra-virgin olive oil

1¼ cups warm water
(100°F to 110°F)

FOR THE TOPPING:

2 medium yellow onions, halved
and thinly sliced

8 ounces Yukon Gold potatoes,
unpeeled, sliced ⅛ to ¼ inch thick

2 tablespoons fresh thyme,
roughly chopped

1 tablespoon honey

5 tablespoons extra-virgin olive oil,
divided, plus more to serve

Kosher salt and ground black pepper

270 grams (1 cup) whole-milk ricotta

In "Tasting Rome," authors Katie Parla and Kristina Gill write about pizza made using an innovative method perfected by Gabriele Bonci of Pizzarium in Rome. Called pizza al contrario, it's pizza turned on its head. The "toppings" are put onto a baking sheet and roasted briefly to give them a head start on cooking. They then are covered with dough and the "pizza" is baked. Once out of the oven, the pie is inverted, revealing ingredients that have melded with the dough, and the browned crust that formed on top during baking becomes a nicely crisp bottom, no pizza stone required. You will, however, need a 13-by-18-inch rimmed baking sheet (the standard size) to make this recipe and a wire rack with roughly the same dimensions on which to invert the pizza after baking (a large heat-safe cutting board works well, too, but may be a bit awkward if the board is heavy). Lining the baking sheet with parchment helps guard against sticking and makes for easier cleanup.

Don't worry if the stretched dough is a little smaller than the dimensions of the baking sheet. When it's laid on top of the hot vegetables, the dough will relax from the warmth, making it easier to stretch. Also, don't worry if the timing of the dough and vegetables doesn't work out perfectly. Either can wait a few minutes for the other to be ready for assembly.

To make the dough, in a stand mixer with the dough hook, mix the flour, sugar, salt and yeast on medium until combined, about 15 seconds. With the mixer running on low, drizzle in the oil followed by the water. Scrape the sides of the bowl. Mix on medium, occasionally scraping the sides of the bowl as well as the hook, until the mixture forms a cohesive, slightly sticky dough that clears the sides of the bowl, 4 to 6 minutes; the dough will not be completely smooth. Using a silicone spatula, scrape the sides of the bowl and gather the dough in the center. Cover with plastic wrap and let rise at room temperature until doubled, 1½ to 2 hours.

About 30 minutes into rising, heat the oven to 475°F with a rack in the lowest position. Mist a 13-by-18-inch rimmed baking sheet with cooking spray, then line it with kitchen parchment and mist the parchment.

In a large bowl, toss together the onions, potatoes, thyme, honey, 3 tablespoons oil and ½ teaspoon each salt and pepper. Distribute the mixture in an even layer on the baking sheet. Bake without stirring until the onions begin to brown and the potato is softened but not yet fully cooked, about 15 minutes. Remove from the oven; leave the oven on.

While the vegetables are roasting, when the dough has doubled, generously flour the counter and turn the dough out onto it. Using your hands, gently stretch the dough into a rough 12-by-16-inch rectangle (slightly smaller than the baking sheet); work from the center outward to help ensure the dough is of an even thickness. If the dough is resistant or shrinks after stretching, let it rest 5 to 10 minutes before resuming.

Using both hands and being careful not to touch the hot baking sheet, lay the dough over the onion-potato mixture, gently stretching it to fill the baking sheet; using a silicone spatula, tuck in the edges. Brush the dough with the remaining 2 tablespoons oil, then use a fork to poke holes every 2 to 3 inches all the way through the dough. Bake until the surface is well browned, 17 to 20 minutes. Meanwhile, in a small bowl, stir the ricotta with salt and pepper, to taste.

Remove the baking sheet from the oven and immediately invert a wire rack onto it. Using potholders, hold the baking sheet and rack together and carefully flip to invert. Lift off the baking sheet (the parchment should remain on the sheet); using a metal spatula, scrape up any onion-potato mixture clinging to it and replace it on the pizza. Dollop with the ricotta, then drizzle with additional oil.

VARIATION

Upside-Down Pizza with Pears, Goat Cheese and Pistachios

Follow the recipe to make the dough, heat the oven and prepare the baking sheet. In a large bowl, toss together **3 medium ripe, but firm pears** (stemmed, halved, cored and cut into ¼-inch wedges), **2 medium shallots** (halved lengthwise and thinly sliced), **2 tablespoons extra-virgin olive oil, 1 tablespoon honey** and **½ teaspoon each kosher salt and ground black pepper.** Distribute in an even layer on the baking sheet and bake without stirring until the pears and shallots begin to brown and soften, about 15 minutes. While the pear mixture is roasting, follow the recipe to stretch the dough and, when the pear mixture is done, fit it into the baking sheet. Brush with an additional **2 tablespoons extra-virgin olive oil,** poke holes with a fork, bake and invert as directed. Scatter **4 ounces (½ cup) crumbled fresh goat cheese** (chèvre) over the pizza, sprinkle with **½ cup roasted salted pistachios** (roughly chopped) and drizzle with additional honey.

VARIATION

Upside-Down Pizza with Fennel, Taleggio and Salami

Follow the recipe to make the dough, heat the oven and prepare the baking sheet. In a large bowl, toss together **2 medium fennel bulbs** (trimmed, cored and sliced ¼ inch thick), **3 medium shallots** (halved lengthwise and thinly sliced), **2 tablespoons extra-virgin olive oil, 1 tablespoon honey, ½ teaspoon kosher salt** and **1 teaspoon ground black pepper.** Distribute in an even layer on the baking sheet, then layer **2 ounces thinly sliced salami** over it. Bake, without stirring, until the fennel begins to brown, 15 to 20 minutes; remove from the oven. While the vegetables are roasting, follow the recipe to stretch the dough and, when the vegetables are done, fit it into the baking sheet. Brush with an additional **2 tablespoons extra-virgin olive oil,** poke holes with a fork, bake and invert as directed. Evenly distribute **6 ounces taleggio cheese** (cut into ¼-inch slices) over the pizza and drizzle with additional honey and oil.

Salami and Cheese Stromboli

Stromboli is an Italian-American invention said to have been created in Philadelphia in the 1950s, but the dish takes its name from an island off the coast of Sicily. Like the calzone, it's a sort of portable pizza—fillings are enclosed in dough and baked—but more often than not, stromboli is cylindrical. A sheet of yeasted dough is topped with ingredients, then rolled up and slid into the oven. Slicing reveals tasty spirals of bread and filling. We use two melty cheeses and sliced salami, all of it layered on a bed of chopped roasted peppers, onion, capers and parsley. Serve slices with a simple spicy tomato sauce (recipe p. 219). Stromboli are fantastic warm, when the cheese is gooey, but also are delicious at room temperature.

Don't fill and roll the dough on the counter. The unbaked stromboli is awkward and difficult to transfer, so it's best to work directly on the baking sheet, as indicated in the recipe. After rolling, don't fold the edges of the stromboli under, or the ends will be too thick and bready. Instead, simply pinch the edges to seal. Finally, be sure to reposition the stromboli diagonally on the baking sheet to give it some room to expand during baking.

In a stand mixer with the dough hook, mix the flour, sugar, salt and yeast on medium until well combined, about 15 seconds. With the mixer on low, drizzle in the oil followed by the water. Scrape the sides of the bowl. Mix on medium, occasionally scraping the sides of the bowl as well as the hook, until the mixture forms a cohesive, slightly sticky dough that clears the sides of the bowl, 4 to 6 minutes; the dough will not be completely smooth. Using a silicone spatula, scrape the sides of the bowl and gather the dough in the center. Cover with plastic wrap and let rise at room temperature until doubled, 1½ to 2 hours.

Meanwhile, in a small bowl, stir together the roasted peppers, onion, capers, parsley, pepper flakes and vinegar; set aside.

About 30 minutes before you are ready to shape and fill the dough, heat the oven to 450°F with a rack in the middle position. Mist a 13-by-18-inch rimmed baking sheet with cooking spray, then line it with kitchen parchment. Mist the parchment, then dust with flour.

When the dough has doubled, turn it onto the prepared baking sheet. With the long edge of the baking sheet nearest you, use lightly oiled hands to press and stretch it into an even layer that covers the surface of the baking sheet; it's fine if the dough doesn't completely fill the corners. Using a large slotted spoon, spread the roasted pepper mixture in an even layer over the dough, leaving a 2-inch border at the top and a 1-inch border on each short side; discard any liquid remaining in the bowl. Lay the salami slices over the pepper mixture, overlapping them to fit. Layer on the provolone slices, then sprinkle evenly with the mozzarella.

Start to finish: 3½ hours (40 minutes active), plus cooling

Makes a 16-inch stromboli, serving 6 to 8

445 grams (3¼ cups) bread flour, plus more for dusting

1 teaspoon white sugar

1¼ teaspoons table salt

1 teaspoon instant yeast

2 tablespoons extra-virgin olive oil

1¼ cups warm water (100°F to 110°F)

¾ cup drained roasted red peppers, patted dry and chopped

¼ cup finely chopped red onion

3 tablespoons drained capers, patted dry and chopped

½ cup lightly packed fresh flat-leaf parsley, finely chopped

¼ to ½ teaspoon red pepper flakes

1 tablespoon balsamic vinegar

4 ounces thinly sliced salami

4 ounces sliced provolone cheese, each slice cut into a half circle

4 ounces whole-milk mozzarella cheese, shredded

1 large egg, beaten

½ ounce Parmesan cheese, finely grated (¼ cup)

Spicy Tomato-Basil Sauce (recipe p. 219), to serve (optional)

Lift up the edge of the parchment closest to you and use it to help fold about 1 inch of the dough over the filling. Continue to roll the dough, without the parchment, until you reach the far edge. Pinch the seam to seal, then pinch the open ends (do not fold them under). Roll the stromboli seam side down and carefully reposition it diagonally on the baking sheet, making sure the seam remains on the bottom. Brush the top and sides with beaten egg and sprinkle evenly with Parmesan. Using a sharp paring knife, cut 5 or 6 shallow diagonal slashes, evenly spaced, into the top so the filling is visible.

Bake until well browned and some of the cheese is bubbling through the slashes, 25 to 30 minutes. Using a wide metal spatula, transfer the stromboli to a cutting board and cool for 15 minutes. Use a serrated knife to cut into slices.

OVER THE TOP

Spicy Tomato-Basil Sauce

Start to finish: 20 minutes
Makes about 1⅓ cups

In a medium saucepan over medium, combine **1 tablespoon extra-virgin olive oil** and **1 medium garlic clove** (minced). Cook, stirring occasionally, until the garlic just begins to brown, 1 to 2 minutes. Stir in **½ teaspoon red pepper flakes,** followed by one **14½-ounce can whole peeled tomatoes** (crushed by hand) with juices, **¼ teaspoon white sugar** and **¼ teaspoon each kosher salt and ground black pepper.** Bring to a simmer and cook, uncovered and stirring occasionally, until the sauce is lightly thickened, 8 to 10 minutes. Off heat, stir in **2 tablespoons finely chopped fresh basil.** Taste and season with salt and black pepper.

Calzone with Caramelized Onions, Anchovies and Raisins

**Start to finish: 3 hours
(1 hour active)**

Servings: 4 to 6

260 grams (2 cups) all-purpose flour, plus more for dusting

2 teaspoons instant yeast

1 teaspoon table salt

3 tablespoons extra-virgin olive oil, divided, plus more for greasing and brushing

¾ cup warm water (110°F)

1½ pounds yellow onions, halved and thinly sliced

Kosher salt and ground black pepper

116 grams (¾ cup) golden raisins

138 grams (1 cup) pitted Kalamata olives, lightly crushed

8 oil-packed anchovy fillets, patted dry

Home cook Tim Donovan of Huntington, New York, has fond memories of a bread roll filled with caramelized onions, olives, raisins and anchovies that his Italian mother and grandmother made. The family called it calzone, though it differs from the North American version of pizza dough folded around meat, cheese and vegetables. Donovan learned that the family calzone was an ancient dish from the Italian region of Puglia called calzone di cipolla alla pugliese, or Puglian onion pie. Lacking a written recipe, typical of generational dishes, Donovan had little success trying to create the family calzone, so he asked Milk Street for help. The filling was straightforward but the dough was a challenge, not least because Donovan's mother "was famous for never making the same recipe twice." We had some clues, like the dough was flaky more than chewy but not like a pie crust. And lots of olive oil. We experimented with basic pizza dough, adjusting the amount of olive oil until we had a dough that was easy to roll out and fold, and not too bready. We call for Kalamata olives, though Donovan's mother and grandmother had only canned black olives. Swapping half the Kalamatas for green olives is a nice way to add color to the filling.

In a stand mixer with the dough hook, mix the flour, yeast and salt on low until combined, about 1 minute. With the mixer on low, drizzle in 1 tablespoon oil followed by the water. Knead on low until the mixture forms a smooth, elastic dough that clears the sides of the bowl, about 7 minutes. Lightly oil a large bowl, transfer the dough to it and turn to coat with the oil. Cover with plastic wrap and let rise in a warm, draft-free spot until doubled in bulk, about 2 hours.

Meanwhile, in a 12-inch skillet over medium, heat the remaining 2 tablespoons oil until shimmering. Add the onions and ½ teaspoon salt. Reduce to low, cover and cook, stirring, until the onions are well browned and jammy, 40 to 50 minutes. Stir in ½ teaspoon pepper, transfer to a large plate and cool to room temperature, about 1 hour. Cover and refrigerate until ready to use.

Put the raisins in a small microwave-safe bowl and add water to cover. Microwave on high until hot, about 1 minute. Drain and let cool.

When the dough is doubled in bulk, heat the oven to 450°F with a rack in the middle position. Lightly coat a rimmed baking sheet with oil. Dust the counter with flour and transfer the dough to the counter. Using your hands, press it into a 9-by-13-inch rectangle of even thickness. With a long side facing you, distribute the

onions evenly along the length of the dough, leaving a 2-inch border along the long sides and a ½-inch border along the short sides. Sprinkle the raisins over the onions, followed by the olives, then lay the anchovy fillets, end to end, down the center of the filling. Starting with one long side, fold the dough over half the filling, then fold the other long side over to meet the first side; firmly pinch the seam closed, then pinch the ends tightly shut. Flip the calzone seam side down. Using your hands, transfer it to the prepared baking sheet and form the calzone into a crescent shape. Lightly brush with oil, then cut 3 vertical 1-inch slits, evenly spaced, in the top of the calzone.

Bake until the crust is well browned and the filling is bubbling, about 40 minutes. Using a large spatula, transfer the calzone to a wire rack and cool completely, about 2 hours. To serve, use a serrated knife to cut the calzone into ½- to ¾-inch slices.

Pizza with Ricotta, Zucchini and Mint

The bright, summery flavors of this pizza are a nice change from rich, cheesy, tomatoey pies. Be sure to choose a medium zucchini or summer squash—that is, one that weighs no more than about 8 ounces. Its texture will be more tender and its core will be less spongy and seedy than larger, more mature fruits. If you prefer to use fresh basil, feel free to swap it for the mint. Basil's sweet, anise-y notes work beautifully with the other ingredients.

Don't use part-skim ricotta cheese for this recipe. The toppings are otherwise lean, so the creaminess of whole-milk ricotta is key for rich, full flavor.

At least 1 hour before baking, heat the oven to 500°F (or 550°F if that's your oven's maximum temperature), with a baking steel or stone on the middle rack. Meanwhile, in a small bowl, stir together the ricotta, pecorino, oil, lemon zest, garlic and ¼ teaspoon each kosher salt and pepper.

When you are ready to shape the dough, heat the oven to broil (use the low setting if your oven offers multiple broiler settings). Generously dust the counter with all-purpose flour and set one portion of dough on top. With your hands, slightly flatten the dough, then with your fingertips, gently press it into an 8-inch round of relatively even thickness. Flip the dough over and press into a 10-inch round, working from the center outward and leaving a ½-inch border around the perimeter; occasionally flip the dough to ensure the bottom is not sticking to the counter.

Dust a baking peel with semolina, then transfer the round to the peel and, if needed, reshape into a 10-inch round; gently shake the peel to ensure the round slides freely. Spread half of the ricotta mixture evenly on the dough, leaving a ½-inch border. Top with half of the zucchini, then drizzle with oil.

Slide the pizza onto the baking steel and bake until the crust is spottily browned and the edges of the zucchini slices begin to curl and brown, 6 to 9 minutes. Using the peel, transfer the pizza to a cutting board. Dust any residual semolina off the peel.

Shape, top and bake the second portion of dough in the same way. While the second pizza is baking, top the first one with half of the pistachios and half of the mint, then sprinkle with additional pecorino and flaky salt (if using). Drizzle with additional oil, then cut into slices and serve.

When the second pizza is done, remove it from the oven and finish it with the remaining pistachios, the remaining mint and additional pecorino; if desired sprinkle with flaky salt. Drizzle with additional oil, then cut into slices and serve.

Start to finish: 45 minutes

Makes two 10-inch pizzas

1 cup whole-milk ricotta

1 ounce pecorino Romano cheese, finely grated (½ cup), plus more to serve

2 tablespoons extra-virgin olive oil, plus more for drizzling

1 tablespoon grated lemon zest

1 medium garlic clove, finely grated

Kosher salt and ground black pepper

All-purpose flour, for dusting the counter

Two portions pizza dough (p. 209)

Semolina flour, for dusting the pizza peel

1 medium (about 8 ounces) zucchini or yellow summer squash, sliced into ⅛-inch-thick rounds

3 tablespoons raw or roasted pistachios, chopped

¼ cup lightly packed fresh mint, torn

Flaky salt, to serve (optional)

Slab Pizza with Sausage, Chard and Onion

**Start to finish: 2½ hours
(1 hour active)**

Servings: 12

FOR THE DOUGH:

6 tablespoons extra-virgin olive oil, divided

2 tablespoons plus 128 grams (¾ cup) semolina flour, divided

514 grams (3¾ cups) bread flour

2 teaspoons white sugar

1¾ teaspoons table salt

1½ teaspoons instant yeast

FOR THE TOPPINGS:

1 pound hot or sweet Italian sausage, casings removed

1 bunch (about 12 ounces) Swiss or rainbow chard, stems thinly sliced, leaves roughly chopped, reserved separately

1 tablespoon extra-virgin olive oil

Simple Tomato Sauce for Pizza (p. 213)

113 grams (1 cup) shredded provolone or fontina cheese

113 grams (1 cup) shredded smoked mozzarella cheese

1 medium red onion, halved and thinly sliced

57 grams (2 ounces) aged Asiago or Parmesan cheese, finely grated (1 cup)

This slab-style pizza boasts a pillowy, focaccia-like dough topped with garlicky tomato sauce, crisp sausage and silky sautéed greens. A flavorful cheese blend brings everything together. We recommend provolone and Asiago for their slightly funkier notes, but if you prefer to keep things mild, melty fontina and Parmesan are delicious. Coating the baking sheet with oil and semolina ensures the pizza develops a crunchy bottom crust, which is especially satisfying in contrast to the dough's tender interior. The pizza's caramelized edges; browned, bubbly cheese; and generous array of toppings make it perfect for a crowd, but if feeding only a few, leftovers reheat well at 350°F for 15 to 20 minutes.

Don't overcook the sausage on the stovetop. Cooking just until the meat no longer is pink gives it a head start so it can brown and crisp up in the oven.

To make the dough, brush a 13-by-18-inch rimmed baking sheet with 3 tablespoons oil and sprinkle with 2 tablespoons semolina; set aside. In a 1-quart liquid measuring cup, combine 2 cups water and 2 tablespoons of the remaining oil.

In a stand mixer with the dough hook, mix the remaining 128 grams (¾ cup) semolina, the bread flour, sugar, salt and yeast on low until combined, about 30 seconds. With the mixer running, gradually add the water-oil mixture, then mix until well combined, about 2 minutes. Increase to medium and knead, scraping the bowl once or twice, until the dough pulls away cleanly from the sides, about 5 minutes. Using a bowl scraper or silicone spatula, scrape the dough onto the center of the prepared baking sheet. Brush the remaining 1 tablespoon oil evenly over the dough's surface. Press a sheet of plastic wrap against the surface of the dough and let rest at room temperature for 30 minutes.

Uncover the dough. With dampened fingertips, gently push and stretch the dough to the edges and into the corners of the baking sheet; try not to press out any bubbles. The dough will not completely fill the baking sheet, but should come close. Re-cover with the plastic wrap and let rest for another 30 minutes.

Again using dampened fingertips and working outward from the center, spread the dough into an even layer to the edges and into corners of the baking sheet. Re-cover and let rest until the dough is bubbly and risen by about half, 20 to 25 minutes. Meanwhile, heat the oven to 500°F with a rack in the lower-middle position.

While the dough rests, prepare the toppings. In a 12-inch skillet over medium-high, combine the sausage, chard stems and oil. Cook, breaking up the sausage

and stirring occasionally, just until the sausage is no longer pink, 4 to 5 minutes. Transfer the sausage mixture to a large plate and set aside. Return the skillet to medium and add the chard leaves and ¼ cup water. Cook, stirring occasionally, until wilted, about 4 minutes. Remove from the heat.

When the dough is ready, uncover it and spread the tomato sauce evenly over its surface, then scatter on the provolone and smoked mozzarella. Sprinkle on the sausage mixture, followed by the chard leaves. Scatter on the onion, followed by the Asiago.

Bake until the pizza is golden brown and the edges are deeply caramelized, about 25 minutes. Cool in the pan on a wire rack for 10 minutes. Using a wide metal spatula, loosen the sides and bottom of the pizza, then slide it onto a cutting board. Slice into 12 pieces and serve warm.

VARIATION

Slab Pizza with Portobello Mushrooms and Lemon-Garlic Ricotta

Follow the recipe to prepare the baking sheet, make the dough and heat the oven, positioning the racks in the upper- and lower-middle positions. While the dough is resting, make the toppings. On another rimmed baking sheet, toss together **1½ pounds portobello mushroom caps** (gills scraped, caps halved and sliced ½ inch thick), **10 medium garlic cloves** (smashed and peeled), **2 tablespoons balsamic vinegar and 2 tablespoons extra-virgin olive oil.** Distribute in an even layer, then roast on the upper rack until lightly browned, about 10 minutes. Remove from the oven and set aside; leave the oven on. While the mushrooms roast, in a medium bowl, stir together a **15- or 16-ounce container whole-milk ricotta, ¼ cup heavy cream, 4 ounces (1 cup) shredded fontina cheese, 1 ounce (½ cup) finely grated Parmesan cheese, 2 medium garlic cloves** (finely grated), **1½ cups lightly packed fresh parsley** (chopped), **1 teaspoon grated lemon zest plus 1 tablespoon lemon juice, ½ teaspoon red pepper flakes, ¼ teaspoon each kosher salt and ground black pepper;** set aside. When the dough is ready, uncover it and evenly spread the ricotta mixture over the surface, then scatter on the mushroom mixture. Sprinkle with an additional **1 ounce (½ cup) finely grated Parmesan cheese.** Bake, cool and remove from the pan as directed. Serve sprinkled with **additional chopped parsley** and a **drizzle of balsamic.**

VARIATION

Slab Pizza with Eggplant, Three Cheeses and Basil

Follow the recipe to prepare the baking sheet, make the dough and heat the oven, positioning the racks in the upper- and lower-middle positions. While the dough is resting, make the toppings. In a large bowl, toss **2 pounds globe eggplant** (peeled lengthwise in strips spaced about an inch apart, then sliced into ½-inch rounds) with **1 teaspoon kosher salt;** let stand, tossing occasionally, for 15 minutes. Brush another rimmed baking sheet with **2 tablespoons extra-virgin olive oil.** Using paper towels, pat the eggplant slices dry and place on the oiled baking sheet, shingling as needed to fit. Brush the eggplant with another **2 tablespoons extra-virgin olive oil** and roast on the upper-middle rack until golden brown, 15 to 18 minutes. Remove from the oven and set aside; leave the oven on. When the dough is ready, uncover it, then scatter **4 ounces (1 cup) shredded fontina cheese** over the surface and top with the eggplant. Spoon **Simple Tomato Sauce for Pizza** (p. 213) evenly over the surface, then layer on **1 pound fresh mozzarella cheese** (sliced ¼ inch thick and patted dry); sprinkle with **½ cup lightly packed fresh basil** (torn, if large) and **2 ounces (1 cup) finely grated Parmesan cheese.** Bake, cool and remove from the pan as directed. Serve sprinkled with **additional torn basil.**

Pissaladière

Start to finish: 2¾ hours
(1 hour active), plus cooling

Servings: 8 to 12

FOR THE DOUGH:

423 grams (3¼ cups)
all-purpose flour

1 teaspoon white sugar

1¼ teaspoons table salt

1 teaspoon instant yeast

2 tablespoons extra-virgin olive oil

1¼ cups warm water
(100°F to 110°F)

**FOR THE TOPPINGS
AND ASSEMBLY:**

4 tablespoons extra-virgin olive oil,
divided

2½ pounds yellow onions, halved
and thinly sliced

2 thyme sprigs, plus 1 tablespoon
minced thyme, reserved separately

2 bay leaves

Kosher salt and ground black pepper

About 10 oil-packed anchovy fillets
(from one 2-ounce can
oil-packed anchovy fillets), patted
dry and roughly chopped (about
4 teaspoons), divided

1 tablespoon white wine vinegar

1 tablespoon semolina flour or
cornmeal

69 grams (½ cup) pitted Niçoise or
Kalamata olives (see headnote),
roughly chopped

¼ cup chopped fresh flat-leaf
parsley

French Provençal pissaladière is a flatbread-like savory tart featuring a thin crust topped generously with onions that are slow-cooked until jammy and sweet, plus briny black olives and umami-rich anchovies. Diminutive Niçoise olives are the traditional choice for pissaladière, but easier-to-source Kalamatas are equally good. Customarily, whole anchovy fillets are arranged decoratively on the onions before baking, but for better flavor integration, we prefer to stir a small portion directly into the onions, then scatter additional chopped anchovies evenly on top. Cut into smallish pieces, pissladière is a great hors d'oeuvre or appetizer, or slice it larger and serve with a vinaigrette-dressed salad as a light meal.

Don't cook the onions until deeply caramelized. Golden brown is the goal. Resist the urge to crank up the heat to hasten the cooking, as the onions need time to fully soften in the time they take to acquire the proper color.

To make the dough, in a stand mixer with the dough hook, mix the flour, sugar, table salt and yeast on medium until well combined, about 15 seconds. With the mixer on low, drizzle in the oil followed by the water. Scrape the bowl. Mix on medium, occasionally scraping the bowl and dough hook, until the mixture forms a shaggy, sticky dough, 4 to 6 minutes. Scrape the sides of the bowl and gather the dough in the center, cover with plastic wrap and let rise at room temperature until doubled, 1½ to 2 hours.

Meanwhile, prepare the toppings. In a 12-inch skillet over medium, combine 2 tablespoons oil, the onions, thyme sprigs, bay and 1 teaspoon kosher salt. Cook, stirring occasionally, until the onions are lightly golden, 30 to 35 minutes. Stir in 1 teaspoon of the chopped anchovies; cook, stirring occasionally, until the onions are golden brown and fully softened, another 5 to 10 minutes. Remove from the heat, then discard the thyme sprigs and bay. Stir in ½ teaspoon pepper, the minced thyme and vinegar; set aside.

Brush the bottom and sides of a 13-by-18-inch rimmed baking sheet with the remaining 2 tablespoons oil, then sprinkle evenly with the semolina. Turn the dough onto the baking sheet, then, using oiled hands, press and stretch it into an even layer that covers the surface of the baking sheet; it's fine if the dough doesn't completely fill the corners. Cover with plastic wrap and let rise at room temperature until puffed and almost doubled, about 30 minutes. Meanwhile, heat the oven to 450°F with a rack in the middle position.

MAKE THE MOST OF YOUR YEAST

Yeast varieties and labels can be confusing, but the good news is that regular active yeast and instant yeast can be substituted for the other, though they are used differently. Regular active yeast can be temperamental and should be proofed before use to ensure it is active. This is done by dissolving it in warm water (a typical ¼-ounce packet of yeast (2¼ teaspoons) should be dissolved in ¼ cup of 110°F to 120°F water) for about 10 minutes. If the mixture bubbles, the yeast is viable and ready to be used in your recipe. Instant yeast (also called rapid-rise, quick-rise or bread machine yeast) is more shelf-stable and doesn't require proofing. In most cases, it can be added directly to dough ingredients during the mixing.

Active dry and instant yeasts can be substituted one for one, but keep in mind a couple things. Active yeast is slower than instant when it comes to dough rising, but will eventually rise just as much as instant yeast by the end of a long rise (two to three hours). For recipes that call for a shorter rise, dough made with active yeast might require an extra 15 or 20 minutes to double in size. Also remember that recipes designed for active yeast account for the extra liquid added with proofing. You will need to compensate for that by adding an equal volume of water. And regardless of the variety of yeast, it's always best to refrigerate it; it's a living organism that can spoil.

While less common, fresh yeast (sometimes called cake yeast) is available in the refrigerated section of some markets. It is a compressed, high-moisture cake, which easily crumbles to incorporate into doughs and batters without the need for additional moisture. Its perishability has made it largely anachronistic, though some bakers claim it provides a stronger aroma and subtle sweetness.

Distribute the onions evenly over the dough, leaving a ½-inch border around the edge. Scatter the remaining chopped anchovies over the onions, followed by the olives. Bake until the edges of the dough are golden brown, 20 to 25 minutes. Using a large metal spatula, slide the pissaladière onto a cutting board and sprinkle with the parsley. Cool for at least 10 minutes. Serve warm or at room temperature.

Tarte Flambée

**Start to finish: 3 hours
(45 minutes active)**

Servings: 4 to 6

FOR THE DOUGH:

260 grams (2 cups) all-purpose flour, plus more for dusting

2 teaspoons white sugar

1 teaspoon table salt

½ teaspoon instant yeast

1 tablespoon extra-virgin olive oil, plus more for the baking sheet

¾ cup warm water (100°F to 110°F)

FOR THE TOPPINGS:

4 ounces thick-cut bacon, cut crosswise into ¼-inch strips

2 medium yellow onions, halved and thinly sliced

8-ounce container crème fraîche (see headnote)

½ teaspoon freshly grated nutmeg

Kosher salt and ground black pepper

½ cup lightly packed fresh flat-leaf parsley, roughly chopped

Tarte flambée, also known as flammekueche, is an onion and bacon-topped flatbread from the Alsace region of northeastern France. Its name translates as "flamed tart," which hints at its method of preparation. The tarts traditionally were prepared as a baker's snack, cooked in the intense heat of a wood-burning oven. The high temperatures resulted in edges that were charred or "flamed." The tart's classic toppings are a soft, fresh, spreadable cheese called fromage blanc, meaty bits of smoky bacon and sliced onions that are sautéed until soft and sweet. Instead of fromage blanc, we use more widely available crème fraîche; its thick, creamy richness works beautifully on the tarts. (However, if you're able to find fromage blanc, use an equal amount.) Slice the tarts into strips to serve as an appetizer, or halve them and pair with a leafy salad for a main course.

Don't worry too much about stretching the dough into a perfect oval. It may shrink back slightly as you are shaping it, but once the toppings are added, it can be stretched and adjusted again. Also, don't worry if the dough seems soft and sticky just after mixing. It will firm up and develop structure as it proofs.

To make the dough, in a stand mixer with the dough hook, mix the flour, sugar, salt and yeast on medium until well combined, about 15 seconds. With the mixer on low, drizzle in the oil, followed by the water. Knead on medium, scraping the bowl once or twice, until the mixture forms a soft, sticky dough that pulls away from the sides of the bowl, 4 to 5 minutes. Cover the bowl with plastic wrap and let rise at room temperature until doubled, 1 to 1½ hours.

Meanwhile, make the toppings. In a 12-inch nonstick skillet over medium, cook the bacon, stirring occasionally, until browned and crisp, about 6 minutes. Using a slotted spoon, transfer to a paper towel–lined plate; set aside. Pour off and discard all but 1 tablespoon fat from the skillet. Add the onions and cook over medium, stirring, until softened and beginning to brown, about 6 minutes. Transfer to a medium bowl and set aside. In a small bowl, stir together the crème fraîche, nutmeg and ½ teaspoon each salt and pepper; cover and refrigerate until ready to use.

About 30 minutes into rising, heat the oven to 450°F with a rack in the upper-middle position. Coat a rimmed baking sheet with oil and line it with kitchen parchment, then coat the parchment with oil.

When the dough has doubled, lightly flour the counter and turn the dough out onto it. Using a chef's knife or bench scraper, divide it in half. With your hands, gently pat and flatten each portion into a 12-by-5-inch oval. Transfer the ovals to the prepared baking sheet, spacing them evenly apart. Using your hands, press and stretch the ovals until they measure about 14-by-5 inches, with at least ½ inch between them. Spread half of the crème fraîche mixture in an even layer over one

oval, leaving a ½-inch border around the edge. Scatter half of the onions evenly over the crème fraîche mixture, followed by half of the bacon. Top the second oval in the same way.

Bake until the edges are golden brown, 18 to 20 minutes, rotating the baking sheet halfway through. Using a wide metal spatula, transfer the tarts to a wire rack. Cool for 10 to 15 minutes, then sprinkle with parsley. To serve, cut crosswise into slices.

Upside-Down Tomato Tart with Parmesan Pastry

**Start to finish: 1½ hours
(30 minutes active), plus cooling**

Servings: 4 to 6

1½ pounds medium plum tomatoes, cored and sliced into ½-inch-thick rounds

Kosher salt and ground black pepper

130 grams (1 cup) all-purpose flour, plus more for dusting

1 ounce Parmesan cheese, finely grated (½ cup)

3 teaspoons minced fresh thyme or finely chopped fresh tarragon, divided

113 grams (8 tablespoons) cold salted butter, cut into ½-inch cubes

3½ tablespoons ice water

1 teaspoon plus 1 tablespoon extra-virgin olive oil, divided, plus more to serve

Flaky sea salt (optional)

This savory tart inspired by classic French tarte tatin stars sweet-tart tomatoes baked until tender and deeply concentrated in a shingled layer on top of a crisp yet tender Parmesan-herb crust. Avoid plump, extra-juicy tomatoes; their moisture quickly turns the crust soggy. Plum tomatoes are best, and we found it best to slice, salt and roast them before adding the dough. After experimenting with different crusts, we settled on a pastry that's rich in butter and accented with Parmesan and thyme. The tart can be baked and left in the pie plate for a couple of hours at room temperature. When ready to serve, if desired, rewarm in a 350°F oven for 10 minutes, then invert it onto a platter. (If any tomato slices stick to the pie plate, simply replace them on the tart.) Serve for brunch, lunch or dinner paired with a bright, fresh salad.

Don't use vine-ripened, heirloom or cherry tomatoes. They contain too much moisture and will turn the crust soggy. Also, don't be shy about allowing the crust to brown deeply. A darker pastry holds up better to the tomatoes' juices and adds toasty notes.

HOW TO MAKE UPSIDE-DOWN TOMATO TART

1. Shingle the salted and patted-dry tomatoes in an oiled pie plate. Add seasoning and oil and bake until most of the liquid has cooked off.

2. Roll out the dough on a lightly floured counter into a 10-inch circle, dusting the dough with flour as needed.

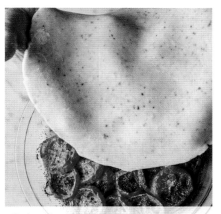

3. Lay the dough on the baked and slightly cooled tomatoes, gently pressing it with your hands.

4. Fold and tuck the edges inside the pie plate. Make slits 1 inch apart all over the dough. Bake until deeply browned. Run a knife around the edge of the pie plate, then cool.

5. Invert a platter onto the pie plate. Holding the platter and pie plate together, carefully re-invert.

6. Lift off the pie plate. Serve warm or cool to room temperature. Just before serving sprinkle with additional pepper, thyme and kosher or flaky sea salt (if using); lightly drizzle with additional oil.

In a large colander set over a bowl, toss the tomato slices with 1 teaspoon salt; let stand for 20 to 30 minutes, occasionally shaking the colander to encourage liquid to drain. Heat the oven to 425°F with a rack in the middle position.

In a food processor, combine the flour, Parmesan, 1 teaspoon of the thyme, ⅛ teaspoon kosher salt and ¼ teaspoon pepper; pulse 3 or 4 times. Scatter about 42 grams (3 tablespoons) butter over the flour mixture and process until the butter is well incorporated, 15 to 20 seconds. Scatter in the remaining butter, then pulse until broken into pieces no larger than small peas, 10 to 12 pulses. Drizzle the ice water over the mixture, then pulse until it forms curdy clumps, 12 to 15 pulses.

Turn the dough out onto the counter. Gather and press it firmly into a disk about 5 inches in diameter. Wrap tightly in plastic, smoothing out the edges and forming the disk into a neat round. Refrigerate at least 30 minutes while you roast the tomatoes (or up to 2 days).

Shake the colander a final time to drain liquid from the tomatoes. Lay out the slices on paper towels, then pat dry with additional paper towels. Brush a 9-inch glass pie plate with 1 teaspoon of the oil. Shingle the tomatoes in concentric circles, packing them tightly. Sprinkle with ½ teaspoon pepper and 1 teaspoon of the remaining thyme, then drizzle with the remaining 1 tablespoon oil. Bake until softened and most of the liquid has cooked off, 30 to 40 minutes, depending on the ripeness of the tomatoes. Remove from the oven and cool on a wire rack for about 10 minutes; leave the oven on.

Remove the chilled dough from the refrigerator. If it is too firm to roll out, let it stand at room temperature for 5 to 10 minutes. Lightly flour the counter, unwrap the dough and set it on the floured surface. Using a rolling pin, roll it into a 10-inch circle, lightly dusting with flour as needed. Lay the dough on the tomatoes, gently pressing it with your hands, then fold and tuck the edges inside the pie plate. Using a paring knife, make slits 1 inch apart all over the dough and all the way through.

Bake until the crust is deeply browned and juices are bubbling at the edges, 30 to 35 minutes. Set the pie plate on a wire rack, then run a knife around the edge of the pie plate to loosen the tart. Cool for 30 minutes.

Invert a platter onto the pie plate and, holding them together, carefully re-invert. Lift off the pie plate. Serve warm or cool to room temperature. Just before serving, sprinkle with additional pepper, the remaining 1 teaspoon thyme and kosher or flaky sea salt (if using); lightly drizzle with additional oil.

Skillet Spanakopita

Spanakopita, the famous Greek phyllo pastry or pie filled with spinach and feta, might be made as small triangular parcels for special occasions or baked in large trays for serving a crowd. This version, baked in and served from a 12-inch cast-iron skillet, is doable for a weeknight dinner, yet is impressive enough for a holiday brunch. For the filling, we combine baby spinach with baby kale, which has a bolder, greener flavor that pairs well with the salty, briny feta. Phyllo is packaged either as 9-by-14-inch sheets or larger 13-by-18-inch sheets. The former can be used as is; the latter should be halved crosswise (use a chef's knife to simply cut through the stack). You will need a total of eight phyllo sheets. As you make the filling, keep the phyllo covered with a sheet of plastic wrap then a damp kitchen towel to prevent drying. If the sheets tear as you work with them, not to worry. Scrunching them to create a pretty ruffled effect hides flaws.

Don't add the egg-greens mixture to the sautéed leek if the skillet is still hot. We've found that about 10 minutes is long enough to cool the pan, but cast iron retains heat exceptionally well, so to be safe and avoid the risk of scrambling the eggs, be sure the skillet is no hotter than warm to the touch before pouring in the egg-greens mixture.

Start to finish: 1 hour 20 mins (40 minutes active), plus cooling

Servings: 6

3 tablespoons salted butter, cut into 1-tablespoon pieces, divided, plus 3 tablespoons salted butter, melted

1-pound container baby spinach

8 ounces baby kale (about 9 cups lightly packed)

1 medium leek, white and light green parts halved lengthwise, thinly sliced, rinsed and drained

4 medium garlic cloves, chopped

Kosher salt and ground black pepper

3 large eggs

8 ounces feta cheese, crumbled (2 cups)

1 cup whole-milk ricotta cheese (8 ounces)

1 cup lightly packed fresh dill, chopped

Eight 9-by-14-inch frozen phyllo sheets, or four 13-by-18-inch frozen phyllo sheets, thawed and halved crosswise, covered to prevent drying (see headnote)

Heat the oven to 375°F with a rack in the middle position. Place a colander in a medium bowl and set near the stove.

In a 12-inch cast-iron skillet over medium-high, melt 1 tablespoon whole butter. Add a few large handfuls of the spinach and kale, then cook, stirring and turning with tongs, until wilted, 1½ to 2 minutes. Transfer to the colander. Wilt the remaining spinach and kale in the same way without adding more butter; set aside.

In the same skillet over medium, melt 2 tablespoons of the remaining whole butter. Add the leek, garlic, ¼ teaspoon salt and ½ teaspoon pepper. Cook, stirring occasionally, until the leek is tender, 4 to 6 minutes (if the leek begins to brown or stick to the skillet, stir in 1 to 2 tablespoons water). Remove the skillet from the heat and let cool for about 10 minutes.

Meanwhile, in a large bowl, whisk the eggs to combine. Add the feta, ricotta and dill, then whisk to combine. Using your hands, squeeze the moisture from the greens; you should have about 3 cups squeezed greens. Add the greens to the egg-cheese mixture and stir until well combined, then transfer to the skillet (it's fine if the skillet is warm to the touch but it should not be hot). Stir to incorporate the leeks, then distribute the filling in an even layer in the pan.

Brush 1 phyllo sheet on both sides with some of the melted butter, then scrunch it loosely and place on top of the filling. Repeat with the remaining phyllo and butter, covering the entire surface of the filling. Drizzle any remaining butter over the top.

Bake until the phyllo is golden brown, about 35 minutes. Cool for about 10 minutes before slicing and serving.

Spinach and Cheese Börek

Börek is a Turkish pie, commonly savory, made with yufka, a thin dough that's slightly sturdier than phyllo, and filled with various combinations of meats, cheeses or vegetables. The term "börek" covers a large category of yufka-based pastries—they may be large and baked, individually sized and fried or formed in a number of different shapes, from spirals to cigars to half moons. For our spinach and cheese börek assembled and baked in a standard 9-by-13-inch baking pan, we use store-bought phyllo instead of hard-to-source yufka, and we modeled it on a recipe from Özlem Warren, author of "Özlem's Turkish Table." Phyllo in the U.S. typically is packaged as 9-by-14-inch sheets or larger 13-by-18-inch sheets. The former can be used as is; the latter need to be halved crosswise to fit neatly into the baking pan (use a chef's knife to simply cut through the stack). You will need a total of 24 phyllo sheets; a 1-pound box will contain more than enough. Make sure to fully thaw the phyllo before you attempt to unroll it otherwise the delicate sheets will crack. We like to sprinkle nigella seeds (also known as kalonji) onto the börek just before baking. Black in color and with a savory, herbaceous, oregano-like flavor and hints of allium, they are worth seeking out. If you cannot find them, however, not to worry; simply use a total of 1½ tablespoons sesame seeds. The börek is delicious served warm or at room temperature. Covered tightly, leftovers will keep in the refrigerator for up to three days; reheat in a 350°F oven for five to 10 minutes.

Don't use precrumbled feta, as it tends to be bland. Purchase a block of good-quality feta and crumble it yourself into small bits that will combine easily with the spinach and mozzarella. When mixing the filling, use your hands to really work the ingredients together so the spinach wilts. Don't add salt to the filling; the cheeses provide lots of salinity. Finally, as you assemble the börek, don't allow the phyllo to dry out; be sure to keep it covered with plastic wrap and a damp towel.

Heat the oven to 350°F with a rack in the middle position. Brush the bottom and sides of a 13-by-9-inch baking pan with 2 tablespoons of oil. In a liquid measuring cup or small bowl, stir together the milk, ½ cup water and 1 tablespoon of the remaining oil (the oil will not fully incorporate); set aside.

In a large bowl, beat 2 of the eggs. Add the spinach, feta, mozzarella and ½ teaspoon pepper. Using your hands, mix well until the spinach is slightly wilted and the ingredients are well combined.

Start to finish: 1¾ hours (40 minutes active), plus cooling

Servings: 6 to 8

4 tablespoons extra-virgin olive oil, divided

½ cup whole milk

3 large eggs, divided

8 ounces baby spinach (18 cups lightly packed)

8 ounces feta cheese, finely crumbled (2 cups)

6 ounces whole-milk mozzarella cheese, shredded (2 cups)

Ground black pepper

Twenty-four 9-by-14-inch frozen phyllo sheets, thawed, or twelve 13-by-18-inch phyllo sheets, thawed and halved crosswise (see headnote)

1 tablespoon nigella seeds (see headnote)

2 teaspoons sesame seeds

Set the stack of phyllo sheets on the counter, then cover with plastic wrap and a damp kitchen towel to prevent drying. Lay 3 phyllo sheets in the bottom of the prepared baking pan; keep the remaining phyllo covered. Brush a generous 2 tablespoons of the milk mixture onto the phyllo. Lay another 3 phyllo sheets on top and brush with another 3 tablespoons milk mixture. Repeat the layering and brushing once more, then place another 3 phyllo sheets on top; you will have used 12 phyllo sheets at this point.

Add the spinach mixture and distribute it in an even layer. Lay another 3 phyllo sheets on top and brush with a generous 2 tablespoons of the milk mixture. Continue layering in the phyllo sheets and brushing with milk mixture in the same way until all the phyllo is used, but do not brush any milk mixture onto the final layer of phyllo.

To the remaining milk mixture, add the remaining 1 egg and the remaining 1 tablespoon oil, then whisk until well combined. Drizzle all of this mixture onto the top layer of phyllo, then brush to coat the entire surface; the mixture may pool in spots. Sprinkle evenly with the nigella and sesame seeds. Bake until puffed and golden brown, about 1 hour, rotating the baking pan once about halfway through.

Cool on a wire rack for at least 15 minutes before cutting into pieces directly in the baking pan. Serve warm or at room temperature.

Milk Street Bakes

Baked Colombian-Style Empanadas

In her book "Colombiana," Mariana Velásquez explains that Colombian empanadas are almost always deep-fried—not baked, as Argentinian empanadas are—creating deeply golden, extra-crisp crusts that conceal any number of fillings. But we opted for baking, as it's simpler and neater than frying, and yields delicious results. A savory mixture of potatoes and ground beef, flavored with alliums, fresh chilies, tomato and spices fill these fantastic empanadas, an adaptation of her recipe. This dough is not traditional, but Velásquez says it is much easier to work with than the classic version made with masarepa (a type of corn flour). This dough combines all-purpose flour and corn flour. Bob's Red Mill is a widely available brand. You will need a 4-inch cutter to stamp out circles of the rolled dough. Serve warm with the Colombian spicy green salsa called ají; recipe p. 241.

Don't over-moisten the edge of the dough when forming the empanadas. When moistening the edge, dip your finger in the water, shake off excess and quickly run your finger over only half of the circle, around the edge; don't moisten the entire perimeter. Once the empanadas are filled, they need at least 30 minutes of chilling to firm up, but don't store them for longer than two hours or the bottoms may become too wet. Also, don't mistake cornmeal or cornstarch for corn flour. To add to the confusion, masa harina is yet another type of ground corn product, and not the type to use here.

To make the filling, in a medium saucepan, combine the potatoes, ½ teaspoon salt and 6 cups water. Bring to a boil over high and cook until a skewer inserted into the potatoes meets no resistance, 15 to 18 minutes. Drain in a colander, shaking to remove as much water as possible, then return the potatoes to the saucepan. Set the pan over low and allow the potatoes to dry for about 1 minute. Remove the pan from the heat, add 1 tablespoon butter and, using a potato masher, mash until the mixture is mostly smooth; set aside.

In a 12-inch nonstick skillet over medium, melt the remaining 1 tablespoon butter. Stir in the onion, cover and cook, stirring occasionally, until lightly browned and softened, about 8 minutes. Add the tomato paste and cook, stirring, until it begins to brown, 1 to 2 minutes. Stir in the jalapeños, garlic and grated tomatoes, followed by the ground beef, cumin, coriander and ½ teaspoon salt. Cook over medium-high, breaking the beef up into small bits, until the meat no longer is pink and the mixture begins to sizzle, about 15 minutes.

Remove the pan from the heat. Add the mashed potatoes and stir until fully integrated, then stir in the cilantro. Taste and season with salt and pepper. Transfer

Start to finish: 2¾ hours, plus chilling and resting

Makes two dozen 3½-inch empanadas

FOR THE FILLING:

8 ounces Yukon Gold potatoes, peeled and cut into 1-inch chunks

Kosher salt and ground black pepper

2 tablespoons salted butter, cut into 1-tablespoon pieces, divided

1 small yellow onion, finely chopped

2 tablespoons tomato paste

2 jalapeño chilies, stemmed, seeded and finely chopped

4 medium garlic cloves, minced

12 ounces ripe tomatoes, halved and grated on the large holes of a box grater, skins discarded

8 ounces 80 percent lean ground beef

2 tablespoons ground cumin

1 tablespoon ground coriander

¼ cup finely chopped fresh cilantro

FOR THE DOUGH AND BAKING:

390 grams (3 cups) all-purpose flour, plus more for dusting

122 grams (1 cup) corn flour (see headnote)

1 teaspoon table salt

170 grams (12 tablespoons) salted butter, melted and slightly cooled

480 grams (2 cups) plain whole-milk Greek yogurt

1 large egg white

to a medium bowl and cool to room temperature, then cover and refrigerate until chilled while you make the dough, or for up to 24 hours.

To make the dough, in a stand mixer with the paddle attachment, mix both flours and the salt on low until combined, about 30 seconds. With the mixer running, drizzle in the butter, then add the yogurt. Mix on low until a smooth dough forms, about 5 minutes; if there are still dry bits at the bottom of the bowl, mix in water 1 tablespoon at a time until the bits are integrated and the dough is smooth. Lightly flour the counter, then turn the dough out onto it. Briefly knead the dough, forming it into a ball. Divide in half, form each piece into a 6-inch disk, wrap in plastic and refrigerate for at least 1 hour or up to 24 hours.

When you are ready to form the empanadas, remove the dough from the refrigerator and let stand at room temperature for 15 minutes to soften slightly. Line 2 rimmed baking sheets with kitchen parchment. Lightly flour the counter, then, using a rolling pin, roll one portion of dough into a round about $\frac{1}{16}$ inch thick. Using a 4-inch round cutter, cut out 12 circles, gathering the scraps and re-rolling the dough as needed. Place the circles in a single layer on one of the prepared baking sheets; cover with a kitchen towel. Repeat with the second portion of dough, placing the circles on the second prepared baking sheet; cover with another kitchen towel.

Remove the filling from the refrigerator. Have ready a small bowl of water. Set one dough circle on the counter. Mound 4 teaspoons filling onto the center of the lower half of the circle and, with your fingers, slightly flatten the mound, keeping the edges of the dough clear. Using your finger dipped into the water, very lightly moisten the edge of half the dough circle along the arc closest to you. Fold the unfilled side over the filling, aligning the edges and forming a half moon; lightly press on the filling to flatten it slightly and remove any air pockets. Press the edges with your fingers, then with the tines of a fork to create a secure seal and a decorative edge. Return the empanada to the baking sheet. Using the remaining dough circles and filling, form additional empanadas; place all 24 empanadas in a single layer on the same baking sheet. Cover with a kitchen towel and refrigerate for at least 30 minutes or up to 2 hours. Reserve the now-empty parchment-lined baking sheet.

When you are ready to bake, heat the oven to 400°F with racks in the upper- and lower-middle positions. In a small bowl, whisk together the egg white and 1 tablespoon water. Transfer half of the empanadas to the reserved parchment-lined baking sheet. Brush the surfaces of all empanadas with egg white mixture and bake both sheets until golden brown, 20 to 25 minutes, rotating the sheets and switching their positions about halfway through. Cool on the baking sheets on wire racks for about 10 minutes. Serve warm or at room temperature.

OVER THE TOP

Colombian Spicy Green Salsa (Ají)

Start to finish: 20 minutes, plus chilling / Makes 2 cups

In a medium bowl, stir together **4 scallions** (finely chopped), **1 jalapeño chili** (stemmed, seeded and minced), **1 small red bell pepper** (stemmed, seeded and finely chopped), **⅓ cup finely chopped fresh cilantro**, **3 tablespoons white vinegar**, **1 tablespoon lime juice** and **kosher salt**, to taste. Cover and refrigerate for at least 1 hour or for up to 1 day.

Chapter 6

Pies and Puddings

Flaky Pie Pastry

Start to finish: 3 hours (40 minutes active)

Makes one 9-inch pie shell

163 grams (1¼ cups) all-purpose flour, plus more for dusting

1 tablespoon white sugar

½ teaspoon table salt

141 grams (10 tablespoons) cold salted butter, cut into 1-tablespoon pieces

4 tablespoons ice water, divided

This pie dough packs in a generous amount of butter, resulting in rich flavor, yet remains workable and holds its shape when baked without a filling. One of the tricks is incorporating the butter in two stages. First, about a third is processed into the dry ingredients until very well combined, then the remainder is pulsed in until the pieces are reduced to pea-sized pieces. This ensures good integration of fat for better workability and tenderness, but leaves enough bits for flaky layers in the baked pastry. After emptying the dough mixture onto the counter, we form it into a rectangle that we cut into thirds, then stack the pieces on top of each other. This builds layers for even more flakiness. A metal bench scraper is a handy tool when working with the dough, but a wide metal spatula works, too. For prebaking, you will need to line the dough-lined pie plate with foil and fill it with pie weights. Ceramic or metal weights work best. Otherwise, use at least 2 cups dried beans or rice, and plan to bake on the longer end of the time ranges. This dough can be doubled for a double-crust pie or to make enough dough for two 9-inch single-crust pies; see the instructions p. 246.

Don't cut the butter into small pieces. Kept in 1-tablespoon chunks, the butter still will be pebbly at the end of processing, not fine and fully incorporated, which is essential for flakiness. Also, be sure the butter is completely cold and firm before you begin; keep it in the refrigerator until ready to use. Finally, after fitting the dough into the pie plate, be sure to poke holes in it with a fork, then freeze for at least one hour. This not only will help the pastry hold its shape during prebaking, it also will allow you to easily line the dough with the foil without marring the surface, sides and edge.

In a food processor, combine the flour, sugar and salt; pulse 3 or 4 times to combine. Scatter 3 tablespoons butter over the flour and process until well incorporated, 10 to 15 seconds. Scatter the remaining butter over the mixture and lock the lid in place. Through the feed tube, add 1 tablespoon ice water and quickly pulse 2 times. Repeat with another 1 tablespoon ice water, quickly pulsing another 2 times. Repeat with the remaining 2 tablespoons ice water, then pulse until the mixture is evenly moistened, has a curdy appearance and the butter is broken down into pea-sized bits, about 10 pulses; the mixture will not have formed a cohesive dough. Pinch a small amount between your fingers; it should hold together.

Working quickly, lightly flour the counter and turn the dough mixture out onto it. Using your hands and a metal bench scraper, gather it together and firmly press it into a rough 9-by-3-inch rectangle of even thickness. With the scraper, block and square the sides, forming a neater rectangle, then cut it into thirds, forming three

3-inch squares. Scrape up one of the end squares and stack it on top of the middle square, aligning the sides. Repeat with the third square.

Cut a 12-inch square of plastic wrap. Scrape up the dough stack, place it in the center of the plastic and wrap the dough. Using the palm of your hand, smash the stack, applying firm, even pressure, until it forms a rough 4½-inch square about 1 inch thick. Round off the corners as best you can by rolling the dough on its side, like a wheel, on the counter, forming a disk, which will be easier than a square to roll out into a circle. Refrigerate for at least 1 hour or up to 2 days.

When you are ready to roll out the dough, if it is too firm to roll, let stand at room temperature 5 to 10 minutes. Dust the counter with flour, unwrap the dough and set it on the floured surface. Dust the dough with flour, then roll the dough into a circle about 13 inches in diameter and of even thickness. Drape the dough over the rolling pin and transfer to a 9-inch pie plate. Gently ease the dough into the plate by lifting the edges while pressing down into the corners. Trim the edges, leaving a ½-inch overhang, then tuck the overhang under itself so the dough is flush with the rim of the pan. Using your fingers, crimp and flute the edge of the dough. With a fork, poke holes every inch or so across the bottom and into the sides. Freeze, uncovered, until firm, about 30 minutes, or cover with plastic wrap and freeze for up to 24 hours.

When you are ready to bake, heat the oven to 375°F with a rack in the middle position. Remove the dough-lined pie plate from the refrigerator. Line the dough with a 12-inch square of foil, pressing the foil into the corners and up the sides, then fold the excess down to cover the fluted edge. Fill evenly with 2 cups pie weights.

Bake until the edges are golden brown, 30 to 35 minutes. Remove from the oven, then carefully lift out the foil and weights. For partially baked pastry, continue to bake until the bottom is dry and lightly browned, 5 to 7 minutes; for fully baked pastry, bake until deep golden brown, 9 to 12 minutes. Transfer to a wire rack to cool.

How to Make A Double Batch of Flaky Pie Pastry

Using doubled ingredients, in a food processor, combine the flour, sugar and salt; pulse 3 or 4 times to combine. Scatter 6 tablespoons butter over the flour mixture and process until the butter is well incorporated, 10 to 15 seconds. Scatter the remaining butter over the flour mixture and lock the lid in place. Through the feed tube, add 1 tablespoon ice water and pulse once. Repeat with another 1 tablespoon ice water. Now add 2 tablespoons ice water through the feed tube and quickly pulse twice. Repeat with another 2 tablespoons ice water. Finally, add the remaining 2 tablespoons ice water through the feed tube, then pulse until the mixture is evenly moistened, has a curdy appearance and the butter is broken down into pea-sized bits, 8 to 10 pulses; the mixture will not have formed a cohesive dough. Working quickly, lightly flour the counter and turn the mixture out onto it. Divide in half, then continue with the recipe to form each portion into a rectangle, cut, stack, smash, refrigerate and roll out the dough.

Brown Sugar Tart

The inspiration for this minimalist but luxurious tart comes from French-Canadian sugar pie, or tarte au sucre, which has roots in the Belgian sweet called tarte de paveû. Our tart has two distinct layers: a rich, lightly sweetened custard on top, and a bed of brown sugar on the bottom. Using only egg yolks in the custard creates a silkier, more sumptuous texture than whole eggs, and adding just a little flour stabilizes the filling and protects it against curdling. Light brown sugar works fine, though we prefer the deeper, more robust flavor of dark brown. Adding the filling to a fully baked and still-warm tart shell helps ensure a crisp bottom crust that contrasts the smoothness of the custard.

Don't use old, hard brown sugar. If your sugar is clumpy and dry, it will resist dissolving in the custard mixture. Also, be sure to allow the tart to fully cool before serving.

Heat the oven to 325°F with a rack in the middle position. In a medium bowl, whisk together the 50 grams (¼ cup) sugar, flour and salt; if needed, break up any clumps of sugar with your fingers. Whisk in the yolks until smooth, then whisk in the cream and vanilla.

Place the tart shell, still on a rimmed baking sheet, in the oven; warm for 5 to 10 minutes. Remove from the oven, then sprinkle the remaining 75 grams (6 tablespoons) sugar over the warm crust and, using a flat-bottomed object such as a dry-ingredient measuring cup, gently press and smooth the sugar into an even layer.

Stir the cream mixture to recombine, then slowly pour it over the sugar, taking care not to disturb the sugar layer. Bake until the edges are set but the center jiggles slightly, 38 to 42 minutes. Let the tart cool completely on the baking sheet on a wire rack. Remove the pan sides and serve at room temperature.

Start to finish: 1¾ hours (30 minutes active), plus cooling

Makes one 9-inch tart

50 grams (¼ cup) plus 75 grams (6 tablespoons) packed dark brown sugar, divided

2 tablespoons all-purpose flour

¼ teaspoon table salt

6 large egg yolks

2 cups heavy cream

1 tablespoon vanilla extract

Whole-wheat tart shell (recipe p. 256), fully baked on a rimmed baking sheet

Pumpkin Pie with Honey-Orange Whipped Cream

We love pumpkin pie, but we don't love how dense, cloying and overspiced it can be. We wanted a lighter, fresher take with a pronounced pumpkin flavor. Canned pumpkin puree was a great place to start, but we intensified its flavor by giving it a quick sauté with dark brown sugar. This cooks off excess moisture and lends caramel notes to the mixture. A little bourbon adds complexity that complements the earthiness of the pumpkin and brown sugar, but an equal amount of orange juice works well, too. To give the filling tang and richness, we add crème fraîche instead of the typical evaporated milk. Honey-sweetened, citrus-scented whipped cream (recipe follows) is the perfect accompaniment.

Don't use canned pumpkin pie filling for this recipe. Look for unsweetened canned pumpkin puree; the only ingredient listed should be pumpkin. After adding the bourbon to the skillet, stir carefully if you're using a gas burner, as splashes may cause the liquid to ignite. If this happens, the flames will extinguish after a few seconds, once the alcohol has burned off.

Heat the oven to 325°F with a rack in the middle position. In a 12-inch nonstick skillet, stir together the pumpkin and sugar. Cook over medium high, stirring, until the mixture is thickened, darkened in color and reduced to about 1½ cups, about 10 minutes. Reduce to medium-low, add the bourbon and scrape up any browned bits. Transfer to a medium bowl.

To the pumpkin mixture, whisk in the crème fraîche and salt. Add the eggs and whisk until homogeneous. Place the pie pastry in the oven; warm for about 10 minutes. Remove from the oven and pour in the filling. Bake until the edges just start to crack and the center sets, 30 to 35 minutes. Cool completely on a wire rack. Serve at room temperature or chilled.

Start to finish: 1 hour 40 minutes (40 minutes active), plus cooling

Makes one 9-inch pie

15-ounce can pumpkin puree

149 grams (¾ cup packed) dark brown sugar

¼ cup bourbon

8-ounce container (1 cup) crème fraîche

⅛ teaspoon table salt

3 large eggs, beaten

Flaky pie pastry, partially baked (recipe p. 244)

Honey-orange whipped cream (recipe follows), to serve

OVER THE TOP

Honey-Orange Whipped Cream

Start to finish: 5 minutes
Makes about 3 cups

In the bowl of a stand mixer, combine **1½ cups cold heavy cream, 3 tablespoons honey** and **½ teaspoon grated orange zest.** Using the whisk attachment, mix on low until frothy, about 30 seconds. Scrape the bowl with a spatula to make sure the honey is incorporated. Mix on medium-high and whip until soft peaks form, 2 to 3 minutes.

Almond Tart Shell

Start to finish: 20 minutes, plus chilling and baking

Makes one 9-inch tart shell

98 grams (¾ cup) all-purpose flour

50 grams (½ cup) almond flour

54 grams (¼ cup) white sugar

¼ teaspoon table salt

85 grams (6 tablespoons) cold salted butter, cut into ½-inch cubes

1 large egg yolk

½ teaspoon vanilla extract

¼ teaspoon almond extract (optional)

This tart shell with a sugar-cookie quality, called pâte sucrée in French, is made from a combination of all-purpose flour and almond flour; the latter lends a subtle sweet, nutty flavor and creates a tender texture. Almond extract accentuates the almond notes, but feel free to omit it if you wish to keep the flavor more neutral. This very "short" dough cannot be rolled with a rolling pin; instead, we press it into the tart pan. To ensure evenly thick walls and base, we first form the sides using about a third of the dough. We then press the remainder into the bottom of the pan and smooth it with a flat-bottomed object, such as a dry-ingredient measuring cup. We typically use foil to line pie and tart shells before filling them with weights in preparation for prebaking, but multiple tries revealed that foil, even if greased, sticks to this pastry and pulls off thin layers upon removal. Kitchen parchment, crumpled up, then smoothed out (this softens the parchment so it better conforms to the shape of the tart shell), is the better liner in this instance. This pastry is a great option for fresh fruit and pastry cream tarts, chocolate fillings and our Lemon-Orange Tart (recipe p. 283).

Don't forget to mist the tart pan with cooking spray, along with the parchment that's pressed into the dough-lined pan before pre-baking. For a delicate dough like this one, cooking spray is added insurance against sticking.

Mist a 9-inch tart pan with removable bottom with cooking spray. In a food processor, combine both flours, the sugar and salt. Process until combined, about 5 seconds. Scatter the butter over the dry ingredients and pulse until the mixture resembles coarse sand, 10 to 12 pulses. Add the egg yolk, vanilla and almond extract (if using), then process in 5- to 10-second bursts until evenly moistened and forms large clumps, 8 to 10 bursts; it will not form a single mass but a small nugget pinched between the fingers should hold together.

Scatter a third of the dough mixture around the perimeter of the prepared tart pan, crumbling it as you go. Using your fingers, press the dough into the sides of the pan, forming sidewalls about ¼ inch thick that are level with the rim of the pan. Pile the remaining dough mixture into the center, then press into an even layer across the bottom, connecting it to the sidewalls. Using a flat-bottomed object such as a dry-ingredient measuring cup, press and smooth the dough. Prick the bottom and sides about every inch or so with a fork. Set the dough-lined pan on a baking sheet and freeze, uncovered, until cold and firm, at least 15 minutes or for up to 1 hour. Meanwhile, heat the oven to 325°F with a rack in the middle position.

DO-AHEAD PIE

As with most baked goods or pastries, pie is best when it's fresh-baked. But if you're making several double-crust pies for a large gathering, there are several options for prepping them ahead of time. One way is to freeze your pie crust. To do this, roll out the bottom crust, position it in the pie plate without trimming the edges, wrap it with plastic wrap, then set it on a baking sheet and freeze. The top crust can be rolled out and frozen flat on a parchment-lined plate. To bake, allow both crusts to thaw at room temperature until pliable but still cold, then proceed with filling and baking the pies. Double-crust pies also can be baked up to three days ahead of serving and re-warmed to freshen them up. In our testing, we found that the reheated pies lost some of their original crispness, but they still were tasty. For this approach, be sure that the fresh-baked pies have cooled completely to room temperature (this can take up to four hours). Once they've fully cooled, wrap them snugly in plastic wrap and refrigerate. To refresh them, heat at 325°F in the center of the oven until the filling is completely warmed through, 25 to 30 minutes (to prevent burning, loosely position a sheet of foil over the top of the pie as it reheats). Let the pies cool at least 10 minutes before serving—for best results, they should be allowed to cool completely before slicing. This process of heating and cooling the pie helps dry out some of the moisture the crust absorbs while in the refrigerator.

When you are ready to bake, cut a large square (at least 12 inches) of kitchen parchment. Crumple the parchment, then flatten and smooth it out. Remove the baking sheet from the freezer. Mist one side of the parchment with cooking spray, then press it oiled side down into the dough-lined pan, smoothing it against the bottom and sides. Pour in 2 cups pie weights and distribute them evenly. Fold the excess parchment over the edge of the pan.

Place the baking sheet in the oven and bake for 35 minutes. Remove from the oven and carefully lift out the parchment with weights, then return to the oven. For a partially baked tart shell, bake until light golden brown, about 5 minutes. For a fully baked tart shell, bake until golden brown, 12 to 15 minutes. Cool on the baking sheet on a wire rack.

Salted Peanut and Caramel Tart

**Start to finish: 2½ hours
(1 hour active)**

Makes one 9-inch tart

**FOR THE PEANUT BUTTER–
MERINGUE FILLING AND
TART SHELL:**

188 grams (¾ cup) creamy (smooth)
peanut butter (see headnote)

2 large egg whites

1 teaspoon vanilla extract

Pinch table salt

164 grams (½ cup) corn syrup

107 grams (½ cup) white sugar

Almond tart shell (recipe p. 250)
or whole-wheat tart shell
(recipe p. 256), fully baked

**FOR THE PEANUT-CARAMEL
TOPPING:**

54 grams (¼ cup) white sugar

3 tablespoons heavy cream

2 tablespoons salted butter,
cut into 2 pieces

68 grams (½ cup) dry-roasted,
salted peanuts, roughly chopped

Flaky sea salt, such as Maldon
(optional)

The peanut butter and marshmallow sandwich—the Fluffernutter—
is inarguably all-American. Le Petit Grain, a Parisian boulangerie
headed by Edward Delling-Williams, created a tartlet riff on that
childhood favorite. A cookie-like pastry is filled with peanut butter
meringue that is topped with caramel-coated roasted peanuts. For
ease, we make a single 9-inch tart instead of individual tartlets.
When making the meringue filling, pay attention to the timing in
the recipe, which can be tricky. The whipped egg whites and sugar
syrup need to be ready at the same time. If your egg whites reach
soft peaks before the syrup is ready, reduce the mixer speed to low
while you wait for the syrup to finish; this prevents the whites from
turning dry and stiff. You'll need a candy or instant thermometer for
gauging the doneness of the sugar syrup. The finished tart will keep
at room temperature for up to 12 hours. If you're storing it longer
than an hour or so, wait to add the flaky salt garnish until just before
serving and cover the tart with plastic wrap or foil.

Don't use natural peanut butter (the variety that requires stirring to mix in the oil
on the surface); even the creamy variety of natural peanut butter has a grittiness
that's detectable in the tart filling. Be sure the mixer bowl and whisk attachment for
whipping the meringue are clean; even a trace of grease will prevent the egg whites
from attaining the proper volume.

To make the peanut butter–meringue filling, put the peanut butter in a small
microwave-safe bowl; set aside. In a clean, dry mixer bowl, combine the egg whites,
vanilla and salt, then attach to the mixer along with the whisk attachment. In a
small saucepan, combine the corn syrup, sugar and ¼ cup water. Bring to a boil
over medium-high and cook until the syrup reaches 238°F, 3 to 4 minutes; swirl
the pan once or twice before the syrup reaches a boil. When the syrup has boiled
for 2 minutes, begin whipping the whites on medium and whip until they hold very
soft peaks when the whisk is lifted, about 1 minute. When the syrup reaches 238°F,
remove the pan from the heat and let stand just until the bubbling slows, no more
than 15 seconds. Then with the mixer running on medium-high, slowly pour the
hot syrup into the egg whites, aiming for the area between the whisk and the sides
of the bowl. After all the syrup has been added, continue whipping on medium-high
until the bowl is just warm to the touch, about 3 minutes; do not overbeat.

Meanwhile, microwave the peanut butter on high until pourable, 30 to 60 seconds,
stirring once about halfway through. When the egg whites are ready, reduce the
mixer to low and pour in the peanut butter. Once all the peanut butter is added, stop
the mixer, then fold with a silicone spatula until homogeneous, taking care not to

deflate the whites. Gently pour the filling into the tart shell and spread in an even layer; set aside.

To make the peanut-caramel topping, place 2 tablespoons water in a small saucepan. Carefully pour the sugar into the center of the pan, and stir gently with a clean spoon just until the sugar is evenly moistened. Bring to a boil over medium and cook, gently swirling the pan (do not stir) until the syrup is deep amber-colored and lightly smoking, 5 to 6 minutes. Carefully pour in the cream (the mixture will bubble and steam vigorously), then stir to combine. Add the butter, remove from the heat and stir until the butter is melted and incorporated. Stir the peanuts into the caramel.

Working quickly, pour the caramel mixture evenly over the filling, then use a small spatula to gently spread it to the edges; be careful not to push the peanuts into the filling. Cool to room temperature. To serve, remove the outer metal ring and set the tart on a platter. Sprinkle lightly with flaky salt (if using).

Chocolate-Orange Tart

**Start to finish: 2 hours
(45 minutes active), plus cooling**

Servings: 8

FOR THE TART SHELL:

130 grams (1 cup) all-purpose flour

50 grams (½ cup) almond flour

71 grams (⅓ cup) white sugar

¼ teaspoon table salt

6 tablespoons salted butter,
cut into ½-inch cubes and chilled

1 large egg yolk

1 teaspoon vanilla extract

FOR THE FILLING:

80 grams (6 tablespoons)
white sugar

2 teaspoons grated orange zest
plus 2 tablespoons orange juice

¼ teaspoon table salt

¼ teaspoon cinnamon

1½ cups (12 ounces) whole-milk
ricotta

1 large egg plus 1 large egg yolk

1 teaspoon vanilla extract

1½ ounces semi-sweet chocolate,
chopped

The filling of this tart was inspired by the chocolate, orange and ricotta tart served at Rose Bakery in Paris, but we found the crust in the pastry case of Vancouver's Beaucoup Bakery—a crisp, slightly crunchy almond meal affair that had us at first bite. Rose Carrarini's decadent cheesecake-style filling is made with ricotta, cream, orange zest and dark chocolate, all bound together with a little flour. We added cinnamon and lightened our take, leaving out cream and flour and reducing the amount of chocolate so the ricotta and orange came through more clearly. For the crust, we used all-purpose and almond flours and pressed the dough right into the tart pan (no rolling). The result had great flavor and texture, and it didn't shrink or slump when blind baked. For do-ahead ease, the tart shell can be prepped, pressed into the pan, pricked all over, then frozen for up to two weeks; do not thaw before baking.

Don't use skim-milk ricotta; whole-milk is needed for a rich, creamy consistency. Some ricottas with more lactose will brown more deeply than others. We liked Calabro, which is low in lactose.

Heat the oven to 300°F with a rack in the middle position. Mist a 9-inch tart pan with removable bottom with cooking spray and set on a baking sheet.

To make the tart shell, in a food processor, combine both flours, the sugar and salt; process until combined, about 5 seconds. Scatter the butter over the dry ingredients and pulse until the mixture resembles coarse sand, 10 to 12 times. Add the yolk and vanilla, then process until the mixture is evenly moistened and cohesive, 20 to 30 seconds; the mixture may not form a single mass.

Crumble the dough into the tart pan, evenly covering the surface. Using the bottom of a dry measuring cup, press the dough into an even layer over the bottom and up the sides of the pan. Use a fork to prick all over the bottom and sides, then freeze until firm, at least 15 minutes or up to 1 hour.

Bake on the baking sheet until the tart shell is deep golden brown, 1 to 1¼ hours. Let cool on the baking sheet on a wire rack for 15 minutes. Increase the oven to 350°F.

Meanwhile, prepare the filling. In the food processor, combine the sugar, orange zest, salt and cinnamon; process until the sugar is moistened and fragrant, about 15 seconds. Add the ricotta and process until smooth, about 30 seconds, scraping the bowl as needed. Add the egg, egg yolk, orange juice and vanilla, then process until combined, another 10 to 15 seconds.

Pour the filling into the still-warm crust, then sprinkle evenly with the chocolate. Carefully slide the baking sheet into the oven and bake until the filling is slightly

puffed at the edges but the center still jiggles lightly, 25 to 35 minutes. Let cool
completely on the wire rack, about 2 hours.

If serving the tart at room temperature, remove the outer ring from the tart pan.
If serving the tart chilled, keep the outer ring in place and refrigerate uncovered for
1 hour, or until the chocolate is set, then loosely cover with plastic wrap. Refrigerate
for up to 2 days; remove the outer ring from the pan before serving.

Whole-Wheat Tart Shell

Start to finish: 20 minutes, plus chilling and baking

Makes one 9-inch tart shell

98 grams (¾ cup) all-purpose flour

70 grams (½ cup) whole-wheat flour

54 grams (¼ cup) white sugar

¼ teaspoon table salt

85 grams (6 tablespoons) cold salted butter, cut into ½-inch cubes

1 large egg yolk

1 teaspoon vanilla extract

A little whole-wheat flour lends this otherwise classic pâte sucrée, or tart pastry, a nutty, earthy quality, yet it remains buttery and cookie-like. The whole-wheat flour makes the dough a little tricky to roll out with a rolling pin, so we use a press-in-the-pan method. To ensure the crust is evenly thick, we first press the dough into the sides of the pan, then form the bottom. For prebaking the pastry, either partially or fully, there's no need to use pie weights or line it with foil. Instead, freeze the dough-lined tart pan before baking to prevent slumping and shrinking in the oven. We like this pastry shell for our sunny, bright Lemon-Orange Tart (recipe p. 283), but it's also a perfect choice for richer, heavier fillings containing nuts and/or chocolate, such as our French Walnut Tart (recipe p. 280). To make a savory version, reduce the sugar to 1 tablespoon and eliminate the vanilla. The dough-lined tart pan can be prepared in advance; once the dough is firm, wrap tightly in plastic and freeze for up to two weeks.

Don't forget that the tart pan has a removable bottom, so it cannot be held or supported by its base. It's best to always have the tart pan on a flat surface, such as a baking sheet, and it should be baked on the baking sheet, too, for easy maneuvering in and out of the oven.

Mist a 9-inch tart pan with removable bottom with cooking spray. In a food processor, combine both flours, the sugar and salt. Process until combined, about 5 seconds. Scatter the butter over the dry ingredients and pulse until the mixture resembles coarse sand, 10 to 12 pulses. Add the egg yolk and vanilla, then process in 5- to 10-second bursts until evenly moistened and comes together in large clumps, 45 to 60 seconds; it will not form a single mass, but a small nugget pinched between the fingers should hold together.

Scatter about one-third of the dough mixture around the perimeter of the prepared tart pan, crumbling it as you go. Using your fingers, press the dough into the sides of the pan, forming sidewalls about ¼ inch thick that are level with the rim of the pan. Pile the remaining dough mixture into the center of the pan, then press it into an even layer across the bottom, connecting it to the sidewalls. Use a flat-bottomed object, such as a dry-ingredient measuring cup, to press and smooth the dough. Prick the bottom and sides about every inch or so with a fork. Set the dough-lined pan on a baking sheet and freeze, uncovered, until cold and firm, at least 15 minutes or for up to 1 hour. Meanwhile, heat the oven to 325°F with a rack in the middle position.

Place the baking sheet with the dough-lined tart pan in the oven. For a partially baked tart shell, bake until pale golden brown, 25 to 30 minutes. For a fully baked tart shell, bake until golden brown, 30 to 35 minutes. Cool on the baking sheet on a wire rack.

Hot Water Pie Crust

This easy-to-make pie crust bakes up with a sturdy, sandy texture instead of the flaky layers of standard pie dough. It uses two types of fat: butter for flavor and shortening to help ensure a tender, cookie-like texture. To prevent shrinking and slipping during baking, the foil-lined pie shell is filled with about 2 cups of pie weights. The weights are removed after about 20 minutes, then the pie shell is returned to the oven to allow it to brown all over.

Don't make the dough in advance. It's easiest to work with when just made. Also, don't roll it too thin; aim for ¼-inch thickness. If the dough tears when putting it into the pie plate, simply patch it; it's very forgiving that way.

Heat the oven to 375°F with a rack in the middle position. In a medium bowl, whisk together the flour and salt, then make a well in the center; set aside.

In a small saucepan, combine the butter, shortening and ¼ cup water. Bring to a simmer over medium-high, stirring to melt the solids. As soon as they're melted and the mixture is simmering, pour it into the well of the dry ingredients. Working quickly, stir with a silicone spatula until the dry ingredients are evenly moistened and without any dry patches; the dough will be very soft and resemble wet mashed potatoes. Turn it out onto a large sheet of plastic wrap and, using your hands, form it into a 6- to 8-inch disk.

Cover the dough disk with another large sheet of plastic wrap and roll it into a 12-inch round of even thickness. Peel off the top sheet of plastic. Using the bottom sheet, carefully flip the round into a 9-inch pie plate, centering it as best you can. Ease the dough, still on the plastic, into the corners and up the sides of the pie plate. Carefully peel off the plastic. If needed, patch any tears in the dough. Trim the excess dough and flute or crimp the edge. Carefully line the dough with a large sheet of foil, gently pressing it into the corners and up the sides, then fill with about 2 cups pie weights.

Bake until the dough is set, about 20 minutes. Carefully lift out the foil with weights, then prick the pie shell all over with a fork to deflate any air bubbles and prevent additional ones from forming. Bake until the shell is lightly browned, another 12 to 15 minutes. Transfer to a wire rack and let cool.

Start to finish: 50 minutes (15 minutes active), plus cooling

Makes 1 baked 9-inch pie crust

195 grams (1½ cups) all-purpose flour

¼ teaspoon table salt

57 grams (4 tablespoons) salted butter, cut into pieces

47 grams (¼ cup) vegetable shortening, cut into pieces

Coconut Macaroon Pie

Start to finish: 1 hour 10 minutes (15 minutes active), plus cooling

Servings: 8 to 10

225 grams (2½ cups) shredded unsweetened coconut, divided

14-ounce can coconut milk

214 grams (1 cup) white sugar

1 tablespoon cornstarch

1 tablespoon lime juice

1 teaspoon vanilla extract

¾ teaspoon table salt

4 large eggs

Hot water pie crust (recipe p. 259), baked and cooled

Inspired by the sold-by-the-slice pies that seaside vendors offer in Yelapa, Mexico, food writer and recipe developer Paola Briseño-González created this pay de coco ("coconut pie" in Spanish). She aptly describes the tropical sweet treat as a coconut macaroon in pie form. Both the filling and crust are sturdy enough that a slice can be eaten sans fork, as one would enjoy a piece while out for a walk on the beach in Yelapa. This pie is best served slightly warm or at room temperature rather than chilled. Store extras well wrapped at room temperature for up to three days.

Don't use sweetened shredded coconut or the filling will wind up too sugary. Also, be sure to use regular (full-fat) canned coconut milk; light coconut milk will yield a filling that's watery in both texture and flavor.

Heat the oven to 350°F with a rack in the middle position. In a blender, combine 135 grams (1½ cups) of the shredded coconut, the coconut milk, sugar, cornstarch, lime juice, vanilla and salt. Puree, scraping the blender jar once or twice, until the mixture is as smooth as possible, 1 to 2 minutes. Add the eggs and blend until combined, about 10 seconds.

Pour the puree into a large bowl. Stir in the remaining 90 grams (1 cup) shredded coconut, then pour the mixture into the pie crust. Bake until the filling is lightly browned and puffed at the edges and the center is slightly domed, 55 to 60 minutes.

Cool on a wire rack; the filling will settle during cooling. Serve slightly warm or at room temperature.

CRACKING THE COCONUT CODE

We love the tropical flavor and richness coconut adds to a dish, but supermarkets stock multiple similarly named coconut products, making it difficult to know which to buy.

Coconut Cream
Coconut cream is a thick, rich cream extracted from the grated meat of mature coconuts. It's about 22 percent fat; heavy coconut cream is 30 percent fat. (Don't confuse it with cream of coconut, a sugary ingredient used in cocktails.)

Coconut Milk
Coconut milk is similar to coconut cream but not quite as thick (full-fat coconut milk is about 17 percent fat). It has a more liquid consistency. Canned coconut milk must be shaken and/or stirred before use; the fat solidifies at the top of the can.

Coconut Water
Coconut water is the clear liquid harvested from young, green coconuts. Typically sold as a beverage in shelf-stable cartons, it's mild and slightly sweet, with a subtle savory salinity. We don't generally use it in baking but often use it in place of some or all of the water when cooking rice.

Banana Custard Pie with Caramelized Sugar

Start to finish: 2¼ hours (40 minutes active), plus cooling

Makes one 9-inch pie

1 pound ripe but firm bananas

Hot water pie crust (recipe p. 259), baked and cooled

2 large eggs, plus 1 large egg yolk

¼ cup whole milk

14-ounce can sweetened condensed milk

1 teaspoon vanilla extract

¼ teaspoon table salt

40 grams (3 tablespoons) white sugar (optional, for caramelizing the surface)

Handmade, freshly baked pies sold by the slice are a specialty of the beach town of Yelapa in Jalisco state on Mexico's west coast. Inspired by those Yelapa delights, recipe writer Paola Briseño-González created a simple, rustic banana custard pie with a sturdy, sandy-textured crust. We adapted her recipe, blending a banana into the custard mixture instead of only studding it with slices, for a creamy filling suffused with tropical flavor. If you own a kitchen torch, this pie is a good reason to dig it out. It's an optional step, but sprinkling the baked, cooled pie with sugar and brûléeing it until caramelized elevates the dessert, giving it a crackly-crisp surface and a lovely dappled look. Serve slices with lightly sweetened, softly whipped cream. Covered well, leftovers will keep in the refrigerator for up to three days (though if you caramelized the surface, the sugar crust will gradually soften).

Don't use underripe bananas, but don't use overripe ones, either. The bananas should be ripe so they're sweet and creamy but not so ripe that they're brown and mushy.

Heat the oven to 325°F with a rack in the middle position. Peel the bananas and slice them into ¼-inch rounds. Lay as many slices in the pie shell as will fit in a single, tightly packed layer, then set the pie plate on a rimmed baking sheet. Add the remaining banana slices to a blender, along with the whole eggs plus yolk, milk, condensed milk, vanilla and salt. Blend until smooth, 15 to 30 seconds.

Pour the mixture into the pie shell, taking care not to overfill it (some of the banana slices will rise to the surface); the pie shell may not hold all of the filling, depending on how much it shrank during prebaking. Carefully transfer the baking sheet to the oven and bake until the filling is puffed and lightly browned at the edges and the filling jiggles only slightly when the pie plate is gently shaken, 55 to 65 minutes. Transfer to a wire rack and cool to room temperature.

If caramelizing the surface, sprinkle the sugar evenly onto the cooled pie. Using a kitchen torch, caramelize the sugar until spotty brown. Serve within an hour, before the sugar crust softens. (The pie also is good served chilled, but if caramelizing the sugar, do so just before serving, as refrigeration will soften the sugar crust.)

Yelapa-Style Sweet Corn Pie

We're big fans of desserts made with sweet corn. Whether in a cake, pudding or custard, the delicate grassy notes of fresh corn pair wonderfully with sugar, eggs and dairy. This unusual pie, developed by food writer Paola Briseño-González, was inspired by the pay de elote (corn pie, translated from the Spanish) sold by the slice in the beach town of Yelapa, Mexico. There, roaming vendors offer treats meant to be eaten on the spot, without the aid of utensils. Fresh corn kernels cut from peak-season just-shucked ears is, of course, best, as their flavor is sweet and texture tender; you'll need three ears to yield the 2½ cups kernels needed for the recipe. Out of season, frozen corn kernels will work, but be sure to fully thaw them before use and pat them dry with paper towels to remove excess moisture. Serve the pie at room temperature or chilled, with or without forks. Store leftovers in the refrigerator for up to three days.

Don't be shy about pressing on the corn puree with the back of a spoon or silicone spatula to extract as much liquid—and flavor—as possible.

Heat the oven to 325°F with a rack in the middle position. In a blender, combine the corn, milk, eggs, sugar and cornstarch. Blend until smooth, about 1 minute.

Set a fine-mesh strainer over a large bowl. Pour the puree into the strainer and press on the solids with a silicone spatula to extract as much liquid as possible; discard the solids. Stir in the lemon juice, vanilla and salt, then pour the mixture into the pie crust. Bake until the filling jiggles only slightly when the pie is gently shaken, 55 to 60 minutes.

Cool completely on a wire rack. Serve at room temperature or refrigerate for about 2 hours (cover if refrigerating longer) and serve chilled.

Start to finish: 1 hour 10 minutes (15 minutes active), plus cooling

Servings: 8 to 10

394 grams (2½ cups) corn kernels (see headnote)

1 cup whole milk

4 large eggs

107 grams (½ cup) white sugar

2 tablespoons cornstarch

1 teaspoon lemon juice

1 teaspoon vanilla extract

¼ teaspoon table salt

Hot water pie crust (recipe p. 259), baked and cooled

Fresh Peach and Raspberry Crostata

**Start to finish: 2 hours
(40 minutes active), plus cooling**

Servings: 8

130 grams (1 cup) all-purpose flour,
plus more for dusting

5 tablespoons white sugar, divided

½ teaspoon table salt, plus a pinch

141 grams (10 tablespoons) cold
salted butter, cut in ½-inch cubes

3½ tablespoons ice water

2 teaspoons grated lemon zest

1 pound (3 medium) ripe but firm
peaches or nectarines, halved, pitted
and cut into ¼-inch wedges

6-ounce container raspberries
(1¼ cups)

This rustic free-form tart is a beautifully delicious way to showcase sweet, summery peaches (or nectarines) and ripe, plump berries. We take a minimalist approach to the filling and mix the fruits with only white sugar, grated lemon zest and a pinch of salt; we skip the spices and thickeners that blunt delicate floral flavors and aromas. The crust that encases the filling is especially high in butter, but it comes together with remarkable ease in a food processor and handles beautifully. After rolling the dough into a round, we dust the surface with a light layer of sugar, then invert the dough sugared side down onto the baking sheet. The sugar coating helps the pastry bake up with a shattering crispness that, along with its rich, buttery flavor, perfectly complements the succulent fruits. We especially like raspberries in this tart, but if you prefer, feel free to substitute blackberries or blueberries. And if you wish to change up the citrus, try orange zest in place of the lemon zest. Serve warm or at room temperature. Ice cream, gelato or lightly sweetened whipped cream are perfect embellishments.

Don't allow the butter to soften before use. Keep the cubes in the refrigerator until the moment you add them to the food processor. When rolling out the dough, if at any point it becomes soft, don't hesitate to put it on a parchment-lined baking sheet and into the refrigerator to cool and firm up. Lastly, don't assemble the filling until the dough is rolled and ready because the sugar will begin to draw out the fruits' juices as soon as they're combined.

In a food processor, combine the flour, 1 tablespoon of the sugar and ½ teaspoon of the salt. Pulse 3 or 4 times to combine. Scatter about 42 grams (3 tablespoons) butter over the flour mixture and process until the butter is well incorporated, 15 to 20 seconds. Scatter in the remaining butter and pulse until it is broken down to pieces about the size of peas, 10 to 12 pulses. Drizzle the ice water over the mixture and pulse until the mixture comes together in large, curdy clumps, 12 to 15 pulses.

Turn the dough out onto the counter. Gather and press it firmly into a disk about 5 inches in diameter. Wrap tightly in plastic, smoothing out any rough edges and forming the disk into a neat round so it will be easier to roll into an even circle. Refrigerate for at least 1 hour or up to 2 days.

When you are ready to bake, heat the oven to 450°F with a rack in the lowest position. Line a rimmed baking sheet with kitchen parchment.

STEPS »

1. In a food processor, combine the flour, 1 tablespoon sugar and ½ teaspoon salt. Scatter 3 tablespoons butter over the mixture.

2. Process until the pieces of butter are incorporated and the mixture resembles finely ground almonds, 15 to 20 seconds.

3. Scatter the remaining 7 tablespoons of chilled butter over the mixture, distributing it as evenly as possible.

4. Pulse the mixture until the largest bits of butter are pea-sized and the mixture resembles damp sand, 10 to 12 pulses.

5. Drizzle ice water over the mixture to keep the butter from melting and fully incorporating into the dough, ensuring a flaky crust.

6. Pulse until the mixture is evenly moistened and forms clumps, 12 to 15 pulses.

If the dough is too firm to roll out, let it stand at room temperature for 5 to 10 minutes until malleable. Lightly flour the counter, unwrap the dough and set it on the floured surface. Dust the dough with flour and, using a rolling pin, roll it into an 11-inch circle of even thickness, lightly dusting with flour as needed to prevent sticking. Sprinkle 1 tablespoon of the remaining sugar on the dough and, using your hands, spread the sugar into an even layer all the way to the edges. Continue to roll the dough, pressing the sugar into the dough, until the circle is 12 inches in diameter.

Flip the dough, sugared side down, onto the center of the prepared baking sheet; it's fine if the edges of the circle slightly climb up the sides of the baking sheet. If the dough is very soft at this point, lay a sheet of plastic wrap against the surface and refrigerate for a few minutes to firm it up, or for up to 24 hours. (If refrigerated until very cold and stiff, let stand at room temperature until the dough is pliable but still cool.)

In a large bowl, combine the remaining 3 tablespoons sugar, remaining pinch of salt and lemon zest. Using your fingers, rub the zest into the sugar until the sugar is evenly moistened. Add the peaches and berries, then toss to combine.

Mound the fruit mixture in the center of the dough, keeping 1½ to 2 inches around the edge uncovered. Working in one direction around the circumference of the dough, fold the edge toward the center and up onto the filling, pleating it at intervals as you go. Gently press the pleats so they remain in place. Refrigerate, uncovered, for 10 to 15 minutes (no longer or the fruit may begin to release too much juice).

Bake until the crust is deep golden brown, 25 to 30 minutes, rotating the baking sheet about halfway through. Let the crostata cool on the baking sheet on a wire rack for about 15 minutes.

Slide a wide metal spatula under the crostata to loosen it from the parchment and transfer it to a platter. Serve warm or at room temperature.

VARIATION

Three-Berry Crostata

Follow the recipe to make, roll and refrigerate the dough. In a large bowl, combine the remaining 3 tablespoons sugar, remaining pinch of salt and lemon zest. Using your fingers, rub the zest into the sugar until the sugar is evenly moistened. Add a **6-ounce container (1¼ cups) each of blackberries, raspberries and blueberries;** toss to combine. Continue with the recipe to fill and bake the crostata.

Peanut Butter Banana Cream Pie

This show-stopping twist on banana cream pie comes to us by way of Chris Taylor and Paul Arguin, authors of "The New Pie." Their three-layer creation, in a peanut and graham cracker crust, elevates the classic diner delight with a salty-sweet peanut butter base, as well as a striking brown sugar meringue topping. Sandwiched between them is a silky-smooth banana cream filling lightened by fluffy whipped cream. For best flavor and texture, make sure your bananas are nice and ripe—the exteriors should show lots of brown spots. Also, opt for regular creamy peanut butter, such as Skippy or Peter Pan. We found that "natural" peanut butter—that is, the type that separates on standing and requires mixing before use—tends to result in a filling with a gritty, granular feel. You can easily prepare the graham cracker crust, peanut butter layer and banana pastry cream ahead of time—just hold off on making and decorating with the meringue until you're ready to serve the pie.

Don't worry if you don't have a kitchen torch to brown the meringue. Heat the oven broiler with a rack 10 inches from the element. Slide the pie into the oven, leaving the door ajar; watch carefully to prevent scorching, broiling just until the meringue reaches your desired level of toasting.

To make the banana cream layer, in a small saucepan, combine the bananas, milk and 1 cup plus 2 tablespoons heavy cream. Bring to a boil over medium-high, stirring occasionally, 3 to 4 minutes; remove from the heat. Cover immediately with the pan lid and cool to room temperature, about 45 minutes, then refrigerate until cold, at least 1 hour.

Gently stir the chilled banana mixture. Strain it through a fine-mesh sieve set over a medium saucepan, shaking the sieve to encourage the liquid to drain off (you should have about 2 cups strained liquid); do not press on the bananas. Discard the bananas in the sieve. Into the liquid, whisk the cornstarch, followed by the white sugar, salt, whole egg and egg yolks.

Set the pan over medium and bring the mixture to a simmer, whisking constantly, then cook, whisking constantly, until very thick, about 2 minutes. Off heat, add the butter and vanilla; whisk until well combined.

Strain the banana cream mixture through a fine-mesh sieve set over a large bowl. Push it through with a silicone spatula, then scrape the bottom of the sieve to collect any pastry cream that clings. Press a piece of kitchen parchment directly against the surface and refrigerate until cold, at least 3 hours or up to 12 hours.

Start to finish: 1½ hours, plus several hours for cooling and chilling

Servings: 8 to 10

FOR THE BANANA CREAM LAYER:

2 very ripe medium bananas, peeled and cut into 1-inch chunks

1¼ cups whole milk

1 cup plus 2 tablespoons heavy cream, plus ⅓ cup cold heavy cream, for whipping

33 grams (¼ cup) cornstarch

120 grams (½ cup plus 1 tablespoon) white sugar

¼ teaspoon table salt

1 large egg, plus 3 large egg yolks

57 grams (4 tablespoons) unsalted butter, cut into 4 pieces

1 teaspoon vanilla extract

FOR THE CRUST:

68 grams (½ cup) roasted salted peanuts

40 grams (3 tablespoons) white sugar

144 grams (9 sheets) graham crackers

85 grams (6 tablespoons) unsalted butter, melted, still warm

FOR THE PEANUT BUTTER LAYER:

4 ounces (113 grams) cream cheese, room temperature

125 grams (½ cup) creamy peanut butter (see headnote)

62 grams (½ cup) powdered sugar

⅛ teaspoon table salt

½ cup cold heavy cream

45 grams (⅓ cup) roasted salted peanuts, chopped

INGREDIENTS CONT. >>

3 large egg whites

145 grams (⅔ cup) packed light brown sugar

⅛ teaspoon table salt

½ teaspoon vanilla extract

To make the crust, heat the oven to 350°F with the rack in the middle position. In a food processor, process the peanuts and white sugar until finely ground, about 30 seconds. Add the graham crackers, breaking them into pieces, and pulse until finely ground, 8 to 10 pulses. Add the melted butter and process until evenly moistened, 10 to 12 pulses.

Transfer the mixture to a 9-inch deep-dish pie plate. Distribute it evenly across the bottom and up the sides of the plate. Use a flat-bottomed ramekin or dry measuring cup to firmly press the crumbs into an even layer in the bottom and up the sides of the pie plate. Freeze uncovered for about 10 minutes.

Bake the chilled crust until lightly browned at the edges, 10 to 12 minutes. Transfer to a wire rack and cool completely, about 30 minutes.

To make the peanut butter layer, in a stand mixer with the paddle attachment, beat the cream cheese on medium until smooth, about 30 seconds. Add the peanut butter, powdered sugar and salt; beat on medium, scraping the bowl as needed, until just barely combined, 15 to 20 seconds; do not overbeat. Fold the mixture a few times by hand, scraping the bottom and side of the bowl to ensure no large pockets of cream cheese remain.

In a medium bowl, whip the cream with a hand mixer or by hand with a whisk until it holds firm peaks. Using a silicone spatula, fold the whipped cream into the peanut butter mixture until no streaks remain. Fold in the peanuts, then scrape the mixture into the cooled crust and spread in an even layer. Refrigerate, uncovered, until chilled, about 1 hour.

To finish the banana cream layer, remove the pastry cream from the refrigerator. In a medium bowl, whip the remaining ⅓ cup cream with a hand mixer or by hand with a whisk until it holds firm peaks. Using the hand mixer or whisk, whip the chilled pastry cream until smooth. Fold the whipped cream into the pastry cream until well combined. Evenly spread the banana cream layer on top of the peanut butter layer. Refrigerate uncovered while you prepare the meringue or cover and refrigerate for up to 12 hours.

To make the meringue, in a medium saucepan, bring about 1 inch of water to a bare simmer. In the bowl of a stand mixer, combine the egg whites, brown sugar and salt. Set the bowl over the saucepan; make sure the bottom does not touch the water. Whisk constantly until the sugar has dissolved and the mixture reaches 160°F on an instant thermometer, 3 to 4 minutes; it will be frothy and almost doubled in volume.

Add the vanilla and attach the bowl to the stand mixer along with the whisk attachment. Beat on medium-high until the meringue holds stiff peaks, about 5 minutes; it's fine if the meringue is still slightly warm. Remove the pie from the refrigerator and spread or, using a large pastry bag fitted with a pastry tip, pipe the meringue onto the banana cream layer. Using a kitchen torch, toast the meringue until caramelized in spots. Serve immediately or refrigerate for up to 2 hours.

Kirsch-Spiked Whipped Cream

Start to finish: 5 minutes
Makes about 3 cups

In the bowl of a stand mixer fitted with the whisk attachment or in a large bowl if using a hand mixer, combine **1 cup cold heavy cream, 60 grams (¼ cup) cold sour cream, 1½ tablespoons white sugar** and **1 teaspoon kirsch.** Mix on low until uniform and frothy, about 30 seconds. Increase to medium-high and whip until soft peaks form, 1 to 2 minutes. Use right away or cover and refrigerate for up to 2 hours.

Brandied Cherry Frangipane Tart

In French baking, frangipane is a mixture of nuts (most commonly almonds), sugar, egg, flour and butter blended to a paste. It's used as a base or filling for a variety of different baked treats, from cakes to croissants. We stud frangipane with dried sour cherries soaked in brandy to make a tart filling perfectly complemented by a sandy-crisp almond flour crust. We prefer to use blanched sliced almonds, so the skins are not visible in the frangipane, but if they're not available, regular sliced almonds work perfectly well. We liked this served warm, topped with whipped cream—sweetened or not—but it's equally delicious at room temperature. Leftovers keep for up to two days in an airtight container at room temperature.

Don't use Kirschwasser in place of the brandy; it will make the filling too sweet.

In a small saucepan, combine the cherries, brandy and 1 tablespoon water. Bring to a simmer over medium-low, then transfer to a large bowl and cool to room temperature, about 30 minutes; the cherries should soak up almost all the liquid. Meanwhile, heat the oven to 350°F with a rack in the middle position.

In a food processor, combine the 93 grams (1 cup) almonds, the sugar, flour and salt. Process until finely ground, about 1 minute. Add the butter and process until just combined, about 30 seconds. Add the egg and both extracts, then process until smooth and well-incorporated, about 10 seconds. Transfer to the bowl with the cherries and fold just until combined.

Place the tart shell, still on a rimmed baking sheet, in the oven; warm for 5 to 10 minutes. Remove from the oven and immediately pour in the almond-cherry mixture. Spread in an even layer and sprinkle the remaining 3 tablespoons almonds on top, around the perimeter. Bake until the top is puffed and golden brown, 30 to 35 minutes.

Cool on the baking sheet on a wire rack for at least 30 minutes. To serve, remove the outer metal ring and set the tart on a platter.

Start to finish: 2 hours (45 minutes active), plus cooling

Makes one 9-inch tart

113 grams (¾ cup) dried sour cherries

3 tablespoons brandy

93 grams (1 cup) sliced almonds, plus 3 tablespoons for sprinkling (see headnote)

71 grams (⅓ cup) white sugar

1 tablespoon all-purpose flour

⅛ teaspoon table salt

85 grams (6 tablespoons) salted butter, cut into ½-inch pieces, room temperature

1 large egg

1 teaspoon vanilla extract

¾ teaspoon almond extract

Almond tart shell (recipe p. 250), fully baked on a rimmed baking sheet

Chocolate-Hazelnut (Gianduja) Crostata

**Start to finish: 1¼ hours
(45 minutes active), plus cooling**

Makes one 9-inch crostata

163 grams (1¼ cups) hazelnuts

65 grams (½ cup) all-purpose flour

35 grams (¼ cup) whole-wheat flour

214 grams (1 cup) white sugar, divided

¼ teaspoon baking powder

Table salt

85 grams (6 tablespoons) cold salted butter, cut into ½-inch cubes

1 large egg yolk, plus 3 large egg whites

2½ teaspoons vanilla extract, divided

4 ounces bittersweet chocolate, chopped

1 teaspoon instant espresso powder

The chewy, rich filling for this dessert was inspired by gianduja, a chocolate-hazelnut paste that originates in Turin, Italy. The crust, made with whole-wheat flour, is simply pressed into the bottom of a springform pan; its nuttiness pairs perfectly with the intense filling. If you like, dust the baked crostata with powdered sugar before serving, or top slices with unsweetened whipped cream or crème fraîche. The crostata is best served the same day, but leftovers can be covered in plastic wrap and refrigerated overnight; bring to room temperature before serving.

Don't underprocess the hazelnut and sugar mixture. Grinding it until fine and paste-like is key to the filling's thick, decadent texture.

Heat the oven to 375°F with a rack in the lowest position. Mist a 9-inch springform pan with cooking spray. Spread the hazelnuts on a rimmed baking sheet, then toast until deep golden brown, about 10 minutes, stirring once about halfway through. Remove from the oven; leave the oven on.

In a food processor, combine both flours, 54 grams (¼ cup) sugar, the baking powder and ⅛ teaspoon salt. Process until combined, about 5 seconds. Scatter the butter over the mixture and pulse until it resembles coarse sand, 10 to 12 pulses. Add the egg yolk and ½ teaspoon vanilla, then process until evenly moistened and clumping together, 20 to 30 seconds.

Transfer the dough to the prepared pan; reserve the food processor bowl and blade. Press the dough into an even layer and prick with a fork about every ½ inch. Bake until golden in the center and slightly darker at the edges, 15 to 20 minutes. Meanwhile, enclose the nuts in a kitchen towel and rub vigorously to remove the skins; set aside.

In a small microwave-safe bowl, microwave the chocolate on 50 percent power, stirring every 30 seconds, until melted and smooth; set aside.

In the food processor, pulse the hazelnuts until roughly chopped, about 8 pulses; measure out ¼ cup and set aside. Add the remaining 160 grams (¾ cup) sugar and process until the nuts are finely ground and the mixture resembles damp sand, about 2 minutes. Scrape the bowl. Add the egg whites, the remaining 2 teaspoons vanilla, the espresso powder and ¼ teaspoon salt. Process until smooth, about 10 seconds. Add the melted chocolate and process until incorporated, about 10 seconds, scraping the bowl as needed.

STEPS »

1. Wrap the toasted hazelnuts in a towel, then rub to remove the skins.

5. Prick all over with a fork to allow steam to escape and keep the crust flat.

9. After processing in the chocolate, the filling's texture should be smooth.

Spread the hazelnut-chocolate mixture in an even layer on the crust, then sprinkle the reserved chopped nuts around the perimeter. Bake until slightly puffed and the edges begin to crack, 20 to 25 minutes.

Let cool in the pan on a wire rack until the edges pull away from the sides of the pan, about 15 minutes. Remove the pan sides. Serve warm or room temperature.

2. Pulse the butter and dry ingredients until they look like coarse, wet sand.

3. Process in the eggs and vanilla until the dough clumps and coats the bowl.

4. Press the dough into a smooth, even layer on the bottom of the pan.

6. Bake the crust until the edges are golden brown. The center will be lighter.

7. Pulse the hazelnuts until roughly chopped. Reserve ¼ cup.

8. Process the remaining nuts and sugar tp a wet sand-like texture.

10. Scatter the reserved nuts around the perimeter of the unbaked crostata.

11. A perfectly baked crostata will have a brownie-like appearance.

12. If baked too long, the hazelnuts and filling will overbrown.

Pies and Puddings

French Walnut Tart

**Start to finish: 2¼ hours
(20 minutes active)**

Makes one 9-inch tart

107 grams (½ cup) white sugar

84 grams (¼ cup) honey

77 grams (⅓ cup) crème fraîche

57 grams (4 tablespoons) salted
butter, cut into 3 or 4 pieces

1 tablespoon cider vinegar

⅛ teaspoon table salt

220 grams (2 cups) walnuts,
roughly chopped

Whole-wheat tart shell
(recipe p. 256), partially baked
on a rimmed baking sheet

2 large egg yolks

Flaky sea salt, to serve (optional)

This simple tart, called tarte aux noix, is from the Perigord region of southwestern France, an area known for its walnuts. A cookie-like pastry shell is filled with the rich, subtly bitter nuts and buttery caramel. Our version tones down what often is cloying sweetness with a small measure of crème fraîche and a dose of cider vinegar (you won't detect it in the finished dessert). The small measure of whole-wheat flour in the crust plays up the earthiness of the walnuts. Be sure to partially bake the tart shell before use and rewarm it as indicated before pouring in the filling; this will set the filling more quickly, which will help guard against sogginess. The tart is superb lightly sprinkled with flaky sea salt and accompanied by crème fraîche or unsweetened whipped cream.

Don't overcook the caramel. Aim for an amber hue; if it gets much darker than that, the finished tart will taste bitter.

Add ¼ cup water to a medium saucepan. Add the sugar and honey to the center, avoiding contact with the sides. Cook over medium, swirling the pan often, until amber, about 8 minutes. Off heat, add the crème fraîche, butter, vinegar and table salt, then whisk until the butter is melted and the mixture is well combined. Cool until just warm, about 30 minutes.

Meanwhile, heat the oven to 325°F with a rack in the lower-middle position. Distribute the walnuts on a rimmed baking sheet. Toast in the oven until fragrant and lightly browned, about 8 minutes, stirring once or twice. Transfer to a plate and cool. Leave the oven on.

When the caramel mixture has cooled until warm, place the tart shell, still on a rimmed baking sheet, in the oven; warm for 5 to 10 minutes. Meanwhile, whisk the egg yolks into the caramel mixture, then add the nuts and stir until evenly coated.

Remove the tart shell from the oven, immediately pour in the nut mixture and gently spread in an even layer. Bake until the edges of the filling begin to puff and the center jiggles only slightly when gently shaken, 25 to 35 minutes.

Cool the tart on the baking sheet on a wire rack for about 1 hour. Remove the pan sides. Serve warm or at room temperature, sprinkled with sea salt, if desired.

CHOCOLATE CHOICES

Chocolate needs little introduction, but selecting the right type to use in a baked good can mean the difference between good and great. This primer briefly explains the varieties of chocolate called for in this book.

Chocolate Chips

Most supermarket chocolate chips contain stabilizers that help the morsels hold their shape during baking, are lower in cocoa butter than bar chocolate, and tend to be too sweet. For these reasons—and despite the convenience they offer—we do not recommend using chocolate chips in baked goods that call for chopped bar chocolate unless the recipe specifically indicates they are fine to use. Even when making chocolate chip cookies, we opt for good-quality dark or bittersweet chocolate chips or chunks. And for best flavor and texture, we prefer to chop bar chocolate with a knife. The resulting bits are always uneven and inevitably we end up with fine, dusty particles, but this lends character to the cookies.

Cocoa Powder

When we call for cocoa powder, we mean the unsweetened variety, not cocoa with added sugar. In general, there are two varieties of cocoa powder: natural and Dutch-processed. Both are made by roasting, then grinding cacao beans, but Dutch-processed cocoa is treated with an alkali, which neutralizes the cacao's natural astringency, resulting in smoother flavor and a deeper, darker color. Black or extra-dark cocoa is Dutch-processed cocoa taken to the extreme; its color is intensely dark, almost black. In some baked goods, natural and Dutch-processed cocoa are interchangeable; in others, it's important to use the variety indicated in order to obtain the desired leavening, color and/or flavor. In our recipes, we specify one or the other if it is important for success. Shopping can be tricky, however, as packages are not always clearly labeled. When in doubt, check the ingredients list—Dutch-processed cocoa likely will read "cocoa processed with alkali" and natural cocoa will list "cocoa powder" as the only ingredient. For information about cacao powder and whether it can be used in place of cocoa powder, see Cacao vs. Cocoa, (p. 393).

Milk, Semi-Sweet and Bittersweet Chocolates

The greater the cocoa content of chocolate, the darker, more bitter and robust its flavor. Milk chocolate is on the mild end of the spectrum, and it features a creamy sweetness that makes it a favorite for eating out of hand. Semi-sweet and bittersweet chocolate both fall under the umbrella of "dark chocolate," but semi-sweet is the milder, sweeter-tasting, more creamy-textured of the two.

Bittersweet chocolate packs a bold, well, bittersweetness and can be quite intense if it's on the far end of the cocoa-solid spectrum. It's the variety we often lean on to deliver deep, rich chocolate flavor. Unsweetened chocolate, as its name indicates, does not contain any added sugar; we rarely use this in baking.

White Chocolate

White chocolate is made with cocoa butter but contains no cocoa solids, hence its ivory color and the reason detractors contend that white chocolate does not actually qualify as chocolate. Its flavor is sweet, milky with vanilla undertones, and has none of the roasty bitterness of dark chocolate; its texture is buttery, unctuous and eminently melty. Note that products labeled "white baking wafers," "white morsels" or "white melting chips" contain no cocoa butter and are made entirely of palm oil, which is more stable at room temperature than cocoa butter, but lacks flavor nuances.

Lemon-Orange Tart

A classic lemon tart requires making a stovetop curd, and too often its flavor winds up harsh and puckery. We found an easier, better way—no stovetop stirring required. We temper the brassiness of lemon with sweeter, gentler orange and simply combine sugar, zest, juice and eggs in a bowl. A little heavy cream softens the sharpness of the citrus. We pour the mixture into a warm prebaked tart shell, then bake it for about 30 minutes. Added to a warm pastry shell, the filling sets more quickly, which helps prevent the crust from becoming soft and soggy. The flavors are boldest if the tart is served at room temperature, but the dessert is more refreshing when lightly chilled. Either way, lightly sweetened whipped cream is a perfect accompaniment.

Don't use bottled citrus juice. Freshly squeezed juices are essential for bright, bracing flavor. Be sure to strain the juices, too, to remove any seeds and bits of pulp. When making the filling, whisk gently, not vigorously, to avoid aeration.

Heat the oven to 325°F with a rack in the middle position. In a medium bowl, combine the sugar, both zests and the salt. Using your fingers, rub the zest into the sugar until fragrant and the mixture begins to clump. Add the whole eggs and yolks; whisk gently just until combined (avoid aerating the mixture). Whisk in the cream and both juices.

Place the tart shell, still on a rimmed baking sheet, in the oven; warm for 5 to 10 minutes. Remove from the oven and immediately add the filling. Bake until the center of the filling jiggles slightly, 25 to 30 minutes.

Cool completely on the baking sheet on a wire rack. The tart can be served at room temperature or chilled. To chill, refrigerate uncovered for 2 hours; if refrigerating for longer (the tart will keep for up to 2 days), tent with foil after about 2 hours. To serve, remove the outer metal ring and set the tart on a platter.

Start to finish: 1 hour 40 minutes (25 minutes active), plus cooling

Makes one 9-inch tart

161 grams (¾ cup) white sugar

2 tablespoons grated lemon zest, plus ½ cup lemon juice

1 teaspoon grated orange zest, plus ¼ cup orange juice

Pinch of table salt

3 large eggs, plus 3 large egg yolks

½ cup heavy cream

Almond tart shell (recipe p. 250) or whole-wheat tart shell (recipe p. 256), fully baked on a rimmed baking sheet

Streusel-Topped Cherry Jam Tart

**Start to finish: 1 hour
(20 minutes active), plus cooling**

Makes one 9-inch tart

71 grams (⅓ cup) white sugar

3 teaspoons grated lemon zest,
divided, plus 1 tablespoon lemon
juice

228 grams (1¾ cups)
all-purpose flour

48 grams (⅓ cup) fine
yellow cornmeal

¼ teaspoon table salt

141 grams (10 tablespoons) cold
salted butter, cut into ½-inch cubes

1 large egg, plus 1 large egg yolk,
lightly beaten

400 grams (1¼ cups) cherry jam

½ teaspoon ground black pepper

Powdered sugar, to serve

This rustic tart is a breeze to prepare with a few pantry staples. The dough, which comes together quickly in a food processor, is dual purpose. Pressed into a tart pan, it forms the bottom crust and, pinched into small bits and scattered onto the filling, bakes into a buttery streusel topping. A little cornmeal in the dough adds textural interest and subtly sweet corn flavor. Just about any type of fruit jam or preserves works well. We particularly like cherry jam, but seedless raspberry preserves and marmalade are great options, too. A little black pepper mixed into the preserves offers a hint of savoriness that balances the sweetness. A scoop of vanilla gelato or ice cream would be a perfect flourish.

Don't worry about being exact when measuring the 1 cup of dough that will form the streusel topping. A little more or less won't make a difference.

Heat the oven to 375°F with a rack in the lowest position. Mist a 9-inch tart pan with a removable bottom with cooking spray.

In a food processor, combine the sugar and 1½ teaspoons of the lemon zest. Process until fragrant and the sugar is moistened, about 15 seconds. Add the flour, cornmeal and salt; process until combined, about 5 seconds. Scatter the butter over the dry ingredients and pulse until the mixture resembles coarse sand, 10 to 12 pulses. Add the beaten whole egg and yolk, then process until the mixture is evenly moistened and begins to clump together, 20 to 30 seconds.

Transfer about 1 cup of the dough mixture to a small bowl; set aside for the streusel. Scatter about one-third of the remaining dough mixture around the perimeter of the prepared tart pan, crumbling it as you go. Using your fingers, press the dough into the sides of the pan, forming sidewalls about ¼ inch thick that are level with the rim of the pan. Pile the remaining dough mixture into the center of the pan, then press it into an even layer across the bottom, connecting it to the sidewalls. Use a flat-bottomed object such as a dry-ingredient measuring cup to press and smooth the dough. Set the tart pan on a rimmed baking sheet.

In a small bowl, stir together the jam, the remaining 1½ teaspoons lemon zest, the lemon juice and pepper. Spread in an even layer in the dough-lined pan. Form the reserved dough into streusel by squeezing bits between your fingers to form cohesive clumps, then crumble and break the clumps into bits of various sizes, scattering them over the jam mixture. Bake until the crust is golden brown and the filling is bubbling in spots, 40 to 45 minutes.

Let the tart cool on the baking sheet on a wire rack for about 1 hour. Remove the pan sides. Serve warm or at room temperature. Dust with powdered sugar just before serving.

Tarte Tatin

Tarte tatin is made by baking apples in sugar under a blanket of pastry, then inverting the tart out of the pan for serving to reveal a stunner of a dessert: velvety, caramel-soaked fruits atop a tender, buttery crust. Said to have been invented by accident by the Tatin sisters in the late 19th century, the rustic tart is a now a classic. For our version, we add a little maple syrup to the sugar mixture; it helps the granules dissolve while also adding subtle woodsy notes that pair perfectly with the apples. Honeycrisp is the apple variety of choice, as the fruits strike a perfect balance of sweet and tangy. And though they soften with cooking, their texture does not turn mealy or mushy. Galas are the runner-up. (See below for variations with pears or peaches.) Many tarte tatin recipes use puff pastry as the crust, but we prefer our homemade pie pastry. It's crisp, flaky and rich in butter, with a sturdiness that can handle the generous caramel and fruit. You will need an oven-safe 10-inch skillet. We caution against cast-iron, as its dark color cooks and bakes differently than a standard skillet and its heft makes it tricky to unmold the tart. Serve warm or at room temperature with vanilla ice cream or gelato or with lightly sweetened whipped cream.

Don't allow the tart to cool for longer than 10 to 15 minutes after removing it from the oven. If the caramel begins to set, it will prevent the tart from unmolding neatly from the pan. If this happens, however, set the skillet over low heat for 30 to 60 seconds to rewarm and loosen the caramel, then try unmolding again.

Dust a sheet of kitchen parchment with flour, set the pie dough on top and dust it with flour. If the dough is too firm to roll, let stand at room temperature for 5 to 10 minutes. Roll the dough into a 10-inch circle about ¼ inch thick. Cut four 1-inch slits in the center that will allow steam to vent (the slits will not be visible in the finished tart), then lay a sheet of plastic wrap against the dough. Slide the parchment with dough onto a baking sheet and refrigerate until ready.

Peel the apples, then cut each into 4 wedges. Using a paring knife, notch out the core from each piece, then cut each wedge in half lengthwise. Heat the oven to 375°F with a rack in the middle position. In a 10-inch oven-safe skillet over medium, melt the butter, then add the sugar and maple syrup; stir with a silicone spatula until the sugar is evenly moistened.

Remove the pan from the heat and arrange most of the apples cut side down and facing the same direction in a tightly packed ring around the circumference the pan, slightly overlapping the wedges. Tuck the remaining wedges into gaps, then sprinkle evenly with the salt.

Start to finish: 1½ hours (35 minutes active)

Makes one 9-inch tart

All-purpose flour, for dusting

Flaky Pie Pastry (p. 244), in a 4½-inch disk and refrigerated (not rolled and fit into a pie plate)

2¼ to 2½ pounds (4 to 6 medium) Honeycrisp apples

57 grams (4 tablespoons) salted butter, cut into 4 or 5 chunks

143 grams (⅔ cup) white sugar

2 tablespoons maple syrup

¼ teaspoon table salt

VARIATION

Peach Tarte Tatin

Follow the recipe to roll out and refrigerate the dough. Halve and pit **2¼ to 2½ pounds (4 to 6 medium) ripe but firm peaches,** then cut each half into 4 wedges. Continue with the recipe to heat the oven and prepare the caramel and fruit, using the peaches in place of the apples; arrange the wedges cut side down and facing the same direction in a tightly packed ring around the circumference of the pan. Arrange the remaining wedges in the center. Cook on the stovetop, bake and unmold as directed.

Set the pan over medium-high and bring to a vigorous simmer. Reduce to medium and cook, without stirring, until the apples release some juice and the liquid forms a bubbly, amber-colored caramel that submerges the fruit about halfway, 25 to 30 minutes; occasionally rotate the pan if you notice hot spots, but do not stir. Remove the pan from the heat.

Working quickly, remove the pastry from the refrigerator. Carefully place the pastry on top of the apples and, using a silicone spatula, tuck the edges into the skillet. Bake until the crust is deep golden brown and the caramel has begun to bubble at the edges, 40 to 50 minutes. Carefully remove the skillet from the oven (the handle will be hot) and set it on a wire rack; let rest for 10 to 15 minutes.

Run the silicone spatula between the sides of the pan and the crust to loosen. Invert a heatproof platter that's about 12 inches in diameter onto the skillet and, using two potholders, hold the two together while carefully inverting them, then lift off the skillet. If needed, carefully reposition any pieces of fruit that were dislodged. Serve warm or at room temperature.

Pear Tarte Tatin

Follow the recipe to roll out and refrigerate the dough. Peel **2¼ to 2½ pounds (4 to 6 medium) ripe but firm Bosc pears,** then cut each one lengthwise into quarters. Using a paring knife, notch out the core from each quarter and slice off the tough center fiber that runs the length the fruit. Continue with the recipe to heat the oven and prepare the caramel and fruit, using the pears in place of the apples; arrange the pieces cut side down and facing the same direction in a tightly packed pinwheel pattern around the circumference of the pan (the narrow end of the pears should point toward the center of the pan). Cut the remaining pears in half crosswise and arrange them in the center. Cook on the stovetop, bake and unmold as directed.

Italian-Style Apple Strudel

Many associate strudel only with Austria, but it also is common in northern Italy's Trentino-Alto Adige region. For this version, we were inspired by the ingredients traditionally used there: golden raisins, citrus zest, pine nuts and, of course, apples. We found that overlapping, buttering and sugaring sheets of store-bought phyllo made a beautifully crisp shell for the tender, fruity filling. But handling delicate phyllo to fill and form a single large strudel can be tricky, so instead we make two smaller ones and bake them side by side on the same baking sheet. The combination of tart Granny Smith apples and a sweet-crisp variety that doesn't disintegrate during baking is best. Honeycrisp, Fuji and Gala all work wonderfully. Phyllo in the U.S. typically is packaged as 9-by-14-inch sheets or larger 13-by-18-inch sheets. The former can be used as is, but the latter need to be halved crosswise (use a chef's knife to simply cut through the stack after unrolling it). You will need a total of about 24 phyllo sheets; a 1-pound box contains more than enough. The strudel is delicious warm or at room temperature, and vanilla ice cream or gelato is an excellent embellishment. Unsliced leftovers, refrigerated for a day, reheat surprisingly well. Place on a parchment-lined baking sheet and bake at 350°F for 15 to 20 minutes.

Don't attempt to unroll the phyllo before it is fully thawed, otherwise the delicate sheets will crack. Also, don't skip the step of letting the juices fall back into the bowl before placing the apples on the phyllo. If the fruit is too wet, it will soak through the phyllo, making the strudel difficult to roll.

In a large bowl, stir together the raisins and brandy. Set aside to allow the raisins to plump, stirring occasionally. In a food processor, process the bread to fine crumbs, about 30 seconds; set aside. In a small bowl, whisk together the white sugar, cinnamon and nutmeg.

In a 10-inch skillet over medium, toast the pine nuts, stirring, until fragrant and lightly browned, 3 to 4 minutes. Transfer to a small plate and set aside. In the same skillet over medium, melt the butter. Pour 113 grams (½ cup) into a small bowl or liquid measuring cup; set aside for brushing. To the butter remaining in the skillet, add the breadcrumbs and cook, stirring, until golden brown, 3 to 5 minutes. Remove from the heat and stir in 2 tablespoons of the sugar mixture; set aside to cool.

**Start to finish: 2 hours
(1 hour active)**

Makes two 12-by-4-inch strudels, serving 8

78 grams (½ cup) golden raisins

2 tablespoons brandy

86 grams (3 ounces) rustic white bread, crusts removed and torn into pieces

214 grams (1 cup) white sugar

1 teaspoon ground cinnamon

½ teaspoon freshly grated nutmeg

70 grams (½ cup) pine nuts or 55 grams (½ cup) chopped walnuts

141 grams (10 tablespoons) salted butter, cut into 4 or 5 chunks

12 ounces (2 medium) Granny Smith apples, peeled, cored and sliced ¼ inch thick

12 ounces (2 medium) crisp, sweet apples, such as Honeycrisp, Fuji or Gala, peeled, cored and sliced ¼ inch thick

1 tablespoon grated orange zest, plus 2 tablespoons orange juice

Twenty-four 9-by-14-inch frozen phyllo sheets, thawed, or twelve 13-by-18-inch phyllo sheets, thawed and halved crosswise (see headnote)

Powdered sugar, for dusting

STEPS »

HOW TO MAKE ITALIAN-STYLE APPLE STRUDEL

1. Working with one stack of phyllo at a time, brush the sheets with melted butter.

2. Sprinkle the phyllo square with ½ teaspoon of the sugar mixture. Continue layering, buttering and sugaring until the phyllo stack is used

3. Mound half of the apple mixture onto the phyllo and sprinkle with half of the breadcrumbs.

4. Using the parchment as assistance, fold the phyllo border at the bottom over the apples.

5. Continue rolling away from you, compacting the apples as you go.

6. The finished roll will measure about 4 inches in diameter.

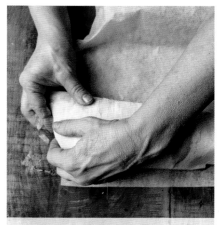

7. Tuck the open ends under the strudel.

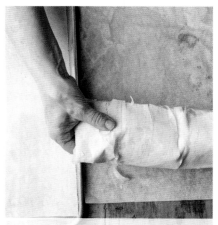

8. Using your hands, carefully transfer the strudel to one side of the lined baking sheet.

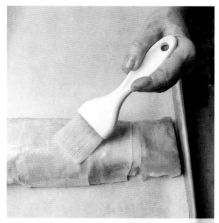

9. Brush the strudel with butter. Using the same sheet of parchment, repeat the process to form a second strudel.

To the bowl with the raisins, add both apples, the orange zest and juice, and the toasted nuts. Add 143 grams (⅔ cup) of the sugar mixture and toss. Reserve the remaining sugar for sprinkling between the phyllo layers. Heat the oven to 375°F with a rack in the middle position. Mist a rimmed baking sheet with cooking spray, then line it with kitchen parchment. Mist again with cooking spray.

Divide the phyllo sheets into 2 equal stacks, then cover each with plastic wrap and a damp kitchen towel to prevent drying. Lay a large (roughly 12-by-16-inch) sheet of kitchen parchment on the counter with a short side nearest you. Working with 1 stack of phyllo at a time, center 1 phyllo sheet on the parchment about 2 inches in from the edge and with a long side facing you (it's OK if the ends of the phyllo sheet extend past the parchment); keep the remaining phyllo covered. Lightly brush the phyllo with melted butter. Place a second phyllo sheet overlapping the first sheet by about 4 inches, creating a square measuring about 13 by 13 inches. Lightly butter the second sheet. Sprinkle the phyllo square evenly with ½ teaspoon of the remaining sugar mixture. Continue layering, buttering and sugaring in the same way until the first stack of phyllo is used.

Using a slotted spoon or your hands, scoop up half of the apple mixture, letting the juices fall back into the bowl, then mound the mixture onto the area of phyllo nearest you and sprinkle with half of the breadcrumbs. Distribute in an even layer across the center of the lower half of the phyllo square, leaving a 3-inch border along the bottom edge and 2-inch borders on each side.

Fold the phyllo border at the bottom over the apples. Lift up the edge of the parchment and use it to help start the roll; gently roll away from you, compacting the apples and forming a log about 4 inches in diameter. Tuck the open ends under the strudel and, using your hands, carefully transfer it to one side of the prepared baking sheet, leaving room for the second strudel. Brush the strudel with butter. Using the same sheet of parchment, repeat the process with the remaining ingredients to form a second strudel; you should, however, have about 2 tablespoons melted butter left for brushing during baking. Place the second strudel on the baking sheet and brush it with butter; bake for 30 minutes. Meanwhile, if the butter has hardened, remelt it.

Remove the baking sheet from the oven and lightly brush the strudels with butter. Return to the oven, rotating the baking sheet 180 degrees. Bake for another 10 minutes. Butter the strudels and rotate the pan once more. Bake until deep golden brown, another 10 to 12 minutes.

Transfer the baking sheet to a wire rack and brush the strudels with any remaining butter. Cool for at least 30 minutes; the outer layers of phyllo will crack and split during cooling. Using a wide metal spatula, transfer to a cutting board or platter. Serve warm or at room temperature. Just before serving, dust with powdered sugar. Using a serrated knife, cut into 1½-inch slices.

Sweet Fresh Corn Pudding

**Start to finish: 1 hour
(40 minutes active)**

Servings: 6

113 grams (8 tablespoons) salted butter, cut into 1-tablespoon pieces, plus more for the ramekins

2 tablespoons plus 107 grams (½ cup) white sugar, divided, plus more for the ramekins

4 teaspoons grated lemon zest, divided

65 grams (½ cup) all-purpose flour

2 cups corn kernels (see headnote)

1 cup heavy cream

⅛ teaspoon table salt

2 large eggs, separated, plus 2 large egg whites, room temperature

2 teaspoons vanilla extract

Powdered sugar, to serve (optional)

This is our adaptation of a recipe from Vivian Howard's "Deep Run Roots" that transforms sweet summer corn into a light, elegant dessert. Fresh corn is best, as the kernels are tender and succulent; you'll need three ears to yield the 2 cups kernels. Frozen corn kernels work, too, but make sure to fully thaw them, then pat dry with paper towels to remove excess moisture. For convenience, the unbaked, sugar-sprinkled soufflés can be covered with plastic wrap and refrigerated up to two hours before baking. Or if you don't plan to serve all six, extras can be covered tightly with plastic wrap then foil and frozen for up to a week. To bake from frozen; simply uncover (do not thaw), set on a baking sheet and bake for 25 to 30 minutes; they may rise slightly less than when baked fresh, but still will be delicious. Serve hot from the oven with fresh blackberries, raspberries and/or blueberries.

Don't forget to thoroughly clean the bowl and beaters you use to whip the egg whites. Any residual oils will prevent the whites from attaining the proper airiness. Don't open the oven during baking; this will cause the soufflés to deflate.

Heat the oven to 400°F with a rack in the middle position. Generously butter six 6-ounce ramekins. Sprinkle each with 1 teaspoon sugar and turn to coat, then tap out the excess. Place the ramekins on a rimmed baking sheet; set aside.

In a small bowl, combine the 2 tablespoons white sugar with 1 teaspoon lemon zest. Using your fingers, rub the zest and the sugar together; set aside.

In a large saucepan, whisk together the flour and 54 grams (¼ cup) of the white sugar. In a blender, combine the corn, cream and salt, then puree just until smooth, about 15 seconds. Whisk the puree into the flour mixture, then set the pan over medium and cook, stirring constantly with a silicone spatula, until the mixture reaches a boil and forms a thick, shiny paste, 5 to 7 minutes. Remove from the heat, then stir in the butter 2 tablespoons at a time until fully incorporated. Transfer to a large bowl and cool to room temperature, about 5 minutes. Whisk in the egg yolks, the remaining 3 teaspoons lemon zest and the vanilla.

In a stand mixer with the whisk attachment, whip the egg whites on medium-high until light and foamy. With the mixer running, slowly add the remaining 54 grams (¼ cup) white sugar, then continue to whip until the whites hold soft peaks when the whisk is lifted, 1 to 2 minutes; do not overwhip. Using a silicone spatula, fold about a quarter of the whites into the corn mixture until just a few streaks remain. Gently fold in the remaining whites, taking care not to deflate them.

Divide the mixture evenly among the prepared ramekins. Run the tip of your thumb along the inside edge of each ramekin to create a small channel; this gives the soufflés better rise. Sprinkle with the lemon sugar, dividing it evenly.

Bake the soufflés until golden brown and well risen, 20 to 22 minutes; they should jiggle slightly when the baking sheet is gently shaken. Do not open the oven door during baking. Transfer the baking sheet to a wire rack. Dust the soufflés with powdered sugar (if using) and serve right away.

Italian Chocolate Custard with Amaretti

Start to finish: 3½ hours (25 minutes active)

Servings: 6 to 8

107 grams (½ cup) plus 71 grams (⅓ cup) white sugar, divided

1½ cups heavy cream

½ cup brewed coffee

100 grams (1 cup) finely crushed amaretti cookies, plus crushed amaretti cookies, to serve

28 grams (⅓ cup) unsweetened cocoa powder

½ teaspoon table salt

3 large eggs, plus 3 large egg yolks

2 tablespoons dark rum

Amaretti are crisp, airy Italian cookies with an almond flavor. In this elegant dessert from Italy's Piedmont region, the cookies are crushed, then soaked and baked into a cocoa-enriched custard. A layer of caramel on the bottom of the pan becomes a sauce once the dessert is unmolded, similar to crème caramel or flan. During baking, the amaretti crumbs rise to the surface of the custard and form a cake-like layer that, after inverting, becomes the base of the dessert. Coffee heightens the chocolatey flavor and a bit of dark rum adds a subtle bite that balances the sweetness. If you can't find amaretti, substitute an equal amount of Stella D'oro Almond Toast. To crush the cookies, place them in a heavy-duty zip-close bag and bash them gently with a rolling pin. Either Dutch-processed or natural cocoa works in this recipe.

Don't let the custard mixture cool before baking or the timing will be off. The baking time may also be affected by the temperature of the water in the water bath, so make sure to use room-temperature, not hot or boiling, water. Don't be surprised if a little caramel remains in the pan after the custard is unmolded; this is normal.

Heat the oven to 350°F with a rack in the middle position. In a medium saucepan, combine ¼ cup water and 107 grams (½ cup) sugar. Cook over medium, occasionally swirling the pan, until the sugar has dissolved, 3 to 4 minutes. Increase to medium-high and cook, gently swirling the pan, until the caramel is lightly smoking and dark amber in color, about 4 minutes. Carefully pour it into a 9-by-5-inch metal loaf pan and gently tilt to coat the bottom of the pan; set aside.

Pour the cream and coffee into the now-empty pan and bring to a bare simmer over medium. Add the crushed amaretti and whisk until the crumbs are softened, about 1 minute. Remove from the heat and set aside.

In a large bowl, whisk together the remaining 71 grams (⅓ cup) sugar, the cocoa and the salt. Whisk in the eggs, yolks and rum. While whisking, gradually add the hot cream mixture. Pour the mixture into the caramel-lined loaf pan, then set the pan in a 9-by-13-inch baking dish.

Pour enough room-temperature water into the outer baking dish to come about halfway up its sides, then carefully transfer to the oven. Bake until the center of the custard jiggles slightly when the loaf pan is gently shaken and a paring knife inserted at the center of the custard comes out mostly clean, 50 to 55 minutes.

Carefully remove the loaf pan from the water bath and set on a wire rack. Remove the baking dish from the oven and discard the water bath. Let the custard cool to

room temperature, then cover with plastic wrap and refrigerate until cold, at least 2 hours or up to 1 day.

To serve, fill a 9-by-13-inch baking dish with about 1 inch of hot tap water. Uncover the loaf pan, place in the baking dish and let stand for about 5 minutes. Run a paring knife around the inside of the pan to loosen the custard. Invert onto a serving platter, then lift off the pan. Garnish with additional crushed amaretti. Cut into slices and serve.

Chapter 7

Loaf Cakes and Small Cakes

Browned Butter and Coconut Loaf Cake

**Start to finish: 5 hours
(45 minutes active)**

Makes one 9-inch loaf

FOR THE CAKE:

141 grams (10 tablespoons) salted butter

45 grams (½ cup) unsweetened shredded coconut

98 grams (¾ cup) all-purpose flour

135 grams (1 cup) spelt flour

1¼ teaspoons baking powder

⅛ teaspoon table salt

1 cup plus 2 tablespoons buttermilk, room temperature

1¼ teaspoons vanilla extract

214 grams (1 cup) white sugar, divided

4 large eggs, room temperature

FOR THE SYRUP:

2 tablespoons coconut milk

2 tablespoons white sugar

FOR THE GLAZE:

62 grams (½ cup) powdered sugar

1 tablespoon plus 1 teaspoon coconut milk

⅛ teaspoon table salt

This moist, dense, buttery loaf cake comes from Briana Holt of Tandem Coffee + Bakery in Portland, Maine. It's baked until the exterior is deeply browned, developing rich, toasty flavors and an amazing aroma. A coconut syrup is brushed on while the cake is still warm and, after cooling, a coconut glaze coats the surface. Holt uses spelt flour, a whole-grain flour with a subtle nuttiness. If you prefer, you can use all-purpose flour instead; if so, the total amount of all-purpose would be 228 grams (1¾ cups). Don't use whole-wheat flour in place of the spelt flour, as it changes the texture of the cake. Stored in an airtight container, the cake will keep at room temperature for up to three days.

Don't attempt to warm the buttermilk to room temperature by heating it in the microwave or in a saucepan. Buttermilk curdles if overheated, so it's best to let it stand on the counter until it reaches room temperature. If you're in a rush, warm it very gently in a warm water bath. Don't be afraid to brown the butter until the milk solids (the bits that separate out to the bottom) are deeply browned—almost black. They won't taste scorched in the finished cake. Rather, they will infuse it with a rich, nutty flavor and aroma.

To make the cake, in a medium saucepan over medium, heat the butter, occasionally swirling the pan and scraping the bottom with a wooden spoon, until dark amber and the milk solids at the bottom are almost black, 8 to 10 minutes. Transfer to the bowl of a stand mixer, making sure to scrape in all of the milk solids. Cool until the butter is opaque, spreadable and cool to the touch, about 1 hour.

While the butter cools, heat the oven to 350°F with a rack in the middle position. Spread the shredded coconut in a 9-by-5-inch loaf pan and toast in the oven until golden brown, 5 to 7 minutes, stirring once about halfway through. Measure 1 tablespoon of the toasted coconut into a small bowl, then transfer the remainder to a medium bowl; set both aside. Let the pan cool.

Mist the loaf pan with cooking spray. Line it with an 8-by-12-inch piece of kitchen parchment, fitting the parchment into the bottom and up the pan's long sides; mist the parchment with cooking spray. To the medium bowl with the coconut, whisk in both flours, the baking powder and salt. In a liquid measuring cup or small bowl, stir together the buttermilk and vanilla.

Add the white sugar to the cooled browned butter. In the stand mixer with the paddle attachment, mix the butter and sugar on medium until well combined, about 2 minutes, scraping the bowl about halfway through. With the mixer running on medium, add the eggs one at a time, scraping the bowl after the first 2 additions. Beat on medium until the mixture is shiny and lightened in color, about 1 minute. With the mixer running on low, add half of the flour, then the buttermilk mixture, followed by the remaining flour mixture. Mix on low for about 10 seconds, then stop the mixer. Using a silicone spatula, fold the batter just until the flour is incorporated, scraping the bottom of the bowl to ensure no pockets of butter or flour remain.

Transfer the batter to the prepared pan and smooth the surface. Bake until the top is deeply browned and a toothpick inserted into the center comes out with a few small crumbs attached, 75 to 80 minutes.

While the cake bakes, make the syrup. In a small microwave-safe bowl, stir together the coconut milk, white sugar and 2 tablespoons water. Microwave on high for 30 seconds, stirring once about halfway through to ensure the sugar is dissolved. Set aside to cool.

When the cake is done, cool in the pan on a wire rack for 15 minutes. Using the parchment overhang as handles, remove the cake from the pan and set on the rack. With a toothpick, poke holes in the top of the cake at 1-inch intervals. Brush all of the syrup onto the cake, allowing it to soak in. Cool to room temperature, about 2 hours. Remove and discard the parchment.

To make the glaze, in a medium bowl, whisk the powdered sugar, coconut milk and salt until smooth. Spoon over the cooled cake, spreading it to cover the surface and allowing it to drip down the sides slightly. Sprinkle with the reserved 1 tablespoon toasted coconut. Allow the glaze to dry for at least 5 minutes before serving.

Upside-Down Cardamom-Spiced Plum Cake

**Start to finish: 1½ hours
(35 minutes active), plus cooling**

Makes one 8½-inch loaf cake

FOR THE CARAMEL-PLUM LAYER:

42 grams (3 tablespoons) salted butter, cut into 3 pieces

145 grams (⅔ cup) packed light brown sugar

2 ripe but firm medium plums (about 5 ounces each), halved, pitted and sliced ¼ inch thick

Pinch table salt

FOR THE CAKE:

125 grams (1¼ cups) almond flour

105 grams (¾ cup) rye flour

2 teaspoons ground cardamom

1 teaspoon baking powder

½ teaspoon baking soda

⅛ teaspoon table salt

2 large eggs, room temperature

2 teaspoons vanilla extract

218 grams (1 cup) packed light brown sugar

2 teaspoons grated orange zest

184 grams (13 tablespoons) salted butter, room temperature

Claire Ptak, proprietor of Violet Cakes, taught us a trio of simple but sumptuous loaf cakes during a visit to her bakery-café in East London. This one, an upside-down affair, features a caramelly layer of sliced fruit that becomes syrupy and supple with baking, and a sturdy, buttery cake made with almond and rye flours (but no wheat flour). Sweetened with brown sugar and aromatic with cardamom and grated orange zest, the dark, moist crumb is more akin to steamed pudding than a light, delicate cake. Ptak used fresh figs, but since figs are highly seasonal, we used plums instead. For an autumnal dessert, pears work beautifully, too; use two ripe but firm small pears (5 to 6 ounces each), peeled, halved, cored and sliced ¼ inch thick. An 8½-by-4½-inch loaf pan is best; if baked in a 9-by-5-inch loaf pan, the cake will sink in the center and also is rather squat. If you like, serve slices dolloped with crème fraîche, which complements the fruity, molasses-y notes with cool, creamy, tangy richness. Store leftovers in an airtight container for up to three days.

Don't skip the step of lining the loaf pan with parchment. The parchment ensures that the cake will invert easily out of the pan and that the fruit layer won't stick.

Heat the oven to 375°F with a rack in the middle position. Mist an 8½-by-4½-inch loaf pan with cooking spray, then line it with an 8-by-14-inch piece of kitchen parchment, allowing the excess to hang over the long sides of the pan.

To make the caramel-plum layer, in a small saucepan, combine the butter and sugar. Cook over medium, stirring occasionally, until thick and well combined, about 2 minutes; the sugar may remain slightly granular. Transfer to the prepared loaf pan and, using a silicone spatula, distribute in an even layer. Place the plum slices in the caramel, overlapping them as needed to fit. Sprinkle the salt over the fruit; set aside.

To make the cake, in a medium bowl, whisk together both flours, the cardamom, baking powder, baking soda and salt. In a small bowl or liquid measuring cup, whisk together the eggs and vanilla.

In a stand mixer with the paddle attachment, beat the sugar and orange zest on medium until fragrant, about 1 minute. Add the butter and beat on medium-high until light and fluffy, scraping the bowl as needed, about 3 minutes. With the mixer running on low, gradually add the egg mixture, then beat on medium until well

STEPS »

1. Transfer the caramel to the prepared loaf pan and, using a silicone spatula, distribute it in an even layer.

2. Place the plum slices in the caramel, overlapping them as needed to fit.

5. Scrape the prepared cake batter onto the fruit in the loaf pan.

6. Spread the batter in an even layer and smooth the surface. Bake until the top is deeply browned, 55 to 50 minutes.

combined, about 1 minute. Scrape down the bowl. With the mixer running on low, add the dry ingredients and mix, scraping the bowl once or twice, just until the mixture is evenly moistened, about 1 minute. Fold the batter by hand with the spatula, scraping the bottom and sides of the bowl to ensure no pockets of flour remain. The batter will be thick.

Scrape the batter onto the fruit in the loaf pan, then spread in an even layer and smooth the surface. Bake until the top is deeply browned and a toothpick inserted at the center comes out clean, 55 to 60 minutes.

Cool in the pan on a wire rack for about 15 minutes; the center of the cake may sink slightly during cooling. Slide a paring knife between the short ends of the cake and the pan to loosen, then invert the cake onto a platter. Lift off the pan and peel off the parchment. Cool to room temperature.

UP YOUR BAKING GAME WITH RYE

Claire Ptak and many other bakers often partially substitute rye flour (made from ground rye berries) for bland all-purpose in order to boost flavor. But how does this substitution work? We tested three recipes: biscuits, pancakes and yellow cake, and we tried variations of each: using 100 percent all-purpose flour, substituting 25 percent rye and, finally, 50 percent rye. Even without adjusting the liquid amount (rye flour absorbs eight times its weight of water, while all-purpose flour absorbs only two times its weight of water), the results were promising. The 50 percent rye flour pancakes were a clear winner, the 25 percent rye yellow cake was the preferred percentage, but the biscuits turned out dry without properly adjusting for liquid. When we did adjust for liquid, the results were much better. Ptak agrees with our results: "For cookies and scones and pancakes, I tend to do 50 percent of a whole-meal flour with a plain all-purpose flour and get great results. Cake is a different beast. It can become dry, so I like to do more of a 33 percent ratio," she says. Two other tips: As a whole-grain flour, rye has more flavor and nutrients. However, it is less able to form gluten. Finally, to adjust the liquid, use whole eggs in place of yolks, if yolks are called for in the recipe. If not, simply increase the liquid by 10 percent if replacing half of the all-purpose flour and by 5 percent if replacing 25 percent.

Double Chocolate Loaf Cake

This loaf cake comes together quickly and easily, and boasts a remarkably deep color, intensely rich flavor and a plush, velvety crumb. The recipe came to us by way of Claire Ptak, of Violet Cakes, a bakery-café in East London. To achieve the cake's deep, complex chocolatiness, she uses a generous amount of bittersweet chocolate and unsweetened cocoa powder. Any type of bittersweet chocolate will work, but we recommend using one that's tasty enough to eat out of hand and contains about 70 percent cocoa solids. Serve slices with spoonfuls of crème fraîche, which has a subtle tang and creaminess that are fantastic foils for the cake. Store leftovers at room temperature, tightly wrapped, for up to three days.

Don't use natural cocoa. Dutch-processed is best because the alkali used in its production gives the cocoa a richer, deeper hue and smoother taste that's important for color and flavor intensity. If your cocoa does not indicate type on the label, check the ingredient list. If it reads "processed with alkali," the cocoa is Dutch-processed.

Heat the oven to 350°F with a rack in the middle position. Mist a 9-by-5-inch loaf pan with cooking spray, then line it with an 8-by-14-inch piece of kitchen parchment, allowing the excess to overhang the long sides of the pan.

In a medium saucepan over medium, bring 1 inch of water to a simmer. Put the chocolate and the butter in a large heatproof bowl and set the bowl on top of the saucepan; be sure the bottom does not touch the water. Stir occasionally until the chocolate and butter are melted. Remove the bowl from the pan and cool until barely warm to the touch, stirring occasionally. Meanwhile, in a medium bowl, whisk together the flour, sugar, cocoa, baking powder and salt.

Add the eggs to the cooled chocolate mixture; whisk until well combined. Add the dry ingredients and stir with a silicone spatula until evenly moistened; the mixture will be dryish and thick. Gradually stir in about half of the boiling water; when fully incorporated, whisk in the remaining boiling water. The batter will be smooth, glossy and fluid. Pour into the prepared pan. Bake until the center of the cake rises, forming deep fissures on the surface, and a toothpick inserted at the center comes out with a few crumbs attached, 55 to 60 minutes.

Cool in the pan on a wire rack for about 20 minutes. Lift the cake out of the pan using the parchment and set it directly on the rack. Cool to room temperature. Peel off and discard the parchment before slicing.

Start to finish: 1¼ hours (20 minutes active), plus cooling

Makes one 9-inch loaf cake

200 grams (7 ounces) bittersweet chocolate (see headnote), finely chopped

198 grams (14 tablespoons) salted butter, cut into several chunks

195 grams (1½ cups) all-purpose flour

214 grams (1 cup) white sugar

43 grams (½ cup) Dutch-processed cocoa powder

2 teaspoons baking powder

¼ teaspoon table salt

3 large eggs, room temperature

1 cup boiling water

Marbled Chocolate-Tahini Cake

**Start to finish: 1½ hours
(30 minutes active), plus cooling**

Makes one 9-inch loaf

FOR THE CAKE:

260 grams (2 cups)
all-purpose flour

1 teaspoon table salt

1½ teaspoons baking powder

½ teaspoon baking soda

1 ounce semi-sweet chocolate,
finely chopped

2 tablespoons tahini

2 tablespoons cocoa powder

113 grams (8 tablespoons) salted
butter, room temperature

321 grams (1½ cups) white sugar

4 large eggs, room temperature

2 teaspoons vanilla extract

80 grams (⅓ cup) plain
whole-milk yogurt

FOR THE GLAZE AND FINISHING:

3 ounces semi-sweet chocolate,
finely chopped

2 tablespoons tahini

2 tablespoons salted butter,
cut into 4 pieces

⅛ teaspoon table salt

1 tablespoon sesame seeds,
toasted

This loaf cake boasts a marbled interior featuring one of our favorite flavor combinations—nutty, savory tahini and rich dark chocolate. The cake's striking design is made by alternating layers of chocolate-enriched batter and plain, lightly colored batter, then using a butter knife to swirl the two together. A buttery chocolate-tahini glaze comes together quickly in the microwave and accentuates the cake's flavors beautifully. Though we often prefer to use bittersweet chocolate in our sweets, for both the batter and glaze in this recipe we find that semi-sweet better complements the earthy, subtly bitter notes of the tahini. Dense and moist, this cake takes about two hours to cool completely. Applying the glaze about halfway through the cooling period ensures it is fully set by the time the cake is ready to serve. While the cake is best enjoyed the day it's made, it can be stored at room temperature in an airtight container or wrapped in plastic for up to two days.

Don't be tempted to spread your batters in even layers after adding them to the pan. Letting them fall on top of each other organically and swirling them together right away yields the most dramatic marbling. Also, don't over-swirl the batters or the cake will have a uniformly colored crumb. Just one swishy zigzag pass from one side of the pan to the other is sufficient.

To make the cake, heat the oven to 350°F with a rack in the middle position. Mist a 9-by-5-inch loaf pan with cooking spray, then line it with an 8-by-14-inch piece of kitchen parchment, allowing the excess to overhang the long sides of the pan. Mist the parchment with cooking spray.

In a medium bowl, whisk together the flour, salt, baking powder and baking soda. In a medium microwave-safe bowl, microwave the chocolate on 50 percent power, stirring every 15 seconds, until melted and smooth. Whisk in the tahini and cocoa powder until smooth; set aside.

In a stand mixer with the paddle attachment, beat the butter and sugar on medium-high until light and fluffy, about 5 minutes. With the mixer running, add the eggs one at a time, scraping the bowl after each addition. Add the vanilla and mix until fully incorporated. With the mixer running on low, add about one-third of the flour mixture followed by about half of the yogurt. Next, add about half of the remaining flour mixture, then the remaining yogurt and finally the remaining flour mixture. Mix on low until just combined, about 1 minute. Fold the batter a few times with the spatula to ensure no pockets of flour remain.

Transfer half of the batter (about 2 cups) to the bowl with the chocolate-tahini mixture. Using a silicone spatula, gently fold until homogeneous. Pour about half of the chocolate batter into the center of the prepared pan; do not spread it. Working quickly, pour in about half of the plain batter followed by the remaining chocolate batter and, finally, the remaining plain batter. Insert a butter knife vertically at one end of the pan until the tip touches the bottom, then swirl the batters by dragging the knife in a swishy zigzag motion to the other end of the pan. Smooth the top with a spatula and rap the pan against the counter to remove any air bubbles.

Bake until the top is deeply browned and a toothpick inserted at the center of the cake comes out with a few small crumbs attached, 50 to 60 minutes. Cool the cake in the pan on a wire rack for 15 minutes. Lift the loaf out of the pan using the parchment and set it directly on the rack. Cool for at least 1 hour.

To make the glaze, in a 2-cup liquid measuring cup, combine the chocolate, tahini, butter and salt. Microwave on 50 percent power, stirring every 15 seconds, until the butter is melted and the chocolate is soft and beginning to melt, about 1 minute. Whisk until smooth and emulsified; the glaze should have the consistency of pourable yogurt. If it is too thick, whisk in water 1 teaspoon at a time.

Drizzle the warm glaze onto the cake, allowing it to run down the sides. (If the glaze cools before pouring, warm it in the microwave on 50 percent power just until pourable, about 10 seconds.) Sprinkle the top of the cake with the sesame seeds. Let the glaze set for about 1 hour before slicing and serving.

Maple-Whiskey Pudding Cakes

Start to finish: 45 minutes (20 minutes active), plus cooling

Servings: 4

113 grams (8 tablespoons) salted butter, cut into 1-tablespoon pieces, divided

¼ cup plus 2 tablespoons maple syrup

¼ cup plus 2 tablespoons whiskey, divided (see headnote)

1 teaspoon cider vinegar

⅛ teaspoon plus ¼ teaspoon table salt, divided

107 grams (½ cup) white sugar

¼ cup whole milk

1 large egg

1 teaspoon vanilla extract

86 grams (¾ cup) pecans, toasted

65 grams (½ cup) all-purpose flour

1 teaspoon baking powder

In the British tradition of self-saucing puddings, these individual desserts bake up with a gooey sauce beneath a layer of rich, tender cake. We tried a few different types of whiskey here: our favorites were Jameson for its clean, bright flavor and Rittenhouse rye for its spicy depth. The alcohol and cider vinegar both work to balance the dessert, ensuring it doesn't become overly sweet. Toasty brown butter was a natural addition—its nuttiness and warmth perfectly complement pecans and maple syrup. If serving a crowd, simply double the recipe to make eight pudding cakes. Enjoy them warm, with vanilla ice cream or lightly sweetened whipped cream.

Don't stir the maple-whiskey syrup into the batter after dividing it among the batter-filled ramekins. With baking, the syrup will form a sauce at the bottom.

In a small saucepan over medium, melt 85 grams (6 tablespoons) of the butter. Cook, swirling the pan, until the milk solids at the bottom are deep golden brown and the butter has the aroma of toasted nuts, about 5 minutes. Transfer to a medium bowl and cool until barely warm to the touch; reserve the saucepan.

Meanwhile, in the same saucepan over medium, combine the remaining 2 tablespoons butter, ½ cup water, the maple syrup, the ¼ cup whiskey, the vinegar and ⅛ teaspoon salt. Bring to a boil, stirring occasionally. Reduce to low and simmer for 5 minutes. Remove from the heat and set aside.

Heat the oven to 325°F with a rack in the middle position. Mist four 6-ounce ramekins with cooking spray and place, evenly spaced, on a rimmed baking sheet.

Into the cooled browned butter, whisk the sugar, milk, egg, vanilla and remaining 2 tablespoons whiskey. In a food processor, process the pecans until finely ground and beginning to clump, 30 to 40 seconds. Add the flour, baking powder and the remaining ¼ teaspoon salt, then pulse until combined, about 5 pulses. Add the browned butter mixture and pulse until a smooth, thick batter forms, about 5 pulses, scraping the bowl once.

Divide the batter evenly among the prepared ramekins. Gently pour the maple mixture over the batter in each ramekin. Do not stir. Bake until the cakes are puffed and the centers jiggle only slightly, 25 to 30 minutes. Let cool on the baking sheet for 10 minutes before serving; the cakes will fall slightly as they cool.

Lemon-Almond Pound Cake

Start to finish: 1½ hours (20 minutes active), plus cooling

Makes one 9-inch loaf

195 grams (1½ cups) all-purpose flour, plus more for the pan

4 large eggs, room temperature

2 teaspoons vanilla extract

2 tablespoons grated lemon zest, plus 3 tablespoons lemon juice, divided

241 grams (1 cup plus 2 tablespoons) plus 54 grams (¼ cup) white sugar

100 grams (1 cup) almond flour

1½ teaspoons baking powder

½ teaspoon table salt

198 grams (14 tablespoons) salted butter, cut into 1-tablespoon pieces, room temperature

3 tablespoons sliced almonds

For this plush, velvety pound cake, we took a cue from Rose Carrarini of Rose's Bakery in Paris and replaced some of the wheat flour with almond flour. Almond flour makes the cake's crumb extra tender and moist and gives it a more interesting texture than wheat flour alone. We finish the cake with a tangy-sweet lemon glaze, brushing it on while the loaf is still hot so the syrup is readily absorbed. Thanks to generous amounts of eggs and butter, this cake keeps well. Store it in an airtight container at room temperature for up to three days.

Don't use cold butter or cold eggs. The butter must be softened to room temperature so it integrates into the sugar-flour mixture. And the eggs must be at room temperature, too, not chilled, so they don't cause the butter to stiffen up when added to the mixer. Lastly, don't rotate the cake as it bakes. Jostling the pan increases the chance the batter will deflate, resulting in a dense, underrisen cake.

Heat the oven to 325°F with a rack in the middle position. Coat a 9-by-5-inch loaf pan with cooking spray, dust evenly with flour, then tap out the excess. In a 2-cup liquid measuring cup or small bowl, beat the eggs and vanilla until combined; set aside.

In a stand mixer with the paddle attachment, mix the lemon zest and 241 grams sugar on low until fragrant, about 1 minute. Add both flours, the baking powder and salt and mix until combined, about 10 seconds. With the mixer on low, add the butter a piece at a time. Once all the butter has been added, continue mixing on low until the mixture is crumbly and no powdery bits remain, 1 to 2 minutes.

With the mixer still running, add the egg mixture in a slow, steady stream and mix for about 10 seconds. Increase to medium-high and beat until the batter is light and fluffy, 1 to 1½ minutes, scraping the bowl once or twice. The batter will be thick.

Transfer the batter to the prepared pan and smooth the surface, then sprinkle evenly with sliced almonds. Bake for 45 minutes, then reduce the oven to 300°F. Continue to bake until the top is deep golden brown and a toothpick inserted at the center of the cake comes out clean, another 30 to 35 minutes.

While the cake is baking, in a small saucepan over medium-low, heat the remaining 54 grams sugar and 2 tablespoons lemon juice, stirring often, until the sugar dissolves and the mixture reaches a simmer. Immediately remove from the heat and stir in the remaining 1 tablespoon lemon juice. Set aside to cool.

When the cake is done, cool in the pan on a wire rack for 10 minutes. Invert the cake onto the rack, then turn it upright. Using a toothpick, poke small holes in the surface at 1-inch intervals. Brush all of the lemon-sugar syrup onto the cake, allowing it to soak in. Cool completely before slicing, about 2 hours.

STEPS »

HOW TO MAKE LEMON-ALMOND POUND CAKE

1. In a stand mixer with the paddle attachment, mix the sugar and lemon zest on low until fragrant, about 1 minute.

2. After adding both flours, the baking powder and salt, keep the mixer on low and add the butter, one piece at a time.

3. After all the butter has been added, continue mixing on low until crumbly and no powdery bits remain, 1 to 2 minutes.

4. With the mixer on low, pour in the egg and vanilla mixture in a steady stream; continue to mix for about 10 seconds.

5. Increase the speed to medium-high and beat until light and fluffy, 1 to 1½ minutes, scraping the bowl once or twice.

6. Transfer the batter to the prepared loaf pan. Smooth the surface, sprinkle with the almonds and bake.

7. Cool the cake in the pan for 10 minutes. Invert the cake onto the rack, turn it upright and poke holes in the surface with a toothpick.

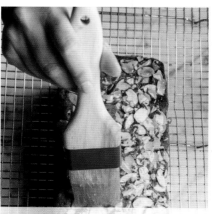

8. Brush the lemon syrup onto the cake, allowing it to soak in. Cool the cake completely before slicing, about 2 hours.

Mini Almond Cakes
with Spiced Chocolate

These three-bite sweets are a riff on classic French financiers, almond cakes baked in a shape that resembles gold bars (hence the name). Their interiors are light and moist and the crusts golden and slightly crisp. We flavored ours with cocoa and spices, then baked them in mini muffin pans. Either Dutch-processed or natural cocoa works, so use whichever you have on hand. Chipotle chili powder gives the cakes an intriguing spiciness; if you don't have any, substitute ⅛ teaspoon cayenne pepper. Once cooled, the cakes keep at room temperature in an airtight container for up to three days.

Start to finish: 1 hour

Makes 24 mini cakes

100 grams (1 cup) almond flour

43 grams (⅓ cup) all-purpose flour

¼ teaspoon table salt

113 grams (8 tablespoons) salted butter, cut into 3 or 4 pieces

28 grams (⅓ cup) cocoa powder

½ teaspoon ground cinnamon

¼ teaspoon chipotle chili powder

1 tablespoon dark rum or bourbon

4 large egg whites

161 grams (¾ cup) white sugar

Don't overbeat the egg whites or they will become dry, stiff and difficult to incorporate into the base. Properly beaten egg whites should hold a soft, droopy peak when the whisk is lifted. When testing for doneness, make sure to test the cakes at the center of the muffin pan, as they bake slightly slower than those at the outside.

Heat the oven to 375°F with a rack in the middle position. Mist one 24-cup or two 12-cup mini muffin pans with cooking spray. In a medium bowl, whisk together both flours and the salt; set aside.

In a small saucepan over medium-high, melt the butter. Once melted, cook, swirling the pan often, until the butter is fragrant and deep golden brown, 4 to 5 minutes. Remove from the heat and let cool for a few minutes. Stir in the cocoa powder, cinnamon, chipotle powder and rum.

In a stand mixer with the whisk attachment, whip the egg whites on medium-high until light and foamy. With the mixer running, slowly add the sugar and continue to whip until the whites are thick and glossy and hold soft peaks, 2 to 4 minutes. Reduce to low, gradually add the flour mixture and mix until incorporated (it's fine if some streaks remain), about 10 seconds.

With the mixer running on low, slowly pour in the butter mixture and mix until homogeneous and no streaks remain, about 10 seconds. Using a silicone spatula, fold the batter by hand a few times to ensure the ingredients are well combined, then divide evenly among the muffin cups.

Bake until a toothpick inserted into the cakes at the center of the pan(s) comes out clean, 10 to 12 minutes. Cool in the pan(s) on a wire rack for 5 minutes. Remove the cakes from the pan(s), then cool completely on the rack, about 30 minutes.

Pistachio-Cardamom Cake

Start to finish: 1 hour 10 minutes (15 minutes active), plus cooling

Makes one 9-inch loaf cake

¼ cup olive oil, plus more for the pan

130 grams (1 cup) all-purpose flour, plus more for the pan

214 grams (1 cup) white sugar

2 teaspoons grated orange zest, plus ¼ cup orange juice

193 grams (1⅓ cups) shelled, unsalted pistachios, toasted and cooled

2 teaspoons baking powder

1½ teaspoons ground cardamom

½ teaspoon table salt

4 large eggs

120 grams (½ cup) plus 2 tablespoons plain whole-milk Greek yogurt, divided

2 teaspoons vanilla extract

93 grams (¾ cup) powdered sugar

Baking a cake can be daunting. Enter the loaf cake, as easy as a quick bread but with more polish. Rose Bakery in Paris, created by Briton Rose Carrarini and her French husband, Jean-Charles, has elevated the style to an art form, producing tempting loaf cakes in all manner of flavors. We were particularly taken by a green-tinged, nut-topped pistachio cake. For our version, we paired toasted pistachios with cardamom and ground orange zest, giving it a distinctly Middle Eastern flavor. Combining ground nuts with rich Greek-style yogurt, olive oil and plenty of eggs ensured a moist, appealingly coarse crumb. We got the best results from grinding the nuts until they were nearly as fine as flour, but still had some texture. If you can't find unsalted pistachios, reduce the salt in the recipe by half. Cooling the cake was essential to maintain the thick consistency of the glaze.

Don't skip toasting the pistachios. The differences in flavor and texture were significant between raw and toasted. Toast the nuts at 300°F until they're quite fragrant and begin to darken, 10 to 15 minutes.

Heat the oven to 325°F with a rack in the middle position. Lightly coat a 9-by-5-inch loaf pan with oil. Dust evenly with flour, then tap out the excess. In a food processor, combine the white sugar and orange zest; process until the sugar is damp and fragrant, 5 to 10 seconds. Transfer to a large bowl and set aside.

Add the pistachios to the processor and pulse until coarse, 8 to 10 pulses. Set aside 2 tablespoons of the nuts for topping. Add the flour, baking powder, cardamom and salt to the processor with the nuts. Process until the nuts are finely ground, about 45 seconds.

To the sugar mixture, whisk in the eggs, the 120 grams (½ cup) yogurt, the oil, orange juice and vanilla. Add the nut-flour mixture and fold until combined. Transfer the batter to the prepared pan and bake until golden brown, firm to the touch and a toothpick inserted at the center comes out with moist crumbs, 50 to 55 minutes. Cool in the pan on a wire rack for 15 minutes. Invert the cake onto the rack, then turn it upright. Let cool completely, about 2 hours.

In a small bowl, whisk the remaining 2 tablespoons yogurt with the powdered sugar until thick and smooth. Spread over the cake. Sprinkle with the reserved nuts. Let set for about 10 minutes before serving.

BAKING BASIC

CARDAMOM 101

A spice that originated in South India, cardamom has been adopted by cuisines around the world. The two most common varieties of cardamom, green and black, are seed pods harvested from plants belonging to the ginger family. But as siblings go, they're very different. Dubbed "the queen of spices" in India, green cardamom is sweetly floral with hints of pine, citrus and eucalyptus, while the black variety is smoky and pungent. The flavor of either can be expressed in different ways, whether simmered whole in liquid to mildly perfume dishes, coarsely cracked to add a sharper note or finely ground to fully meld with other flavors. And then there's white cardamom, which is in fact green cardamom that has been bleached; this type is used only when cooks want a uniform white color with a hint of cardamom flavor. As with many spices, freshly ground cardamom is more potent than preground. One convenient way to get more robust cardamom flavor is to search out "decorticated" cardamom—which are seeds that have been removed from the inedible pod shell—and grind them as needed.

Puddings Chômeur

This gooey Québecois dessert is said to have been created during the Great Depression, when many people were au chômage, or unemployed. The individual "puddings" have the texture of a cake-like biscuit, with crusty edges moistened by maple and cream. The vanilla ice cream may seem unnecessary, but its cold creaminess is the perfect foil for the rich, warm puddings. You'll need four 6-ounce ramekins for this recipe. If you like, it can be doubled to serve eight.

Don't use maple-flavored syrup. This dessert gets its flavor from pure maple syrup. We especially liked the puddings made with darker syrups, which tend to have a deeper, richer taste. But lighter "amber" syrups were good, too.

Heat the oven to 400°F with a rack in the middle position. In a medium saucepan over medium, whisk together the maple syrup and cream. Bring to a simmer and cook, stirring, for 1 minute. Off heat, whisk in the vinegar; set aside.

In a small bowl, whisk together the flour, baking powder, cinnamon and salt. In a stand mixer with the paddle attachment, beat the butter and sugar on medium-high until light and fluffy, 2 to 4 minutes, scraping the bowl as needed. With the mixer on low, add the egg and beat until well combined, 1 to 2 minutes. With the mixer running, gradually add the flour mixture and beat until incorporated, about 30 seconds, scraping the bowl as needed; the mixture will resemble sticky cookie dough. Cover and refrigerate for 15 minutes. Meanwhile, generously butter four 6-ounce ramekins, then place them on a rimmed baking sheet.

Into each prepared ramekin, spoon 2 tablespoons of the maple mixture. Scoop the dough into the ramekins, dividing it evenly (about ⅓ cup in each). Spoon another 2 tablespoons of the maple mixture over each; reserve the remaining maple mixture for serving.

Bake until the puddings are deep golden brown and bubbling at the edges, about 25 minutes. Transfer the ramekins to a wire rack and cool for 10 minutes. Serve warm, topped with ice cream and with the reserved maple mixture on the side.

Start to finish: 1 hour (15 minutes active), plus cooling

Servings: 4

1 cup maple syrup (see headnote)

¼ cup plus 2 tablespoons heavy cream

2 tablespoons cider vinegar

130 grams (1 cup) all-purpose flour

¾ teaspoon baking powder

½ teaspoon ground cinnamon

Pinch of table salt

85 grams (6 tablespoons) salted butter, room temperature, plus more for the ramekins

93 grams (¼ cup plus 3 tablespoons) white sugar

1 large egg

Vanilla ice cream, to serve

Lemon and Caraway Butter Cake

**Start to finish: 1¼ hours
(20 minutes active), plus cooling**

Makes one 9-inch loaf cake

280 grams (2⅓ cups) cake flour

2 teaspoons caraway seeds

2 teaspoons baking powder

¼ teaspoon table salt

214 grams (1 cup) white sugar

1 tablespoon grated lemon zest

254 grams (18 tablespoons) salted butter, room temperature

3 large eggs, plus 1 large egg yolk, room temperature

¼ cup whole milk, room temperature

Claire Ptak made us this elegantly simple cake when we paid her a visit at Violet Cakes, her bakery-café in London. She explained that it is an old-fashioned British teacake known, rather plainly, as "seed cake" and that she first encountered it after moving from the U.S. to England in 2005. In addition to caraway, Ptak also includes lemon zest; its bright, fresh notes lift the richness of the butter, the sweetness of the sugar and the earthiness and anise-like hints of the seeds. She recommends serving the light, tender cake with glasses of Madeira. Leftovers will keep tightly wrapped at room temperature for up to three days.

Don't forget to fold the batter by hand with a spatula before turning it into the loaf pan. The batter is thick and heavy, so scraping the mixer bowl, especially along the bottom, will ensure the flour mixture is fully incorporated.

Heat the oven to 350°F with a rack in the middle position. Mist a 9-by-5-inch loaf pan with cooking spray, then line it with an 8-by-14-inch piece of kitchen parchment, allowing the excess to overhang the long sides of the pan. In a medium bowl, whisk together the flour, caraway, baking powder and salt; set aside.

In a stand mixer with the paddle attachment, beat the sugar and lemon zest on medium until fragrant, about 1 minute. Add the butter and beat on medium-high until the mixture is light and fluffy, scraping the bowl as needed, about 3 minutes.

With the mixer running on low, beat in the eggs one at a time, adding the yolk with the third egg; beat until combined, about 15 seconds, and scrape the bowl after each addition. With the mixer still running on low, gradually add the flour mixture; mix just until combined, about 45 seconds, then scrape the bowl. Again with the mixer running on low, slowly add the milk; mix just until incorporated, about 30 seconds. Fold the batter by hand with the spatula, scraping the bottom and sides of the bowl to ensure no pockets of flour remain. The batter will be thick.

Scrape the batter into the prepared pan and spread in an even layer. Tap the pan on the counter a few times to remove any large air bubbles. Bake until golden brown and a skewer inserted at the center of the cake comes out clean, 55 to 60 minutes.

Cool in the pan on a wire rack for about 20 minutes. Lift the cake out of the pan using the parchment and set it directly on the rack. Cool to room temperature. Peel off and discard the parchment before slicing.

SHELF-STABLE MILK

Whether you don't regularly stock conventional dairy milk or are just prone to running out, shelf-stable milks can be handy to have around. We wondered whether it was possible to keep shelf-stable dairy milk on hand for when baking needs arise. We put several varieties to the test: canned evaporated milk (which sometimes is sold as "unsweetened condensed milk"); ultra-high temperature (UHT) processed milk (sold in shelf-stable cartons); powdered milk (both whole and nonfat); and fresh whole milk we froze for storage, then thawed for use. We used each as a substitute for whole milk in cupcakes, custard and pancakes.

Both the UHT milk and thawed frozen milk performed well in all tests—the UHT milk in fact produced the fluffiest, lightest cupcakes. One of the worst performers was the nonfat milk powder, which resulted in gummy, unappetizing cupcakes. By contrast, however, the whole milk powder—an ingredient that is less common than nonfat milk powder, but relatively easy to find online—produced solid results: The pancakes and cupcakes were tender and the custard set up nicely, with a smooth, velvety texture. Somewhere in the middle was the evaporated milk, which is whole milk that has had up to 60 percent of its water removed, a process that concentrates its natural sugars. In every test, baked goods made with evaporated milk came out dense. (This is why some bakers "reconstitute" evaporated milk by mixing it with equal parts water, adjusting the sugar and fat levels to be on par with regular whole milk.) Overall, we found that UHT milk might be the best option to keep on hand (and freeze any leftovers for future baking).

Invisible Apple Cake (Gâteau Invisible)

**Start to finish: 2 hours
(45 minutes active), plus cooling**

Makes one 9-inch loaf cake

2½ pounds (5 or 6 medium) Honeycrisp apples (see headnote), peeled

130 grams (1 cup) all-purpose flour

1 teaspoon baking powder

¾ teaspoon table salt

½ teaspoon ground allspice

½ teaspoon ground cardamom

½ teaspoon ground cinnamon

⅛ to ¼ teaspoon freshly grated nutmeg

3 large eggs

107 grams (½ cup) white sugar

½ cup whole milk

57 grams (4 tablespoons) salted butter, melted and slightly cooled

Caramel sauce with allspice (recipe p. 323), to serve

Brown sugar whipped cream (recipe p. 323), to serve

"Cake" is somewhat of a misnomer for this elegant dessert. Instead of open, airy and crumby, the texture is rich and dense, with slices of sweet-tart apples set in an egg-rich batter. During the long oven-bake, the fruit slices and custard-like layers meld and become nearly indistinguishable from each other, giving the cake its name. We especially like Honeycrisp apples for this, as they have an ideal balance of sweetness and acidity, along with a texture that softens without turning mushy. Gala apples are the next best variety. To slice the fruits thinly and evenly, a mandoline is the tool of choice. If you prep them by hand, the slices should be no thicker than $1/16$ inch. The cake is best the day it is baked, but make sure it has time to cool to room temperature before slicing and serving. Spiced caramel sauce and tangy whipped cream (recipes p. 323) are perfect accompaniments.

Don't try to shortcut the layering of apples and batter in the loaf pan. Though it takes some time to arrange the fruit and batter, doing so ensures the slices are compact and the cake will not have air pockets that cause it to fall apart when sliced.

Heat the oven to 375°F with a rack in the middle position. Mist a 9-by-5-inch loaf pan with cooking spray. Line it with an 8-by-14-inch piece of kitchen parchment, allowing the excess to overhang the long sides of the pan, then mist the parchment.

Adjust the blade of your mandoline to slice $1/16$ inch thick. Slice an apple lengthwise against the mandoline until you reach the core. Rotate the apple a quarter turn and again slice lengthwise to the core. Continue in this way until only the core remains; discard the core. The apple slices will have different shapes; this is fine. Transfer to a large bowl and slice the remaining apples as you did the first; add them to the bowl.

In a small bowl, whisk together the flour, baking powder, salt, allspice, cardamom, cinnamon and nutmeg. In a stand mixer with the whisk attachment, beat the eggs and sugar on medium-high until pale and thick, about 4 minutes. Reduce to medium-low, then add half of the flour mixture and mix, scraping the sides of the bowl as needed, until combined, about 30 seconds. Increase to medium-high and slowly add the milk; mix until fully incorporated, about 30 seconds. Reduce to medium-low, add the remaining flour mixture and mix until just combined, about 30 seconds. With the mixer running, slowly add the melted butter, then mix until homogeneous, about 30 seconds; the batter will be thick but pourable.

Add about one-third of the batter to the apples. Using a silicone spatula, gently fold until the apples are lightly but evenly coated. Pour about ½ cup of the remain-

STEPS »

HOW TO MAKE INVISIBLE APPLE CAKE

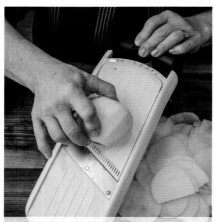

1. Adjust the blade of a mandoline to slice 1/16 inch thick. Slice an apple lengthwise until you reach the core.

2. Rotate the apple a quarter turn, again slice lengthwise to the core. Continue until only the core remains; discard the core.

3. Add about one-third of the batter to the apples. Gently fold until lightly but evenly coated.

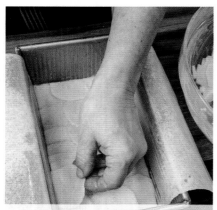

4. Pour 1/2 cup batter into the pan and layer one-third of the apples over it. Aim to arrange the straight edges against the pan sides.

5. Spread another 1/2 cup batter over the apples.

6. Repeat the layering of batter and apples, and spread the remaining batter on top. Smooth the surface.

ing batter into the prepared pan and spread it in an even layer. Layer one-third of the batter-coated apples (about 2 cups) in the pan; as much as possible, arrange the slices with a straight edge against the sides of the pan to minimize the gaps between fruit and pan around the perimeter. Spread another ½ cup batter over the apple layer, then arrange half of the remaining apples on top. Repeat the layering of batter and apples, then spread the remaining batter on top. Smooth the surface, then rap the pan against the counter to remove any air bubbles.

Bake until the cake is golden brown, well risen and a skewer inserted at the center meets no resistance, 80 to 90 minutes. Cool completely in the pan on a wire rack, at least 2 hours; the cake will settle during cooling.

Run a thin-bladed knife between the cake and short edges of the pan. Using the parchment overhang as handles, lift the cake out of the pan and set it on a cutting board. Carefully slide the cake off the parchment, then cut it into 1-inch slices. Serve with caramel sauce and whipped cream.

OVER THE TOP

Caramel Sauce with Allspice

Start to finish: 20 minutes
Makes about 1 cup

Place 2 tablespoons water in a small saucepan. Carefully pour **107 grams (½ cup) white sugar** into the center of the pan, and stir gently with a clean spoon just until the sugar is evenly moistened. Bring to a boil over medium and cook, gently swirling the pan (do not stir) until the syrup is deep amber-colored and lightly smoking, 5 to 6 minutes. Carefully add **½ cup heavy cream** (the mixture will bubble and steam vigorously), then stir to combine. Add **3 tablespoons cold salted butter** (cut into ½-inch pieces), **1 teaspoon vanilla extract, 1 teaspoon bourbon** (optional), **¼ teaspoon table salt** and **¼ teaspoon ground allspice.** Remove from the heat and stir until the butter is melted and incorporated. Transfer to a small bowl and cool to room temperature. (The caramel will keep in an airtight container in the refrigerator for up to 5 days; bring to room temperature for serving.)

OVER THE TOP

Brown Sugar Whipped Cream

Start to finish: 5 minutes
Makes about 3 cups

In the bowl of a stand mixer, combine **1 cup cold heavy cream, 60 grams (¼ cup) cold sour cream, 2 tablespoons packed light or dark brown sugar, ½ teaspoon vanilla extract and ⅛ teaspoon table salt.** Using the whisk attachment, mix on low until uniform and frothy, about 30 seconds. Increase to medium-high and whip until soft peaks form, 1 to 2 minutes. Use right away or cover and refrigerate for up to 2 hours.

Raspberry Friands

**Start to finish: 55 minutes
(25 minutes active), plus cooling**

Makes 24 mini cakes

113 grams (8 tablespoons)
salted butter

2 teaspoons grated orange zest

½ teaspoon almond extract

155 grams (1¼ cups) powdered
sugar, plus more for dusting

125 grams (1¼ cups) almond flour

33 grams (¼ cup) all-purpose flour

¾ teaspoon table salt

6 large egg whites

24 raspberries (from a 1-pint
container)

A relative of French financiers, Australian friands are miniature cakes. Like financiers, they feature nutty almond flour and get their light, chewy texture from egg whites. What sets friands apart is the addition of fresh fruit, and instead of a bar shape, they're baked in small ovals or rounds. We opted for an easy-to-find mini muffin pan. Browned butter elevates the flavor, adding richness and complexity that complement the nuttiness of the almond flour. We love the bright, floral combination of raspberries and orange zest, but blueberries and lemon are a fantastic combination, too. (Simply substitute lemon zest for the orange zest and drop 2 or 3 blueberries in the batter in each cup before baking.) These cakes are best the day of baking, when the crispness of the exteriors contrasts with the chewiness of the crumb, but extras can be stored at room temperature in an airtight container for a couple days.

Don't skip sifting the dry ingredients. Almond flour and powdered sugar both tend to clump, so sifting is essential for a smooth batter and light, even texture in the baked cakes.

Heat the oven to 375°F with a rack in the middle position. Mist two 12-cup mini muffin pans or one 24-cup mini muffin pan with cooking spray. In a small saucepan over medium, cook the butter, swirling the pan often, until the milk solids at the bottom are golden brown and the butter has a nutty aroma, 3 to 5 minutes. Remove from the heat and cool for a few minutes. Stir in the orange zest and almond extract; set aside.

Sift the powdered sugar, both flours and the salt into a large bowl; whisk to combine and set aside. In a medium bowl, whisk the egg whites until frothy and opaque but not to the soft-peak stage, 2 to 3 minutes. Add the whites to the dry ingredients and, using a silicone spatula, gently fold until there are no dry bits but lots of white streaks remain. Add the butter mixture and fold until homogeneous.

Evenly divide the batter among the muffin cups. Place 1 raspberry, pointed end up, in the center of each cup and gently press it into the batter until it only peeks out the top. Bake until deep golden brown, 25 to 30 minutes. Cool in the pan(s) on a wire rack for 5 minutes. One at a time, gently pry the cakes loose with a butter knife, lift them out of the pan and set them directly on the rack. Cool completely. Dust with powdered sugar just before serving.

VARIATION

Blackberry and Ginger Friands

Cut **12 large blackberries** in half crosswise; set aside. Follow the recipe to make the batter, omitting the orange zest and stirring **½ teaspoon grated fresh ginger** and **½ teaspoon ground ginger** into the browned butter with the almond extract. Divide the batter among the muffin cups, then replace each raspberry with a blackberry half, inserting it cut side down and gently pressing it into the batter until it only peeks out the top. Bake, cool and remove from the pan as directed.

Chapter 8

Cheesecakes,
Bundt Cakes,
Tortes and More

Chèvre Cheesecake with Black Pepper–Graham Crust

Angie Mar, chef/owner of Beatrice Inn in New York City, may be best known for her artistry with all things meat, but we're smitten with her chèvre cheesecake, the recipe for which is found in her book "Butcher + Beast." Made with equal parts chèvre (fresh goat cheese) and cream cheese plus a generous measure of crème fraîche, the cake has the perfect amount of savoriness and tanginess—and a surprisingly light texture despite its richness. In addition to scaling Mar's recipe to fit into a standard 9-inch springform, we mixed lemon zest into the filling to lift the flavor and add citrusy notes that play off the black pepper in the crust. The best way to gauge doneness of the cake is with an instant thermometer inserted through the side (in the area where the filling has risen above the pan), with the probe angled slightly down and to the center; 145°F to 150°F is the finished temperature. To cut clean slices, warm the knife blade by dipping it into a pitcher of hot water; wipe the blade dry before and after each cut and rewarm it as needed. Covered tightly with foil and refrigerated, the cheesecake keeps well for up to four days, though the crust softens over time.

Don't forget to allow the cheeses to warm to cool room temperature before mixing. If they're refrigerator-cold, the filling is more likely to wind up with lumps. Note that this recipe involves multiple oven settings: 300°F, 450°F, off (with the cake still inside and the door propped open) and 250°F. Don't forget to run a knife around the cheesecake after the cake has cooled for 10 minutes—this helps prevent cracking.

Heat the oven to 300°F with a rack in the lower-middle position. Brush the bottom of a 9-inch round springform pan with melted butter; reserve the brush. In a large bowl, stir together the cracker crumbs, pepper, 1 teaspoon sugar and ¼ teaspoon salt. Add the melted butter and stir until evenly moistened. Transfer to the prepared pan and use the bottom of a ramekin or dry measuring cup to firmly press into an even layer. Bake until the crust is fragrant and golden, 15 to 17 minutes. Let cool on a wire rack until barely warm, 15 to 20 minutes.

Brush the inside walls of the pan with melted butter, then set on a rimmed baking sheet. Increase the oven temperature to 450°F. In a stand mixer with the paddle attachment, beat the goat cheese and cream cheese on medium until creamy, airy and well combined, about 3 minutes, scraping the bowl and paddle once or twice. Add the remaining 161 grams (¾ cup) sugar and the remaining ¼ teaspoon salt, then beat on medium-high until the mixture is smooth and fluffy, about 1 minute, scraping the bowl and paddle halfway through.

Start to finish: 2½ hours (40 minutes active), plus cooling and refrigerating

Servings: 12 to 16

85 grams (6 tablespoons) salted butter, melted and cooled slightly, plus more for the pan

210 grams (1¾ cups) graham cracker crumbs

1 teaspoon ground black pepper

1 teaspoon plus 161 grams (¾ cup) white sugar, divided

½ teaspoon table salt, divided

1 pound fresh goat cheese (chèvre), cool room temperature

Two 8-ounce packages cream cheese, cool room temperature

Two 8-ounce containers crème fraîche, cool room temperature

111 grams (⅓ cup) honey

4 large eggs, plus 2 large egg yolks, cool room temperature

1 tablespoon grated lemon zest

STEPS »

HOW TO MAKE CHÈVRE CHEESECAKE WITH PEPPER-GRAHAM CRUST

1. Brush the bottom of a 9-inch round springform pan with 1½ teaspoons melted butter; reserve the brush.

2. In a large bowl, mix the cracker crumbs, black pepper, sugar and salt until well combined.

3. Add the melted butter and stir until moistened. Transfer to the prepared pan, press into an even layer and bake.

4. After the crust has cooled, brush the inside walls of the pan with the remaining 1½ teaspoons melted butter.

5. In a stand mixer, beat the cheeses until creamy and well combined. Add the sugar and salt and beat until fluffy.

6. After incorporating the crème fraîche to the mixture, beat in the honey, then scrape the bowl and paddle.

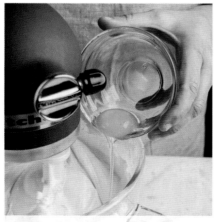

7. Add the whole eggs one at a time, scraping the bowl and paddle after the first 2 eggs. Beat in the yolks.

8. Add the lemon zest and stir with a spatula, scraping the bottom of the bowl, until the zest is evenly distributed.

9. Pour the mixture into the pan over the crust. If necessary, smooth the surface with the spatula.

330   Milk Street Bakes

With the mixer on medium-low, gradually add the crème fraîche, followed by the honey. Scrape the bowl and paddle. With the mixer on low, add the whole eggs one at a time, beating until combined after each addition and scraping the bowl and paddle after the first 2 eggs. Add the yolks and beat until fully incorporated.

Detach the bowl from the mixer, and use a spatula to stir in the lemon zest, scraping the bottom of the bowl, until evenly distributed. Pour into the springform pan; the pan may be filled to the rim. If necessary, smooth the surface with the spatula.

Bake the cheesecake on the baking sheet for 20 minutes; the filling will have risen above the rim of the pan and the surface will be golden. Turn off the oven and prop open the door with the handle of a wooden spoon for 10 minutes; the surface of the cake will darken slightly during this time.

Close the oven door and heat the oven to 250°F. Continue to bake until the center reaches 145°F to 150°F (insert an instant-read thermometer through the side of cake, in the area where it has risen above the pan, with the probe slightly angled down so the tip is at the center of the cake), 35 to 40 minutes.

Set the baking sheet with the cheesecake on a wire rack and cool for 10 minutes. Run a narrow-bladed knife around the edge of the cheesecake to loosen the sides, then cool for 1½ to 2 hours; the cake will deflate slightly as it cools. Refrigerate uncovered until cold, at least 6 hours or up to overnight (if refrigerating for longer than 3 hours, cover tightly with foil after the cheesecake is fully chilled). Remove the pan sides before slicing.

Triple Crème Cheesecake with Guava Sauce

**Start to finish: 1½ hours
(30 minutes active), plus cooling**

Servings: 16 to 20

5 tablespoons (71 grams) salted butter, cut into 1-tablespoon pieces, cool room temperature, plus more for the pan

71 grams (⅓ cup) plus 214 grams (1 cup) white sugar, divided

87 grams (⅔ cup) plus 24 grams (3 tablespoons) all-purpose flour, divided

75 grams (¾ cup) almond flour

1 pound cream cheese, room temperature

1¼ pounds Saint André cheese (see headnote), trimmed of rind (1 pound without rind), room temperature

1 tablespoon vanilla extract

7 large eggs, room temperature

2 cups heavy cream, room temperature

Guava sauce (recipe p. 334)

At Maximo Bistrot, chef Eduardo García's acclaimed Mexico City restaurant, we tasted an exceptionally delicious guava cheesecake. In addition to standard cream cheese, the cake is made with French triple crème cheese—plus heavy cream and a good dose of eggs—but the light, almost lilting, texture belies its richness. Guava sorbet and compote accompanied the cake, the tropical fruitiness complementing and balancing the savoriness of the cheeses. We adapted the recipe, adjusting the cheesecake formula just slightly and creating an easy guava sauce to take the place of the sorbet and compote. Saint André cheese is a widely available type of French triple crème and what we call for in this recipe. The rind from the cheese must be removed before use, so you'll need to purchase about 1¼ pounds in order to obtain 1 pound, trimmed. To make the sauce, (recipe p. 334) you will need guava nectar, which is sold in cans, aseptic packaging (like boxed broth) or refrigerated cartons (like orange juice); if you have a choice of pink or white guava nectar, the former will yield a more attractive sauce. Note that a nonstick springform pan with a dark finish requires a slightly lower oven temperature to compensate for the heat absorption properties of the pan. (We advise against using a springform with a lip or moat around the bottom intended for containing leaks; during testing, we found the unusual raised bottom of this type of pan to affect the browning of the crust and baking time for the filling in unpredictable ways.) Both the cheesecake and sauce can be made up to three days in advance.

Don't begin making the cheesecake until the cheeses, eggs and cream are at room temperature. If the ingredients are cold, they won't mix easily and the batter may wind up lumpy. However, it's easiest to remove the rind from the soft, buttery Saint André cheese while it's cold, so do the trimming before allowing it to come to room temperature.

Butter the bottom and sides of a 9-inch springform pan. If the pan is nonstick with a dark finish, heat the oven to 400°F with a rack in the lower-middle position; if it is not, heat the oven to 425°F.

In a medium bowl, whisk together the 71 grams (⅓ cup) sugar, the 87 grams (⅔ cup) all-purpose flour and the almond flour. Sprinkle 2 tablespoons of the mixture into the prepared springform pan and turn to evenly coat the bottom and sides, then tap any excess back into the bowl. Set the pan on a square of extra-wide foil and fold the foil up the sides, pressing it against the pan.

To the flour mixture, add the butter, then, using your fingers, rub it into the dry ingredients until the mixture resembles wet sand. Transfer to the prepared pan and press firmly into an even layer in the bottom. Set the pan on a rimmed baking sheet; set aside.

Cheesecakes, Bundt Cakes, Tortes and More

In a small bowl, whisk the remaining 24 grams (3 tablespoons) all-purpose flour to remove any lumps; set aside. In a stand mixer with the paddle attachment, mix both cheeses, the remaining 214 grams (1 cup) sugar and the vanilla on low until combined, about 1 minute; scrape the bowl once or twice. Increase to medium-high and beat until the mixture is smooth and fluffy, scraping the bowl as needed, 3 to 4 minutes.

With the mixer running on low, add the flour and mix just until combined, about 30 seconds; scrape the bowl. With the mixer running on low, add the eggs one at a time, mixing until incorporated, 10 to 15 seconds, after each addition. After all the eggs have been added, scrape the bowl, then beat on medium until well combined, about 1 minute. With the mixer running on low, slowly pour in the cream; this should take about 1 minute. Remove the bowl from the mixer and stir with a silicone spatula, making sure to scrape the bottom and sides of the bowl; the batter will be thin.

Pour the batter into the prepared pan; it will be quite full. Place the baking sheet in the oven and bake for 40 minutes; the cake will rise above the rim of the pan and the surface will be deeply browned. Turn off the oven, prop open the door with the handle of a wooden spoon and continue to bake the cake with the oven's residual heat for 15 minutes. The center of the cake should reach 150°F to 160°F; if it does not, return it to the oven, close the door and continue to bake with the oven's residual heat until the center comes up to temperature.

Transfer the baking sheet with the cheesecake to a wire rack; the center of the cake will still be wobbly. Cool for 1 hour; the cake will deflate as it cools. Refrigerate, uncovered, until fully chilled, for at least 4 hours or up to 3 days. Once fully chilled, cover the cake with foil or plastic wrap.

To serve, let the cheesecake stand at room temperature for about 30 minutes. Run a narrow-bladed knife around the edge of the cake to loosen the sides. Remove the pan sides, then cut the cake into slices. Serve with the chilled guava sauce.

OVER THE TOP

Guava Sauce

Start to finish: 20 minutes
Makes about 1¾ cups

In a small bowl, whisk together **71 grams (⅓ cup) white sugar, 1 teaspoon cornstarch** and **⅛ teaspoon table salt.** In a 12-inch skillet, bring **3 cups guava nectar** to a simmer over medium-high, then reduce to medium-low and simmer, stirring occasionally, until reduced to about 1½ cups, 12 to 15 minutes. Whisk the sugar mixture into the guava nectar, return to a simmer, stirring constantly, and cook for about 1 minute; the mixture will thicken very slightly. Pour into a nonreactive container and whisk in **3 tablespoons lime juice.** Cool to room temperature, then cover and refrigerate for at least 1 hour or up to 3 days.

Basque-Style Cheesecake

Created in the 1990s by Spanish chef Santiago Rivera, Basque cheesecake, or tarta de queso vasca, has garnered global acclaim for its blistered, "burnt" surface and creamy-smooth center. The crustless cake bakes in a parchment-lined pan in a hot oven—no water bath needed—until the center is just barely set. Room-temperature dairy is key for ensuring a lump-free batter, but then thoroughly chilling the batter (at least six hours) before baking allows the cake to spend enough time in a hot oven to achieve dramatic coloring without overcooking. After much trial and error, we found that the style of springform pan makes a huge difference in how the cake bakes. For a pan with a light-colored finish, bake at 450°F; for a dark-colored pan, such as nonstick, 425°F is best. Start checking doneness after 40 minutes; a digital thermometer is best for testing the temperature. The cake keeps well in the refrigerator for at least three days. Basque cheesecake sometimes is served at room temperature, but we prefer it with a bit of a chill.

Start to finish: 1 hour (20 minutes active), plus cooling and chilling

Servings: 12 to 16

4 large eggs, plus 3 large egg yolks, room temperature

321 grams (1½ cups) white sugar

1 teaspoon grated lemon zest

½ teaspoon table salt

2 pounds cream cheese, cut into chunks, room temperature

8-ounce (226-gram) container crème fraîche, room temperature

STEPS »

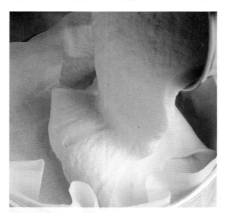

1. Once the oven is at temperature, remove the chilled batter from the refrigerator and pour into the prepared pan. If needed, spread it in an even layer.

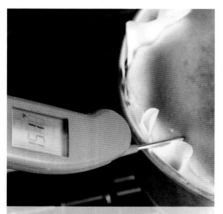

2. Bake until browned and an instant thermometer inserted at an angle so the tip is at the center of the cake reaches 150°F to 155°F, 40 to 55 minutes.

3. Remove the sides of the pan, then set the chilled cake, still on the springform base, on a platter. Gently pull the parchment away from the sides of the cake and cut the cake into slices.

Don't begin making the batter until the cream cheese, eggs and crème fraîche are at room temperature. Also, be sure to use the paddle attachment, not the whisk, to avoid incorporating excess air into the batter. Finally, don't be alarmed by how jiggly the cheesecake is when it comes out of the oven. As it cools and chills, it will set up beautifully.

In a liquid measuring cup or small bowl, whisk together the whole eggs and yolks. In a stand mixer with the paddle attachment, mix the sugar, lemon zest and salt on low until fragrant, about 30 seconds. Add the cream cheese and beat on medium-low until no lumps remain, 2 to 3 minutes, scraping the bowl and paddle attachment a few times. With the mixer on low, slowly add the beaten eggs in 4 or 5 additions, occasionally scraping the bowl and mixing after each addition until fully incorporated, 15 to 20 seconds, before adding more. Scrape the bowl. With the mixer on low, add the crème fraîche a spoonful at a time. Detach the bowl from the mixer and stir with a silicone spatula, making sure to scrape the bottom and sides of the bowl. Cover and refrigerate until thoroughly chilled, at least 6 hours or up to 24 hours.

About 30 minutes before you are ready to bake the cake, adjust an oven rack to the lower-middle position. If your pan is light in color, heat the oven to 450°F; if your pan has a dark finish, heat to 425°F. Cut a 14- to 15-inch round of kitchen parchment. Line a 9-inch springform pan with the parchment round, pushing the paper into the edges and against the sides of the pan, allowing it to form folds and pleats; set aside.

When the oven is at temperature, pour the cold batter into the prepared pan; if needed, spread in an even layer. Rap the pan against the counter a few times to remove any large air bubbles. Bake until the cake is deeply browned and an instant thermometer inserted at the edge with the probe angled so the tip is at the center of the cake reaches 150°F to 155°F, 40 to 55 minutes; once the cake nears 150°F, the temperature tends to rise quickly, so check every 3 to 4 minutes. Even when done, the center of the cake will jiggle when the pan is gently shaken. Transfer to a wire rack and cool for 1 to 2 hours; the cake will deflate as it cools.

Refrigerate the cake, uncovered (it will still be warm), until chilled, at least 4 hours or up to 3 days (if storing for more than a day, cover with foil once the cake no longer is warm). Let stand at room temperature for about 30 minutes before serving. To serve, remove the sides of the pan, then set the cake, still on the springform base, on a platter. Pull the parchment away from the sides of the cake and cut the cake into slices.

Hot Milk Sponge Cake

When Linda White's grandmother was a young woman, she started a book of recipes that she had clipped from the newspaper or had gotten from friends and family. Now White, who lives in Fort Washington, Pennsylvania, has inherited that book. "Most of the recipes have titles attributed to someone significant in her life," she says, and the cake named Adena's Hot Milk Sponge was comfort food for the family. "She made it for happy occasions, but I associate it more with times when I was under the weather or was just feeling down." Both White and her mother tried to replicate the sponge cake, but her grandmother's handwritten recipe was sketchy and vague. They had no luck. "The flour is listed as the last ingredient, after the baking instructions," White says. "The ingredients include egg yolks, but later on it says to fold in the whites. I think this might be a case of making sure no one can duplicate it!" White contacted Milk Street to help her recreate this old-fashioned cake, which she described as light and tender and flavored with a little orange zest; it was always baked in a tube pan and never iced. Sponge cakes like this incorporate beaten egg whites, which, along with baking powder for added leavening, produce a light, fluffy crumb.

Don't grease the tube pan. The batter clings more readily to the sides and the center tube if the pan is ungreased, resulting in better rise. Beat the egg whites just until very droopy peaks form; if they are stiff, the cake won't rise as high. Finally, to prevent the baked cake from falling, after removal from the oven, immediately invert the pan with the cake still in it and let cool completely in the pan.

Heat the oven to 325°F with a rack in the middle position. Have ready an ungreased 9-inch or 10-inch tube pan with a removable bottom or, if using a 1-piece pan, line it with kitchen parchment cut to fit into the bottom, with a center hole to accommodate the tube. In a medium bowl, whisk together the flour, baking powder and salt; set aside.

In a small saucepan over medium, heat the milk to just below a simmer (185°F), 2 to 3 minutes. Set aside off heat.

In a stand mixer with the paddle attachment, beat the egg yolks, 214 grams (1 cup) of the white sugar and the orange zest on medium-high until the mixture is pale yellow and doubled in volume, 3 to 4 minutes. Scrape down the bowl. With the mixer running on low, very slowly drizzle in the warm milk, then add the vanilla and beat until combined, about 1 minute. Scrape down the bowl. With the mixer running on low, add the flour mixture in three additions, mixing until almost fully incorporated, about 30 seconds, after each addition. Remove the bowl from the

Start to finish: 1½ hours (30 minutes active), plus cooling

Servings: 10 to 12

260 grams (2 cups) all-purpose flour

1 teaspoon baking powder

¼ teaspoon table salt

1 cup whole milk

4 large eggs, separated, room temperature

428 grams (2 cups) white sugar, divided

1 tablespoon grated orange zest

1 teaspoon vanilla extract

Powdered sugar, for dusting (optional)

Citrus-macerated strawberries, for serving (recipe p. 338)

Citrus-Macerated Strawberries

Start to finish: 15 minutes, plus standing
Makes about 4 cups

In a large bowl, toss together **2 pounds strawberries** (hulled and quartered), **54 grams (¼ cup) white sugar, 4 teaspoons grated orange, lemon or lime zest** and a pinch of table salt. Let stand at room temperature until the berries have softened slightly and released some juices, at least 15 minutes or up to 1 hour, tossing the mixture a few times.

mixer and fold with the spatula to ensure no dry pockets remain. Transfer the mixture to a large bowl; set aside. Thoroughly wash and dry the mixer bowl.

In the clean mixer bowl, using the whisk attachment, whip the egg whites on medium-high until light and foamy, about 1 minute. With the mixer running, slowly sprinkle in the remaining 214 grams (1 cup) white sugar and continue to whip until the whites are thick and glossy and hold very droopy, soft peaks, about 2 minutes. Remove the bowl from the mixer.

Using the spatula, fold one-third of the egg whites into the batter until mostly combined. Gently fold in the remaining whites until no streaks remain; the batter will be light and airy but pourable. Pour the batter into the tube pan and spread it into an even layer.

Bake until the cake is golden brown and a toothpick inserted 2 inches from the edge comes out clean, 50 to 55 minutes if using a nonstick pan, or 55 to 60 minutes if using a conventional pan. Immediately invert the pan onto a heatproof surface and let the cake cool to room temperature, about 1 hour.

Invert the pan again. Run a long, thin knife between the cake and the sides of the pan as well as between the cake and the center tube. If you've used a pan with a removable bottom, lift out the center tube with the cake attached and set it on a surface. Slide the knife between the cake and the base to loosen. Invert the cake still on the base onto a platter, then lift off the base. If you've used a one-piece pan, after loosening the sides of the cake, invert the pan onto a platter, lift off the pan and peel off the parchment. If desired, dust the cake with powdered sugar just before serving, and serve with the citrus-macerated strawberries.

BAKING BASIC

TO SCALD OR NOT TO SCALD

Some baking recipes call for scalded milk, some don't. To test whether it really makes a difference, we first had to turn to the history books. For the home cooks of yesteryear, this was a critical step to kill off potentially harmful pathogens—a common concern in the days before pasteurized milk solved the problem by heating milk to just below the boiling point, typically to around 180°F. Today, this is less of an issue, and therefore it's far less common to need to scald milk. But we learned that scalding milk still has a role in modern baking. Turns out, scalding also affects gluten development and how that gluten influences the final texture of baked goods. That's because the whey proteins in milk can impact the gluten proteins in flour, ultimately weakening the elasticity of the dough. But the scalding process denatures the whey proteins, allowing for stronger gluten development that ensures a better crumb in breads and other baked goods. Unfortunately, working with hot milk can be tricky. If added to flour too quickly, the heated liquid tends to cause clumping, resulting in an unappealingly lumpy dough. But there is an easy solution: Just let the milk cool first, then mix it with the flour. This works because once the whey protein is deactivated by scalding, it can no longer interact with the gluten, even when cooled.

Almond-Coconut Cake with Cherries and Pistachios

**Start to finish: 1¼ hours
(20 minutes active), plus cooling**

Servings: 10 to 12

141 grams (10 tablespoons) salted butter, melted and cooled, plus more for the pan

100 grams (1 cup) almond flour

87 grams (⅔ cup) all-purpose flour

45 grams (½ cup) shredded unsweetened coconut

1 teaspoon baking powder

½ teaspoon table salt

3 large eggs, room temperature

107 grams (½ cup) plus 1 tablespoon white sugar

73 grams (⅓ cup) packed light brown sugar

½ teaspoon almond extract

1½ cups pitted fresh or frozen sweet cherries, thawed and patted dry

48 grams (⅓ cup) unsalted roasted pistachios, chopped

Powdered sugar, to serve (optional)

This rustic cake is our adaptation of a recipe from "Honey & Co.: The Cookbook" by London restaurateurs and chefs Itamar Srulovich and Sarit Packer. Dense, moist and filled from top to bottom with fruity, nutty flavor and texture, the cake is great as dessert, brunch or with coffee or tea. Honey & Co. flavors it with mahleb, a baking spice made from the seeds from a variety of cherry; we use easier-to-source almond extract. Store leftovers in an airtight container at room temperature for up to three days.

Don't use sweetened shredded coconut, as it will make the cake too sugary. Unsweetened shredded coconut—not wide shavings—is the right variety. If fresh cherries are out of season, don't hesitate to use thawed frozen cherries—they're equally tasty on the cake. Lastly, don't worry that inverting the cake out of the pan will cause the toppings to fall off. The fruit and nuts are baked in, so only a couple small pieces may come loose, if any.

Heat the oven to 350°F with a rack in the middle position. Butter a 9-inch round cake pan, line the bottom with a round of kitchen parchment, then butter the parchment.

In a medium bowl, whisk together both flours, the coconut, baking powder and salt. In a large bowl, combine the eggs, the 107 grams (½ cup) white sugar, brown sugar and almond extract, then whisk until well combined. Whisk in the melted and cooled butter. Whisk in the dry ingredients until homogeneous; the batter will be thick but pourable.

Pour the batter into the prepared pan. Using your hands, tear the cherries in half over the batter, allowing the juice to fall onto the surface, then drop the pieces onto the surface in an even layer. Sprinkle with the pistachios and the remaining 1 tablespoon white sugar.

Bake until a toothpick inserted at the center of the cake comes out clean, 50 to 55 minutes. Cool on a wire rack until barely warm to the touch, about 1 hour. Run a paring knife around the inside edge of the pan to loosen the cake, then invert onto a platter. Lift off the pan and peel off the parchment. Re-invert the cake onto a platter. If desired, dust with powdered sugar just before serving.

Spanish Almond Cake

This flourless cake from Galicia, Spain, traditionally is leavened with whipped egg whites and flavored with citrus and/or cinnamon. We liked it made more simply, with whole eggs beaten with a few additional whites and just a small measure of vanilla and almond extracts. A sprinkling of chopped almonds and coarse raw sugar on top of the batter gives the surface a chewy-crisp crust that contrasts wonderfully with the dense, plush crumb of the cake's interior. Crème fraîche and fresh berries are perfect accompaniments. Allow the cake to cool to room temperature before serving.

Don't underbake the cake. Rather than use a skewer or toothpick to test the center for doneness, check the browning and crust development. The cake is ready when the surface is deeply browned and the crust feels firm when gently pressed with a finger.

Heat the oven to 350°F with a rack in the middle position. Mist the bottom and sides of a 9-inch round cake pan with cooking spray, line the bottom with a round of kitchen parchment, then mist the parchment.

In a large bowl, combine the white sugar, whole eggs and egg whites, salt and both extracts. Whisk vigorously until well combined, 30 to 45 seconds; the mixture will be slightly frothy and the sugar will not be fully dissolved. Add the almond flour and whisk until incorporated. Pour the batter into the prepared pan, then sprinkle evenly with the turbinado sugar and chopped almonds. Bake until deeply browned and the crust feels firm when gently pressed with a finger, 45 to 55 minutes. Let cool in the pan on a wire rack for 10 minutes.

Run a knife around the edges of the cake, then invert onto a plate. Remove the pan and parchment then re-invert the cake onto a serving plate. Let cool completely before serving.

Start to finish: 1 hour 10 minutes, plus cooling (10 minutes active)

Servings: 8

241 grams (1 cup plus 2 tablespoons) white sugar

3 large eggs, plus 3 large egg whites

¼ teaspoon table salt

¼ teaspoon almond extract

¼ teaspoon vanilla extract

250 grams (2½ cups) blanched almond flour

37 grams (3 tablespoons) turbinado or demerara sugar

31 grams (⅓ cup) sliced almonds, chopped

French Almond-Rum Cake

**Start to finish: 3¼ hours
(25 minutes active)**

Servings: 12

FOR THE CAKE:

226 grams (16 tablespoons) salted butter, room temperature, plus more for the pan

6 large eggs

285 grams (1⅓ cups) white sugar

2 tablespoons grated lemon zest

250 grams (2½ cups) almond flour

¼ teaspoon table salt

81 grams (½ cup plus 2 tablespoons) all-purpose flour

¼ cup plus 2 tablespoons dark rum

FOR THE RUM SYRUP:

40 grams (3 tablespoons) white sugar

1 tablespoon whole allspice

1 teaspoon black peppercorns

½ cup dark rum

**FOR THE LEMON GLAZE
AND GARNISH:**

186 grams (1½ cups) powdered sugar

¼ teaspoon table salt

3 tablespoons lemon juice, plus more if needed

47 grams (½ cup) sliced almonds, toasted

Gâteau Nantais originated in Nantes in western France. Made with generous amounts of butter, eggs and almond flour, the cake's crumb is rich, moist and pleasantly dense, and becomes even more so after it's brushed with a rum syrup. The classic finish is a rum icing, but we opted instead for a bracing lemon glaze that brings out the lemon zest in the cake. You can serve the cake as soon as the glaze sets, but its flavor and texture improve if allowed to rest overnight at room temperature. If storing for longer, cover and refrigerate (up to three days), but bring to room temperature before serving. If you have a dark, non-stick cake pan (which transfers heat more quickly than lighter aluminum) reduce the temperature to 325°F and bake for the same time.

Don't use a small saucepan to make the syrup, and don't forget to remove the pan from the burner before pouring in the rum. These steps help ensure that the alcohol won't ignite. After removing the cake from the pan, don't re-invert it—leave it bottom side up, as the perfectly flat surface is easy to glaze. Finally, don't allow the cake to cool before brushing on the syrup; absorption is better if the cake is still hot.

To make the cake, heat the oven to 350°F with a rack in the middle position. Generously butter the bottom and sides of a 9-inch round cake pan. In a small bowl or liquid measuring cup, beat the eggs.

In a stand mixer with the paddle attachment, beat the butter, white sugar and lemon zest on medium until light and fluffy, 2 to 3 minutes, scraping the bowl as needed. Add the almond flour and salt, then beat on medium just until incorporated. With the mixer running, gradually add the eggs and beat until homogeneous, scraping the bowl as needed. Increase to medium-high and continue to beat until the mixture is light and fluffy, about 3 minutes, scraping the bowl once or twice. With the mixer running on low, gradually add the all-purpose flour and mix until incorporated, then slowly add the rum and beat just until combined. Scrape the bowl to ensure no pockets of flour or rum remain. The batter will be thick.

Scrape the batter into the prepared pan, then spread in an even layer and smooth the surface. Bake until deep golden brown and the center of the cake springs back when gently pressed, 50 to 55 minutes.

Meanwhile, to make the rum syrup, in a large saucepan combine the white sugar, ⅓ cup water, allspice and peppercorns. Bring to a boil over medium-high, stirring to dissolve the sugar, then boil for 3 minutes. Remove the pan from the heat and stir in the rum. Bring to a simmer over medium and cook for 2 minutes. Pour the mixture through a fine mesh strainer set over a small bowl; discard the solids and set the syrup aside.

When the cake is done, let cool in the pan on a wire rack for 5 minutes. Invert the cake onto another wire rack; do not re-invert. Immediately brush the top and sides of the cake with all of the rum syrup. Cool to room temperature, about 1 hour. Transfer the cooled cake to a platter.

To make the lemon glaze, in a medium bowl, whisk together the powdered sugar and salt, then gradually whisk in the lemon juice; the glaze should be smooth, with the consistency of yogurt. If it is too thick, whisk in additional lemon juice ½ teaspoon at a time to attain the proper consistency.

Pour the glaze onto the center of the cake, then use an offset spatula or the back of a spoon to spread the glaze toward the edges, allowing just a small amount to drip down the sides. Sprinkle with the toasted almonds. Let stand at room temperature to set the glaze, about 1 hour.

Greek Apple Cake with Honey and Cinnamon

Start to finish: 1½ hours, plus cooling

Servings: 12 to 16

1 cup apple cider

Two 3-inch strips orange zest, plus ¼ cup orange juice

2 tablespoons honey, divided

3-inch cinnamon stick

268 grams (1¼ cups) plus 2 tablespoons white sugar, divided

325 grams (2½) cups all-purpose flour

2 teaspoons baking powder

½ teaspoon baking soda

½ teaspoon table salt

3 large eggs

½ cup extra-virgin olive oil

120 grams (½ cup) plain whole-milk Greek yogurt

1 pound (2 medium) firm, crisp, sweet-tart apples, such as Honeycrisp or Gala, peeled, cored and cut into ¼-inch chunks

1 teaspoon grated nutmeg

½ teaspoon ground cinnamon

Powdered sugar, to serve (optional)

There are many types of apple cakes, but Greek milopita is unique in that it often is made with two very Mediterranean ingredients: olive oil and yogurt. It's a homey, rustic treat, with a moist, dense crumb studded with chunks of fruit. Our take on milopita is an easy no-mixer affair. The spicing is simple but warm, balanced by the brightness of orange, and we amp up the apple flavor by reducing apple cider to a syrup that's used in the batter as well as a lustrous glaze on the cooled cake. Heavy cream mixed with a little Greek yogurt, sweetened with honey and whipped to soft peaks is a perfect accompaniment. Store leftovers in an airtight container at room temperature for up to three days.

Don't use an apple variety that breaks down when cooked. Choose one or two that are firm and crisp, with a flavor that's sweet-tart rather than just sugary. Honeycrisp and Gala are two widely available varieties that work well in the cake. Don't toss the apples with sugar too far in advance or the fruit will begin to soften and release juices.

In a small saucepan, combine the cider, orange zest and juice, 1 tablespoon of the honey and the cinnamon stick. Bring to a simmer over medium-high and cook, stirring occasionally, until reduced to ½ cup, 8 to 10 minutes. Transfer to a medium bowl. Remove and discard the orange zest and cinnamon stick. In a small bowl, whisk together 1 tablespoon of the syrup and the remaining 1 tablespoon honey; set aside for glazing the cake. Cool the syrup and glaze to room temperature, about 20 minutes.

Meanwhile, heat the oven to 350°F with a rack in the middle position. Mist a 9-inch springform pan with cooking spray and line the bottom with a round of kitchen parchment.

In a medium bowl, whisk together the 268 grams (1¼ cups) sugar, flour, baking powder, baking soda and salt. To the syrup in the medium bowl, add the eggs, oil and yogurt; whisk to combine. In a large bowl, toss together the apples, nutmeg, ground cinnamon and remaining 2 tablespoons sugar.

Add the egg mixture to the dry ingredients and stir with a silicone spatula until mostly smooth. Add the batter to the apples and fold until the fruit is evenly distributed throughout. Transfer to the prepared pan, then gently shake the pan to level the batter. Bake until well browned and a toothpick inserted at the center comes out clean, 60 to 65 minutes. Cool completely in the pan on a wire rack, about 2 hours.

Run a paring knife around the inside edge of the pan to loosen the cake, then remove the pan sides. Invert the cake onto the rack, lift off the springform base, then peel off and discard the parchment. Re-invert onto a serving platter, then evenly brush the glaze onto the surface. If desired, dust with powdered sugar just before serving.

French Apple Cake

**Start to finish: 1 hour
(25 minutes active), plus cooling**

Servings: 8

113 grams (8 tablespoons) salted butter, cut into 3 or 4 chunks, plus more for the pan

¼ teaspoon ground allspice

1½ pounds Granny Smith apples, peeled, cored and cut into ¼-inch slices

1 pound Braeburn or Golden Delicious apples, peeled, cored and cut into ¼-inch slices

2 tablespoons plus 120 grams (½ cup plus 1 tablespoon) white sugar, plus more for sprinkling

¼ teaspoon table salt

2 tablespoons brandy or Calvados

87 grams (⅔ cup) all-purpose flour, plus more for the pan

1 teaspoon baking powder

2 large eggs

2 teaspoons vanilla extract

This simple dessert is less cake than sautéed apples set in a thick, buttery custard encased in a golden crust. We liked using two varieties of apples, one tart and one sweet—the variation in the apples' sweetness give the cake a full, complex flavor. The cake is delicious served unadorned, but it's equally wonderful accompanied with crème fraîche or ice cream.

Don't use a spatula to scrape the browned butter out of the skillet—simply pour it into the bowl. A skim coat of butter in the pan is needed for cooking the apples. And don't slice the cake until it has fully cooled; if it is at all warm, the texture at the center will be too soft.

Heat the oven to 375°F with a rack in the middle position. Coat a 9-inch springform pan with butter, dust evenly with flour, then tap out the excess.

In a 12-inch skillet over medium, cook the butter, swirling the pan often, until the milk solids at the bottom are golden brown and the butter has a nutty aroma, 4 to 6 minutes. Pour into a small heatproof bowl without scraping out the skillet. Stir the allspice into the butter and set aside.

Add all of the apples, the 2 tablespoons sugar and the salt to the still-hot skillet and set over medium-high. Cook, stirring occasionally, until all moisture released by the apples has evaporated and the slices are beginning to brown, 12 to 15 minutes. Add the brandy and cook until evaporated, 30 to 60 seconds. Transfer to a large plate, spread in an even layer and refrigerate uncovered until cool to the touch, 15 to 20 minutes.

In a small bowl, whisk together the flour and baking powder. In a large bowl, whisk together the eggs, vanilla and the remaining 120 grams (9 tablespoons) sugar. Gradually whisk in the butter. Add the flour mixture and stir with a silicone spatula until smooth; the batter will be very thick. Add the cooled apples and fold until evenly coated. Transfer to the prepared pan, spread in an even layer and sprinkle with 1 tablespoon sugar.

Bake until the cake is deeply browned, 35 to 40 minutes. Let cool completely in the pan on a wire rack, about 2 hours. Run a knife around the inside of the pan and remove the sides before slicing.

German Apple Cake

Start to finish: 1½ hours, plus cooling

Servings: 8

130 grams (1 cup) all-purpose flour, plus more for the pan

1½ teaspoons baking powder

214 grams (1 cup) white sugar, plus 2 tablespoons for sprinkling

113 grams (4 ounces) almond paste, broken into rough ½-inch pieces

¼ teaspoon table salt

113 grams (8 tablespoons) salted butter, cool room temperature

3 large eggs, room temperature

2 teaspoons vanilla extract

2 small Granny Smith apples (about 12 ounces total), peeled, cored and halved lengthwise

Powdered sugar, to serve

Apfelkuchen, or apple cake, is a classic German sweet of which there are numerous versions. We were particularly fond of Luisa Weiss's recipe in "Classic German Baking," which is her adaptation of a recipe she found on a package of almond paste. Almond paste gives the cake's crumb a custardy richness, a moist, tender texture and a pleasant—but not overpowering—almond fragrance and flavor. Tangy-sweet sliced apples are fanned on top of the batter and baked into the surface to elegant effect. You will need an apple corer to punch out the cores from the apples before halving them. If you don't own one, halve the apples, then notch out the cores with a paring knife. This recipe was developed with a conventional (that is, not nonstick) springform pan. If yours is nonstick or otherwise has dark finish, to prevent overbaking, heat the oven to 350°F and begin checking for doneness on the low end of the time range.

Don't use marzipan in place of the almond paste. Marzipan is sweeter than almond paste. Also, make sure the almond paste is fresh and pliable, not dried out and hard, or it won't break down properly during mixing. The apples can be peeled, cored and halved before you make the cake batter, but don't slice the apple halves until the batter is in the pan. If sliced sooner, the apples may discolor.

Heat the oven to 375°F with a rack in the middle position. Mist a 9-inch springform pan with cooking spray, then dust with flour; tap out the excess. In a small bowl, whisk together the flour and baking powder.

In a stand mixer with the paddle attachment, mix the 214 grams (1 cup) white sugar, almond paste and salt on low until the paste has broken into crumbly bits, 2 to 3 minutes. Add the butter and mix until combined, about 30 seconds. Increase to medium-high and beat until the mixture is pale and fluffy, about 3 minutes, scraping the bowl as needed. Reduce to medium, then add the eggs, one at a time, beating for about 20 seconds after each addition.

Scrape down the bowl, then add the vanilla and continue mixing on medium until well-combined, about 2 minutes. Reduce to low, add the flour mixture and mix just until the batter is evenly moistened, about 10 seconds; it will be thick. Using the spatula, scrape the bottom and sides of the bowl and give the batter a few folds to ensure no pockets of butter or flour remain. Transfer to the prepared pan and spread in an even layer, smoothing the surface.

Slice each apple half into ⅛-inch-thick half circles; do not separate the slices. With your hand, gently press down on each half to fan the slices. Divide the fanned apples into 8 equal portions without undoing the fanned effect. Slide a thin spatula or butter knife under the apples, then slide the slices off the spatula near the outer edge of the cake with the slices fanning outward from the center. One at a time,

STEPS »

1. Mix the sugar, almond paste and salt on low until crumbly, then add the butter and mix until well combined.

5. Reduce to low, add the flour mixture and mix just until the batter is evenly moistened; it will be thick.

position another 6 sets of slices on the cake, creating an evenly spaced spoke pattern. Place the last set of apple slices in the center. Sprinkle the remaining 2 tablespoons sugar evenly over the top.

Bake until the edges of the cake are deep golden brown and a toothpick inserted at the center comes out clean, 50 to 60 minutes. Cool in the pan on a wire rack for 30 minutes. Run a paring knife around the inside of the pan to loosen, then remove the pan sides. Serve warm or at room temperature; dust with powdered sugar just before serving.

9. With your hand, gently press down on each half of the apple slices in order to spread them out in a fan shape.

2. Increase to medium-high and beat until the mixture is pale and fluffy, scraping the bowl as needed.

3. Reduce to medium and add the eggs, one at a time, beating for about 20 seconds after each addition.

4. Scrape down the bowl then add the vanilla and continue mixing on medium until well combined.

6. Scrape the sides of the bowl and give the batter a few folds to ensure no pockets of butter or flour remain.

7. Transfer the batter to a prepared springform pan and spread in an even layer, smoothing the surface.

8. Slice each of the apple halves into ⅛-inch-thick half circles; do not separate the slices.

10. Carefully divide the fanned apples into 8 equal portions, making sure not to undo the fanned effect.

11. Position the sets of slices on the cake, one set at a time, creating an evenly spaced pattern.

12. Place the last set of apple slices in the center, then sprinkle sugar evenly over the top of the cake before baking.

Cheesecakes, Bundt Cakes, Tortes and More

Orange-Anise Bundt Cake

Start to finish: 1 hour 15 minutes (30 minutes active), plus cooling

Servings: 12

293 grams (2¼ cups) all-purpose flour

50 grams (½ cup) almond flour

2 teaspoons baking powder

½ teaspoon table salt

268 grams (1¼ cups) white sugar

1 tablespoon grated orange zest, plus 2 tablespoons and 1 teaspoon orange juice

2 teaspoons anise seed, coarsely ground

3 large eggs

¾ cup extra-virgin olive oil

¾ cup whole milk

3 tablespoons Sambuca liqueur

1 teaspoon vanilla extract

124 grams (1 cup) powdered sugar

1 teaspoon honey

Italian ciambella is a ring-shaped cake, though the term is also used for certain types of doughnuts. There are countless variations on the sweet; our cake is based on ciambella all'arancia, made with olive oil and orange juice or zest (arancia means orange). We use a standard Bundt pan rather than the traditional ring mold, and we add anise seed for aromatic, licorice-like flavor; make sure to coarsely grind the aniseed so it retains some texture. Sambuca, an anise liqueur, gave us a second layer of flavor; ouzo and pastis are fine substitutes. To skip the alcohol, substitute ½ teaspoon anise extract plus 3 table-spoons orange juice. In an airtight container at room temperature, the cake will keep for up to three days.

Don't use regular cooking spray to coat the Bundt pan. Baking spray, which contains flour, ensures the cake releases easily. Don't overmix the batter after adding the flour; it's fine if a few small lumps remain.

Heat the oven to 350°F with a rack in the middle position. Generously coat a nonstick 12-cup Bundt pan with baking spray. In a medium bowl, whisk together both flours, the baking powder and salt.

In a large bowl, combine the white sugar, orange zest and anise seed. Rub the mixture between your fingertips until the sugar is moistened and beginning to clump. Add the eggs and whisk until lightened in color and slightly thickened, about 30 seconds. While whisking, gradually pour in the oil; whisk until completely incorporated. Whisk in the milk, Sambuca and vanilla. Add the flour mixture and whisk until smooth with a few small lumps.

Pour into the prepared pan. Bake until golden brown and a toothpick inserted at the center comes out clean, 40 to 50 minutes. Let cool in the pan on a wire rack for 15 minutes, then invert the cake onto the rack. Let cool completely, about 2 hours.

In a small bowl, whisk the powdered sugar, orange juice and honey until smooth. Brush evenly over the cake. Let sit until dry, 1 hour.

BUNDT PAN PROBLEMS

Bundt cakes may be beautiful, but they also can be a challenge to get out of the pan intact. That's because the distinctive shape of Bundt pans—designed for a round, tube-shaped cake, with a hollow center and a decorative fluted pattern around the body—makes them especially susceptible to sticking. Ensuring a smooth release starts before the batter goes in the pan. Coating the pan with baking spray (a type of cooking spray that contains oil and flour) is the best bet for Bundts; it works far better than standard cooking spray. Or, try brushing on a thin paste made of softened butter or oil and flour.

Next, focus on the baking itself. A cake won't release well if it hasn't baked properly. And for that, a digital thermometer is best. The traditional toothpick or skewer test for doneness can be misleading and often doesn't reach the center of the cake, so the results can be off. We recommend inserting the thermometer probe into the center of the cake. When it reads 200°F, it's done. If it's 190°F or below, try baking for another 10 minutes, then test again. A good visual cue is when the cake pulls away from the sides of the pan, but a thermometer still is most reliable. After baking, our go-to expert Cheryl Day says cakes should cool in the pan for 25 minutes, just long enough to still be slightly warm to the touch. This lets the cake firm up a bit, making it less likely to break apart. During this resting period—which also allows any steam or moisture to better distribute throughout the cake—the cake will contract slightly, pulling away from the sides of the pan. This can create a small gap between the cake and the pan, making it easier to release.

Cheesecakes, Bundt Cakes, Tortes and More

Amalfi-Style Lemon Cake

**Start to finish: 1 hour
(25 minutes active), plus cooling**

Servings: 10 to 12

428 grams (2 cups) white sugar, divided

2 tablespoons grated lemon zest, plus ¾ cup lemon juice

260 grams (2 cups) all-purpose flour

2 teaspoons baking powder

½ teaspoon table salt

198 grams (14 tablespoons) salted butter, room temperature

3 large eggs, room temperature

½ cup whole milk, room temperature

Giovanna Aceto, whose family owns a generations-old lemon farm on the Amalfi Coast of Italy, showed us how to make torta al limone, a simple lemon cake popular throughout the region. Naturally, Aceto used farm-grown lemons, a variety called sfusato amalfitano that mature to the size of softballs; the fruits are wonderfully fragrant and have a subtle sweetness. Lucky for us, in recipes such as torta al limone, regular supermarket lemons work perfectly well, as their tartness can be offset by adding a little more sugar. Lemon zest perfumes the cake, then a lemon syrup is poured on after baking to keep the crumb moist and add a layer of tangy-sweet flavor. We use a Bundt pan as a substitute for the conical fluted pan that Aceto uses for her torta. The fastest, simplest way to prep the Bundt pan is with baking spray, which is similar to cooking spray, but with added flour. Alternatively, mix 2 tablespoons melted butter and 1½ tablespoons flour, then brush the mixture onto the pan, making sure to coat all the peaks and valleys.

Don't forget to grate the zest before juicing the lemons; grating is much easier when the fruits are whole. Also, don't allow the cake to cool for more than about 10 minutes before the first application of syrup. Absorption is better and more even when the crumb is warm. But after pouring on the second half of the syrup, don't let the cake cool for longer than 30 minutes or it may be difficult to remove it from the pan.

Heat the oven to 350°F with a rack in the middle position. Mist a 12-cup nonstick Bundt pan with baking spray. In a small saucepan, combine 214 grams (1 cup) of the sugar and the lemon juice. Cook over medium-high, stirring, until the sugar dissolves, 4 to 5 minutes. Pour into a 2-cup glass measuring cup or small bowl; you should have about 1¼ cups syrup. Cool while you make and bake the cake.

In a medium bowl, whisk together the flour, baking powder and salt. In a stand mixer with the paddle attachment, beat the remaining 214 grams (1 cup) sugar and the lemon zest on medium until fragrant, 1 to 2 minutes, scraping the bowl once or twice. Add the butter and beat on medium-high until the mixture is light and fluffy, scraping the bowl as needed, 3 to 5 minutes.

With the mixer running on low, add the eggs one at a time, beating until combined after each addition and scraping down the bowl as needed. Increase to medium and beat until well aerated, about 3 minutes. With the mixer running on low, add about one-third of the flour mixture followed by about half of the milk. Next, add about half of the remaining flour mixture, then the remaining milk and

finally the remaining flour mixture. Mix on low until just combined, about 1 minute. Fold the batter a few times with a spatula to ensure no pockets of flour remain; the batter will be thick.

Scoop the batter into the prepared pan and spread in an even layer. Bake until golden brown and a toothpick inserted into the cake about 2 inches from the edge comes out clean, 35 to 40 minutes.

Cool in the pan on a wire rack for 10 minutes. Poke the cake with a toothpick every ½ inch or so, inserting the toothpick as deep as possible into the cake. Slowly pour half of the syrup evenly over the cake, then let stand for about 5 minutes to allow the syrup to soak in.

Slowly pour the remaining syrup onto the cake, then cool for 30 minutes. If the cake looks stuck to the sides in any spots, including the center tube, carefully loosen those areas by inserting a thin-bladed knife between the cake and the pan. Invert the cake onto a platter, lift off the pan and cool to room temperature.

Cheesecakes, Bundt Cakes, Tortes and More

Mexican Sweet Corn Cake

**Start to finish: 1¼ hours
(25 minutes active), plus cooling**

Servings: 8 to 10

3 medium ears fresh corn,
preferably yellow, husked

36 grams (¼ cup) fine yellow
cornmeal

14-ounce can sweetened
condensed milk

60 grams (¼ cup) plain whole-milk
yogurt

179 grams (1¼ cups plus
2 tablespoons) all-purpose flour

2 tablespoons cornstarch

2 teaspoons baking powder

¼ teaspoon table salt

2 large eggs, plus 2 large egg yolks

½ cup grapeseed or other neutral oil

Powdered sugar, to serve

This simple baked treat is ubiquitous in Mexican food markets, street stalls and restaurants. Called panqué de elote, pan de elote or pastel de elote, its texture lands somewhere between cake and cornbread while hinting at custard. At La Cocina de Mi Mamá in Mexico City, we had it for breakfast, but finished with a dusting of powdered sugar, it also makes a casual, homey dessert. Cornmeal is not a typical ingredient in panqué de elote; we add a small amount to account for the fact that the fresh Mexican corn used for making this type of cake is starchier and drier than the fresh corn available in the U.S. If you have more than 250 grams (1½ cups) corn after cutting the kernels from the ears, it's best to save the extra for another use rather than use it in this recipe; the additional moisture may make the cake too wet. Though we've previously advised against using frozen corn kernels in this recipe, we've since adapted it to use either. To use frozen corn, thaw 225 grams (1⅔ cups) cut kernels—frozen corn weighs a little more per cup than fresh—and be sure to thoroughly pat dry before use.

Don't whisk the corn puree into the flour mixture vigorously. Gentle mixing, just until no pockets of flour remain, will minimize gluten development so the cake bakes up tender.

Heat the oven to 350°F with a rack in the middle position. Mist a 9-inch round cake pan with cooking spray. Using a chef's knife, cut the kernels from the ears of corn. Measure 250 grams (1½ cups) kernels and add to a blender; if you have extra corn, reserve it for another use. To the blender, add the cornmeal, condensed milk and yogurt, then puree until smooth, 15 to 20 seconds, scraping down the blender as needed. Let stand for 10 minutes. Meanwhile, in a small bowl, whisk together the flour, cornstarch, baking powder and salt.

To the blender, add the whole eggs and yolks, and the oil; blend on low until smooth, 5 to 10 seconds. Pour the puree into a large bowl. Add the flour mixture and whisk just until evenly moistened and no lumps of flour remain. Transfer to the prepared cake pan and bake until golden and a toothpick inserted into the center of the cake comes out clean, 40 to 45 minutes.

Cool in the pan on a wire rack for 30 minutes. Run a paring knife around the pan to loosen the cake, then invert directly onto the rack and lift off the pan. Re-invert the cake onto a serving platter and cool completely, about 1 hour. Serve dusted with powdered sugar.

Plum Cake with Spiced Almond Crumble

**Start to finish: 1½ hours
(30 minutes active), plus cooling**

Servings: 12 to 14

FOR THE CRUMBLE:

47 grams (½ cup) sliced almonds

65 grams (½ cup) all-purpose flour

109 grams (½ cup) lightly packed
light brown sugar

½ teaspoon ground cardamom

½ teaspoon ground coriander

¼ teaspoon ground allspice

¼ teaspoon table salt

57 grams (4 tablespoons) salted
butter, cut into ½-inch cubes, cool
room temperature

FOR THE CAKE:

195 grams (1½ cups) all-purpose
flour

1½ teaspoons baking powder

½ teaspoon baking soda

½ teaspoon table salt

120 grams (½ cup) sour cream,
room temperature

1½ teaspoons vanilla extract

¼ teaspoon almond extract

170 grams (1½ sticks) salted butter,
room temperature

268 grams (1¼ cups) white sugar

3 large eggs, room temperature

1½ pounds ripe, semi-firm red or
black plums (4 to 6 medium-large),
halved, pitted and each half cut into
4 wedges

In this adaptation of a recipe from the award-winning book "Suqar" by Greg Malouf and Lucy Malouf, wedges of sweet-tart fresh plums melt into a rich, buttery cake, the whole thing finished with a nutty brown sugar and spice crumble that complements the plush, tender crumb hiding just beneath. This fruit-forward cake is ideal for a weekend brunch, but is special enough to serve as dessert after a summery meal. For prepping the baking pan or dish, we use baking spray, which is a mixture of oil and flour, to help guarantee that slices of the cake are easy to remove for serving. If you don't have baking spray, butter the pan or dish, dust it with flour, then tap out the excess. Note that if you use a glass or ceramic baking dish rather than a metal pan, the baking times are slightly longer. If you like, dust the cake with powdered sugar just before serving, or spoon on a little whipped cream, gelato or ice cream.

Don't leave the crumble mixture at room temperature while you make the cake batter. Freezing it, as the recipe instructs, helps ensure the crumble bakes up with a pleasantly pebbly texture. The chilled crumble mixture is sprinkled onto the cake midway through baking so it remains on the surface and does not sink into the batter. Note that the butter for the streusel should be cool room temperature, but the butter for the cake must be at room temperature so it creams easily and yields a light, aerated batter.

To make the crumble, in a 10-inch skillet over medium, toast the almonds, stirring often, until lightly browned and fragrant, 3 to 4 minutes. Transfer to a small plate and let cool.

In a medium bowl, stir together the flour, brown sugar, cardamom, coriander, allspice and salt. Add the butter and toss to coat the pieces, then, using your fingers, rub the butter into the flour mixture until it is mostly incorporated and in pea-sized pieces. Stir in the almonds. Transfer to a pie plate and, using your hands, press the mixture into an even layer about ¼ inch thick. Freeze uncovered until ready to use.

To make the cake, heat the oven to 350°F with a rack in the middle position. Mist a 9-by-13-inch baking pan or baking dish with baking spray; set aside. In a medium bowl, whisk together the flour, baking powder, baking soda and salt. In a small bowl, whisk together the sour cream, vanilla and almond extract.

In a stand mixer with the paddle attachment, beat the butter and white sugar on medium until light and fluffy, 3 to 4 minutes, scraping the bowl as needed. With the mixer running on medium-low, add the eggs one at a time, beating until combined after each addition and scraping the bowl as needed. Increase to medium and beat until the mixture is fluffy and aerated, about 1 minute.

With the mixer running on low, add about one-third of the dry ingredients followed by about half of the sour cream mixture. Next, add about half of the remaining dry ingredients, then the remaining sour cream mixture and finally the remaining dry ingredients. Mix on low until just combined, about 1 minute. Fold a few times with the spatula to ensure no pockets of flour remain. The batter will be thick.

Transfer the batter to the prepared baking pan and spread it in an even layer. Arrange the plum wedges on the surface in three rows along the length of the pan, overlapping them slightly if needed. Bake for 25 minutes if using a metal pan or for 30 minutes if using a glass or ceramic dish; the cake will be lightly browned on top and have enveloped some or all of the fruit.

Remove the crumble mixture from the freezer and the cake from the oven (close the oven door). Working quickly, sprinkle the crumble mixture evenly onto the cake, breaking it up into pieces no larger than ½ inch (the topping should resemble a mixture of damp sand and pebbles). Continue to bake until the crumble is deep golden brown and a toothpick inserted at the center of the cake comes out clean, another 20 to 25 minutes if using a metal pan or another 25 to 30 minutes if using a glass or ceramic dish. Cool on a wire rack for at least 1 hour before cutting and serving.

Sticky Toffee Pudding

To update Britain's sticky toffee pudding—a steamed, too-often bland dessert hidden under a cloying syrup—we worked backward, starting with the sauce. Instead of the traditional cream, we gave the toffee glaze a twist by spiking it with rye whiskey. The whiskey's spice and heat cut through the sweetness of the dark brown sugar and corn syrup; orange zest added brightness. For the cake itself, we wanted to mirror the flavor of the rye, so we used a blend of rye and all-purpose flours. Dates that are steeped in coffee, then pureed, gave body and an earthiness that boosted the rye flavor. Together, the nutty rye and bitter coffee balanced the cake's sweetness. To up the dessert's elegance, we made it in a Bundt pan. Covering the pan with foil kept the cake rich and moist. This mimicked the gentle heat of steaming in a water bath (bain marie), but was far less fussy.

Don't chop the dates. Their texture was unpleasant in the finished dish. The food processor is the best bet. And be sure to check your dates for pits.

To make the cake, heat the oven to 325°F with a rack in the middle position. Lightly coat a 12-cup nonstick Bundt pan with butter, then dust with flour, tapping out the excess. In a medium saucepan over medium-high, bring the dates and coffee to a boil. Remove from the heat and let stand for 15 minutes. Meanwhile, in a large bowl, whisk together both flours, the baking powder, salt and baking soda.

Transfer the coffee-date mixture to a food processor, add the sugar and process until smooth, about 1 minute. Add the eggs, vanilla and allspice. With the processor running, add the butter. Pour the date mixture over the flour mixture and whisk gently until thoroughly combined. Transfer to the prepared pan, cover tightly with foil and bake until firm and a toothpick inserted at the center comes out clean, 55 to 65 minutes. Remove the foil and cool in the pan on a rack for 15 minutes.

While the cake cools, make the sauce. In a medium saucepan over medium-high, combine the sugar, corn syrup, orange zest and salt. Bring to a boil, then cook until the mixture reaches 240°F, 2 to 3 minutes. Reduce to low and add the whiskey, 2 tablespoons at a time, allowing the bubbling to subside before adding more. Whisk in the butter 2 tablespoons at a time until melted and smooth.

Invert the cake onto a platter. Brush the top and sides generously with the warm toffee sauce. Slice and serve drizzled with additional sauce. The cooled, brushed cake can be wrapped tightly in plastic wrap and kept at room temperature for up to 3 days. Cooled sauce can be refrigerated for up to 1 week. To reheat, wrap the cake in foil and place in a 300°F oven until warmed. Microwave the sauce until bubbling.

Start to finish: 1½ hours (30 minutes active), plus cooling

Servings: 10

FOR THE CAKE:

170 grams (12 tablespoons) salted butter, melted and slightly cooled, plus more for the pan

130 grams (1 cup) all-purpose flour, plus more for the pan

227 grams (1½ cups) pitted dates

1 cup brewed coffee

105 grams (¾ cup) rye flour

1 teaspoon baking powder

½ teaspoon table salt

½ teaspoon baking soda

199 grams (1 cup) packed dark brown sugar

4 large eggs

2 teaspoons vanilla extract

1 teaspoon ground allspice

FOR THE TOFFEE SAUCE:

199 grams (1 cup) packed dark brown sugar

218 grams (⅔ cup) light corn syrup

2 teaspoons grated orange zest

⅛ teaspoon table salt

¼ cup plus 2 tablespoons rye whiskey

113 grams (8 tablespoons) cold salted butter, cut into 8 pieces

Glazed Guinness Gingerbread

Start to finish: 1¾ hours (30 minutes active), plus cooling and drying

Servings: 12

FOR THE GINGERBREAD:

418 grams (1¼ cups) light/mild molasses

1 cup Guinness or other stout beer (see headnote)

2 teaspoons instant espresso powder

1 teaspoon baking soda

358 grams (2¾ cups) all-purpose flour, plus more for the pan

25 grams (¼ cup) ground ginger

2 teaspoons ground cinnamon

1 teaspoon ground nutmeg

1 teaspoon baking powder

½ teaspoon table salt

3 large eggs

214 grams (1 cup) white sugar

1 cup grapeseed or other neutral oil

FOR THE GLAZE AND TOPPING:

155 grams (1¼ cups) powdered sugar

2 tablespoons stout beer

1 tablespoon light/mild molasses

2 tablespoons chopped crystallized ginger

This spicy gingerbread is our adaptation of a recipe in "Soframiz" by Ana Sortun and Maura Kilpatrick, chef/owners of Sofra Bakery and Café in Cambridge, Massachusetts. The molasses and Guinness (you can use another type of stout, if you prefer) share smoky, roasty, bittersweet notes that are further deepened by the addition of espresso powder. A simple glaze made with some of the molasses and stout left over from the cake adds sweetness and shine to the surface, and bits of crystallized ginger scattered on top offer an extra hit of spice and texture. If you can, make and glaze the cake a day in advance—its flavor and texture improve overnight. Covered tightly, leftovers will keep for up to three days at room temperature.

Don't use robust/full-flavored molasses or blackstrap molasses; the flavor will overpower the other ingredients. After pouring the stout into the measuring cup, be sure to allow the foam to subside in order to get an accurate measurement. Be sure to use a large saucepan to heat the molasses and stout. When the baking soda is stirred in, the mixture bubbles vigorously and will flow over if the saucepan is too small.

To make the cake, in a large saucepan over medium-high, simmer the molasses, stout and espresso powder, stirring well. Remove from the heat and immediately stir in the baking soda; the mixture will foam energetically. Stir until the foam subsides, then transfer to a medium bowl and cool until barely warm to the touch, about 20 minutes, stirring occasionally for faster cooling.

Heat the oven to 350°F with a rack in the middle position. Mist a 9-by-13-inch pan with cooking spray, dust evenly with flour, then tap out the excess. In a medium bowl, whisk together the flour, ginger, cinnamon, nutmeg, baking powder and salt, breaking up any clumps of spices.

In a stand mixer with the whisk attachment, beat the eggs on medium until combined, about 15 seconds. Add the white sugar, increase to high and beat until well aerated and tripled in volume, about 5 minutes. Reduce to medium-low and slowly add the oil; continue to beat until homogeneous, about 15 seconds. With the mixer still running on medium-low, gradually add the cooled stout-molasses mixture, then beat until fully incorporated, about 30 seconds.

With the mixer running on low, add the dry ingredients, then increase to medium and mix until just incorporated, about 10 seconds; do not overmix. Using a silicone spatula, fold the batter, scraping the bottom and sides of the bowl, to ensure that no pockets of flour or egg remain. The batter will be thin.

Pour into the prepared pan and bake until a toothpick inserted at the center comes out clean, 45 to 55 minutes. Cool to room temperature in the pan on a wire rack. Once cooled, make the glaze. In a medium bowl, whisk together the powdered sugar, stout and molasses. Pour onto the cake and spread in an even layer, then sprinkle with the crystallized ginger. Let the glaze dry for at least 30 minutes.

Cheesecakes, Bundt Cakes, Tortes and More

Portuguese Sponge Cake

Start to finish: 45 minutes (25 minutes active), plus cooling

Servings: 8 to 10

120 grams (1 cup) cake flour

1 teaspoon baking powder

⅜ teaspoon table salt

4 large eggs, plus 4 large egg yolks

2 teaspoons vanilla extract

214 grams (1 cup) white sugar

¼ cup extra-virgin olive oil

Outside Lisbon, home cook Lourdes Varelia baked for us a classic Portuguese sponge cake called pão de ló. Its outward appearance was, to us, unusual—deeply browned, wrinkly and sunken, and the dessert was brought to the table in the parchment in which it was baked. And another surprise was in store: slicing revealed a layer of gooey, barely baked batter between the upper crust and the airy, golden-hued crumb. Sweet, eggy and tender, the unadorned cake was simple yet supremely satisfying. When attempting to re-create pão de ló at Milk Street, we turned to a recipe from "My Lisbon" by Nuno Mendes, who, in an uncommon twist, adds olive oil, giving the cake subtle fruity notes along with a little more richness. We adjusted ingredient amounts and added some baking powder as insurance for a lofty rise; we also modified the mixing method and the baking time and temperature. The cake is delicious with Mendes' suggested garnishes—a drizzle of additional olive oil and a sprinkle of flaky sea salt—but it also is excellent with fresh berries and lightly sweetened whipped cream. Leftovers will keep in an airtight container at room temperature for up to three days.

Don't overbake the cake. The best way to test for doneness is to insert a toothpick 2 inches from the edge, not into the center of the cake; the toothpick should come out clean. The type of cake pan—dark-colored nonstick or conventional light-toned metal—affects how quickly the cake bakes, so the recipe includes two different baking times, one for dark pans and one for light. Don't be alarmed if the cake sinks and shrinks dramatically and forms folds and creases as it cools; this is normal.

Heat the oven to 375° with a rack in the middle position. Cut a 12- to 14-inch round of kitchen parchment. Mist a 9-inch springform pan with cooking spray and line the pan with the parchment round, pushing the paper into the edge and against the sides of the pan, allowing it to form folds and pleats. In a small bowl, whisk together the flour, baking powder and salt.

In a stand mixer with the whisk attachment, beat the whole eggs, egg yolks and vanilla on medium until frothy, about 2 minutes. With the mixer running, gradually stream in the sugar. Increase to medium-high and beat until very thick, pale and tripled in volume, about 6 minutes.

Reduce to medium-low and, with the mixer running, add the flour mixture 1 spoonful at a time, then slowly drizzle in the oil. Immediately stop the mixer (the oil will not be fully incorporated), detach the bowl and fold with a silicone spatula just until the batter is homogeneous; it will be light, airy and pourable.

Pour the batter into the prepared pan and bake until the cake is domed and well-browned, the center jiggles slightly when the pan is gently shaken and a toothpick inserted 2 inches in from the edge comes out clean, 22 to 25 minutes if using a dark-colored pan or 30 to 33 minutes if using a light-colored pan.

Cool in the pan on a wire rack until barely warm, about 1 hour; the cake will deflate as it cools. If areas of the cake's circumference stick to the sides of the pan, run a knife around the inside of the pan to loosen. Lift the cake out of the pan using the edges of the parchment or remove the sides of the springform pan. When ready to serve, carefully pull the parchment away from the sides of the cake, then cut into wedges.

Danish Dream Cake

Start to finish: 50 minutes, plus cooling

Servings: 12

210 grams (1¾ cups) cake flour, plus more for the pan

1½ teaspoons baking powder

4 large eggs

214 grams (1 cup) white sugar

2 teaspoons vanilla extract

¼ teaspoon table salt

1¾ cups whole milk, divided

299 grams (1½ cups) packed dark brown sugar

170 grams (12 tablespoons) salted butter, cut into 3 or 4 chunks

338 grams (3¾ cups) unsweetened shredded coconut

In our version of drømmekage (dream cake), a light, fluffy vanilla cake meets a buttery coconut–brown sugar topping. The topping is spread onto the still-warm cake, then a brief stint under the broiler caramelizes the surface. When applying the topping, spoon it onto the cake's edges, which are sturdier than its center, then spread inward to cover the entire cake. You will need a broiler-safe 9-by-13-inch baking pan for this recipe (note that neither nonstick nor Pyrex is considered broiler-safe). For slicing, use a serrated knife to make clean cuts. Wrapped well and stored at room temperature, leftovers will keep for up to two days.

Don't underwhip the eggs and sugar. The mixture should be beaten with the whisk attachment until pale and thick. The air incorporated during whipping is in part what makes the cake light. Also, don't forget to tent the finished cake with foil after broiling. It's an unusual step, but the foil traps a little moisture and prevents the topping from forming a brittle crust so the cake is easier to cut for serving.

Heat the oven to 350°F with a rack in the middle position. Mist a broiler-safe 9-by-13-inch baking pan with cooking spray, dust evenly with flour, then tap out the excess. In a small bowl, whisk together the flour and baking powder, then sift into a medium bowl or onto a large sheet of kitchen parchment.

In the bowl of a stand mixer with the whisk attachment, beat the eggs, white sugar, vanilla and salt on low until the sugar dissolves, about 20 seconds. Increase to medium-high and whip until the mixture is pale and thick, 5 to 6 minutes. Reduce to low, add about one-third of the flour mixture and mix until almost incorporated, about 10 seconds. With the mixer running, slowly pour in ½ cup milk. Repeat with half of the remaining flour mixture and another ½ cup of the remaining milk. With the mixer still running, add the remaining flour mixture and mix just until no flour clumps remain, about 20 seconds. Using a silicone spatula, fold the batter, scraping along the bottom of the bowl, to ensure the ingredients are well combined. The batter will be very thin.

Pour the batter into the prepared pan. Bake until just beginning to brown and a toothpick inserted into the center of the cake comes out clean, about 22 minutes. Set the pan on a wire rack and heat the broiler.

In a medium saucepan, combine the remaining ¾ cup milk, the brown sugar and butter. Bring to a boil over medium-high, stirring to dissolve the sugar, then boil for 4 minutes. Remove from the heat, add the coconut and stir until evenly moistened. Spoon the topping onto the outer edges of the warm cake, then gently spread into an even layer over the surface. Broil until the top is bubbling and deep golden brown, 2 to 3 minutes, rotating the pan if needed for even browning.

Set the pan on a wire rack and tent with foil. Let cool for at least 30 minutes. Cut into pieces and serve warm or at room temperature.

Tangerine-Almond Cake with Bay-Citrus Syrup

Start to finish: 1 hour 10 minutes (20 minutes active), plus cooling

Servings: 8

FOR THE CAKE:

170 grams (12 tablespoons) salted butter, room temperature, plus more for the pan and parchment

225 grams (2¼ cups) almond flour

87 grams (⅔ cup) all-purpose flour

½ teaspoon baking powder

214 grams (1 cup) white sugar

1½ tablespoons grated tangerine zest

2 teaspoons grated lemon zest

¼ teaspoon table salt

4 large eggs, room temperature

3 tablespoons sliced almonds

FOR THE SYRUP:

71 grams (⅓ cup) white sugar

3 tablespoons tangerine juice

2 tablespoons lemon juice

3 small bay leaves

Syrup-soaked cakes are common throughout eastern Mediterranean countries. Easy to make, the cakes also keep well because of the hygroscopic (water retaining) nature of the syrup. Our tangerine-almond cake has a moist, pleasantly dense texture thanks in part to almond meal. (Use blanched almond flour; unblanched almond meal makes for a drier and less appealing cake.) We infuse our citrus syrup with bay leaves, adding an herbal note. We loved the unique flavor of tangerines in this cake, but oranges also work. If you can't find them, substitute orange zest and juice. If you don't have an 8-inch round cake pan, use a 9-inch pan and reduce the baking time to about 45 minutes.

Don't invert the cake without the buttered parchment. The cake's exterior is tacky and will easily stick to other surfaces, peeling off the crust and almonds.

To make the cake, heat the oven to 325°F with a rack in the middle position. Butter the bottom and sides of an 8-inch round cake pan. Line the bottom with kitchen parchment, then butter the parchment. In a medium bowl, whisk together both flours and the baking powder.

In a stand mixer with the paddle attachment, mix the sugar, both zests and the salt on low until the sugar appears moistened and clumps, about 1 minute. Add the butter and mix on medium-low until combined, then increase to medium-high and beat until pale and fluffy, about 3 minutes. Reduce the mixer to low and add the eggs, one at a time, scraping the bowl after each.

Add the dry ingredients and mix on low just until combined, 10 to 15 seconds. Using a silicone spatula, fold until no streaks of flour remain; the batter will be very thick. Scrape the batter into the prepared pan and spread it into an even layer. Sprinkle the almonds on top. Bake until golden brown and the center feels firm when lightly pressed, about 55 minutes, rotating the pan halfway through.

Meanwhile, make the syrup. In a small saucepan over medium, combine all ingredients. Bring to a simmer, stirring until the sugar dissolves. Remove from heat and set aside.

When the cake is done, return the syrup to a simmer over medium. Use a toothpick or skewer to poke holes all over the cake's surface. Brush all of the syrup evenly over the cake. Cool the cake in the pan until barely warm to the touch, about 30 minutes.

Lightly butter a sheet of kitchen parchment, then place it on the cake buttered side down. Invert a large plate on top of the parchment, then invert the plate and cake

BAKING WITH NUT FLOURS

As the name suggests, nut flours are made by grinding nuts to a fine, flour-like consistency. These days, there are many types of nut flours on the market, but we tend to turn to the most prolific of the bunch: almond flour.

Across the board, nut flours contain no gluten and are high in flavorful fats. As a result, they lend baked goods a rich, tender texture and moist, dense crumb.

Desserts that require a lighter interior—like Lemon-Almond Pound Cake (p. 310)—benefit from being made with a blend of flours. Nut flour ensures tenderness, while wheat flour supplies structure. On the other hand, sweets such as Italian Flourless Chocolate Torta (p. 387) are dense enough to maintain their shape sans gluten. This style of baked good can be made entirely with nut flour.

When baking with nut flours, it's best to trust the ratios laid out in the recipe. If inclined to experiment, start by substituting small amounts of wheat flour for nut flour—about a quarter of the total flour volume should be a safe place to start—and increase from there.

pan together. Lift off the pan and remove the parchment round. Re-invert the cake onto a serving platter, remove the parchment and cool completely.

Coconut Layer Cake

**Start to finish: 1½ hours
(45 minutes active), plus cooling**

Servings: 16 to 20

FOR THE CAKE:

330 grams (2¾ cups) cake flour, plus more for dusting

1 teaspoon baking powder

½ teaspoon baking soda

¼ teaspoon table salt

5 large eggs, room temperature

¾ cup buttermilk, room temperature

1 teaspoon vanilla extract

283 grams (20 tablespoons/ 2½ sticks) salted butter, room temperature

482 grams (2¼ cups) white sugar

**FOR THE FROSTING
AND ASSEMBLY:**

678 grams (48 tablespoons/6 sticks) salted butter, room temperature

744 grams (6 cups) powdered sugar

½ cup coconut milk or half-and-half

2 teaspoons vanilla extract

140 grams (2 cups) sweetened shredded coconut or 150 grams (2 cups) grated fresh coconut

Growing up in Los Angeles, Karen Clay lived around the corner from her grandmother, Margaret Newborn. Before and after school, when her parents were at work, she'd stay with Newborn—a born-and-raised Southerner and excellent cook who, as a mother of 10, was incredibly skilled at making a little go a long way. Clay treasures her memories of Newborn's coconut cake: a beautiful, towering creation she describes simply as "dreamy." It was always baked on a whim rather than for celebratory occasions, making the sumptuous treat seem especially magical. Newborn usually prepared the rich, moist cake and melt-in-your-mouth frosting without a recipe and entirely by hand, deeming most tools "too fancy." Whenever possible, she used fresh coconut, which Clay recalls her teenaged uncle cracking open out in the garage. Now living outside Atlanta with her husband and children, Clay has tried recreating the cake, but found her layers too dense, frosting too sweet and the cake lacking in coconut flavor. To replicate Newborn's impressive dessert, with the help of Savannah baker Cheryl Day, we've developed a tall, proud cake, featuring four fluffy layers and airy buttercream. Sweetened shredded coconut works well, but you also can shred raw coconut on the small holes of a box grater; you will need about 150 grams (2 cups), the yield of roughly half a coconut. Though Newborn probably did not use coconut milk in her frosting, we found that mixing just a little into the buttercream not only makes for a perfectly spreadable consistency, it also brings more coconutty goodness along with depth of flavor; half-and-half, if that's what you have on hand, yields a delicious result, too. The cake can be served right away or kept at room temperature for up to two hours before serving. Covered loosely with plastic wrap, the cake can be refrigerated for up to three days; just bring to room temperature before serving.

To make the cake, heat the oven to 350°F with racks in the upper- and lower-middle positions. Mist four 8-inch round cake pans with cooking spray. Line the bottoms with rounds of kitchen parchment, then mist the parchment. Dust the pans with flour, then knock out the excess.

In a medium bowl, whisk together the flour, baking powder, baking soda and salt. In another medium bowl or a 1-quart liquid measuring cup, whisk together the eggs, buttermilk and vanilla; set aside.

In a stand mixer with the paddle attachment, beat the butter and white sugar on medium until light and fluffy, 4 to 5 minutes. With the mixer running on low, add

about one-third of the flour mixture, followed by about half of the egg mixture. Next, add about half of the remaining flour mixture, then the remaining egg mixture and finally the remaining flour mixture; scrape the bowl as needed. After the final addition, increase to medium and beat until well combined, about 1 minute. Fold the batter with the spatula, scraping along the bottom and sides of the bowl to ensure no pockets of flour remain; the batter will be thick.

Divide the batter evenly among the prepared pans, then spread in an even layer and smooth the surface. Gently rap each pan against the counter to remove any air bubbles. Place 2 pans on the upper rack and 2 on the lower, spacing them evenly. Bake for 15 minutes, then quickly move the pans on the upper rack to the lower rack and the pans on the lower rack to the upper rack. Continue to bake until the center of the cakes spring back when touched and a toothpick inserted at the center comes out clean, 10 to 12 minutes. Let the cakes cool in the pans on wire racks for about 15 minutes.

Run a paring knife around the edge of each pan to loosen the cakes. One at a time, invert the cakes onto the racks and lift off the pans. Peel off and discard the parchment, then cool the cakes to room temperature.

To make the frosting, in a stand mixer with the paddle attachment, beat the butter on medium until smooth and creamy, about 1 minute. With the mixer running on low, add about one-third of the powdered sugar and beat until fully incorporated, 2 to 3 minutes, scraping the bowl as needed. Gradually add the remaining powdered sugar; continue beating until smooth and creamy, about 2 minutes. Add the coconut milk and vanilla; beat on low until combined and the frosting is smooth, about 1 minute, scraping the bowl as needed. Increase to medium and beat for 1 minute to aerate slightly.

To assemble the cake, if the layers domed in the center during baking, turn them upright. Using a long-bladed serrated knife held parallel to the counter and a sawing motion, carefully trim off the domes. (If the cakes baked up flat, there is no need to trim them.)

Set 1 cake layer on the center of a cake plate. (If desired, to keep the plate clean as you frost the cake, cut 5 kitchen parchment strips, each measuring roughly 6 by 3 inches, and tuck them under the edges of the bottom cake layer so they cover the plate). Scoop about ¾ cup frosting onto the center of the cake and, using an icing spatula, spread in an even layer to the edges of the cake. Sprinkle about 2 tablespoons coconut evenly over the frosting. Place a second cake layer on top, aligning it with the bottom layer, then frost in the same way and sprinkle with 2 tablespoons of the remaining coconut. Repeat with the third layer. Place the final cake layer, bottom side up, on top. Spread the remaining frosting on the top and sides of the cake. (Remove and discard the parchment strips, if used.)

Add the remaining coconut to a medium bowl and toss with your hands to separate the shreds. Pick up a handful and gently press it against the side of the cake; repeat until the sides are completely coated. Return any coconut that falls off to the bowl, then sprinkle it over the top of the cake to cover.

Swedish "Sticky" Chocolate Cake

This gooey-centered chocolate cake, a popular sweet in Sweden, is called kladdkaka, which translates as "sticky cake." With only seven ingredients and an easy dump-and-stir mixing method, it's easy to love. For our version, we brown the butter to add a subtle nuttiness, and we use brown sugar for its molasses notes. The cake can be served warm or at room temperature. Top slices with whipped cream, ice cream or gelato.

Don't whisk the eggs into the cocoa-sugar mixture while the mixture is still hot or the eggs may begin to cook on contact.

Heat the oven to 325°F with a rack in the middle position. Mist a 9-inch spring-form pan with cooking spray and line the bottom with a round of kitchen parchment.

In a medium saucepan over medium-high, cook the butter, stirring, until the milk solids at the bottom of the pan are browned and the butter has a nutty aroma, 1 to

**Start to finish: 45 minutes
(20 minutes active), plus cooling**

Servings: 10 to 12

170 grams (12 tablespoons) salted butter, cut into 1-tablespoon pieces

43 grams (½ cup) unsweetened cocoa powder, plus more to serve

249 grams (1¼ cups) packed dark brown sugar

4 large eggs

¼ teaspoon table salt

98 grams (¾ cup) all-purpose flour

85 grams (½ cup) chocolate chips

3 minutes. Whisk in the cocoa and sugar; transfer the mixture to a medium bowl and let cool until barely warm to the touch.

One at a time, whisk the eggs into the cocoa-sugar mixture, followed by the salt. Whisk in the flour, add the chocolate chips and stir until evenly distributed. Spread the batter evenly in the prepared pan. Bake until the edges of the cake spring back when lightly pressed, 30 to 35 minutes. Cool in the pan for 30 minutes, then remove the pan sides. Serve dusted with cocoa powder.

OVER THE TOP

Flavored Whipped Creams

Plain whipped cream is fine, but a cake this rich begs for a topping spiked with bright balancing flavors. And making those tweaks to your typical whipped topping is easy.

Tangy Whipped Cream
Mix **1 cup heavy cream, ¼ cup Greek yogurt or sour cream** and **1½ tablespoons confectioners' sugar** until uniform and frothy, then whip until soft peaks form.

Brown Sugar Whipped Cream
Mix **1 cup heavy cream** and **1 tablespoon light brown sugar** until uniform and frothy, then whip until soft peaks form.

Boozy Whipped Cream
Mix **1 cup heavy cream, 1½ tablespoons confectioners' sugar** and **1 teaspoon kirsch or triple sec** until uniform, then as usual.

Chocolate, Prune and Rum Cake

Claire Ptak has a fairly revolutionary approach to baking—soft-whipped egg whites! undermixed batter!—that sets her apart from most bakers. We were smitten with her chocolate, prune and whiskey cake when we tasted it at her Violet bakery in East London. When we got the recipe back to Milk Street, we knew we needed to adjust it to be more approachable for the American home cook. Ptak uses almond flour in her batter, but we preferred the lighter, more mousse-like texture we got by leaving it out. We followed her lead in under whipping the egg whites and just barely mixing them into the batter. We found dark rum was delicious warm or cool and complemented the molasses. We preferred bar chocolates with 60 to 70 percent cacao. Chocolate chips contain stabilizers that can change the cake's texture; it's best to avoid them. Serve with whipped cream.

Don't use blackstrap molasses in this recipe, as its flavor is too bitter. Regular, non-blackstrap molasses is often sold in two varieties but brands label them differently. "Original," "mild," "robust" or "full" will all work in the cake.

Start to finish: 1 hour and 20 minutes (30 minutes active), plus cooling

Servings: 12

113 grams (8 tablespoons) salted butter, cut into 3 or 4 chunks, plus 1 tablespoon salted butter, room temperature, for the pan

113 grams (1½ cups) pitted prunes, finely chopped

⅓ cup dark rum

1 tablespoon molasses

12 ounces bittersweet chocolate, finely chopped

6 large eggs, separated

71 grams (⅓ cup) plus 54 grams (¼ cup) white sugar, divided

¼ teaspoon table salt

Heat the oven to 325°F with a rack in the middle position. Coat the bottom and sides of a 9-inch springform pan evenly with the 1 tablespoon room-temperature butter.

In a microwave-safe 2-cup liquid measuring cup or small bowl, combine the prunes, rum and molasses. Microwave until the rum is bubbling, 45 to 60 seconds. Let stand for 15 minutes, stirring occasionally.

In a medium saucepan over medium, melt the remaining 113 grams (8 tablespoons) butter. Remove from the heat and immediately add the chocolate, then whisk until melted and completely smooth. In a large bowl, whisk together the egg yolks and 71 grams (⅓ cup) sugar until pale and glossy, about 30 seconds. Slowly add the melted chocolate mixture and continue whisking until smooth. Stir in the prune mixture.

Using a stand mixer with the whisk attachment, whip the egg whites and salt on medium-high until light and foamy, about 1 minute. With the mixer running, slowly sprinkle in the remaining 54 grams (¼ cup) sugar and continue to whip until the whites are thick and glossy and hold soft peaks, about 1 minute.

Whisk one-third of the whipped egg whites into the chocolate mixture to lighten it. Using a silicone spatula, gently fold in the remaining egg whites until the batter is marbled and not fully blended.

Pour the batter into the prepared pan and, if needed, smooth the surface with a spatula. Bake until the edges of the cake are firm and cracked, 35 to 40 minutes; the center will be mostly set, with a slight jiggle when the pan is gently shaken. Let cool in the pan on a wire rack for at least 1 hour; the cake will settle and sink as it cools. To serve, remove the pan sides.

Bête Noire

The creation of cookbook author Lora Brody, bête noire is a flourless chocolate cake that gets its silky, ultrasmooth, almost custard-like texture from the sugar syrup in the base, as well as from gentle baking. We bring a uniquely complex flavor to our version by caramelizing sugar with black peppercorns before dissolving the caramel with orange juice and bourbon. A combination of bittersweet and semi-sweet chocolate yields a rounder, richer finish than just one type of chocolate, while Angostura bitters lend a spiciness and depth that balance the sweetness of the dessert. We forgo the classic ganache coating and opt to use quickly candied orange zest for a garnish that adds contrasting color and texture. Though the cake requires at least four hours of chilling to fully set, it's best served at room temperature, so be sure to remove the cake from the refrigerator at least two hours before serving. For neat slices, dip the knife in hot water, then wipe it dry before each cut.

Don't use a whisk to combine the ingredients for the batter; a large silicone spatula is better. A whisk incorporates air, which leads to bubbles rising to the surface during baking and marring the smooth, shiny surface. Also, don't forget to run a knife around the edges of the cake the moment it comes out of the oven; loosening the edges from the sides of the pan prevents the cake from cracking as it cools. Finally, don't cover the cake before refrigerating, as a cover may trap condensation that can drip onto the cake.

Heat the oven to 275°F with a rack in the middle position. Coat the bottom and sides of a 9-inch springform pan with butter. Line the bottom of the pan with kitchen parchment, then butter the parchment. Set a wire rack in a rimmed baking sheet. In a large bowl, combine the bittersweet and semi-sweet chocolate and the butter; set a fine-mesh strainer across the bowl, then set aside.

Using a vegetable peeler, remove just the outer zest of the orange, not the white pith beneath, in long strips; set the strips aside. Halve the orange and juice it into a liquid measuring cup. Measure 3 tablespoons of the juice into a medium saucepan. Add the bourbon to the remaining juice in the measuring cup, then add enough water to equal 1 cup total liquid; set aside.

Add the 161 grams (¾ cup) sugar to the juice in the saucepan, then add the zest strips and peppercorns. Set over medium-high and cook, without stirring but occasionally swirling the pan, until the sugar dissolves, 1 to 2 minutes. Continue cooking, swirling the pan often, until the sugar caramelizes to deep mahogany brown and the peppercorns begin to pop, 4 to 5 minutes. Remove the pan from the heat and carefully pour in the orange juice–bourbon mixture; the caramel will bubble up and harden. Set the pan over medium, bring to a simmer and cook,

8 tablespoons (1 stick) salted butter, cut into 16 pieces, plus more for the pan

12 ounces bittersweet chocolate, finely chopped

4 ounces semi-sweet chocolate, finely chopped

1 large navel orange

161 grams (¾ cup) plus 71 grams (⅓ cup) white sugar

½ cup bourbon

3 tablespoons black peppercorns

2 tablespoons Angostura bitters

6 large eggs, beaten

Whole-milk Greek yogurt, to serve

stirring, until the caramel has dissolved and the peppercorns no longer stick together, 1 to 2 minutes. Remove from the heat and stir in the bitters.

Immediately pour the hot sugar syrup through the strainer into the chocolate-butter mixture; reserve the strained solids. Jostle the bowl to ensure the chocolate and butter are fully covered with syrup, then let stand for 2 to 3 minutes. Using a silicone spatula, gently stir until the mixture is well combined and completely smooth; it should be barely warm.

Add the beaten eggs to the chocolate mixture and stir with the spatula until homogeneous and glossy, 2 to 3 minutes. Pour into the prepared springform pan. Gently tap the sides of the pan to remove any air bubbles, then use the back of a spoon to smooth the surface. Set the pan on the prepared baking sheet and bake until the cake barely jiggles when the pan is gently shaken, about 45 minutes.

While the cake is baking, transfer the zest strips from the strainer to a small, shallow bowl, removing and discarding any peppercorns stuck to them. Sprinkle the strips with the 71 grams (⅓ cup) sugar, then toss until the strips are completely coated. Cover loosely and store at room temperature until ready to serve.

Remove the cake from the oven and immediately run a thin, sharp knife around the edges to loosen the sides of the cake from the pan. Cool to room temperature in the pan, then refrigerate uncovered for at least 4 hours or up to 24 hours.

About 2 hours before serving, remove the cake from the refrigerator. Remove the zest strips from the sugar and shake off excess sugar; reserve the sugar for another use. Cut the strips lengthwise into thin strips. Remove the sides of the springform pan. Arrange the zest slivers on the cake around the edges. Slice the cake and serve with small spoonfuls of yogurt.

Chocolate-Hazelnut Cream Cake

Start to finish: 1¾ hours, plus cooling and chilling

Servings: 12

FOR THE WHIPPED GANACHE:

170 grams (6 ounces) white chocolate, finely chopped

1 packet (7 grams) unflavored gelatin

2 cups heavy cream

8-ounce container mascarpone cheese

2 tablespoons honey

FOR THE CAKE:

43 grams (½ cup) unsweetened Dutch-processed cocoa powder (see headnote), plus more for the pan

217 grams (1⅔ cups) all-purpose flour

321 grams (1½ cups) white sugar

½ teaspoon baking powder

½ teaspoon baking soda

¼ teaspoon table salt

2 large eggs

1 cup buttermilk, preferably low-fat

⅔ cup grapeseed or other neutral oil

2 teaspoons vanilla extract

FOR THE SOAKING SYRUP:

71 grams (⅓ cup) white sugar

1 teaspoon instant espresso powder

FOR ASSEMBLY:

95 grams (⅓ cup) chocolate-hazelnut spread, such as Nutella

35 grams (¼ cup) toasted skinned hazelnuts, half roughly chopped, half very finely chopped, reserved separately

This impressive and sumptuous special-occasion dessert, composed of two "go-to" recipes from Dominique Ansel's book "Everyone Can Bake," is easier to make than you might think. We did modify both his chocolate cake and the mascarpone whipped ganache, and we also added a coffee syrup for moistening the cake before assembly. We fold a chocolate-hazelnut spread (such as Nutella) into half of the whipped ganache to sandwich between the cake layers; the remaining whipped ganache is spread on top, creating a unique striped effect. The cake itself has the deepest, richest flavor and color when made with a good-quality dark Dutch-processed cocoa powder—we had the best results with Valrhona. Part of the beauty of this dessert is that the cake and filling can be made ahead; even after assembly, the dessert will hold nicely for up to 24 hours. We recommend making the ganache base and the cake a day in advance and refrigerating them separately. The following day, whip the ganache, assemble the dessert and refrigerate for at least two hours or for up to an entire day. For neat slices, cut the cake with a serrated knife that's been warmed in hot water and wiped dry. To store leftovers, press plastic wrap directly against the cakes' cut sides and refrigerate for up to two days.

Don't whip the ganache before the mixture is completely cold and set. If whipped too soon, it won't attain the proper light, fluffy volume. When spreading the whipped ganache on the top layer of cake, the less you manipulate it, the better. Overworking may cause the ganache to become grainy and lose its velvety smoothness. Finally, don't allow the cake to stand for more than about 30 minutes before serving; if it loses too much of its chill, the filling softens and the layers may begin to slide apart.

To make the ganache, put the white chocolate in a medium bowl; set aside. In a small bowl, stir together the gelatin and 2 tablespoons water; set aside. In a medium saucepan over medium, combine the cream, mascarpone and honey. Cook, stirring often, until the mascarpone is fully melted and the mixture begins to bubble at the edges, 6 to 8 minutes. Remove from the heat, add the gelatin mixture and whisk until completely dissolved. Immediately pour the cream mixture over the white chocolate, then let stand for about 1 minute.

Whisk the chocolate mixture until completely smooth. Press plastic wrap directly against the surface and cool to room temperature, then refrigerate until well chilled and fully set, at least 4 hours or up to 24 hours.

To make the cake, heat the oven to 350°F with a rack in the middle position. Mist the bottom and sides of a 9-by-2-inch round cake pan with cooking spray, line the bottom with a round of kitchen parchment, then mist the parchment. Using a paper towel, evenly spread the oil. Dust the pan evenly with cocoa and knock out any excess.

In a large bowl, whisk together the cocoa, flour, sugar, baking powder, baking soda and salt. In a medium bowl, whisk the eggs, buttermilk, oil and vanilla until homogeneous. Add the liquid ingredients to the dry ingredients, and, using a large silicone spatula, fold until the batter is completely smooth.

Pour the batter into the prepared pan, then rap the pan 4 or 5 times against the counter to release any large air bubbles. Bake until a toothpick inserted at the center of the cake comes out clean, about 45 minutes. Cool in the pan on a wire rack for

STEPS »

Cheesecakes, Bundt Cakes, Tortes and More

1. Using a pastry brush, brush the sides of the cake evenly with about one-fourth of the syrup.

2. Using a serrated knife and a gentle sawing motion, slice off the domed surface of the cake, creating a level top.

3. Slice the cake horizontally into two even layers. Carefully lift off the top layer and set aside.

5. Brush the surface of both cake layers with the remaining syrup. The layers should be well moistened but not soggy.

6. Transfer the chilled ganache to the bowl of a stand mixer fitted with a whisk attachment.

7. Using the whisk attachment, whip on high until light and fluffy, 5 minutes, scraping the bowl once.

9. Scoop the chocolate-hazelnut ganache onto the center of the bottom cake layer; use an offset icing spatula to spread into an even layer to the edges.

10. Using a wide metal spatula, lift the top cake layer and gently center it on the chocolate-hazelnut ganache layer; do not press on the cake.

11. Re-whip the remaining ganache until smooth, then scoop it onto the top layer of the cake. Spread in an even layer, or create swirls in the surface.

4. Transfer the other layer to a cake platter, this will become the bottom layer of the cake.

8. Add half of the ganache to the bowl containing the chocolate-hazelnut spread, and fold until homogeneous.

12. Scatter the finely chopped hazelnuts over the top, followed by the roughly chopped hazelnuts. Refrigerate uncovered for at least 2 hours or for up to 24 hours. Before serving, let the cake stand at room temperature for 20 to 30 minutes.

about 20 minutes. Run a paring knife around the edge of the cake to loosen, then invert it onto the rack and lift off the pan. Remove and discard the parchment, then carefully re-invert the cake and let cool completely. Wrap the cake in plastic wrap and set on a large, flat plate. Refrigerate for at least 4 hours or up to 24 hours.

When ready to assemble, make the soaking syrup. In a 1-cup liquid measuring cup or small microwave-safe bowl, stir together the sugar and ¼ cup water. Microwave on high for 30 seconds, then stir until the sugar is fully melted and the syrup is clear. Add the instant espresso and whisk until dissolved. Cool to room temperature.

Unwrap the chilled cake and set it on a cutting board or other flat surface. Using a pastry brush, brush the sides of the cake evenly with 1½ tablespoons of the syrup. Using a serrated knife and a gentle sawing motion, carefully slice off and remove the domed surface of the cake, creating a level top. Now slice the cake horizontally into 2 even layers. Carefully lift off the top layer and set aside; transfer the bottom layer to a cake platter. Brush the surface of both cake layers with all of the remaining syrup, dividing it evenly; the layers should be well moistened but not soggy.

Transfer the chilled ganache to the bowl of a stand mixer. Using the whisk attachment, whip on high until lightened and fluffy, about 5 minutes, scraping the bowl once. Meanwhile, put the chocolate-hazelnut spread in a large bowl and stir to smooth and soften. Scoop half (about 440 grams/3 cups) of the whipped ganache into the bowl containing the chocolate-hazelnut spread, and, using a silicone spatula, gently fold until homogeneous. Scoop the chocolate-hazelnut ganache onto the center of the bottom cake layer, then use an offset icing spatula to spread it in an even layer, all the way to the edges of the cake.

Using a wide metal spatula, lift the top cake layer and gently center it on the chocolate-hazelnut ganache layer; do not press on the cake. Using the whisk attachment, re-whip the remaining ganache on high until smooth, about 30 seconds. Scoop it onto the center of the top layer of the cake and spread it in an even layer or, if desired, create swirls in the surface. Scatter the finely chopped nuts over the top, followed by the roughly chopped nuts. Refrigerate uncovered for at least 2 hours or for up to 24 hours. Before serving, let the cake stand at room temperature for 20 to 30 minutes, but no longer or the filling may become too soft.

Cheesecakes, Bundt Cakes, Tortes and More

Italian Flourless Chocolate Torta

Pasticceria Gollini in Vignola, Italy, not far from Modena, is home to the sumptuous flourless chocolate cake known as torta Barozzi. Created in 1886 by pastry chef Eugenio Gollini and named for Jacopo Barozzi da Vignola, a 16th-century architect, the much-loved sweet continues today to be produced according to a closely guarded secret recipe. Impostor recipes abound, as professional and home bakers alike have attempted to re-create the dessert, and we ourselves set out to devise a formula. It's well known that torta Barozzi is made without wheat flour (and is therefore gluten free). Instead, a combination of ground peanuts and almonds—along with whipped egg whites—deliver a structure that's somehow rich and dense yet remarkably light. We found that we could skip the peanuts, as almond flour alone worked well. To achieve a complex chocolatiness, we use both cocoa powder and bittersweet chocolate (ideally, chocolate with about 70 percent cocoa solids). Instant espresso powder accentuates the deep, roasty, bitter notes and a dose of dark rum lifts the flavors with its fieriness. Serve with lightly sweetened mascarpone or whipped cream, or with vanilla gelato.

Don't use natural cocoa. The recipe will still work, but the cake will be lighter in color and not quite as deep in flavor as when made with Dutch-processed cocoa. Take care not to overbake the cake. Remove it from the oven when a toothpick inserted at the center comes out with a few sticky crumbs clinging to it. After 30 to 45 minutes of cooling, the cake is inverted out of the pan; don't worry about re-inverting it. True torta Barozzi is left upside-down for cutting and serving; we do the same with ours.

Heat the oven to 350°F with a rack in the middle position. Butter an 8-inch square pan, line the bottom with a parchment square and butter the parchment.

In a medium saucepan over medium, melt the butter. Remove from the heat and add the chocolate, cocoa and espresso powder. Let stand for a few minutes to allow the chocolate to soften, then whisk until the mixture is smooth; cool until barely warm to the touch.

In a large bowl, vigorously whisk the egg yolks and 107 grams (½ cup) of the sugar until lightened and creamy, about 30 seconds. Add the chocolate mixture and whisk until homogeneous. Add the almond flour and salt, then whisk until fully incorporated. Whisk in the rum; set aside.

In a stand mixer with the whisk attachment or in a large bowl with a hand mixer, whip the egg whites on medium-high until frothy, 1 to 2 minutes. With the mixer

141 grams (10 tablespoons) salted butter, cut into 10 pieces, plus more for the pan

6 ounces bittersweet chocolate, chopped

21 grams (¼ cup) Dutch-processed cocoa powder, plus more for dusting

1 tablespoon instant espresso powder

4 large eggs, separated, room temperature

161 grams (¾ cup) white sugar, divided

100 grams (1 cup) almond flour

½ teaspoon table salt

3 tablespoons dark rum

STEPS »

1. Add chocolate, cocoa and espresso powder to melted butter, let stand a few minutes, then whisk until smooth.

2. In a large bowl, vigorously whisk together 4 egg yolks and ½ cup sugar until lightened and creamy, about 30 seconds.

3. Add the chocolate mixture, cooled until barely warm, and whisk until homogeneous.

4. Add the almond flour and salt, then whisk until fully incorporated. Whisk in the rum; set aside.

5. Using a mixer, whip the egg whites on medium-high until frothy. With the mixer running, gradually add ¼ cup of sugar.

6. Beat the whites until they hold soft peaks, about 2 minutes. They should cling to the beater, but droop when lifted.

7. Add a third of the whites to the chocolate mixture and fold with a silicone spatula to lighten and loosen the base.

8. Scrape in the remaining whites and gently fold in until no streaks remain.

9. Transfer the batter to the prepared baking pan and gently shake or tilt the pan to level the batter.

running, gradually add the remaining 54 grams (¼ cup) sugar, then beat until the whites hold soft peaks, about 2 minutes. Add about a third of the whipped whites to the yolk-chocolate mixture and fold with a silicone spatula to lighten and loosen the base. Scrape on the remaining whites and gently fold in until well combined. Transfer to the prepared pan and gently shake or tilt the pan to level the batter.

Bake until the cake is slightly domed and a toothpick inserted at the center comes out with a few crumbs attached, 30 to 35 minutes. Cool in the pan on a wire rack for 30 to 45 minutes; the cake will deflate slightly as it cools.

Run a paring knife around the inside edge of the pan to loosen the cake, then invert onto a platter; if needed, peel off and discard the parchment. Cool completely. Dust with cocoa before serving.

Cheesecakes, Bundt Cakes, Tortes and More

Chocolate Olive Oil Cake

**Start to finish: 1¼ hours
(35 minutes active), plus cooling**

Servings: 10 to 12

43 grams (⅓ cup) all-purpose flour

½ teaspoon baking soda

½ teaspoon table salt

113 grams (4 ounces) bittersweet chocolate, finely chopped

¾ cup olive oil (see headnote)

21 grams (¼ cup) cocoa powder, preferably Dutch-processed (see headnote), plus more to serve (optional)

1 teaspoon instant espresso powder

214 grams (1 cup) white sugar, divided

4 large eggs, separated

¼ cup plus 2 tablespoons lemon juice

This rustic chocolate cake is made with two surprising ingredients: olive oil and lemon juice. Extra-virgin olive oil lends fruity, peppery flavor notes. For a less prominent flavor, use light olive oil ("light" indicates the oil is refined, not lower in fat). You could even use a combination of oils—for example, a robust extra-virgin olive oil tempered with a little neutral oil. The lemon juice brings a brightness that balances the richness of the oil and chocolate, and its acidity reacts with the baking soda to provide lift. We prefer the deeper, darker color that Dutch-processed cocoa gives the cake, but natural cocoa works fine, too, if that's what you have on hand. Serve with lightly sweetened whipped cream or with ice cream or gelato. Store leftovers well wrapped at room temperature for up to three days.

Don't overbake the cake. Be sure to test it by inserting a toothpick into the center; it should come out with a few moist crumbs attached, as if baking brownies. Don't be alarmed when the center of the cake deflates as it cools; this is normal.

Heat the oven to 325°F with a rack in the lower-middle position. Mist a 9-inch springform pan with cooking spray. In a small bowl, whisk together the flour, baking soda and salt.

In a medium saucepan over medium, bring about 1 inch of water to a simmer. Put the chocolate in a heatproof large bowl and set the bowl on top of the saucepan; be sure the bottom does not touch the water. Stir occasionally until the chocolate is completely melted. Remove the bowl from the pan. Add the oil, cocoa, espresso powder and 107 grams (½ cup) sugar; whisk until well combined. Add the egg yolks and lemon juice; whisk until smooth. Add the dry ingredients and gently whisk until fully incorporated.

In a stand mixer with the whisk attachment or in a large bowl with a hand mixer, whip the egg whites on medium-high until frothy, 1 to 2 minutes. With the mixer running, gradually add the remaining 107 grams (½ cup) of the sugar, then beat until the whites hold soft peaks, 1 to 2 minutes. Add about one-third of the whipped whites to the yolk-chocolate mixture and fold with a silicone spatula to lighten and loosen the base. Scrape in the remaining whites and gently fold in until well combined and no white streaks remain; the batter will be light and airy.

Gently pour the batter into the prepared pan and smooth the surface. Bake until well risen, the surface is crusty and a toothpick inserted into the center of the cake comes out with a few crumbs attached, 45 to 50 minutes; do not overbake.

Set the pan on a wire rack and immediately run a narrow-bladed knife around the edge of the cake to loosen the sides. Cool in the pan for at least 1 hour before serving; the cake will deflate as it cools. When ready to serve, remove the pan sides and, if desired, dust with cocoa.

Stovetop Chocolate Cake

**Start to finish: 35 minutes
(10 minutes active), plus cooling**

Servings: 8

130 grams (1 cup) all-purpose flour

28 grams (⅓ cup) cocoa powder

1 teaspoon baking soda

¼ teaspoon table salt

218 grams (1 cup) packed light brown sugar

2 large eggs

1 teaspoon instant espresso powder

120 grams (½ cup) sour cream

85 grams (6 tablespoons) salted butter, melted and cooled slightly

1½ teaspoons vanilla extract

Steaming a standard chocolate cake batter produces a light, moist cake, and lets us avoid having to turn on the oven. To elevate the cake above the water that steams it, we fashion a ring from foil. Brown sugar and espresso powder give the cake complexity, while sour cream adds richness and a welcome tang. If your Dutch oven has a self-basting lid—bumps or spikes on the underside—lay a sheet of foil across the top of the pot before putting the lid in place to prevent water from dripping onto the surface. We like serving this cake dusted with powdered sugar or topped with whipped cream.

Don't open the Dutch oven too often while steaming, but do ensure that the water is at a very gentle simmer. You should see steam emerging from the pot. If the heat is too high, the water will boil away before the cake is cooked.

Cut an 18-inch length of foil and gently scrunch together to form a snake about 1 inch thick. Shape into a ring and set it in a large Dutch oven. Add enough water to reach three-quarters up the coil. Mist the bottom and sides of a 9-inch round cake pan with cooking spray, line the bottom with a round of kitchen parchment and mist the parchment. Place the pan in the pot on top of the foil ring.

Sift the flour, cocoa, baking soda and salt into a medium bowl. In a large bowl, whisk the sugar and eggs until slightly lightened, about 30 seconds. Whisk in ½ cup water, the espresso powder, sour cream, butter and vanilla. Add the flour mixture and whisk gently until just combined.

Pour the batter into the prepared pan. Cover the pot and heat on high until the water boils. Reduce to low and steam, covered, until the center of the cake is just firm to the touch, about 23 minutes.

Turn off the heat and remove the lid. Let stand until the cake pan is cool enough to handle. Transfer the pan to a wire rack, then run a paring knife around the edge of the cake to loosen. Let cool completely.

Invert the cake directly onto the rack, lift off the pan and remove and peel off the parchment. Re-invert onto a platter.

CACAO VS. COCOA

It was hard enough knowing which cocoa powder to use when we had two choices—Dutch-processed and natural. Now there's a third option—cacao powder. Since all three are made by processing the dried, fermented beans of cacao pods, we wanted to know whether cacao powder could be used in place of either of the other two. The differences arise in how they are processed. Natural cocoa powder is extracted from beans that have been roasted at high temperature, which removes much of the bitterness. Dutch-process cocoa powder is made much the same, but the beans are treated with alkali, giving them (and the resulting powder) a darker hue and neutralizing their natural astringency. For this reason, many recipes that specify natural cocoa powder also include an alkaline such as baking soda to balance the acidity.

Cacao powder is made using a cold-pressing process, which exposes the beans to significantly less heat. That allows the cacao's bitterness—and depth—to come through clearly. To see how all three compared, we used each in recipes for brownies and chocolate cake. Tasters overwhelmingly preferred the intense chocolate flavor cacao powder gave the brownies; its bitter notes balanced the sweetness of the brownies better than either cocoa powder. For chocolate cake, the results were less straightforward. The smooth taste of Dutch-process cocoa was the favorite, with cacao and natural cocoa roughly tying for second place. In general, we found cacao powder can be substituted for natural cocoa when a more robust chocolate flavor is desired. But the lack of an alkali makes it a poor substitute in recipes that call for Dutch-processed cocoa.

Cheesecakes, Bundt Cakes, Tortes and More

Caprese Chocolate and Almond Torte

This flourless chocolate cake from Capri, Italy (where it is called torta caprese), gets its rich, almost brownie-like texture from ground almonds and a generous amount of egg. Before grinding the nuts, we toast them to intensify their flavor and accentuate the deep, roasted notes of the chocolate. We preferred the cake made with bittersweet chocolate containing 70 to 80 percent cocoa solids. You can, of course, use a lighter, sweeter bittersweet chocolate, but the cake will have less chocolate intensity. Serve slices warm or at room temperature dolloped with unsweetened whipped cream.

Don't forget to reduce the oven to 300°F after toasting the almonds. Also, don't overbake the cake or its texture will be dry and tough. Whereas many cakes are done when a toothpick inserted at the center comes out clean, a toothpick inserted into this one should come out with sticky, fudgy crumbs, similar to brownies.

Heat the oven to 350°F with a rack in the middle position. Spread the almonds in an even layer on a rimmed baking sheet and toast in the oven until golden brown, 8 to 10 minutes, stirring once about halfway through. Cool to room temperature.

While the almonds cool, reduce the oven to 300°F. Mist the bottom and sides of a 9-inch round cake pan with cooking spray, line the bottom with a round of kitchen parchment, then mist the parchment. Crack the eggs into a liquid measuring cup and add the vanilla; set aside.

In a food processor, process 186 grams (2 cups) of the almonds until finely ground, 20 to 30 seconds. Add the chocolate and pulse until the chocolate is finely ground, 10 to 15 pulses. Add the sugar and salt, then process until well combined, about 30 seconds, scraping the bowl as needed. With the machine running, gradually pour in the egg mixture. Continue processing until the batter is smooth and homogeneous, about another 15 to 20 seconds. Remove the blade and scrape the bowl.

Pour the batter into the prepared pan, then sprinkle evenly with the remaining 31 grams (⅓ cup) almonds. Bake until the center feels firm when gently pressed and a toothpick inserted at the center comes out with moist, fudgy crumbs attached, 30 to 35 minutes.

Let cool in the pan on a wire rack for 30 minutes. Run a knife around the sides of the cake, then invert onto a rack. Peel off the parchment and reinvert the cake onto a platter. Serve warm or at room temperature.

Start to finish: 1 hour 10 minutes (20 minutes active)

Servings: 10

217 grams (2⅓ cups) sliced almonds

5 large eggs

2 teaspoons vanilla extract

8 ounces bittersweet chocolate (see headnote), roughly chopped

199 grams (1 cup) packed dark brown sugar

½ teaspoon table salt

1-2-3-4 Yogurt Cake

Start to finish: 1 to 1¼ hours (15 minutes active), plus cooling

Makes a 9-inch loaf cake or 9-inch round cake

4-ounce or 5.3-ounce container plain whole-milk yogurt

1 container grapeseed or other neutral oil

2 containers white sugar

4 large eggs

3 containers all-purpose flour, plus more for the pan

1 tablespoon baking powder

½ teaspoon table salt

In France, gâteau au yaourt is a cake that uses an entire container of yogurt, then cleverly employs the empty container as the measuring cup for the flour, sugar and oil. It's easy to throw together and a perfect recipe to make with children. If you've got a 4-ounce container of yogurt, bake the cake in a 9-by-5-inch loaf pan; if it's a 5.3-ounce container, use a 9-inch round cake pan. The cake is a blank canvas, so feel free to flavor it to your liking with vanilla or other extracts, ground spices or grated citrus zest, but it's also delicious plain, especially accompanied by ice cream. Wrapped well in plastic, leftovers will keep for up to three days at room temperature.

Don't alter the number of eggs, nor the amounts of baking powder and salt. Whether using a 4-ounce or 5.3-ounce container of yogurt, these ingredients remain the same. The 4-ounce loaf-pan version bakes up slightly fluffier than the 5.3-ounce cake-pan version, but the difference is subtle and both are moist and tender.

Heat the oven to 350°F with a rack in the middle position. If using a 4-ounce container of yogurt, mist a 9-by-5-inch loaf pan with cooking spray. If using a 5.3-ounce container, mist a 9-inch round cake pan with cooking spray. Dust the pan evenly with flour, then tap out the excess.

In a large bowl, whisk together the yogurt, oil, sugar and eggs. Add the flour, baking powder and salt; whisk gently until well combined. Scrape the batter into the prepared pan, then spread it in an even layer and smooth the surface.

Bake until golden brown and a toothpick inserted at the center comes out clean, 45 to 50 minutes for a loaf pan or 60 to 65 minutes for a round pan. Cool in the pan on a wire rack for about 30 minutes. Invert the cake out of the pan, then turn it upright. Cool completely before serving.

Chocolate Cake with Vietnamese Coffee Sauce

Start to finish: 50 minutes, plus cooling

Servings: 12

FOR THE CAKE:

½ cup grapeseed or other neutral oil, plus more for the pan

160 grams (1⅓ cups) cake flour, plus more for the pan

43 grams (½ cup) cocoa powder, plus more to serve

1½ teaspoons Chinese five-spice powder

1½ teaspoons baking powder

½ teaspoon table salt

4 large eggs, separated

285 grams (1⅓ cups) white sugar, divided

1 tablespoon vanilla extract

FOR THE SAUCE:

2 tablespoons hot water

2 tablespoons instant espresso powder

14-ounce can sweetened condensed milk

2 tablespoons whole milk

1 tablespoon vanilla extract

⅛ teaspoon table salt

FOR THE WHIPPED CREAM:

¾ cup cold heavy cream

60 grams (¼ cup) mascarpone cheese

1 tablespoon powdered sugar

1 teaspoon vanilla extract

Pinch of table salt

This light but moist chiffon cake pairs cocoa powder with warm, subtly sweet Chinese five-spice, plus a generous dose of vanilla. Baked in a 9-by-13-inch pan, the cake is minimalist in its appearance, so to transform it into a memorable dessert, we created two simple embellishments. First, we took inspiration from Vietnamese iced coffee and created a rich, sticky sauce with sweetened condensed milk and instant espresso powder; the chilled sauce is spooned onto individual pieces. As a final flourish, we whip up a mascarpone-enriched whipped cream for dolloping on top.

Don't substitute instant coffee for the instant espresso powder. Its flavor is less intense and less balanced.

To make the cake, heat the oven to 350°F with a rack in the middle position. Trace the bottom of a 9-by-13-inch baking pan on kitchen parchment, then cut inside the line to create a piece to fit inside the pan. Brush the bottom of the pan with oil and line it with the parchment. Brush the parchment and the sides of the pan with oil and dust lightly with flour, then tap out the excess.

In a large bowl, whisk together the flour, cocoa, five-spice powder, baking powder and salt. In a separate bowl, whisk together the egg yolks, 214 grams (1 cup) sugar, ½ cup water, the oil and vanilla. Add the dry ingredients to the wet and whisk until well combined; set aside.

In a stand mixer with the whisk attachment, whip the egg whites on medium-high until light and foamy, about 1 minute. With the mixer running, slowly add the remaining 71 grams (⅓ cup) sugar and whip until the whites are thick, glossy and hold soft peaks, about 3 minutes.

Using a silicone spatula, fold one-third of the whipped egg whites into the batter to lighten it, then fold in the remaining whites until just combined. Transfer to the prepared pan and bake until a toothpick inserted into the center of the cake comes out clean, about 25 minutes. Cool in the pan on a wire rack for at least 1 hour.

Meanwhile, to make the sauce, in a medium bowl, stir together the water and espresso powder until dissolved. Whisk in both milks, the vanilla and salt. Cover and refrigerate.

When you are ready to serve, make the whipped cream. In a stand mixer with the whisk attachment, whip all ingredients on low until frothy, about 30 seconds. Increase to medium-high and whip until it holds soft peaks, about 1 minute.

Run a thin-bladed knife between the cake and the sides of the pan. Invert the cake onto the rack, lift off the pan and, if needed, peel off and discard the parchment. Re-invert onto a cutting board. Cut the cake into 12 squares and transfer to individual serving plates. Spoon about 1 tablespoon of the sauce over each piece, then dollop with whipped cream. Dust with cocoa powder and serve with additional sauce on the side.

VANILLA 101

Floral, aromatic vanilla is derived from the tiny seeds found in vanilla "beans"—actually the seedpods of a tropical orchid. This powerful flavor enhancer is most commonly used in American kitchens as an extract, made by steeping specially cured vanilla beans in an alcohol solution to infuse it with vanillin, a flavor compound that gives vanilla its characteristic taste and scent. (Vanillin also can be synthesized to create artificial vanilla extract). Double-strength vanilla extract simply uses twice the amount of vanilla beans for the same volume of conventional extract.

However, there are many other forms of vanilla available to home cooks. In general, extract is best in recipes where you want vanilla flavor, but not the telltale flecks that announce its presence. Conversely, vanilla paste is an easy-to-measure option for items enhanced by both the flavor and appearance of vanilla, such as homemade ice cream. Vanilla seeds and pure vanilla powder (made from pulverized vanilla beans) are especially useful for applications where moisture is a consideration. For example, the seeds are ideal as additions to baking recipes in which extra liquid would destabilize a delicate dough, while vanilla powder can be a great ingredient for custom spice blends. Both can be used to make vanilla sugar. (However, vanilla paste and some vanilla powders contain added sweetener, so sugar-sensitive recipes may need adjustment.)

Broken Phyllo Cake with Orange and Bay

**Start to finish: 2 hours
(30 minutes active), plus cooling**

Servings: 10 to 12

FOR THE SYRUP:

214 grams (1 cup) white sugar

Four 3-inch strips orange zest,
plus ½ cup orange juice

3-inch cinnamon stick

2 cardamom pods, lightly smashed

3 bay leaves

FOR THE CAKE:

227 grams (8 ounces) phyllo, thawed

214 grams (1 cup) white sugar

1 tablespoon grated orange zest

240 grams (1 cup) whole-milk
Greek yogurt

1 cup grapeseed or other neutral oil

5 large eggs

1 tablespoon baking powder

¼ teaspoon table salt

In "Aegean," chef Marianna Leivaditaki tells of her attempts at portokalopita, a cake made with dry, broken-up bits of phyllo dough in place of flour. Like many Mediterranean sweets, the cake is doused with syrup after emerging from the oven, which partly explains the tendency toward a heavy, sodden texture. She recounts that it was a friend's mother who baked the best, lightest version of portokalopita she'd ever had, and she obtained the recipe. The phyllo, cut into strips and dried in the oven, creates a layered structure in the cake that, when soaked with syrup takes on a moist, pudding-like consistency. Greek yogurt and oil add richness while eggs bind and lift, with an assist from baking powder. The cake is citrusy with grated orange zest, and the soaking syrup is infused with cinnamon, cardamom and bay for added flavor and fragrance. (Leivaditaki suggests dusting the cake with bay dust, but we put the bay into the syrup.) If you like, serve slices of the cake topped with a spoonful of lightly sweetened cream whipped with a little Greek yogurt (recipe p. 403). Leftovers will keep well wrapped in the refrigerator for up to four days; serve slices slightly chilled or at room temperature.

Don't forget to zest the orange before juicing it. To remove the zest in strips, a Y-style peeler is the best tool. You will need two large oranges for this recipe—one to provide the zest strips and juice for the syrup and one to supply the grated zest for the cake. Also, don't use a cake pan that's less than 2 inches deep. In a shallower pan, the syrup may overflow the rim. Lastly, don't allow the cake to cool before pouring on the syrup, and after the second half of the syrup is poured on, don't be alarmed if the syrup floods the pan. As the cake cools, it will absorb the syrup.

To make the syrup, in a small saucepan, combine the sugar, orange zest strips and juice, cinnamon, cardamom, bay and ½ cup water. Bring to a simmer over medium-high, stirring to dissolve the sugar, then transfer to a 2-cup liquid measuring cup or small bowl; you should have about 1⅔ cups. Cool to room temperature.

Meanwhile, to make the cake, heat the oven to 350°F with a rack in the middle position. Mist a 9-by-2-inch round cake pan with cooking spray, line the bottom with a round of kitchen parchment, then mist the parchment.

Roll the thawed phyllo lengthwise, then slice the roll crosswise ½ inch thick. Transfer to a rimmed baking sheet, using your hands to unfurl and separate the strips. Distribute in an even layer and bake until brittle and light golden brown, 15 to 18 minutes, scraping up and flipping the phyllo once about halfway through;

STEPS »

1. Combine the syrup ingredients in a saucepan, bring to a simmer, then transfer to a 2-cup liquid measuring cup or small bowl. Cool to room temperature.

2. Roll the stack of thawed phyllo sheets lengthwise. Using a chef's knife, cut the roll crosswise into slices ½ inch wide.

3. Transfer the phyllo to a baking sheet, separating the strips. Bake until light golden, scraping up and flipping the phyllo once. Cool to room temperature.

4. Using a stand mixer, beat the sugar and grated zest, then add the yogurt, oil, eggs, baking powder and salt. Beat until well combined, scraping the bowl as needed.

5. Add half of the phyllo to the batter base and fold until almost evenly moistened. Add the remaining phyllo and fold until well combined.

6. Pour the batter into the prepared pan and spread in an even layer without compressing the phyllo. Bake until golden brown and a toothpick comes out clean.

7. While the cake is baking, remove and discard the solids from the syrup. When the cake is done, using a toothpick, poke holes into it about every ½ inch.

8. Pour half of the syrup onto the warm cake; let stand 5 minutes. Pour on the remaining syrup. Cool to room temperature.

it's fine if many of the pieces break as they're turning. Cool to room temperature on the baking sheet.

In a stand mixer with the paddle attachment, beat the sugar and grated orange zest on medium until fragrant, about 30 seconds. With the mixer running on low, add the yogurt, oil, eggs, baking powder and salt. Increase to medium and beat until the mixture is well combined, about 1 minute, scraping the bowl as needed. Remove the bowl from the mixer and, if needed, scrape any zest that is stuck to the paddle attachment back into the bowl.

Add half of the phyllo to the batter base and, using a silicone spatula, fold until the phyllo is reduced in volume and almost evenly moistened. Add the remaining phyllo and fold until well combined and no dry patches of phyllo remain. Pour the batter into the prepared pan and spread in an even layer without compressing the phyllo. Bake until deep golden brown and a toothpick inserted at the center of the cake comes out clean, 45 to 50 minutes. When the cake is almost done, remove and discard the zest strips, cinnamon, cardamom and bay from the syrup.

Set the cake on a wire rack. Using a toothpick, immediately poke holes into the cake every ½ inch or so. Slowly pour half the syrup evenly onto the warm cake, then let stand for about 5 minutes to allow the syrup to soak in. Slowly pour on the remaining syrup. The cake will not immediately take in all of the syrup, so liquid will flood the pan; this is normal. Cool until room temperature and all the syrup has been absorbed, at least 2 hours.

Run a paring knife around the inside edge of the pan to loosen the cake, then invert onto a platter. Lift off the pan and peel off the parchment. Re-invert the cake onto a serving plate.

OVER THE TOP

Yogurt Whipped Cream

Start to finish: 5 minutes
Makes about 3 cups

In the bowl of a stand mixer, combine **1 cup cold heavy cream, 60 grams (¼ cup) cold plain whole-milk Greek yogurt** and **1½ tablespoons white sugar.** Using the whisk attachment, mix on low until uniform and frothy, about 30 seconds. Increase to medium-high and whip until soft peaks form, 1 to 2 minutes. Use right away or cover and refrigerate for up to 2 hours.

Cheesecakes, Bundt Cakes, Tortes and More

Brazilian-Style Chocolate-Glazed Carrot Cake

Start to finish: 1½ hours (30 minutes active), plus cooling

Servings: 12 to 14

FOR THE CAKE:

260 grams (2 cups) all-purpose flour

2 teaspoons baking powder

½ teaspoon table salt

12 ounces carrots, peeled and cut into rough 1-inch chunks (about 2 cups)

321 grams (1½ cups) white sugar

¾ cup coconut cream (from a 5.4-ounce can)

½ cup grapeseed or other neutral oil

3 large eggs

2 teaspoons grated orange zest

2 teaspoons vanilla extract

FOR THE GLAZE AND FINISHING:

113 grams (4 ounces) semi-sweet chocolate (see headnote), finely chopped

¼ cup strained orange juice

1 teaspoon grapeseed or other neutral oil

Chocolate or colored sprinkles, chocolate pearls or roughly chopped cocoa nibs, for sprinkling (optional)

The Brazilian baked sweet bolo de cenoura—which translates from the Portuguese as, simply, "carrot cake"—is a homey, nearly failsafe dessert that finishes a brilliantly hued orange cake with a glossy chocolate glaze. To make the batter, raw carrots, sugar, oil and eggs are blitzed in a blender, then whisked into dry ingredients. We swapped in coconut cream for some of the oil to give the crumb rich, tropical notes and added orange zest to brighten the flavor. It's best to measure the carrots by weight; too much makes the cake heavy and dense. The classic glaze is similar to the Brazilian chocolate truffle confections called brigadeiros, but we opted for an easier mixture of chocolate thinned with orange juice. Though we usually prefer bittersweet chocolate, the milder flavor of semi-sweet is better here. Store leftovers in an airtight container for up to three days.

Don't use regular nonstick cooking spray instead of baking spray, as the cake has a tendency to stick. If you don't have baking spray, mix 2 tablespoons flour and 1½ tablespoons oil to form a thin paste, then use a pastry brush or paper towel to coat the entire inside of the pan. Be sure to use coconut cream, not cream of coconut or coconut milk. And don't skip straining any pulp out of the orange juice.

Heat the oven to 350°F with a rack in the middle position. Mist a 12-cup nonstick Bundt pan with baking spray, including the center tube and all crevices. In a large bowl, whisk together the flour, baking powder and salt.

In a blender, combine the carrots, sugar, coconut cream, oil, eggs, orange zest and vanilla. Blend until smooth, 1 to 2 minutes, scraping the jar as needed. Pour into the dry ingredients and whisk gently until smooth; the batter will be thin. Transfer to the prepared pan.

Bake until the cake is golden brown and a toothpick inserted about 2 inches from the edge comes out clean, 40 to 45 minutes. Cool in the pan on a wire rack for 30 minutes. Run a small silicone spatula between the edges of the cake and the pan to loosen the sides; invert the cake onto the rack and lift off the pan. Cool completely, about 2 hours.

To make the glaze, place the chocolate in a medium bowl. In a microwave-safe liquid measuring cup or small bowl, heat the orange juice on high until just beginning to simmer, about 40 seconds. (Alternatively, in a small saucepan over medium, bring the juice to a bare simmer.) Immediately pour 3 tablespoons juice over the chocolate, then gently shake the bowl to fully submerge the chocolate; let stand until the chocolate softens, about 2 minutes.

Gently whisk the chocolate mixture until smooth. Add the oil, then whisk again until smooth and shiny. Let stand, stirring occasionally, until cooled to room temperature, about 10 minutes. The glaze should have the consistency of pourable yogurt. If it is too thick, whisk in the remaining orange juice 1 teaspoon at a time (it's fine if the juice has cooled).

Transfer the cake to a platter. Using a large spoon, drizzle the glaze onto the cake, allowing it to run down the sides. Garnish with sprinkles (if using), then dust off any sprinkles that landed on the platter. Let the glaze set for at least 15 minutes before serving.

Cheesecakes, Bundt Cakes, Tortes and More

Cranberry and Candied Ginger Buckle

A buckle is a fruit-studded cake with a buttery crumb topping; it's a great breakfast treat, an excellent midday sweet alongside tea or coffee, or a casual, not-too-heavy dessert. Our version is loosely based on a recipe in "Rustic Fruit Desserts" by Cory Schreiber and Julie Richardson. Instead of making an entirely separate crumb topping, we remove a portion of the flour-sugar-butter mixture that is the base of the cake, then mix in a few additional ingredients to create a mixture that bakes up with just the right texture. Covered tightly, leftovers keep for up to three days at room temperature

Don't forget to thaw the cranberries if using frozen. If they are freezer-cold, they will cause the batter to stiffen, which will make mixing difficult.

Heat the oven to 375°F with a rack in the middle position. Mist a 9-by-13-inch baking pan with cooking spray, dust evenly with flour, then tap out the excess.

In a food processor, combine the flour, white sugar, baking powder, cinnamon and salt. Pulse until well combined, 6 to 8 pulses. Scatter the 12 tablespoons butter over the dry ingredients and pulse until the mixture resembles coarse crumbs, about 20 pulses. Transfer to a large bowl, then measure out 165 grams (1 cup) of the mixture and return it to the food processor. To the food processor, add the brown sugar, almonds and remaining 2 tablespoons butter, then pulse until the mixture begins to clump and resembles wet sand, about 20 pulses; transfer to a medium bowl and set aside.

In another medium bowl, whisk together the eggs, sour cream and vanilla. Pour into the large bowl of flour-butter mixture and fold the batter with a silicone spatula until only a few streaks of flour remain. Add the cranberries and crystallized ginger, then fold until evenly distributed; the batter will be thick. Transfer to the prepared pan and spread in an even layer.

Using your hands, squeeze the almond-flour mixture into rough ½-inch clumps, then scatter evenly over the batter in the pan. Bake until the topping is golden brown and a toothpick inserted at the center comes out clean, 40 to 45 minutes. Cool in the pan on a wire rack for at least 30 minutes before slicing. Dust with powdered sugar just before serving, if desired.

Start to finish: 1 hour 10 minutes (30 minutes active), plus cooling

Servings: 12

390 grams (3 cups) all-purpose flour, plus more for pan

214 grams (1 cup) white sugar

1 tablespoon baking powder

1 teaspoon ground cinnamon

¼ teaspoon table salt

170 grams (12 tablespoons), plus 2 tablespoons cold salted butter, cut into ½-inch cubes, reserved separately

42 grams (3 tablespoons) packed dark brown sugar

31 grams (⅓ cup) sliced almonds

3 large eggs

240 grams (1 cup) sour cream

1 tablespoon vanilla extract

12-ounce bag fresh or thawed frozen cranberries (3 cups)

68 grams (½ cup) finely chopped crystallized ginger

Powdered sugar, to serve (optional)

Chapter 9

Cookies, Bars and Brownies

Italian Almond Crumb Cookie

**Start to finish: 50 minutes
(25 minutes active), plus cooling**

Servings: 4 to 6

184 grams (1¼ cups) whole almonds

3 large egg yolks

2 tablespoons whole milk

130 grams (1 cup) all-purpose flour

214 grams (1 cup) white sugar

¼ teaspoon table salt

85 grams (6 tablespoons) cold salted butter, cut into ½-inch cubes

Fregolotta, a Venetian cookie akin to buttery streusel topping, takes its name from "fregola," the Italian word for "crumb." The sweet gets its name not only from the pebbly, crumby appearance of the unbaked mixture, but the cookie also is broken into rustic shards or coarse crumbs for serving. Offer pieces of fregolotta alongside coffee, tea or dessert wine, or crumble it onto bowls of ice cream or gelato. In an airtight container, fregolotta will keep for up to a week.

Don't worry if the almonds are not in uniform pieces after chopping. Uneven bits add to the charm of the cookie. For the crispiest texture, make sure to allow the fregolotta to cool completely before serving.

Heat the oven to 350°F with a rack in the lower-middle position. Place the almonds in a 9-by-13-inch metal baking pan and toast in the oven until lightly browned, 5 to 7 minutes, stirring once. Transfer the nuts to a cutting board and cool; reserve the pan and leave the oven on. Meanwhile, in a small bowl, whisk together the egg yolks and milk.

When the almonds are cooled, roughly chop them and add them to a large bowl along with the flour, sugar and salt; stir to combine. Scatter the butter over the top and, using your fingers, rub the butter into the dry ingredients until the mixture resembles coarse crumbs. Drizzle on the yolk-milk mixture and stir with a silicone spatula until it resembles a combination of pebbles and sand; it should not form a cohesive dough.

Mist the bottom and sides of the reserved baking pan with cooking spray. Transfer the mixture to the reserved pan and distribute in an even layer but do not compress or compact it.

Bake until light golden brown, 25 to 30 minutes. Cool in the pan on a wire rack for about 10 minutes. Using a metal spatula, carefully pry the fregolotta out of the pan and transfer directly to the rack; it's fine if it breaks during removal. Cool to room temperature. To serve, break the fregolotta into pieces of the desired size.

HOW THE FROZEN COOKIE CRUMBLES

For an easier way to satisfy cookie cravings without dragging out the mixer each time, we experimented to find the best way to prep them in advance. Is it better to freeze raw dough and bake as needed or freeze baked cookies and thaw a few at a time? The answer, it turns out, depends on the style of cookie. We tested two varieties—oatmeal drop cookies and slice-and-bake sugar cookies. And in each case, we tried two approaches. First, we baked the cookies and let them cool, then froze them and later thawed them at room temperature. Second, we divided the raw doughs into individual portions, froze them, then baked them from frozen. With the sugar cookies—which are made by rolling the dough into a log, then slicing it into rounds—we found that freezing already baked cookies left them dry and crumbly when thawed. We had far better results when we froze raw slices of the log, then baked those direct from the freezer. But with the drop cookies, we found the difference in freezing methods was negligible. Frozen portions of raw dough baked directly from the freezer and frozen, then thawed fully cooked cookies were equally delicious. Our suggestion: Since cookie recipes vary greatly in sugar and dairy content—the likely sources of the differences in our tests—we suggest freezing individual portions of raw dough and baking those as needed, the technique that gave us reliable results in both cases.

Cookies, Bars and Brownies

Tahini and Browned Butter Cookies

Start to finish: 45 minutes, plus cooling

Makes 18 cookies

260 grams (2 cups) all-purpose flour

1 teaspoon baking soda

½ teaspoon table salt

141 grams (10 tablespoons) salted butter, cut into 8 to 10 pieces

120 grams (½ cup) tahini

299 grams (1½ cups) packed dark brown sugar

54 grams (¼ cup) white sugar

2 large eggs

Tahini isn't just for hummus and sauces. Here, it gives rich, chewy cookies a nutty flavor and pleasant bitterness that plays off the sweetness of the sugar. Browned butter is butter that is cooked until the milk solids caramelize, which infuses the fat with a flavor reminiscent of toasted nuts. In these cookies, browned butter accentuates the sesame notes of the tahini. The cookies will keep in an airtight container at room temperature for up to five days.

Don't forget to stir the tahini. The oil separates and rises to the surface on standing, so before use, tahini requires mixing until the paste is creamy and homogeneous.

Heat the oven to 350°F with racks in the upper- and lower-middle positions. Line 2 rimmed baking sheets with kitchen parchment. In a medium bowl, whisk together the flour, baking soda and salt; set aside.

In a 10-inch skillet over medium-high, melt the butter. Cook, swirling the pan often, until the milk solids at the bottom are golden brown and the butter has a nutty aroma, 1 to 3 minutes. Pour into a large heatproof bowl, being sure to scrape in the browned bits. Whisk in the tahini. Cool, stirring occasionally, until just warm to the touch.

Add both sugars and the eggs, then whisk until homogeneous. Add the flour mixture and stir until no streaks remain.

Scoop the dough into 18 even portions (a generous 2 tablespoons each), placing 9 on each prepared baking sheet, spaced evenly apart. Using the palm of your hand, flatten each portion into a round about ½ inch thick. Bake until the cookies are light golden brown at the edges, 16 to 18 minutes, switching and rotating the baking sheets halfway through.

Let the cookies cool on the baking sheets for about 5 minutes. Using a wide metal spatula, transfer to wire racks and cool completely, about 30 minutes.

Chocolate-Dipped Tahini and Browned Butter Cookies

Once the cookies are fully cooled, in a medium saucepan over medium, bring about 1 inch of water to a bare simmer. Put **170 grams (6 ounces) bittersweet chocolate** (chopped) in a heatproof medium bowl and set the bowl on top of the saucepan; be sure the bottom does not touch the water. Stir occasionally until the chocolate is completely melted. Remove the bowl from the pan. Dip half of the surface of a cookie in the chocolate and return dipped side up to the wire rack. If desired, sprinkle the chocolate-coated area with **sesame seeds** (toasted). Dip the remaining cookies in the same way. Let stand until the chocolate sets, about 1 hour.

Cherry-Almond Coconut Macaroons

Start to finish: 25 minutes, plus cooling

Makes about 12 cookies

120 grams (1⅓ cups) shredded unsweetened coconut

2 large egg whites

54 grams (¼ cup) white sugar

1 teaspoon aniseed

⅛ teaspoon table salt

2 tablespoons cherry jam (see headnote)

23 grams (¼ cup) sliced almonds

Cloyingly sweet, one-dimensional coconut macaroons get a makeover with this simple recipe. We use shredded unsweetened coconut and grind it in a food processor into a coarse flour. We then add cherry jam for color and tangy notes and aniseed for licorice-like fragrance and flavor. Sliced almonds are pulsed in at the end to add texture. If you prefer, substitute apricot preserves or orange marmalade for the cherry jam. The macaroons are best eaten within several hours of baking, but extras will keep in an airtight container at room temperature for up to two days.

Don't overprocess the almonds in the food processor. Pulse only a few times to roughly chop them so they lend texture. Also, be sure to use the upper-middle oven rack for baking. On the middle or lower rack, the bottoms of the cookies had a tendency to overbrown.

Heat the oven to 400°F with a rack in the upper-middle position. Line a rimmed baking sheet with kitchen parchment.

In a food processor, process the coconut until finely ground, about 1 minute. Add the egg whites, sugar, aniseed and salt. Pulse until evenly moistened, about 5 pulses. Add the jam and almonds, then pulse until just incorporated, about 5 pulses.

Using a small ice cream scoop or 2 spoons, drop heaping 1-tablespoon mounds of the mixture onto the prepared baking sheet, spaced evenly apart. Bake until golden brown, about 10 minutes. Cool on the baking sheet on a wire rack for 10 minutes. Using a wide metal spatula, transfer directly to the rack and cool completely.

Benne Seed Cookies

Sesame seeds are known as benne seeds in the South, and these cookies are a nod to traditional Southern benne wafers. The addition of tahini reinforces the nutty notes of the toasted sesame seeds, and browned butter brings richness. We like these cookies made with a mixture of black and white sesame seeds. Black sesame seeds are sold in natural foods stores, Asian markets and in the international aisle of well-stocked supermarkets. Try to purchase seeds that are not pretoasted; if they are, use them straight from the package and toast only the white sesame seeds. If you cannot find black sesame seeds, use just white. Turbinado sugar is a coarse raw sugar; it gives the cookies interesting texture as well as hints of molasses.

Don't toast the black and white sesame seeds separately. Since the black sesame seeds won't darken as they cook, the color of the white seeds will help you gauge doneness. As you toast, stir frequently and pay attention, as they burn easily.

Heat the oven to 350°F with racks in the upper- and lower-middle positions. Line 2 baking sheets with kitchen parchment.

In a 12-inch skillet over medium, combine both sesame seeds. Toast, stirring often, until the white seeds are fragrant and golden brown, 8 to 10 minutes. Transfer to a medium bowl and cool completely; wipe out but do not wash the skillet.

Set the now-empty skillet over medium and melt the butter. Cook, swirling the pan often, until the milk solids at the bottom are browned and the butter has a nutty aroma, 1 to 3 minutes. Immediately pour into a medium heatproof bowl and let cool until barely warm to the touch, 10 to 15 minutes. Meanwhile, add the flour and baking soda to the toasted sesame. Whisk to combine, then set aside.

Into the cooled butter, whisk the tahini, sugar and salt; the sugar will not fully dissolve. Whisk in the egg. Add the flour-sesame mixture; using a silicone spatula, stir until no dry patches remain and the dough is well combined.

Form the dough into thirty 1-inch balls (1 rounded tablespoon each); roll each portion between the palms of your hands while compressing and compacting the dough so the ball holds together. Arrange 15 balls on each prepared baking sheet, evenly spacing them. Using your hand, flatten each into a disk about ¼ inch thick.

Bake until the cookies are light golden brown at the edges, 12 to 14 minutes, rotating the baking sheets and switching their positions about halfway through. Let cool on the baking sheets for about 5 minutes. Using a wide metal spatula, transfer the cookies to wire racks and cool completely.

Start to finish: 45 minutes, plus cooling

Makes 30 cookies

80 grams (½ cup) white sesame seeds

80 grams (½ cup) black sesame seeds

113 grams (8 tablespoons) salted butter

130 grams (1 cup) all-purpose flour

¼ teaspoon baking soda

60 grams (¼ cup) tahini

198 grams (1 cup) turbinado sugar

⅛ teaspoon table salt

1 large egg

Triple Chocolate and Almond Cookies

Start to finish: 50 minutes, plus cooling

Makes 30 cookies

70 grams (¾ cup) sliced almonds

227 grams (8 ounces) milk chocolate, chopped

130 grams (1 cup) all-purpose flour

164 grams (¾ cup) packed light brown sugar

16 grams (3 tablespoons) cocoa powder

½ teaspoon table salt

3 large eggs, beaten, plus 1 large egg white, divided

170 grams (⅔ cup) almond butter

1 teaspoon vanilla extract

170 grams (6 ounces) semi-sweet chocolate, chopped

Flaky sea salt, for sprinkling

These chewy, rich chocolate cookies use an unorthodox one-bowl mixing method that is easy and cuts down on cleanup. Instead of dairy butter, we use almond butter, which makes these cookies especially moist, fudgy and almost brownie-like. We liked them with toasted sliced almonds pressed onto the tops before baking, but they can be left off, if you prefer. If the dough is very sticky when you try to shape the cookies, allow it to stand for five to 10 minutes. As the flour hydrates and the chocolate solidifies, the dough becomes easier to work with. The cookies will keep in an airtight container at room temperature for up to five days.

Don't forget to stir the almond butter before measuring. And don't use inexpensive milk-chocolate candy bars, which will make these cookies too sweet. Opt for good-quality bar chocolate for baking; we liked Guittard. Don't forget to stir the chocolate as it warms in the microwave, and take care not to overheat it, which will cause the chocolate to seize.

Heat the oven to 350°F with racks in the upper- and lower-middle positions. Line 2 baking sheets with kitchen parchment.

Distribute the almonds in an even layer on a prepared baking sheet. Toast in the oven on the upper rack until lightly browned, 6 to 7 minutes, stirring once about halfway through. Transfer to a large plate and let cool. Reserve the parchment-lined baking sheet; leave the oven on.

Put the milk chocolate in a medium microwave-safe bowl. Microwave on 50 percent power for 1½ to 2 minutes, stirring every 30 seconds, until completely smooth and melted.

In a medium bowl, whisk together the flour, sugar, cocoa and salt. Add the whole eggs and mix thoroughly with a silicone spatula. Add the melted chocolate, almond butter, vanilla and chopped semi-sweet chocolate; stir until well combined. In a small bowl, beat the remaining egg white with a fork.

Form the dough into thirty 1½-inch balls (about 1½ tablespoons each), rolling each portion between the palms of your hands. Lightly press each ball into the almonds to coat one side and flatten them into 2-inch disks. Arrange the portions almond side up on the prepared baking sheets, dividing them evenly and spacing them about 2 inches apart. Brush the tops lightly with the egg white and sprinkle with sea salt.

Bake until the centers of the cookies are set and the edges are no longer glossy, 10 to 13 minutes, rotating the baking sheets and switching their positions about halfway through. Cool completely on the baking sheets on wire racks.

Venetian Cornmeal and Currant Cookies

Zaletti are buttery, crisp Italian cornmeal cookies studded with raisins or currants. The dried fruit usually is first plumped in grappa, a fiery Italian brandy, but we opted instead to use orange liqueur for its more nuanced flavor. We then upped the citrus notes with grated orange zest. The cooled cookies will keep in an airtight container for up to one week.

Don't use coarsely ground cornmeal or polenta. Their rough texture will result in crumbly, rather than crisp, cookies.

Heat the oven to 350°F with racks in the upper- and lower-middle positions. Line 2 baking sheets with kitchen parchment. In a small saucepan over medium, bring the currants and orange liqueur to a simmer. Cover, remove from the heat and set aside.

Meanwhile, in a stand mixer with the paddle attachment, beat the butter and sugar on medium until light and fluffy, 1 to 2 minutes, scraping the bowl as needed. Add the zest and beat until combined, about 30 seconds. Add the cornmeal, salt, egg yolk and vanilla; mix on medium until combined, about 30 seconds. Scrape the bowl. Add the flour and mix on low until incorporated, about 30 seconds, then mix in the currants and their liquid.

Form the dough into 1-tablespoon balls (each about 1 inch in diameter) and space evenly on the prepared baking sheets. Using your hand, flatten each to a 2-inch round about ¼ inch thick. Bake until the cookies are golden brown at the edges, 15 to 20 minutes, rotating the baking sheets and switching their positions halfway through. Cool on the baking sheets for about 5 minutes. Using a wide metal spatula, transfer the cookies to a wire rack and cool completely.

Start to finish: 30 minutes (10 minutes active), plus cooling

Makes about 40 cookies

70 grams (½ cup) dried currants

3 tablespoons orange liqueur, such as Cointreau

170 grams (12 tablespoons) salted butter, room temperature

107 grams (½ cup) white sugar

1 tablespoon grated orange zest

73 grams (½ cup) fine yellow cornmeal

¼ teaspoon table salt

1 large egg yolk

1 teaspoon vanilla extract

195 grams (1½ cups) all-purpose flour

Chocolate Biscotti with Pistachios, Almonds and Dried Cherries

Start to finish: 1¾ hours (45 minutes active), plus cooling

Makes about 3 dozen biscotti

110 grams (¾ cup) whole almonds

228 grams (1¾ cups) all-purpose flour, plus more for dusting

214 grams (1 cup) white sugar

28 grams (⅓ cup) Dutch-processed cocoa powder

1 tablespoon instant espresso powder

1 teaspoon baking soda

½ teaspoon table salt

227 grams (8 ounces) bittersweet chocolate, finely chopped (see headnote), divided

3 large eggs

1½ teaspoons vanilla extract

½ teaspoon almond extract

109 grams (¾ cup) roasted pistachios

75 grams (½ cup) dried cherries, roughly chopped

The late Maida Heatter had about a dozen cookbooks to her name, all of them focused on baking sweets. These biscotti, our adaptation of a recipe from "Maida Heatter's Best Dessert Book Ever," are made with a combination of cocoa powder and bittersweet chocolate. With a flavor boost from instant espresso powder, they're dark and rich and not too sugary. Each satisfyingly crunchy slice—perfect with coffee or dessert wine—is studded with pistachios, almonds and dried cherries. We prefer to use Dutch-processed cocoa here, as it lends the cookies a deeper, darker color than natural cocoa, but natural cocoa works, if that's what you have. Once the biscotti are fully cooled, they will keep in an airtight container for a few weeks. If they soften slightly during that time, put them into a 250°F oven for about 10 minutes; they will crisp as they cool.

Don't use chocolate chips in place of the bittersweet chocolate, as chips contain additives that help them retain their shape but give them a waxiness and affect their flavor. Rather, opt for bittersweet chocolate sold in bars or chunks. When chopping the chocolate, aim for pieces no larger than ¼ inch. Large chunks create big pockets of chocolate in the biscotti that reduce their structural integrity.

Heat the oven to 375°F with the racks in the upper- and lower-middle positions. Distribute the almonds in an even layer on a rimmed baking sheet. Toast on the upper oven rack, stirring once, until lightly browned and fragrant, 6 to 8 minutes. Let cool on the baking sheet; reduce the oven to 300°F. When the almonds are cool, transfer to a small bowl; set aside. Line the same baking sheet as well as a second baking sheet with kitchen parchment.

In a large bowl, whisk together the flour, sugar, cocoa, espresso powder, baking soda and salt. In a food processor, combine ½ cup of the flour mixture and 114 grams (4 ounces) of the chopped chocolate. Process until the chocolate is finely ground, about 25 seconds; do not overprocess or the chocolate may begin to melt. Whisk the mixture into the dry ingredients.

In a small bowl, whisk together the eggs and vanilla and almond extracts. Add the egg mixture to the dry ingredients and, using a silicone spatula, stir and fold, mashing the mixture against the bowl with the spatula, until the dry ingredients are evenly moistened and no streaks of flour remain. Add the remaining chopped chocolate, the almonds, pistachios and cherries. Lightly flour your hands and knead gently until the ingredients are evenly distributed.

Lightly flour the counter, then turn the dough out on it and divide it in half. Moisten your hands with water and roll one portion into a 14-inch log. Place the log on one side of one of the prepared baking sheets. Shape the remaining dough in the same way and place on the other side of the baking sheet, spacing the logs about 4 inches apart.

Bake on the lower rack until the dough has spread into flat, fissured loaves that are firm on the surface and appear dry in the cracks, 45 to 50 minutes. Let the loaves cool on the baking sheet on a wire rack for 20 to 25 minutes; immediately after removing from the oven, reduce the temperature to 275°F.

Using a wide metal spatula, carefully transfer the loaves to a cutting board; reserve the baking sheet and its parchment. Using a serrated knife, cut each still-warm loaf on the diagonal into ⅜- to ½-inch slices; use a gentle sawing motion to slice about halfway through the thickness of the loaf, then bear down on the knife, slicing straight down to complete the cut. (This slicing technique helps prevent breakage, as sawing through the entire thickness of the loaf has a greater chance of dislodging nuts, causing the biscotti to break apart.)

Place the biscotti cut side up in a single layer on the prepared baking sheets. Bake until firm and dry, about 20 minutes, rotating the baking sheets and switching their positions about halfway through. Let cool on the baking sheets on wire racks for about 10 minutes. Transfer the biscotti directly to the racks and cool completely.

Chocolate-Almond Spice Cookies

**Start to finish: 1¼ hours
(30 minutes active), plus cooling**

Makes about 24 cookies

¾ teaspoon ground cinnamon

½ teaspoon ground cardamom

½ teaspoon ground ginger

54 grams (¼ cup) plus 285 grams
(1⅓ cups) white sugar

250 grams (2½ cups) almond flour

21 grams (¼ cup) cocoa powder

½ teaspoon table salt

4 large egg whites, lightly beaten

1½ teaspoons vanilla extract

5 ounces bittersweet chocolate,
finely chopped

This recipe is a loose interpretation of the Swiss chocolate-almond holiday cookie known as Basler brunsli. Traditionally, the dough is rolled and cut into shapes before baking, but we opted for an easier drop cookie studded with bits of chocolate. Even without butter, these cookies are intensely rich—and they happen to be gluten-free, too. Both Dutch-processed cocoa and natural cocoa work. If you have a 2-tablespoon spring-loaded scoop, use it for portioning the dough; otherwise, two soup spoons get the job done. The dough can be made ahead and refrigerated in an airtight container for up to 24 hours; bring to room temperature before shaping and baking. The baked and cooled cookies keep well in a well-sealed container at room temperature for up to two days.

Don't skip toasting the almond flour; it gives the cookies a fuller, deeper flavor. But don't forget to allow the almond flour to cool after toasting; if the flour is too hot when the egg whites are added, the whites will cook. Take care not to overbake the cookies or they will become tough.

Heat the oven to 375°F with racks in the upper- and lower-middle positions. Line 2 baking sheets with kitchen parchment. In a small bowl, stir together the cinnamon, cardamom and ginger. Measure ¼ teaspoon of the spice mixture into another small bowl, stir in 54 grams (¼ cup) sugar and set aside.

In a 12-inch skillet over medium, combine the almond flour and remaining spice mixture. Cook, stirring frequently and breaking up any lumps, until fragrant and lightly browned, 5 to 7 minutes. Transfer to a large bowl and let cool until barely warm to the touch, 15 to 20 minutes.

Into the almond flour mixture, whisk in the remaining 285 grams (1⅓ cups) sugar, the cocoa and salt. Use a spatula to stir in the egg whites and vanilla until evenly moistened. Stir in the chocolate.

Form a few 2-tablespoon portions of dough, drop them into the spiced sugar, then gently roll to coat evenly. Arrange on the prepared baking sheets about 2 inches apart. Repeat with the remaining dough.

Bake until the cookies' surfaces are cracked, 12 to 15 minutes, switching and rotating the pans halfway through. Cool for 5 minutes. Transfer to a rack and cool completely.

Dried Cherry and Chocolate Chunk Cookies

Bourke Street Bakery began in Sydney, Australia, and now has multiple locations in New York City. The bakery's dark chocolate sour cherry cookies, one of their most popular creations, were the inspiration for these fudgy treats. Dried cherries hydrated in balsamic vinegar punctuate the cookies with bites of tangy, fruity flavor that offsets the richness of the butter, sugar and dark chocolate. If you like, you can substitute dried cranberries for the dried cherries. Either Dutch-processed or natural cocoa powder works, though we think natural cocoa gives a slightly more intense chocolate flavor.

Don't add the melted butter-chocolate mixture to the beaten eggs until the mixture has cooled until barely warm to the touch otherwise it will overheat the eggs.

Heat the oven to 325°F with the racks in the upper- and lower-middle positions. Line 2 baking sheets with kitchen parchment.

In a small microwave-safe bowl, stir together the cherries and vinegar. Microwave uncovered on high until the cherries are warm and absorb the vinegar, about 1 minute; set aside.

In a 10-inch skillet over medium, melt the butter. Add 1 ounce (¼ cup) of the chopped chocolate and the cocoa, then remove the pan from the heat. Whisk until the chocolate is melted and the mixture is smooth. Let cool until barely warm to the touch. Meanwhile, in a medium bowl, whisk together the flour, baking soda and salt.

In a stand mixer with the paddle attachment, beat the egg and both sugars on medium until light and fluffy, 2 to 3 minutes. With the mixer running on low, add the vanilla, then slowly pour in the chocolate-butter mixture. Beat on medium until homogeneous, 3 to 5 minutes, scraping down the bowl once or twice. With the mixer running on low, add the dry ingredients, then mix just until combined, about 30 seconds. Using a silicone spatula, stir in the remaining chopped chocolate, the pecans and the cherries, along with any remaining liquid, until the ingredients are evenly distributed.

Form the dough into 24 balls (about 2 tablespoons each), rolling each portion between the palms of your hands. Place 12 balls on each prepared baking sheet, spacing them evenly. Bake until the cookies are slightly cracked on top and the edges feel firm, 14 to 16 minutes, rotating the baking sheets and switching their positions halfway through. Cool on the baking sheets for about 10 minutes. Using a wide metal spatula, transfer the cookies to a wire rack, cool to room temperature.

Start to finish: 40 minutes, plus cooling

Makes 24 cookies

150 grams (1 cup) dried cherries, roughly chopped

2 tablespoons balsamic vinegar

113 grams (8 tablespoons) salted butter, cut into 8 pieces

4 ounces bittersweet chocolate, chopped

21 grams (¼ cup) cocoa powder

130 grams (1 cup) all-purpose flour

½ teaspoon baking soda

¼ teaspoon table salt

1 large egg

100 grams (½ cup) packed dark brown sugar

54 grams (¼ cup) white sugar

1 teaspoon vanilla extract

57 grams (½ cup) pecans, chopped

Dutch Butter Cake

**Start to finish: 1¼ hours
(15 minutes active), plus cooling**

Servings: 10 to 12

217 grams (1⅔ cups) all-purpose flour, plus more for the pan

1 large egg, plus 1 large egg, separated

1 teaspoon vanilla extract

226 grams (16 tablespoons) salted butter, cool room temperature

214 grams (1 cup) white sugar

1 teaspoon grated lemon zest

⅜ teaspoon table salt

Cross shortbread with pound cake and you have the classic Dutch baked treat known as boterkoek, which translates as "butter cake." This is definitely the place to splurge on high-fat, European-style butter or cultured butter, if you're so inclined. But whatever butter used, make sure it's salted or the flavor of this cake-like cookie will fall flat. If you find it tricky to gauge doneness, keep in mind it's best to err on the side of overbaking, as the crumb will have a raw, starchy flavor if underdone. We use a springform pan, but a standard 9-inch round cake pan misted with cooking spray and dusted with flour works well, too. After baking, cool the cake completely in the pan, invert it onto a wire rack, then turn it right side up for serving.

Don't beat the butter and sugar until the butter is at cool room temperature, but also don't allow the butter to become so soft and warm that it has a slick, greasy appearance. And when beating, be sure to cream the mixture for a full three minutes, until very light and fluffy, before adding the eggs. This helps ensure the cake doesn't bake up too dense.

Heat the oven to 375°F with a rack in the middle position. Mist the bottom and sides of a 9-inch springform pan with cooking spray, then dust evenly with flour and tap out the excess. In a small bowl, whisk together the whole egg, the second egg yolk and the vanilla. In another small bowl, lightly beat the remaining egg white.

In a stand mixer with the paddle attachment, beat the butter, sugar, lemon zest and salt on medium-high until light and fluffy, a full 3 minutes, scraping the bowl as needed. With the mixer running on medium-low, gradually add the egg-vanilla mixture. Increase to medium-high and beat until fully incorporated, about 10 seconds, scraping the bowl as needed. With the mixer on low, gradually add the flour and mix until just combined, 10 to 15 seconds. Scrape the bowl to ensure no pockets of flour remain.

Transfer the batter to the prepared pan. Using a small offset spatula, spread in an even layer to the edges of the pan, then smooth the surface. Lightly brush with the beaten egg white. Using a fork, score the surface with a crosshatch pattern.

Bake for 15 minutes, then reduce the oven to 325°F. Bake until the cake is golden brown and the center is firm when gently pressed with a finger, another 25 to 30 minutes. Cool in the pan on a wire rack for 30 minutes. Remove the pan sides. Serve warm or at room temperature, cut into wedges.

Rye Chocolate Chip Cookies

**Start to finish: 1 hour
(20 minutes active), plus cooling**

Makes about 24 cookies

140 grams (1 cup) rye flour
(see headnote)

170 grams (12 tablespoons) cold
salted butter, cut into 6 to 8 pieces

130 grams (1 cup) all-purpose flour

½ teaspoon baking soda

¼ teaspoon table salt

2 large eggs

268 grams (1¼ cups) white sugar

1 tablespoon molasses

1 tablespoon vanilla extract

213 grams (1¼ cups) good-quality
dark chocolate chips or chopped
bittersweet chocolate

114 grams (1 cup) pecans, toasted
and chopped (optional)

We've eaten plenty of Toll House chocolate chip cookies. And while they're good, we wanted something more complex, with a robust flavor that could balance the sugar and chocolate. We found inspiration on a visit to Claire Ptak's Violet bakery in London, where she's a fan of switching things up (think rye flour for an apricot upside-down cake). Rye is a little bitter, a little savory, and it makes the perfect counterpoint for the sugary high notes of a chocolate chip cookie. First, though, we had to make a few adjustments. Rye has less gluten than all-purpose flour so it bakes differently and requires more liquid. We decided to go almost equal parts rye and all-purpose flours and recommend that you weigh for best results. Toasting the rye flour added complex, nutty flavor that balanced the sweetness of the cookies. Rye flour texture and flavor varies brand to brand; we preferred the cookies' spread and chew when made with Arrowhead Mills Organic Rye, with Bob's Red Mill Dark Rye as a close second. A touch of molasses (preferably blackstrap, if available) deepened the flavor and added slight bitterness. These cookies continue to firm up after they come out of the oven; it is best to check them early and err on the side of underbaking.

Don't use coarsely ground rye flour, as it absorbs moisture differently than finely ground, causing these cookies to spread too much during baking. Unfortunately, labels usually do not specify, but if the flour is visible in its packaging, coarsely ground has a granularity similar to cornmeal; finely ground rye has a powderiness much like all-purpose flour.

Heat the oven to 350°F with a rack in the upper-middle and lower-middle positions. Line 2 baking sheets with kitchen parchment.

In a 12-inch skillet over medium-high, toast the rye flour, stirring constantly, until fragrant and darkened by several shades, 3 to 5 minutes. Remove the skillet from the heat, add the butter and stir until melted, then transfer to a small bowl. Let the mixture cool until barely warm to the touch, about 10 minutes, stirring once or twice. Meanwhile, in a medium bowl, whisk together the all-purpose flour, baking soda and salt.

In a large bowl, combine the eggs, sugar, molasses and vanilla; whisk until smooth, about 30 seconds. Gradually stir in the rye-butter mixture. Add the flour mixture and stir until combined. Stir in the chocolate chips and pecans (if using). Let the dough rest at room temperature until a finger pressed into the mixture comes away cleanly, about 5 minutes.

Drop 2-tablespoon mounds of dough about 2 inches apart on the prepared baking sheets. Bake until the edges of the cookies feel set when gently pressed but the centers are still soft, 13 to 15 minutes, rotating the baking sheets and switching their positions halfway through. Let cool on the baking sheets for 5 minutes. Using a wide metal spatula, transfer the cookies to a wire rack and cool for at least 10 minutes.

FOR BIGGER FLAVOR, TOAST YOUR FLOUR

Want more flavor from your flour? Toast it! Thanks to the Maillard effect—a heat-triggered chemical reaction that deepens the flavors of foods with proteins and sugars as it browns them—flour can take on deeply rich nutty, roasted flavors. The gluten (protein) and starches (sugar) in most flours make them ideal ingredients for this technique. And toasting affects more than flavor. The heat also deactivates the proteins, weakening the ability of wheat flours to form gluten. Though not appropriate for yeasted breads, this is great for cookies, cakes and quick breads, which benefit from minimal gluten development. We love to toast rye flour for chocolate chip cookies, while toasted semolina elevates Basque-inspired polvorones, and toasted buckwheat flour upgrades Russian blinis. Toasting also increases a flour's liquid absorption, so we've found it best to limit toasted flour to no more than half of a recipe's total flour volume. More than that, and the recipe likely will need additional liquid.

The benefits of toasting are not limited to wheat flour. Besan, a toasted chickpea flour, seasons Burmese salads. In Ecuador, soups often are enhanced with toasted masa. Japanese kinako, a flour of roasted soybeans, lends sweet-savory notes to mochi desserts. And toasted almond flour is essential for Italian amaretti. Though toasting flours is simple, it does require attention, as flour can go quickly from toasted to burnt. The optimal range for Maillard browning is 284°F to 330°F; charring starts at 350°F. We recommend toasting flour in a skillet over medium-high heat. As you toast, stir constantly until the flour is fragrant and darkened by several shades, three to five minutes.

Swedish Gingersnaps

**Start to finish: 3½ hours
(30 minutes active), plus cooling**

Makes 24 cookies

113 grams (8 tablespoons) salted butter, cut into 3 or 4 pieces

100 grams (½ cup packed) dark brown sugar

80 grams (¼ cup plus 2 tablespoons) white sugar

82 grams (¼ cup) dark corn syrup

2½ tablespoons ground ginger

1 tablespoon finely grated fresh ginger

1 teaspoon ground cinnamon

¾ teaspoon grated orange zest

¼ teaspoon table salt

½ teaspoon ground cloves

¼ teaspoon ground black pepper

⅛ teaspoon cayenne pepper (optional)

217 grams (1⅔ cups) all-purpose flour

¼ teaspoon baking soda

1 large egg

Turbinado sugar, for sprinkling

In search of a cookie that would deliver grown-up gingerbread flavor, we came across pepparkakor, or Swedish gingersnaps. With a deep, smoldering spiciness and a texture that actually "snaps," these cookies pair as well with wine as they do coffee or tea. A combination of dark brown and white sugars plus dark corn syrup makes a workable dough that crisps properly. Baking soda helps with browning and gives the cookies lift, making them crunchy but not hard. The pepparkakor's distinctive spice came from ground and fresh ginger, black pepper and cayenne, and we pump up all of them. The dough can be made up to two days in advance. The cookies keep for up to a week in an airtight container.

Don't portion the dough right after mixing; it will be too soft and sticky. Because it is made with melted butter and corn syrup, the dough has to chill before it is firm enough to portion and shape.

In a medium saucepan over medium, combine the butter, both sugars, corn syrup, both gingers, the cinnamon, orange zest, salt, cloves, black pepper and cayenne (if using). As the butter melts, whisk until the sugar dissolves and the mixture begins to simmer. Remove from the heat and let cool until just warm to the touch, about 30 minutes. Meanwhile, in a medium bowl, whisk together the flour and baking soda.

Add the egg to the cooled butter-spice mixture and whisk until well combined. Add to the flour mixture and stir until no dry patches remain. Cover and refrigerate for at least 2 hours or up to 2 days.

Heat the oven to 350°F with racks in the upper- and lower-middle positions. Line 2 baking sheets with kitchen parchment. Divide the dough into 24 portions (heaping 1 tablespoon each). Moisten your hands with water to prevent sticking, then roll each portion between the palms of your hands into a ball. Arrange 12 dough balls on each baking sheet, spacing evenly.

Drape a sheet of plastic wrap over one of the baking sheets, then use a flat-bottomed object such a ramekin or dry-ingredient measuring cup to flatten each dough ball to a ¼-inch thickness. Peel off the plastic wrap and use it to flatten the remaining dough balls. Sprinkle each cookie with a generous pinch of turbinado sugar.

Bake until deep golden brown, 16 to 18 minutes, rotating the baking sheets and switching their positions about halfway through. Cool on the baking sheets for about 10 minutes. Using a wide metal spatula, transfer to a wire rack and cool completely.

Polish Gingerbread Cookies with Honey and Rye

Start to finish: 1 hour, plus chilling and cooling

Makes about 40 cookies

251 grams (¾ cup) buckwheat or clover honey

113 grams (8 tablespoons) salted butter, cut into 6 to 8 pieces

1¼ teaspoons ground black pepper

1 teaspoon ground cinnamon

1 tablespoon ground ginger

½ teaspoon ground cardamom

210 grams (1½ cups) rye flour

195 grams (1½ cups) all-purpose flour

½ teaspoon baking soda

1 tablespoon finely grated fresh ginger

109 grams (½ cup) packed light brown sugar

¼ teaspoon table salt

1 large egg

198 grams (1 cup) turbinado sugar or Espresso Glaze (recipe facing page)

Pierniki, Poland's honey-based gingerbread cookie, is heavily spiced. To replicate that and get the most flavor from our spices, we infuse them into the honey. This both draws out their flavors and distributes them more evenly through the cookies. A dark, robust honey stands up nicely to the intensity of the spices and the nuttiness of the rye flour. Our favorite is buckwheat honey, which has notes of molasses. Clover honey works well, too, but avoid honeys with a distinct floral sweetness, such as orange blossom and wildflower. Traditional pierniki dough is aged for days or even weeks, but we opted to chill the dough for only two hours or up to overnight; if time allows, bake the cookies the day before serving, as their flavor improves with resting. These can be decorated in a couple different ways. Rolling the dough balls in turbinado sugar before baking creates a pretty, crackled appearance. Alternatively, you can drizzle the baked and cooled cookies with an espresso glaze that pairs well with the spices.

Don't chill the cookie dough for longer than 12 hours or the cookies will bake up cakey and thick.

In a small saucepan over medium, combine the honey, butter, pepper, cinnamon, ground ginger and cardamom. Bring to a simmer, stirring occasionally, then transfer to a medium bowl. Let cool until warm, 20 to 30 minutes. Meanwhile, in a medium bowl, whisk together both flours and the baking soda.

Into the cooled honey mixture, stir the fresh ginger, brown sugar and salt. Add the egg and whisk until well combined. Add the flour mixture and stir until no dry patches remain and the dough is well combined. Shape the dough into a disk, wrap in plastic wrap and refrigerate until firm, at least 2 hours or up to 12 hours.

Heat the oven to 350°F with the racks in the upper- and lower-middle positions. Line 2 rimmed baking sheets with kitchen parchment. Put the turbinado sugar, if using, in a small bowl.

Pinch off 1-tablespoon bits from the chilled dough disk and roll them between the palms of your hands into 1-inch balls. If using turbinado sugar, roll each ball in the sugar to coat evenly. Divide the dough balls between the prepared baking sheets, spacing them evenly. Lightly press each one with your hand to flatten to a ¼-inch thickness.

Bake until the cookies are light golden brown at the edges and slightly cracked on top, 10 to 12 minutes, switching and rotating the baking sheets halfway through.

Cool on the baking sheets for about 5 minutes. Using a wide metal spatula, transfer the cookies to a wire rack and cool completely.

If using espresso glaze, use a spoon to drizzle the glaze over the cooled cookies. Let the glaze dry for about 30 minutes.

Espresso Glaze

Start to finish: 5 minutes
Makes enough glaze for
40 cookies

In a medium bowl, combine **2 tablespoons instant espresso powder** and **3 tablespoons plus 1 teaspoon whole milk;** whisk until the espresso dissolves. Add **248 grams (2 cups) powdered sugar;** whisk until the glaze is thick and smooth.

Maple-Glazed Hermits with Cranberries

**Start to finish: 1½ hours
(30 minutes active), plus cooling
and drying**

Makes 24 cookies

293 grams (2¼ cups)
all-purpose flour

1 teaspoon baking soda

1 teaspoon ground cinnamon

1 teaspoon ground allspice

½ teaspoon ground black pepper

¼ teaspoon table salt

113 grams (8 tablespoons) salted
butter, room temperature

299 grams (1½ cups) packed dark
brown sugar

2 large eggs

140 grams (1 cup) dried cranberries

93 grams (¾ cup) powdered sugar

⅓ cup pure maple syrup

Hermits are quintessential New England cookies, and there are many variations. Some are heavy with molasses while others, like ours, are richly spiced. But all hermits are moist and chewy. They're often baked as bar cookies, but we liked ours shaped into rounds and drizzled with a simple maple glaze. The finished cookies keep well in an airtight container for up to two days.

Don't drizzle the glaze on the cookies while they're warm. The cookies need to be fully cooled for the glaze to set.

In a medium bowl, whisk together the flour, baking soda, cinnamon, allspice, pepper and salt. In a stand mixer with the paddle attachment, beat the butter and brown sugar on medium until light and fluffy, about 5 minutes. Add the eggs one at a time, mixing well after each and scraping down the bowl as needed. Add the flour mixture in 2 additions, mixing on low after each until only a few streaks of flour remain. Using a silicone spatula, fold in the cranberries.

Cut a 20-inch length of plastic wrap and lay it on the counter with a long side nearest you. Scrape half of the dough onto the center of the wrap and use the spatula to shape it into a rough log. Starting with the long edge nearest you, use the plastic to lift and roll the dough into a 1-by-12-inch log, compressing as you go to remove air. Wrap the log in the plastic wrap and tightly twist the ends to seal. Repeat with the remaining dough. Set the wrapped logs on a rimmed baking sheet and freeze until firm, at least 1 hour or up to overnight.

Heat the oven to 350°F with racks in the upper- and lower-middle positions. Line 2 rimmed baking sheets with kitchen parchment. Unwrap each dough log and cut it into 1-inch-thick rounds. Arrange 12 rounds, evenly spaced, on each baking sheet

Bake until golden brown and slightly domed, 15 to 20 minutes, rotating the baking sheets and switching their positions about halfway through. Let cool on the baking sheets for 5 minutes, then transfer to a wire rack to cool completely.

To make the glaze, in a small bowl, whisk the powdered sugar and maple syrup until smooth and thick. Using a small spoon, drizzle the glaze over the cookies and let stand until dry, 30 to 40 minutes.

Meringue Cookies with Salted Peanuts and Chocolate

**Start to finish: 2½ hours
(35 minutes active), plus cooling**

Makes 12 small or 6 large meringues

34 grams (¼ cup) salted roasted peanuts, chopped

57 grams (2 ounces) bittersweet, semi-sweet or milk chocolate, finely chopped

6 large egg whites

½ teaspoon cream of tartar

¼ teaspoon table salt

214 grams (1 cup) white sugar

1 teaspoon vanilla extract

1 teaspoon grated orange zest

These light, crisp, cloud-like meringue cookies are the perfect way to use egg whites left over from other recipes. And if you have chocolate chips in the pantry, feel free to swap them in for the bar chocolate. You'll need 57 grams (⅓ cup) of bittersweet, semi-sweet or milk chocolate chips (or use a combination); make sure to chop them so there's enough for good distribution. The meringues can be made into a dozen 3-inch cookies or six oversized 6-inch puffs. Serve them alone or split them open and fill them with whipped cream and scattered with fresh berries. The cookies will keep in an airtight container for up to five days, though if you live in a humid climate, it's best to eat them right away.

Don't add the orange zest earlier than instructed. If it's added before the egg whites attain full volume, the oils in the zest will prevent the meringue from whipping properly. Also, don't underbeat the meringue after adding the sugar. We found that if we didn't adequately whip the meringue, it had a tendency to deflate slightly in the oven. Five minutes gave us good results every time.

Heat the oven to 250°F with a rack in the middle position. Line a rimmed baking sheet with kitchen parchment. In a small bowl, toss together the nuts and chocolate.

In a stand mixer with the whisk attachment or in a large bowl with a hand mixer, whip the egg whites, cream of tartar and salt on medium until frothy and opaque, 1 to 2 minutes. With the mixer running, gradually add the sugar. Add the vanilla, then increase to high and beat for 5 minutes; the whites will be thick, shiny and hold stiff peaks. Remove the bowl from the mixer. Using a silicone spatula, fold in the orange zest and half of the peanut-chocolate mixture.

Anchor the parchment onto the baking sheet by lifting each corner, dabbing meringue onto the baking sheet and replacing the parchment. Scoop the meringue into mounds onto the prepared baking sheet, dividing it into 12 portions of about ½ cup each or 6 portions of about 1 cup each; space the mounds evenly apart. Slightly smooth the tops and sprinkle with the remaining peanut-chocolate mixture.

Bake for 1¼ hours for small meringues or 1½ hours for large; they will be very pale golden brown and have expanded slightly. Turn off the oven, prop open the door with the handle of a wooden spoon and allow to fully dry and crisp, about 45 minutes. Remove from the oven and transfer the meringues from the baking sheet to a wire rack. Cool to room temperature.

VARIATION

Golden Meringue Cookies with Pistachios and Candied Ginger

Follow the recipe, **using salted roasted pistachios** instead of the peanuts, replacing the chocolate chips with **¼ cup chopped candied ginger** and adding **1 teaspoon ground turmeric** and **½ teaspoon ground cinnamon** to the egg whites along with the cream of tartar and salt.

Chocolate Meringue Cookies

**Start to finish: 1 hour 10 minutes
(40 minutes active)**

Makes about 24 cookies

227 grams (8 ounces) bittersweet chocolate, finely chopped, divided

57 grams (4 tablespoons) salted butter, cut into 4 pieces

21 grams (¼ cup) cocoa powder

½ teaspoon instant espresso powder

3 large egg whites

145 grams (⅔ cup) packed light brown sugar

1 teaspoon vanilla extract

¼ teaspoon table salt

These rich, yet airy flourless chocolate cookies have crisp edges and chewy interiors. They rely on whipped egg whites for their structure. To ensure your whites attain the proper volume with beating, they must not contain any bits of egg yolk, and make sure the mixer bowl, whisk and the whisk attachment are perfectly clean and have no trace of oil or fat. Either Dutch-processed or natural cocoa works well in this recipe, but bittersweet chocolate, rather than semi-sweet, will give the cookies more intense flavor. Extras can be stored in an airtight container for up to three days; the edges will lose their crispness but the cookies will still taste good.

Don't omit the step of heating the egg whites and sugar over the saucepan of simmering water. This ensures the sugar fully dissolves so the cookies bake up with shiny, crisp exteriors. But also make sure you don't overheat the mixture (100°F is the ideal temperature), which can cause the whites to cook. Also, the melted chocolate mixture should still be warm when you fold in the whipped egg whites. If it has cooled and thickened, it will be impossible to fold in the whites without deflating them. If needed, before folding in the whites, return the bowl of chocolate to the saucepan and re-melt the mixture.

Heat the oven to 350°F with racks in the upper- and lower-middle positions. Line 2 rimmed baking sheets with kitchen parchment. Measure out 71 grams (2½ ounces) of the chopped chocolate and set aside.

In a medium saucepan over high, bring 1 inch of water to a boil, then reduce heat to a bare simmer. In a medium heatproof bowl, combine the remaining 156 grams (5½ ounces) chopped chocolate, the butter, cocoa and espresso powder. Set the bowl on top of the saucepan; make sure the bottom does not touch the water. Stir occasionally with a silicone spatula until the mixture is completely smooth. Remove the bowl from the pan and cool slightly; keep the saucepan and water over the heat.

In the bowl of a stand mixer, whisk together the egg whites, sugar, vanilla and salt. Set the bowl on top of the saucepan over the simmering water and, while whisking constantly, heat the mixture to 100°F. Attach the bowl to the mixer fitted with the whisk attachment and whip on medium-high until the mixture holds soft peaks when the whisk is lifted, 3 to 4 minutes.

Using a silicone spatula, fold about one-third of the egg white mixture into the chocolate mixture until almost completely combined. Add the remaining egg whites and fold until a few streaks of white remain. Add the reserved chopped chocolate and fold gently until no white streaks remain.

Drop the batter in 2-tablespoon mounds spaced 1½ inches apart on the prepared baking sheets. Bake until the tops have cracked but the interiors still look moist, 12 to 14 minutes, switching and rotating the sheets halfway through. Cool on the baking sheets for 10 minutes, then transfer the cookies to a wire rack to cool completely, about 30 minutes.

Chewy Molasses Spice Cookies with Browned Butter Icing

Start to finish: 1¼ hours (45 minutes active), plus drying

Makes about 18 cookies

390 grams (3 cups) all-purpose flour

1 teaspoon ground cinnamon

1 teaspoon ground ginger

1 teaspoon baking powder

½ teaspoon baking soda

334 grams (1 cup) molasses (see headnote)

66 grams (⅓ cup) packed dark brown sugar

57 grams (4 tablespoons) salted butter, melted

¼ cup buttermilk

2 large eggs

Browned butter icing, (recipe facing page)

These generously sized cookies are soft and cake-like. Spiced with cinnamon and ground ginger and made with only 4 tablespoons of butter, their flavor is mostly about the bittersweet, subtly smoky notes of molasses. Use either mild or "robust" (or "full") molasses, but avoid blackstrap molasses; its potent flavor will overpower the spices and make the cookies taste harsh and bitter. A browned butter icing gives the cookies a rich, elegant finish. Refrigerate leftovers in an airtight container for up to three days.

Don't ice the cookies until they have cooled to room temperature. If they are still warm, the icing may become too soft to spread.

Heat the oven to 350°F with racks in the upper- and lower-middle positions. Line 2 rimmed baking sheets with kitchen parchment. In a medium bowl, whisk together the flour, cinnamon, ginger, baking powder and baking soda; set aside.

In a large bowl, combine the molasses, brown sugar and melted butter. Whisk to combine, then whisk in the buttermilk. Add the eggs and whisk until smooth. Add the flour mixture and fold with a silicone spatula just until no streaks of flour remain; the dough will be thick.

Using a ¼-cup dry measuring cup or a 1½-inch spring-loaded ice-cream scoop, drop scant ¼-cup mounds of dough onto the prepared baking sheets, spacing them evenly. Bake until the cookies are domed and a toothpick inserted at the center comes out clean, 12 to 15 minutes, rotating the baking sheets and switching their positions about halfway through. Cool completely on the baking sheets on wire racks, about 30 minutes. Using a metal spatula, transfer the cookies directly to the racks.

Using the back of a spoon or a small spatula, spread 1 tablespoon icing evenly onto each cookie. Let dry for about 30 minutes before serving.

Browned Butter Icing

**Start to finish: 10 minutes
Makes about 1 cup**

In a 10-inch skillet over medium-high, melt **57 grams (4 table-spoons) salted butter** (cut into 4 pieces). Cook, swirling the pan often, until the milk solids at the bottom are golden brown and the butter has a nutty aroma, 1 to 3 minutes. Transfer to a medium bowl. Add **248 grams (2 cups) powdered sugar, ¼ cup butter-milk** and **2 teaspoons vanilla extract;** whisk until smooth. The icing should have the consistency of smooth peanut butter; if it is too thick, whisk in additional buttermilk 1 teaspoon at a time until spreadable.

Australian Oat-Coconut Cookies

These cookies, known as Anzac biscuits, are one of the traditions associated with Anzac Day, April 25, the day the Australian and New Zealand Army Corps (known as ANZAC) landed at Gallipoli in Türkiye during World War I. They're typically made with golden syrup but we found honey and dark brown sugar were good stand-ins. Toasting the coconut and the oats deepened the cookies' flavor. Be sure to have all the ingredients measured beforehand; it's important to combine everything as soon as possible after the baking soda has been incorporated into the wet ingredients or the leavening will not be as effective. A greased 1-tablespoon measuring spoon helps portion out the dough for evenly sized cookies.

Don't roll the portioned dough into balls. Doing so will knock the air out of the dough, resulting in dense cookies. Also, don't overbake the cookies or they won't have moist, chewy centers.

Heat the oven to 350°F with racks in the upper- and lower-middle positions. Line 2 baking sheets with kitchen parchment.

In a 12-inch skillet over medium-high, toast the oats, stirring often, until fragrant and beginning to brown, about 5 minutes. Reduce to medium-low and add the coconut, then toast, stirring constantly until the oats are golden and the coconut is fragrant, 1 to 2 minutes. Transfer to a large bowl and stir in the flour. Wipe out the skillet.

In the same skillet over medium-low, combine the butter, sugar, coffee, honey, vanilla, orange zest and salt. Cook, whisking, until the butter melts and the mixture reaches a simmer. Remove from the heat, add the baking soda and whisk until pale, foamy and well combined. Immediately scrape the mixture into the oatmeal mixture, then stir until just combined. Scoop up and drop 2-tablespoon mounds of dough, spaced about 2 inches apart, onto the prepared baking sheets.

Bake until the cookies have risen and are deep golden brown but still soft at the center, 8 to 10 minutes, switching and rotating the baking sheet halfway through. Cool the cookies on the baking sheets on wire racks for 5 minutes. Using a wide metal spatula, transfer the cookies directly to the racks and cool completely.

Start to finish: 40 minutes, plus cooling

Makes about 2 dozen cookies

125 grams (1¼ cups) old-fashioned rolled oats

113 grams (1¼ cups) unsweetened shredded coconut

140 grams (1 cup) whole-wheat flour

141 grams (10 tablespoons) salted butter

100 grams (½ cup) packed dark brown sugar

¼ cup brewed coffee

63 grams (3 tablespoons) honey

2 teaspoons vanilla extract

1 teaspoon grated orange zest

¼ teaspoon table salt

1 teaspoon baking soda

Peanut Butter–Miso Cookies

Start to finish: 50 minutes, plus chilling and cooling

Makes 1½ dozen cookies

252 grams (1¾ cups plus 3 tablespoons) all-purpose flour

1 teaspoon baking powder

1 teaspoon baking soda

8 tablespoons (1 stick) salted butter, room temperature

199 grams (1 cup) packed dark brown sugar

122 grams (½ cup plus 1 tablespoon) white sugar

94 grams (¼ cup plus 2 tablespoons) chunky peanut butter (see headnote), room temperature

75 grams (¼ cup) white miso

2 teaspoons toasted sesame oil or roasted peanut oil

1 large egg

2 teaspoons vanilla extract

66 grams (⅓ cup) turbinado sugar

These sweet-salty, chewy-crunchy treats are our adaptation of the wildly popular peanut butter–miso cookies from Falco Bakery in Melbourne, Australia. Umami-rich white miso makes the cookies taste full and complex. Because sodium content varies greatly among different brands of miso, look for one with about 300 milligrams per 12 grams of miso (check the nutrition facts on the label). Turbinado sugar is a coarse sugar with a golden hue; the granules give the cookies a glittery appearance and an appealing crunch.

Don't use natural peanut butter; differences in fat and sugar content from brand to brand may impact the cookies' texture and flavor. Regular chunky/crunchy peanut butters such as Skippy or Jif are best.

In a medium bowl, whisk together the flour, baking powder and baking soda. In a stand mixer with the paddle attachment, beat the butter, brown sugar and white sugar on medium-high until well combined, about 3 minutes. Add the peanut butter, miso and oil, then beat, scraping the bowl once or twice, until light and fluffy, about 2 minutes. Add the egg and vanilla and beat again, then scrape the bowl.

With the mixer on low, gradually add the flour mixture. Mix, scraping the bowl as needed, just until the dough is evenly moistened, 1 to 2 minutes. Using a spatula, mix the dough by hand to ensure no pockets of flour remain; the dough will be very soft. Press a sheet of plastic wrap against the surface of the dough and refrigerate for at least 2 hours or up to 24 hours.

When ready to bake, heat the oven to 350°F with a rack in the middle position. Line 2 baking sheets with kitchen parchment. Put the turbinado sugar in a small bowl. Divide the dough into 18 portions, about 3 tablespoons each, then roll into 1½-inch balls. Dip each in the turbinado sugar to coat one side; set sugared side up on the prepared baking sheet, 9 per sheet. Bake 1 sheet for 10 minutes.

Remove the baking sheet from the oven and firmly rap it twice against the counter to deflate the cookies. Bake for another 5 to 7 minutes, or until the cookies have fissured and are golden at the edges. Cool the cookies on the baking sheet on a wire rack for 10 minutes. Using a metal spatula, transfer the cookies to the cooling rack and cool completely. Meanwhile, repeat with the second batch of cookies.

Rosemary–Pine Nut Cookies

This cookie contains enough sugar to track as a sweet, but it's equally at home on a cheese platter as it is with a glass of milk or a cup of coffee. Our inspiration was a hazelnut-rosemary biscotti by Claudia Fleming, the former pastry chef of New York's Gramercy Tavern who famously blended savory seasonings into classically sweet treats. We chose to reimagine Fleming's biscotti as a buttery, pat-in-the-pan shortbread. A similar firm, sturdy texture without the hassle of rolling, slicing and twice-baking. The cookies can be stored in an airtight container at room temperature for up to a week.

Don't use dried rosemary. Fresh has a better flavor and aroma. Also, don't allow the slab to cool completely before cutting or it'll break into shards. Allow it to cool for about 15 minutes; it will firm up slightly but will still be sliceable.

Heat the oven to 325°F with a rack in the lower-middle position. Line a 9-by-13-inch metal baking pan with foil so the ends overhang the long sides of the pan. In a medium bowl, whisk together the flour and cornmeal.

In a stand mixer with the paddle attachment, mix the sugar, rosemary and orange zest on low until the sugar is moistened and begins to clump, 1 to 2 minutes. Add the room-temperature butter, increase to medium-high and beat until light and fluffy, 3 to 5 minutes, scraping the bowl twice. Reduce to low and gradually add the flour mixture. Scrape the bowl and continue to mix on low until the dough forms around the paddle, about 1 minute.

Crumble the dough evenly into the prepared pan. Coat the bottom of a flat-bottomed object such as a ramekin or dry-ingredient measuring cup with oil, then use it to press the dough into an even layer. Evenly sprinkle the pine nuts onto the dough and press down firmly.

In a small bowl, stir together the melted butter and the honey. Brush the mixture onto the nut-topped dough, then bake until deep golden brown, 40 to 45 minutes.

Let cool in the pan for 15 minutes. Using the foil overhang as handles, lift the slab out of the pan and set on a cutting board. Cut while warm into 24 pieces, then cool completely on a wire rack.

Start to finish: 1½ hours (30 minutes active), plus cooling

Makes 24 cookies

195 grams (1½ cups) all-purpose flour

73 grams (½ cup) fine cornmeal

107 grams (½ cup) white sugar

1 tablespoon minced fresh rosemary

2 teaspoons grated orange zest

198 grams (14 tablespoons) salted butter, cut into 1-tablespoon pieces, room temperature, plus 28 grams (2 tablespoons) salted butter, melted, divided

140 grams (1 cup) pine nuts

63 grams (3 tablespoons) honey

Linzer Bars

Start to finish: 1¾ hours (35 minutes active), plus cooling

Makes 16 bars

161 grams (¾ cup) white sugar

55 grams (½ cup) walnuts

228 grams (1¾ cups) all-purpose flour

1 tablespoon unsweetened cocoa powder

1 teaspoon ground cinnamon

½ teaspoon ground black pepper

¼ teaspoon ground cloves

¼ teaspoon ground allspice

¼ teaspoon table salt, plus a pinch

4 teaspoons grated lemon zest, divided

141 grams (10 tablespoons) cold salted butter, cut into ½-inch cubes

1 large egg, separated

240 grams (¾ cup) seedless raspberry jam (see headnote)

Turbinado sugar, for sprinkling

Linzertorte is from Linz, Austria, but these more casual bars were inspired by ones we tasted in Frankfurt, Germany. Whereas the classic dessert requires a tart pan, a lattice top and deftness with delicate doughs, this bar cookie comes together easily using an 8-inch square baking pan, a pat-in-the-pan bottom crust and simple cutouts for a top crust. Linzer pastry is made with nuts, which adds extra-rich flavor and a tender texture; we chose walnuts for their butteriness. Warm spices and a tablespoon of cocoa provide a little color and a lot of complexity. Seedless raspberry jam is our favorite, but cherry (make sure it's not too chunky)—or a combination—is excellent, too. You can create a minimalist pattern in the top crust by stamping out circles and lining them up on the jam layer, or you can create a more intricate design. The bars will keep in an airtight container at room temperature for a few days; the crust will soften, but the flavor blooms.

Don't forget to mist the parchment-lined baking pan with cooking spray. The jam becomes sticky at the edges and this ensures the paper peels away easily. Don't forget to reduce the oven temperature to 325°F after removing the bottom crust from the oven. Finally, when placing the dough cutouts on the filling, don't overlap them, which will create areas that are too thick. But do make sure the filling is mostly covered so the jam won't scorch.

Heat the oven to 350°F with a rack in the middle position. Mist an 8-inch square metal baking pan or glass baking dish with cooking spray, then line it with two 7-by-14-inch pieces of kitchen parchment placed perpendicular to each other and with excess hanging over the edges of the pan. Mist with cooking spray.

In a food processor, combine the white sugar and walnuts; process until finely ground, about 30 seconds. Add the flour, cocoa, cinnamon, pepper, cloves, allspice, the ¼ teaspoon salt and 2 teaspoons lemon zest; pulse until combined, 10 to 12 pulses. Scatter the butter over the mixture, then pulse until incorporated and resembles damp sand, 8 to 10 pulses. Add the egg yolk and process until it forms large, evenly moistened clumps (it will not come together into a ball), 45 to 60 seconds.

Turn the mixture out onto the counter. Using your hands, firmly press into a rough log, then use a chef's knife or bench scraper to cut off a third of it. Place the smaller piece on the center of a 12-by-16-inch sheet of kitchen parchment; set the remainder aside at room temperature. Using a rolling pin, roll out the smaller piece to a rough 8-inch square about ¼ inch thick. Use cookie cutters to cut shapes into the dough; leave the shapes in place with the scraps. Slide the parchment onto a baking sheet and refrigerate, uncovered.

Break the remaining dough into bits, evenly scattering them in the prepared pan. Using your fingers, press into an even layer. Bake until slightly puffed and just set, about 30 minutes. Meanwhile, in a small bowl, stir together the jam, the pinch of salt and the remaining 2 teaspoons lemon zest.

When the crust is done, cool on a wire rack for 20 minutes. Reduce the oven to 325°F. In a small bowl, beat the egg white until slightly foamy; set aside.

Scrape the jam mixture onto the center of the cooled crust and spread in an even layer. Remove the dough from the refrigerator. Working quickly, peel away the dough scraps and reserve. Lift off each cutout by sliding a small offset spatula or butter knife under it, then place on the jam, creating the design of your choice. If more cutouts are needed, gather the scraps, roll them into a ¼-inch thickness, stamp out additional shapes and position on the jam. Lightly brush the cutouts with the beaten egg white, then sprinkle with turbinado sugar.

Bake until the top is golden brown and the jam is bubbling, about 50 minutes. Cool completely in the pan on a wire rack, about 1½ hours. Using the parchment overhang as handles, lift the bars out of the pan and set on a cutting board. Cut into 16 squares.

Cookies, Bars and Brownies

Turkish Crescent Cookies with Spiced Walnut Filling

Start to finish: 1½ hours (1 hour active), plus cooling

Makes eighteen 3½-inch cookies

FOR THE DOUGH:

½ cup whole milk

1 large egg

390 grams (3 cups) all-purpose flour, plus more for dusting

40 grams (3 tablespoons) white sugar

1 teaspoon instant yeast

½ teaspoon table salt

141 grams (10 tablespoons) salted butter, cut into 1-tablespoon pieces, room temperature

FOR THE FILLING:

½ cup whole milk

110 grams (1 cup) walnuts, finely chopped

40 grams (⅔ cup) panko breadcrumbs

1 tablespoon grated lemon zest

78 grams (½ cup) raisins, finely chopped

1 teaspoon ground cinnamon

1 teaspoon ground allspice

1 teaspoon vanilla extract

214 grams (1 cup) white sugar

FOR FINISHING:

1 large egg

1 teaspoon powdered sugar, plus more for dusting

47 grams (½ cup) sliced almonds, very roughly chopped

During a trip to Istanbul, we tasted ay çöreği, generously sized moon-shaped pastry-like cookies with an aromatic nut and spice filling. Rustic yet refined, the crescents were a perfect not-too-sweet treat with a cup of tea or coffee. The otherwise basic dough includes a little yeast. The leavener does not provide airiness as it would in a yeasted bread, but it does make the crumb a bit lighter and more tender. To make the filling, Turkish bakeries are said to use cake scraps, mixing them with nuts, dried fruits and sometimes cocoa. We use fluffy, coarse panko breadcrumbs, plus walnuts, raisins, spices, sugar and lemon zest to brighten the flavors. The baked crescents keep well; after cooling, store in an airtight container at room temperature for up to five days. Dust with powdered sugar just before serving.

Don't use regular fine, dry breadcrumbs in the filling. Their dusty, powdery texture will make the mixture too thick and pasty. Panko is the best type of breadcrumbs to use here.

Line 2 rimmed baking sheets with kitchen parchment; set aside. To make the dough, in a small bowl, whisk the milk and egg. In a stand mixer with the paddle attachment, mix the flour, sugar, yeast and salt on low, 15 to 20 seconds. Add the butter and mix until the mixture is sandy and the butter is in pea-size bits, about 1 minute. With the mixer on low, gradually add the milk-egg mixture. Increase to medium and mix, scraping the bowl once or twice, until the ingredients come together and start to pull away from the sides of the bowl, about 1 minute.

Lightly flour the counter and turn the dough out onto it. Knead by hand several times until smooth, then form the dough into a ball. Wipe out the mixer bowl and the paddle attachment; set both aside for making the filling.

Divide the dough into thirds. Cover 2 portions with a kitchen towel. Using your hands, roll the third against the counter into a log roughly 6 inches long, then cut it into 6 pieces. Place the pieces on one of the prepared baking sheets; cover with a kitchen towel. Divide the remaining dough in the same way. Set aside at room temperature while you make the filling.

To make the filling, in a small saucepan, combine the milk and walnuts. Bring to a gentle simmer over medium and cook, stirring occasionally, until most of the milk has been absorbed, about 3 minutes. Transfer to the mixer bowl. Add the panko, lemon zest, raisins, cinnamon, allspice and vanilla; mix on low with the paddle attachment until well combined, about 1 minute. With the mixer running, gradually

STEPS »

HOW TO MAKE TURKISH CRESCENT COOKIES WITH SPICED WALNUT FILLING

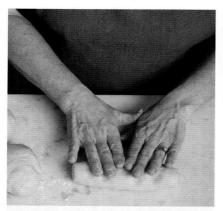

1. Using your hands, roll one third of the dough against the counter in a log roughly 6 inches long.

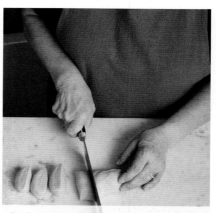

2. Cut the log into sixths, place the pieces on a prepared baking sheet and cover with a kitchen towel. Repeat with the remaining dough.

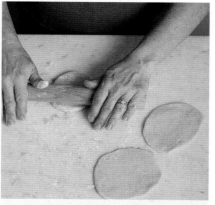

3. Using a rolling pin, roll each piece into a 3-by-5-inch oval, dusting as needed to prevent sticking. Scoop 1 heaping table-spoon filling onto each oval.

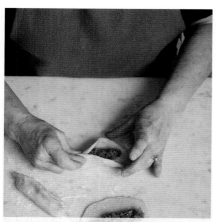

4. Working with one oval at a time, bring the long edges of the dough together to cover the filling, pinch the seams to seal.

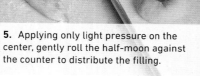

5. Applying only light pressure on the center, gently roll the half-moon against the counter to distribute the filling.

6. Place seam side down on the baking sheet, forming a crescent. Brush with egg mixture and sprinkle with almonds.

add the sugar; increase to medium and mix, scraping the bowl once or twice, until the ingredients form a thick, sticky, coarse-textured paste, about 1 minute.

Heat the oven to 350°F with a rack in the middle position. Have ready a small bowl of water for moistening your fingers.

Lightly flour the counter and set 1 piece of dough on top. With your hands, press into a 3-inch round. Using a rolling pin, roll the dough into a 3-by-5 inch oval, dusting with flour as needed. Shape 2 more pieces in the same way.

Scoop 1 heaping tablespoon of filling onto each oval. Using fingers lightly moistened with water, shape the filling into a log about 1 by 4 inches in the center of the dough. For each oval, bring the long edges of the dough together to enclose the filling, firmly pinching the seams to seal; the sealed dough will be a half-moon shape. Applying only light pressure on the center section, use your hand to gently roll the half-moon against the counter a few times to distribute the filling within the dough; you should have a cigar shape 5½ to 6 inches long with ends that taper to a point. Place seam side down on the other prepared baking sheet, forming the cigar into a crescent. Cover with a kitchen towel. Repeat with the remaining ingredients.

To finish the cookies, in a small bowl, whisk together the egg and powdered sugar. Brush the surface of the crescents with the egg mixture and sprinkle with the almonds. Bake until golden brown, 30 to 35 minutes. Cool completely on the baking sheet on a wire rack, about 1 hour. Just before serving, dust with additional powdered sugar.

VARIATION

Turkish Crescent Cookies with Spiced Walnut and Chocolate Filling

Follow the recipe to make the dough and filling, adding **2 tablespoons cocoa powder** with the spices. After the filling forms a coarse paste in the mixer, by hand fold in **1 ounce bittersweet or semi-sweet chocolate**, finely chopped.

Cinnamon-Sugared Chocolate and Orange Mandelbrot

**Start to finish: 1¾ hours
(45 minutes active), plus cooling**

Makes about 4 dozen cookies

1 large egg, plus 2 large egg yolks

1 tablespoon vanilla extract

¼ teaspoon almond extract (optional)

2 teaspoons grated orange zest

214 grams (1 cup) white sugar, divided

130 grams (1 cup) slivered almonds, divided

55 grams (¼ cup) packed light brown sugar

390 grams (3 cups) all-purpose flour

2 teaspoons ground cinnamon, divided

1 teaspoon baking powder

½ teaspoon baking soda

½ teaspoon table salt

170 grams (12 tablespoons) cold salted butter, cut into ½-inch cubes

113 grams (4 ounces) bittersweet chocolate, chopped into bits no larger than ¼ inch

Mandelbrot, which means "almond bread" in both Yiddish and German, is a Jewish cookie similar to biscotti. It is baked as a loaf that is sliced, then the cookies are returned to the oven to crisp and dry. But because of the fat in the dough, mandlebrot has a richer flavor and more tender texture than biscotti. Almonds are the classic choice, and traditionally the cookies are quite plain. But these days spruced-up versions are common and might include any nut along with dried fruit or pomegranate seeds and flavor accents such as espresso or citrus. Orange zest, along with vanilla and almond extract, adds fragrance, and chopped chocolate brings bittersweet notes. The final flourish is a coating of cinnamon sugar. Stored in an airtight container, these keep well for at least a week.

Don't leave the chocolate in large chunks when chopping. Larger pieces won't mix in well. Also, don't remove the loaves from the baking sheet while hot. Give them 20 minutes to cool and set up so there's less risk of breakage.

Heat the oven to 350°F with racks in the upper- and lower-middle positions. Line 2 baking sheets with kitchen parchment. In a liquid measuring cup or small bowl, whisk the whole egg, yolks, vanilla, almond extract (if using) and orange zest.

In a food processor, combine 160 grams (¾ cup) white sugar, 65 grams (½ cup) almonds and the brown sugar; process until finely ground, about 30 seconds. Add the flour, 1 teaspoon cinnamon, baking powder, baking soda and salt; process until well combined, about 10 seconds. Scatter in the butter, then pulse until it is in pea-sized bits, about 20 pulses. With the machine running, drizzle in the egg mixture and process until it forms large clumps (it will not come together into a single mass), 30 to 45 seconds.

Transfer the dough to a large bowl. Add the remaining 65 grams (½ cup) almonds and the chocolate. Using your hands, gently knead in the bowl just until the dough comes together and the nuts and chocolate are evenly distributed. Turn the dough out onto the counter and form it into a ball, then divide in half. Using your hands, roll each portion into a 14-inch log, pressing in any bits that come loose. Place the logs, about 4 inches apart, on one of the prepared baking sheets. With your hands, flatten the logs until 1 inch thick and 2 inches wide.

Bake on the lower rack until the dough has spread into flat, fissured loaves that are firm on the surface and appear dry in the cracks, 25 to 30 minutes. Cool on the baking sheet on a wire rack for 20 minutes; leave the oven on. Meanwhile, in

a wide, shallow bowl or on a medium plate, stir together the remaining 54 grams (¼ cup) white sugar and the remaining 1 teaspoon cinnamon.

Using a wide metal spatula, carefully transfer the still-warm loaves to a cutting board; reserve the baking sheet and its parchment. Using a serrated knife and a gentle sawing motion, cut each loaf on the diagonal into ½-inch slices. Dredge the cut sides of each cookie in the cinnamon sugar, pressing so the sugar adheres (the cinnamon sugar will adhere better if the cookies are warm), then place them sugared side up on the baking sheets, dividing them between both baking sheets.

Place both baking sheets in the oven and bake until the cookies are firm and dry, about 15 minutes, flipping each cookie and also rotating the baking sheets and switching their positions halfway through. Let cool on the baking sheets on wire racks for about 10 minutes. Transfer the mandelbrot directly to the racks and cool completely.

THE RIGHT CINNAMON FOR THE RIGHT JOB

There are two main classes of cinnamon: cassia cinnamon and Ceylon cinnamon. Both are harvested in sheets from trees, which curl into bark-like "sticks." Sticks of cassia cinnamon are rougher, darker and thicker than Ceylon cinnamon, with a more potent flavor. Cassia comes in different varieties. Indonesian cassia is the type most common in American grocery stores, and it is milder than Saigon cassia (also known as Vietnamese cinnamon), which is intensely flavorful, almost spicy. Ceylon cinnamon (sometimes referred to as Mexican cinnamon, due to its popularity there) is lighter in color and has thinner bark and the mildest, most delicate flavor of all the varieties. To compare them, we made cinnamon-dusted snicker-doodles, but there was no clear winner. Some tasters loved the subtlety of Ceylon cinnamon. Others preferred the spicier punch of the Saigon cinnamon. And for some, Indonesian cinnamon offered the best of both worlds—neither understated nor overpower-ing. In general, we recommend Saigon cinnamon for spice-forward baked goods such as cinnamon rolls, and for savory dishes. Ceylon is better for more delicate recipes, such as rice pudding or custard. But if you plan to keep just one cinnamon, medium-strength Indonesian cassia is the most versatile. As with any spice, freshness is important. Look for single-source spices from companies that work with farmers directly. This cuts down on the time between when the cinnamon is harvested and when it appears on store shelves.

Corn and Cinnamon Butter Cookies

Start to finish: 40 minutes, plus cooling

Makes about 3 dozen cookies

270 grams (2¼ cups) masa harina (see headnote)

1½ teaspoons baking powder

1 teaspoon ground cinnamon

½ teaspoon table salt

170 grams (12 tablespoons) salted butter, room temperature

107 grams (½ cup) white sugar, plus more for sprinkling

1 large egg, room temperature

1½ teaspoons vanilla extract

These buttery cookies, with the warm, sweet fragrance and flavor of cinnamon and the subtly nutty notes of ground corn, are food writer and recipe developer Paola Briseño-González' re-creation of the galletas de maíz (corn cookies) from a home bakery in the town of El Tuito, in the Mexican state of Jalisco. Made without wheat flour and therefore lacking gluten, the cookies' texture is quite "short," similar to shortbread, but more delicate. It's important to use masa harina here, the type of ground-corn product used to make corn tortillas. Masa harina is processed differently from cornmeal or corn flour, and even from masarepa, which is used to make empanadas and arepas; these different meals and flours are not interchangeable. If masa harina is not sold near the all-purpose flour and cornmeal, check the international aisle. Maseca is a widely available brand. In an airtight container, the cookies will keep for up to four days.

Don't worry if the dough feels softer than standard cookie dough, but it should not be wet and sticky. If it is, knead in a little more masa harina, adding only enough so the dough is workable during shaping. These cookies are wheat-free, so there's no risk of overmixing and making the cookies tough.

Heat the oven to 375°F with a rack in the middle position. Line a rimmed baking sheet with kitchen parchment. In a medium bowl, whisk together the masa harina, baking powder, cinnamon and salt.

In a stand mixer with the paddle attachment, beat the butter, sugar, egg and vanilla on medium, scraping the bowl once or twice, until the mixture is light and creamy, 1 to 2 minutes. With the mixer running on low, gradually add the dry ingredients, then mix until they are evenly moistened, about 1 minute. With the mixer still running on low, stream in ¼ cup water and mix until the dough is soft and pliable but not sticky, about 30 seconds.

Scoop up 1 tablespoon of the dough and roll it into a 3-inch log, then bring the ends together to form a ring. If the dough cracks, it is too dry and needs more water. Return the shaped portion to the mixer bowl and knead in 1 to 2 teaspoons additional water (there is no gluten in the dough and therefore no risk of overworking it). Test the dough by shaping another portion; knead in more water, if needed. When the dough is properly hydrated, form it into rings as you did the first portion; place the rings on the prepared baking sheet, spacing them evenly apart.

Bake until the edges of the cookies are golden brown, 13 to 15 minutes. Remove from the oven and immediately sprinkle with about 2 tablespoons additional sugar. Cool on the baking sheet for about 10 minutes. Using a wide metal spatula, transfer the cookies to a rack; cool completely before serving.

Semolina Polvorones

**Start to finish: 3 hours
(45 minutes active), plus cooling**

Makes 24 cookies

54 grams (¼ cup) white sugar

1½ teaspoons grated orange zest

55 grams (½ cup) roughly chopped walnuts

128 grams (¾ cup) semolina flour

½ teaspoon ground cinnamon

2 large egg yolks

½ teaspoon vanilla extract

Pinch of table salt

87 grams (⅔ cup) all-purpose flour

141 grams (10 tablespoons) cold salted butter, cut into ½-inch pieces

Powdered sugar, for coating

Polvorones are Spanish cookies popular across Latin America, Spain and the Philippines. With a firm yet crumbly texture, they're similar to shortbread. Our take on the popular cookies was inspired by a lesser-known Basque version made with semolina and spiced with orange zest and cinnamon. To give the cookies deep, complex flavor, we toast both the walnuts and semolina in a skillet before making the dough. Adding the ground cinnamon to the hot semolina bloomed it, bringing out its aroma. Flattening the dough into very thin rounds resulted in cookies that were too delicate; ½-inch-thick disks held up best, especially when tossed in powdered sugar after baking. The cookies are fragile when hot out of the oven, so let them cool several minutes before transferring to a wire rack.

Don't be alarmed if the semolina smokes slightly during toasting. And don't coat the cookies with powdered sugar until you're ready to serve them; they look best immediately after they're sugared.

In a food processor, pulse the white sugar and orange zest until combined. In a 10-inch skillet over medium heat, toast the walnuts, stirring, until lightly browned and fragrant, 3 to 5 minutes. Transfer to the food processor. Wipe the skillet clean, then add the semolina and toast, stirring, until beginning to brown, 2 to 3 minutes. Reduce heat to medium-low and toast, stirring constantly, until golden brown and fragrant, another 2 to 3 minutes. Off the heat, stir in the cinnamon, then transfer to a plate and cool to room temperature.

In a small bowl, combine the yolks and vanilla; beat with a fork. Add the salt to the walnuts and sugar, then process until coarsely ground, about 10 seconds. Add the flour and the semolina mixture, then process until combined, about 5 seconds. Add the butter and pulse until the mixture resembles damp sand, 10 to 12 pulses. Drizzle in the yolk mixture and pulse until large clumps gather around the blade. Transfer the dough to the counter and knead briefly, then wrap in plastic wrap and refrigerate for at least 1 hour and up to 2 days.

Heat the oven to 325°F with a rack in the middle position. Line 2 baking sheets with kitchen parchment. Form the dough into 24 balls (1 tablespoon each) and arrange evenly on the baking sheets. Press the balls into disks about ½ inch thick.

Bake the cookies one baking sheet at a time until well browned, 23 to 28 minutes, rotating halfway through. Let cool on the baking sheet for about 10 minutes, then transfer to a wire rack and cool completely. Just before serving, gently drop each cookie into powdered sugar to coat.

Belgian Spice Cookies

Start to finish: 1 hour, plus cooling

Makes about 6 dozen cookies

¾ teaspoon ground cinnamon

¾ teaspoon ground coriander

¾ teaspoon ground allspice

2 tablespoons white sugar

320 grams (2⅔ cups) cake flour, plus more for dusting

1½ teaspoons baking soda

⅛ teaspoon ground cloves

170 grams (12 tablespoons) salted butter, cool room temperature

218 grams (1 cup) packed light brown sugar

¼ teaspoon table salt

2 tablespoons dark corn syrup

Speculoos are Belgian spice cookies with a light, airy crispness. Creaming the butter and sugar until light and fluffy is important, so make sure the butter is softened to cool room temperature, then beat in the stand mixer for the full five minutes. The dough can be cut in any shape, but the baking time may need to be adjusted if the cookies are much smaller or larger than 2 inches.

Don't use light corn syrup in place of dark; light corn syrup lacks the caramel notes that mimic the flavor of the type of brown sugar (made from beets) traditionally used to make speculoos.

Heat the oven to 350°F with a rack in the middle position. Line 2 baking sheets with kitchen parchment. In a small bowl, stir together the cinnamon, coriander and allspice. Measure 1 teaspoon of the mixture into another small bowl, whisk the white sugar into it and set aside. In a medium bowl, whisk together the cake flour, baking soda, cloves and remaining spice mixture.

In a stand mixer with the paddle attachment, beat the butter, brown sugar and salt on low until combined, about 30 seconds. Increase to medium-high and beat until fluffy and pale, about 5 minutes. With the mixer running, gradually add the corn syrup and 2 tablespoons water. Using a silicone spatula, scrape the sides of the bowl, then mix for another 30 seconds. Reduce to low, add the flour mixture and mix until the ingredients just begin to form an evenly moistened dough, about 15 seconds.

Dust the counter liberally with flour and scrape the dough onto it. Gently knead the dough, giving it 2 or 3 turns, until smooth; it should feel moist and supple but should not be sticky. Divide the dough in half; wrap 1 piece in plastic and set aside. With your hands, pat the second piece into a rough 8-by-6-inch rectangle.

Using a well-floured rolling pin, roll the dough rectangle to an even ⅛-inch thickness. With a 2-inch rectangular or round cookie cutter (ideally with a fluted edge), cut out cookies as close together as possible. Use an offset spatula to carefully transfer the cutouts to one of the prepared baking sheets, spacing them about ½ inch apart.

Gently pat the dough scraps together, then re-roll and cut out additional cookies; transfer the cutouts to the baking sheet. If desired, use a slightly smaller cutter of the same shape to imprint a decorative border (do not cut all the way through the dough) and use a toothpick to poke a few holes in the centers. Sprinkle the cookies evenly with half of the spiced sugar, then refrigerate uncovered for 15 minutes.

While the first sheet of cookies chills, repeat with the remaining dough and second baking sheet. Place the first sheet of cookies in the oven, then immediately refrigerate the second sheet. Bake until the cookies are firm and beginning to brown, 16 to 18 minutes, rotating once halfway through. Cool on the baking sheet for 10 minutes, then use a wide metal spatula to transfer them to a wire rack. Repeat with the second sheet of cookies. Cool completely before serving.

Catalan Biscotti

These simple, rustic cookies are our spin on carquinyolis, or Catalan biscotti. They're a perfect accompaniment to a cup of coffee or a glass of dessert wine. Classic carquinyolis are twice baked, like Italian biscotti, which makes them dry, brittle and crunchy. We, however, follow the lead of chef and cookbook author Daniel Olivella and bake the cookies only once so they have a satisfying crispy-chewy texture. Store in an airtight container for up to a week.

Don't use marzipan in place of the almond paste (marzipan is sweeter and softer than almond paste). And don't discard the egg yolk after separating the second egg to make the dough—you'll need it to brush onto the cookies so they bake up with a rich golden sheen.

Heat the oven to 350°F with racks in the upper- and lower-middle positions. Line 2 baking sheets with kitchen parchment. In a medium bowl, whisk together the flour and baking soda.

Distribute the almonds in an even layer on one of the prepared baking sheets. Toast in the oven until golden brown, 4 to 5 minutes, stirring once about halfway through. Cool on a wire rack.

In a food processor, combine the sugar, almond paste, lemon zest and salt. Process until the almond paste has broken down and the mixture is sandy, about 30 seconds. Add the whole egg, the egg white and the vanilla, then process until the mixture is smooth and lightened in color, 20 to 30 seconds, scraping the bowl as needed.

Transfer the almond paste mixture to the bowl with the flour mixture; stir with a silicone spatula until the flour is mostly incorporated. Add the toasted almonds and stir until incorporated; reserve the parchment-lined baking sheet. Turn the mixture out onto a lightly floured counter and knead a few times to bring the dough together.

Form the dough into a log about 14-inches long and 2 inches wide. Cut the log into fourths, then cut each quarter into 6 slices, each about ½ inch thick. Place the slices on the baking sheets, spacing them evenly apart. In a small bowl, whisk together the remaining egg yolk and 1 teaspoon water, then lightly brush onto the slices.

Bake until the cookies are golden brown, 20 to 25 minutes, switching and rotating the baking sheets about halfway through. Cool on the baking sheets for 5 minutes, then transfer to a wire rack and cool completely, about 30 minutes.

Start to finish: 50 minutes, plus cooling

Makes about 24 cookies

195 grams (1½ cups) all-purpose flour, plus more for dusting

¾ teaspoon baking soda

93 grams (1 cup) sliced almonds

214 grams (1 cup) white sugar

113 grams (4 ounces) almond paste, broken into rough 1-inch pieces

1 teaspoon grated lemon zest

½ teaspoon table salt

1 large egg, plus 1 large egg, separated

1 teaspoon vanilla extract

Turkish Date-Filled Semolina Cookies

**Start to finish: 1½ hours
(1 hour active), plus cooling**

Makes 20 large cookies

FOR THE DOUGH:

170 grams (1 cup) semolina flour

130 grams (1 cup) all-purpose flour

54 grams (¼ cup) white sugar

½ teaspoon ground cinnamon

¼ teaspoon table salt

141 grams (10 tablespoons) cold salted butter, cut into 1-tablespoon pieces

60 grams (¼ cup) plain whole-milk yogurt or 45 grams (3 tablespoons) plain whole-milk Greek yogurt mixed with 1 tablespoon water

½ teaspoon grated orange zest

FOR THE FILLING:

454 grams (1 pound) pitted dates

28 grams (2 tablespoons) salted butter, cut into 4 pieces

2 teaspoons grated orange zest, plus 1 or 2 tablespoons orange juice, if needed

1 teaspoon ground cinnamon

¼ teaspoon table salt

FOR SHAPING AND FINISHING:

Extra-virgin olive oil or neutral oil, if needed for greasing

40 grams (¼ cup) sesame seeds, if not using a kömbe mold

Powdered sugar, for dusting (optional)

During a visit to Türkiye, we became fans of kömbe, buttery, pastry-like cookies made with spices and semolina, filled with nuts or dates and imprinted with delicate patterns or designs. Similar to Middle Eastern ma'amoul, kömbe are a specialty of Antakya in the country's southernmost province. Our version adds cinnamon and orange zest to the dough, along with a little yogurt to help bind the ingredients. The cookies can be formed simply, using only your hands, but for unique shapes and filigree-esque details, a kömbe mold is essential. Made from wood or plastic, the molds are spoon-like, with flutes, scallops or ridges that imprint the dough with intricate designs. Our recipe includes instructions for shaping by hand as well as using a mold with a capacity of about 2½ tablespoons. Whichever method you choose, filling and shaping becomes easier with each cookie you form. The dough is clay-like and manageable; if you're shaping by hand, you may even wish to experiment with creating designs using the tines of a fork. The cookies are excellent served with tea or coffee. Stored in an airtight container at room temperature, kömbe will keep for up to a week.

Don't use the dates without first checking for pits, even if you purchased pitted dates. Date variety doesn't matter for these cookies—medjools are likely what you'll find in grocery stores—but do seek out ones that are soft and plump. Dry and leathery dates may resist processing; adding 1 or 2 tablespoons of orange juice will help them break down.

Heat the oven to 325°F with a rack in the middle position. Line 2 baking sheets with kitchen parchment.

To make the dough, in a food processor, combine both flours, the sugar, cinnamon and salt. Process until combined, about 5 seconds. Scatter the butter over the flour mixture and process until the mixture resembles coarse sand, 15 to 20 seconds. Add the yogurt and orange zest, then process until the ingredients come together in large, evenly moistened clumps, 45 to 60 seconds. Turn the dough out onto a clean counter; return the food processor bowl and blade, unwashed, to the base. Gently knead the dough by hand just until smooth and cohesive. Wrap in plastic wrap and set aside at room temperature while you make the filling.

To make the filling, in the food processor, combine the dates, butter, orange zest, cinnamon and salt. Pulse until the dates are chopped, about 20 pulses. If the dates

are dryish and resistant to breaking down, add 1 to 2 tablespoons orange juice. Scrape the bowl, then process until the mixture forms a thick paste, 45 to 60 seconds, scraping the bowl as needed. Remove the bowl from the food processor base, then remove the blade from the bowl. Scoop the filling into 20 portions (1 slightly mounded tablespoon each), dropping them onto one of the prepared baking sheets. If the filling is sticky, lightly oil the measuring spoon and your hands. Roll each portion between your palms into a ball and return it to the baking sheet, placing the balls on one side (to leave room for the portioned dough).

Divide the dough into 20 portions (1 generously mounded tablespoon each), roll each into a ball between your palms and place on the other side of the same baking sheet. If needed to prevent sticking, lightly coat your hands with oil. Cover the baking sheet with a kitchen towel. If you are not using a kömbe mold, place the sesame seeds on a small plate.

Set a dough ball in your palm; keep the remaining dough covered. Using your other hand, press the dough into a slightly concave round about 3 inches in diameter; don't worry if the round is not perfect and if the edges split a bit. Drop a ball of filling into the center, gather the edges to enclose the filling and pinch to seal; the dough will not form a sphere. Roll it between your palms into a ball (it's fine if a little filling peeks through the dough).

If using a kömbe mold (see headnote), place the filled dough ball in the mold, then gently flatten it with your fingers so it fills the mold. Invert the dough out of the mold into your hand; if it does not easily unmold, gently rap the tip of the mold against a clean counter and allow the dough to fall out. Place the cookie decorative side up on the second prepared baking sheet. Fill and shape the remaining dough in the same way, evenly spacing the cookies on the baking sheet.

If you are not using a mold, drop the ball into the sesame seeds, then gently flatten it with your hand to a round about 2 inches in diameter. Set the cookie seeded side up on the second prepared baking sheet. Fill and shape the remaining dough in the same way, evenly spacing the cookies.

Bake until the cookies are pale golden on top and a few shades darker on the bottom, 30 to 35 minutes. Cool on the baking sheet on a wire rack for about 5 minutes. Using a wide metal spatula, transfer the cookies directly to the rack. Serve warm or at room temperature. If desired, dust with powdered sugar just before serving.

Coconut Bars with Almonds and Chocolate

These treats are an adaptation of a recipe from "Golden" by Itamar Srulovich and Sarit Packer of London's Honey & Co. The bars are akin to coconut macaroons, but studded with nuts and dried fruit and cut into squares. For the chocolate bottom, chips are convenient—they can be used straight from the bag—but 9 ounces of bar chocolate works, too. Be sure to chop it finely so it melts readily. Store leftovers in an airtight container in the refrigerator for up to five days.

Don't skip the step of lining the baking pan with foil or the bars will be difficult to remove from the pan. Although we sometimes use kitchen parchment to line baking pans, in this case, foil works better because it conforms to the shape of the pan and lays very flat against the surface.

Heat the oven to 350°F with the rack in the middle position. Mist an 8-inch square baking pan with cooking spray, then line it with a 7-by-14-inch piece of foil; allow the excess to hang over the sides.

Distribute the chocolate chips in an even layer in the prepared pan. Put the pan in the oven and warm until the chocolate is softened, 3 to 5 minutes. Remove the pan from the oven; leave the oven on. Using a silicone spatula, spread the chocolate in an even layer; set aside.

In a small microwave-safe bowl, combine the cherries and 1 tablespoon water. Microwave, uncovered, on high for 1 minute, stirring once halfway through. Stir again, then let cool slightly.

In a large bowl, stir together the coconut, almonds, butter and cherries. In the same bowl used to microwave the cherries, whisk together the eggs, vanilla and salt. Add the egg mixture to the coconut mixture and stir until the ingredients are well combined. Transfer to the prepared pan and, using a spatula, lightly compact into an even layer. Bake until the surface is light golden brown, 15 to 18 minutes.

Cool in the pan on a wire rack until barely warm, about 45 minutes. Refrigerate uncovered until completely chilled and set, about 2 hours.

Remove the bars from the pan using the foil overhang as handles and set on a cutting board. Using a chef's knife, cut into 16 squares, wiping the knife blade after each cut for the cleanest slices. Serve chilled or at room temperature.

Start to finish: 40 minutes (20 minutes active), plus cooling and chilling

Makes 16 bars

255 grams (1½ cups) dark chocolate, semi-sweet or milk chocolate chips

75 grams (½ cup) dried cherries or 70 grams (½ cup) dried cranberries, roughly chopped

225 grams (2½ cups) unsweetened shredded coconut

74 grams (½ cup) salted roasted almonds, chopped

71 grams (5 tablespoons) salted butter, melted and slightly cooled

2 large eggs

2 teaspoons vanilla extract

¼ teaspoon table salt

Tahini Swirl Brownies

Start to finish: 40 minutes

Makes 16 brownies

57 grams (4 tablespoons) salted butter, plus more for the pan

4 ounces bittersweet chocolate, finely chopped

16 grams (3 tablespoons) cocoa powder

3 large eggs

241 grams (1 cup plus 2 tablespoons) white sugar

1 tablespoon vanilla extract

½ teaspoon table salt

180 grams (¾ cup) tahini

43 grams (⅓ cup) all-purpose flour

Tired of one-note brownies, we loved the halvah brownie from Tatte Bakery & Cafe in Cambridge, Massachusetts. Halvah is fudge-like candy from the Middle East made from tahini, a rich sesame seed paste. At Milk Street, we fiddled with how much tahini to use—its fat content was the major problem. To start, we reduced the tahini and the amount of butter, substituted cocoa powder for some of the chocolate and added an egg to cut through the rich brownie base. Then, we reversed our thinking and instead of trying to add tahini to a classic brownie batter, we added chocolate to a tahini base. For a final touch, we swirled reserved tahini batter into the chocolate to create a visual and textural contrast and let the tahini flavor shine. The best way to marble the brownies was to run the tip of a paring knife through the dollops of batter. Be sure to fully bake these brownies—they are extremely tender, even wet, if not baked through. The tahini's flavor and color will intensify over time, so make a day ahead for a more pronounced sesame taste.

Don't forget to stir the tahini before measuring. Upon standing, the solids sink to the bottom and the oil rises to the top.

Heat the oven to 350°F with a rack in the middle position. Line an 8-inch-square baking pan with two 7-by-14-inch pieces of foil placed perpendicular to each other and with excess hanging over the edges of the pan. Lightly coat with butter.

In a medium saucepan over medium, melt the butter. Remove from the heat and add the chocolate and cocoa, then whisk until smooth.

In a large bowl, whisk the eggs, sugar, vanilla and salt until slightly thickened, about 1 minute. Add the tahini and whisk to combine. Add the flour and fold until just incorporated. Transfer ½ cup of the mixture to a small bowl. Add the chocolate mixture to the batter remaining in the large bowl and fold until homogeneous.

Pour the chocolate batter into the prepared pan, spreading evenly. Dollop the reserved tahini mixture over the top, then, using the tip of a butter knife or paring knife, swirl the batters together; do not overmix. Bake until the edges are set but the center remains moist, 28 to 32 minutes.

Cool in the pan on a wire rack for 30 minutes. Using the foil overhang as handles, lift the brownies out of the pan and set on the rack. Cool for at least another 30 minutes; the longer they cool, the easier they cut. Peel away the foil and transfer to a cutting board. Cut into 2-inch squares.

Walnut Pakhlava with Pomegranate Syrup

Start to finish: 1¾ hours (45 minutes active)

Makes about 40 pieces

375 grams (1¾ cups) plus 2 tablespoons white sugar

88 grams (¼ cup) pomegranate molasses

2 tablespoons lemon juice

339 grams (24 tablespoons or 3 sticks) salted butter, each stick cut into 4 to 6 chunks

330 grams (3 cups) walnuts

1 teaspoon ground cinnamon

¼ teaspoon table salt

1-pound box frozen phyllo, thawed

Similar to baklava, Armenian pakhlava features layers of crisp, well-buttered phyllo and finely chopped nuts, but there are a few key differences. For one, the filling is always made with walnuts, never pistachios or almonds. Also, it relies on a warmly spiced syrup that is sweetened with sugar, as opposed to honey, and a hit of lemon juice for bright acidity. We were inspired by Irina Georgescu's recipe from "Tava," in which she adds pomegranate molasses to the soaking syrup. Though not traditional in pakhlava, tangy pomegranate molasses complements the pastry's nutty, spiced filling and wonderfully balances its sweetness. To keep the layers crisp and for rich, even browning, it's important to use clarified butter, which is pure butterfat, with none of the water and milk solids found in whole butter. Many grocery stores sell jars of ghee that are also labeled "clarified butter." Ghee is indeed a type of clarified butter used in South Asian cooking, but we've found its flavor and aroma to be too strong for this pakhlava, so it's worth the few minutes to clarify your own butter. Just like baklava, pakhlava holds well covered at room temperature for up to a week and is delicious paired with coffee or tea.

Don't bring the syrup to room temperature before using it and don't allow the pakhlava to cool before pouring on the chilled syrup. The more viscous consistency of refrigerated syrup makes it easier to pour into the cuts; it also is more readily absorbed by the hot pakhlava. But do cool the pakhlava completely before serving. This gives time for even saturation and for the layers and flavors to meld.

In a medium saucepan, combine the 375 grams (1¾ cups) sugar, ¾ cup water and the pomegranate molasses. Bring to a simmer over medium-high, then reduce to medium and simmer, stirring occasionally, until thickened slightly, 5 to 7 minutes. Pour the syrup into a 2-cup liquid measuring cup; you should have about 1¾ cups. Stir in the lemon juice and set aside.

In a small saucepan over medium-low, melt the butter without stirring. Once melted, cook until a layer of white foam forms on the surface, 4 to 5 minutes. Remove from the heat and let stand for 5 minutes. Using a spoon, skim off and discard the foam. Slowly pour the clear, yellow liquid into a 2 cup-liquid measuring cup or microwave-safe small bowl (in case the butter needs remelting), leaving the milk solids and water in the pan; you should have about 1⅓ cups. Discard the solids and water.

In a food processor, pulse the walnuts, the remaining 2 tablespoons sugar, the cinnamon and salt until finely chopped, 10 to 12 pulses. Transfer 2 tablespoons of the mixture to a small bowl and set aside; transfer the remainder to a medium bowl.

Heat the oven to 325°F with a rack in the middle position. Brush the bottom and sides of a 9-by-13-inch metal baking pan with clarified butter.

Unroll the phyllo. If the sheets measure 13-by-18 inches, cut the stack in half crosswise, forming two 9-by-13-inch stacks, then place one stack on top of the other. If the sheets measure 9-by-14 inches, simply leave them as they are. Cover the phyllo stack with plastic wrap and a damp kitchen towel to prevent drying.

Lay 1 sheet of phyllo in the bottom of the baking pan; keep the remaining sheets covered. Lightly brush with clarified butter. Repeat the layering and brushing until you have a total of 10 stacked and brushed sheets. Sprinkle evenly with about 1 cup of the walnut mixture.

One at a time, layer in 8 phyllo sheets, brushing each with butter. Top with half of the remaining nut mixture. Layer on another 8 phyllo sheets, brushing each with butter, then top with the remaining walnut mixture. If the butter cools and begins to solidify as you work, remelt it so it can be lightly brushed onto the phyllo.

Lay a phyllo sheet on the final nut layer and lightly brush it with butter. Continue layering and brushing up to an additional 9 or 10 phyllo sheets. Drizzle 2 tablespoons of the remaining butter over the final sheet of phyllo, then brush it evenly over the surface (if you have leftover clarified butter, reserve it for another use).

Using a sharp paring knife, cut the pakhlava in the pan into eighths on the diagonal; start by cutting from one corner to the opposite corner, then cutting 3 evenly spaced parallel lines on each side of the center diagonal. Be sure to slice through all the layers, down to the pan bottom. Now cut from and to the other two corners, cutting across the first set of parallel lines and forming diamond shapes.

Bake until well browned and crisp, 50 to 60 minutes. Transfer the pan to a wire rack. Immediately and quickly run a knife around the inside edge of the pan to loosen the phyllo from the edges. While the pakhlava is hot, slowly pour about two-thirds of the chilled syrup (about 1⅓ cups) into the cut lines, then drizzle the remainder all over the top. Sprinkle with the reserved nut mixture, then cool to room temperature. Serve right away or leave in the pan, covered tightly and stored at room temperature for up to 5 days.

Sesame and Oat Bars with Dates and Dried Apricots

**Start to finish: 1 hour
(20 minutes active), plus cooling**

Makes 16 bars

37 grams (¼ cup) whole almonds, chopped

20 grams (2 tablespoons) sesame seeds

375 grams (3¾ cups) old-fashioned rolled oats

113 grams (8 tablespoons) salted butter, cut into 6 or 8 pieces

167 grams (½ cup) Lyle's Golden Syrup (see headnote) or honey

218 grams (1 cup) packed light brown sugar

120 grams (½ cup) tahini

1 teaspoon table salt

½ teaspoon ground cinnamon

½ teaspoon ground cardamom

113 grams (¾ cup) pitted dates, chopped

83 grams (½ cup) dried apricots, chopped

Flaky sea salt, for sprinkling (optional)

In the U.K., oat bars such as these are known as "flapjacks." They're sturdy, chewy-crisp and unapologetically rich. We love the earthy, nutty, pleasantly resinous flavor of sesame and incorporate the ingredient two ways: toasted seeds dot the oat mixture while tahini helps hold the bars together. Lyle's Golden Syrup, an amber-hued sweetener common in the U.K., imparts nuances of butterscotch and caramel, but if it is difficult to source, honey works nicely, though it adds floral notes. We also toss in dates and dried apricots for a satisfying chew; the latter also offers tartness to balance the bars' sweetness. Stored in an airtight container at room temperature, the bars keep well for up to five days.

Don't use quick-cooking or instant oats in this recipe. These have a finer texture than old-fashioned oats and absorb moisture differently; bars made with them will be too soft and lack chewiness. After baking, make sure the oat slab has cooled completely before cutting it into bars. If it's at all warm, it may not hold together as you cut.

Heat the oven to 325°F with a rack in the middle position. In a medium saucepan over medium, toast the almonds and sesame seeds, stirring, until golden brown and fragrant, about 5 minutes. Transfer to a large bowl and cool; reserve the saucepan.

On a rimmed baking sheet, distribute the oats in an even layer. Toast in the oven until light golden brown, 10 to 12 minutes, stirring once about halfway through. Cool completely on the baking sheet on a wire rack; leave the oven on.

Mist an 8-inch square metal baking pan or glass baking dish with cooking spray, then line it with two 7-by-14-inch pieces of kitchen parchment placed perpendicular to each other and with excess hanging over the edges of the pan. Mist the parchment with cooking spray.

In the reserved saucepan over medium, combine the butter, golden syrup, sugar and tahini. Bring to a simmer and cook, whisking occasionally, until the butter has melted and the sugar has dissolved, 3 to 5 minutes. Set aside off heat.

In a food processor, pulse half of the toasted oats until coarsely ground, about 5 pulses. Transfer to the bowl containing the almonds and sesame seeds, then add the remaining toasted oats, the salt, cinnamon, cardamom, dates, and apricots; stir well. Pour the butter mixture over the oat mixture; using a silicone spatula, fold until evenly moistened.

Scrape the mixture into the prepared pan and press firmly into a compact, even layer. Bake until golden brown, about 30 minutes. Set the pan on a wire rack, sprinkle with flaky sea salt (if using) and cool until barely warm, about 1 hour.

Using the parchment overhangs as handles, lift the slab out of the pan and set it directly on the rack. Cool completely, about 1 hour. Peel away the parchment, transfer to a cutting board and cut into sixteen 2-inch squares.

GOLDEN SYRUP

Many recipes for sticky-sweet baked goods call for corn syrup, but there's another product to consider in the baking aisle of most supermarkets—golden syrup. The two products have similarities but are inherently different. Corn syrup is a sugary liquid derived from corn. Common in American baking, corn syrup's hygroscopic nature (it draws in water) makes it a good choice for ensuring a moist texture. It also does not require additional dissolving the way granulated sugar does. (It is worth noting that corn syrup is not the same as high-fructose corn syrup, a more processed and controversial food additive.) Golden syrup, also known as "light treacle," is a sweetener from the U.K. that is made by boiling sugar cane juice down to a thick, amber-colored syrup. It tastes less sweet than corn syrup and has a hint of caramel. To test whether it can be substituted for corn syrup, we used both to make pecan pies and marshmallows and were pleased with the results. Both pies were equally gooey, and the marshmallows were nearly identical—the golden syrup marshmallows were only slightly creamier. The biggest difference was in flavor. The versions made with golden syrup had toasty, caramel notes, while those made with corn syrup did not. Ultimately, we find the choice comes down primarily to taste preference.

Salty Honey and Browned Butter Bars

Start to finish: 1 hour 20 minutes
(25 minutes active), plus cooling

Makes 20 to 24 bars

FOR THE CRUST:

390 grams (3 cups) all-purpose flour

109 grams (½ cup packed) light
brown sugar

½ teaspoon table salt

283 grams (20 tablespoons) salted
butter, melted and slightly cooled

FOR THE FILLING:

113 grams (8 tablespoons) salted
butter, cut into 8 pieces

107 grams (½ cup) white sugar

167 grams (½ cup) honey

2 tablespoons fine cornmeal

¾ teaspoon table salt

3 large eggs, plus 1 large egg yolk

111 grams (⅓ cup) Lyle's Golden
Syrup (see headnote)

½ cup heavy cream

2 teaspoons vanilla extract

2 teaspoons cider vinegar

1 teaspoon flaky sea salt

Cheryl Day — cookbook author, pastry chef and co-owner of Back in the Day Bakery in Savannah, Georgia — knows a thing or two about Southern baking. So it's no surprise that these sweet and salty bars, adapted from her book, "Cheryl Day's Treasury of Southern Baking," are reminiscent of rich, custardy chess pie. But Day brings a new twist to the Southern classic by using browned butter for its notes of toasted nuts and giving the treats a nuanced sweetness with a combination of white sugar, Lyle's Golden Syrup and floral honey. She also balances the sugariness and heightens the flavors with a good dose of salt. Lyle's Golden Syrup is a cane syrup with a light caramel flavor that's popular in the U.K. It's sold in most well-stocked grocery stores here in the U.S., but if it's not available, you can mimic its flavor by combining 3 tablespoons light corn syrup and 2½ tablespoons pure maple syrup. Refrigerate leftover bars in an airtight container for up to three days; bring to room temperature before serving.

Don't skip the step of poking holes in and refrigerating the crust before baking. The holes allow steam to escape, thereby minimizing the amount the baked good puffs in the oven. Chilling the crust before baking will help prevent the side walls from slumping in the oven. Also, don't use a nonstick skillet to brown the butter for the filling. A pan with a light-colored surface will allow you to better see the color of the milk solids and fat so you can monitor their progress. If you don't own a conventional (i.e., not nonstick) skillet, use a conventional saucepan instead.

Mist a 9-by-13-inch baking pan with cooking spray. Line the pan with a 16-inch length of foil perpendicular to the pan's length; fold the foil widthwise so it fits neatly in the bottom of the pan and allow the excess to overhang the sides. Mist the foil with cooking spray.

To make the crust, in a large bowl, whisk together the flour, sugar and salt, breaking up any lumps of sugar. Drizzle in the butter and stir with a silicone spatula until the mixture is evenly moistened and crumbly. Transfer the mixture to the prepared pan and, using your hands, press the dough into an even layer in the bottom of the pan and 1 inch up the sides; the side walls should be about ¼ inch thick (it's fine if the sides are not perfect). Using a fork, poke holes in the bottom of the crust. Refrigerate, uncovered, until the crust is firm to the touch, 30 to 45 minutes. Meanwhile, heat the oven to 350°F with a rack in the middle position.

Bake the chilled crust until lightly browned, 12 to 15 minutes. Cool on a wire rack while you make the filling; leave the oven on.

To make the filling, in a 10-inch skillet over medium-high, melt the butter. Cook, swirling the pan frequently, until the milk solids at the bottom are golden brown and the butter has a nutty aroma, 1 to 3 minutes. Pour into a large heatproof bowl, making sure to include the milk solids. Cool, stirring occasionally, until just warm to the touch.

To the browned butter, whisk in the sugar, honey, cornmeal and table salt. Add the whole eggs and yolk, then gently whisk to combine. Whisk in the syrup, cream, vanilla and vinegar until homogeneous. Pour the filling into the crust. Bake until the edges are puffed and the center wobbles slightly when the pan is gently jiggled, 30 to 35 minutes.

Transfer to a wire rack and sprinkle the surface with the flaky salt. Cool for at least 3 hours. Remove the bars from the pan, using the foil overhang as handles, and set on a cutting board. Using a chef's knife, cut into 16 to 20 pieces.

Browned Butter Oatmeal Chocolate Chip Cookies

Start to finish: 1 hour
(15 minutes active), plus cooling

Makes twelve 4-inch cookies

113 grams (8 tablespoons) salted butter, cut into 8 pieces

100 grams (1 cup) old-fashioned rolled oats

86 grams (¾ cup) pecans, chopped

107 grams (½ cup) white sugar

100 grams (½ cup) packed dark brown sugar

1 large egg, plus 1 large egg yolk

2 teaspoons vanilla extract

130 grams (1 cup) all-purpose flour

½ teaspoon table salt

½ teaspoon baking powder

½ teaspoon baking soda

170 grams (1 cup) bittersweet chocolate chunks (see headnote)

113 grams (4 ounces) milk chocolate, finely chopped (see headnote)

Flaky sea salt (optional)

These cookies deliver big flavor because the key ingredients get special attention. We toast both the oats and pecans to coax out their nuttiness, then grind the oats in a food processor so the finished cookies have a more refined texture than your standard oatmeal cookie. The butter is deeply browned to add deep, butterscotch notes that carry flavor throughout the dough. Chunks of bittersweet chocolate create pockets of gooeyness, while finely chopped milk chocolate lends creaminess and milky sweetness that melts into the cookies. (You can use store-bought chocolate chunks sold in bags alongside the chocolate chips, or chop your own from a bar. And you can grate the milk chocolate on a box grater if you find that easier than finely chopping it.) The recipe doubles easily, and the portioned dough can be frozen for up to a month. Bake the cookies directly from the freezer, without thawing, for 20 minutes, rotating the baking sheet halfway through.

Don't skip the step of refrigerating the dough after mixing. Not only will the dough be easier to portion because it has had a chance to firm up and hydrate, the cookies will spread less during baking. Chill it for a minimum of 30 minutes or for up to one hour. If refrigerated longer, the dough will harden and be difficult to scoop unless allowed to soften at room temperature.

Heat the oven to 375°F with racks in the upper- and lower-middle positions. Line 2 rimmed baking sheets with kitchen parchment. In a 10-inch skillet over medium, cook the butter, swirling the pan occasionally, until the milk solids at the bottom are deeply browned, 4 to 6 minutes. Pour into a large bowl and set aside.

Distribute the oats in an even layer on one of the prepared baking sheets; distribute the pecans in an even layer on the second baking sheet. Place the oats on the lower rack and pecans on the upper rack. Toast until the pecans are fragrant, about 2 minutes; remove from the oven and set aside to cool. Stir the oats, then toast until light golden brown, another 3 to 5 minutes. Transfer the oats to a food processor and cool until barely warm. Reserve the parchment-lined baking sheets.

Meanwhile, whisk both sugars into the browned butter. Whisk in the whole egg plus egg yolk and the vanilla until the mixture is aerated and pale in color.

To the cooled oats in the processor, add the flour, salt, baking powder and baking soda. Pulse until the oats are finely ground, 7 to 10 pulses. Add the oat-flour mixture to the egg mixture; fold with a silicone spatula until well combined and no dry patches remain. Add both chocolates and the toasted pecans (reserve the parchment-lined baking sheet); fold until evenly distributed. Cover and refrigerate for at least 30 minutes or up to 1 hour.

Using a ¼-cup dry measuring cup or a 2-inch spring-loaded scoop, drop six mounds of dough, evenly spaced, onto each reserved baking sheet. Bake until golden brown, 12 to 15 minutes, rotating the baking sheets and switching their positions about halfway through.

Set the baking sheets on wire racks. Sprinkle each cookie with flaky salt (if using). Cool for 5 minutes. Using a wide metal spatula, transfer the cookies directly to the racks. Cool completely before serving.

Cookies, Bars and Brownies

Brown Sugar Butter Mochi

Start to finish: 2 hours (20 minutes active), plus cooling

Makes sixteen 2-inch squares

42 grams (3 tablespoons) salted butter, cut into 3 pieces

14-oz can light coconut milk

227 grams (about 1½ cups) sweet rice flour (see headnote)

½ teaspoon baking powder

½ teaspoon table salt

218 grams (1 cup) packed light brown sugar

2 large eggs

1 teaspoon vanilla extract

3 tablespoons unsweetened shredded coconut

Butter mochi, a riff on traditional Japanese mochi (rice cakes made with sweet rice) is a popular baked treat in Hawaii. Its defining characteristic is a uniquely chewy, satisfyingly sticky texture, and though it's rich with butter and coconut milk, its taste is something of a blank canvas. We use brown sugar and deeply browned butter; together they give the mochi delicious notes of caramel and butterscotch. A sprinkle of shredded coconut onto the batter just before baking adds contrasting crisp texture. Sweet rice flour, also known as glutinous rice flour or mochiko (the Japanese term for the ingredient), is essential for achieving the correct chewiness. Koda Farms brand, sold in a white box with a distinctive blue star, is widely available. Half of the 1-pound box works perfectly in this recipe. We found Bob's Red Mill sweet rice flour to be too coarse to yield good results. We prefer light coconut milk here; regular coconut milk is too rich. Leftovers will keep in an airtight container at room temperature for a couple days.

Don't underbake the mochi or the center will taste starchy and raw. It's best to err on the side of overdone. For easiest slicing, allow the mochi to cool completely. A plastic utensil, such a disposable knife or plastic dough scraper with a sharp edge, is ideal for cutting the mochi, as it sticks less than the metal blade of a conventional knife.

Heat the oven to 350°F with a rack in the middle position. Mist an 8-inch square baking pan or glass baking dish with cooking spray. In a small saucepan over medium, cook the butter, swirling the pan often, until the milk solids at the bottom are deeply browned and the butter has a rich, nutty aroma, 4 to 6 minutes. Remove from the heat and pour in about ¼ cup of the coconut milk, swirling the pan to stop the cooking. Transfer to a large bowl and cool until barely warm.

In a medium bowl, whisk together the rice flour, baking powder and salt. To the bowl containing the butter mixture, whisk in the sugar, eggs and vanilla, then whisk in the remaining coconut milk. Add the dry ingredients and whisk until smooth; the batter will be fluid.

Pour the batter into the prepared pan. Rap the pan against the counter a few times to remove any large air bubbles, then sprinkle evenly with the coconut. Bake until the mochi pulls away from the sides of the pan, the center springs back when gently pressed with a finger and a toothpick inserted into the center comes out clean, 1 to 1¼ hours. Cool completely in the pan on a wire rack; the mochi will deflate slightly.

Invert the cooled mochi out of the pan, then turn it upright onto a cutting board. Cut into sixteen 2-inch squares.

VARIATION

Browned Butter Mochi with Mango

Thaw **340 grams** (**2 cups**) **frozen mango chunks,** then cut the chunks into ½- to ¾-inch cubes and pat dry. Follow the recipe; after transferring the batter to the pan and rapping the pan against the counter, scatter the mango chunks over the batter (they will sink into the batter). Sprinkle with the coconut, then bake, cool and cut as directed.

VARIATION

Coffee and Browned Browned Butter Mochi

Follow the recipe, adding **1 tablespoon instant espresso powder** to the browned butter along with the ¼ cup coconut milk and whisking **2 teaspoons cocoa powder** into the rice flour, baking powder and salt. Substitute **21 grams** (**3 tablespoons**) **cocoa nibs** for the shredded coconut; bake, cool and cut as directed.

Whole-Wheat Apricot Bars with Almond Crumble

To create apricot bars packed top to bottom with flavor and texture, we start with a buttery dough made from equal parts all-purpose and whole-wheat flours, then add ground toasted almonds, sugar, warm spices and vanilla. The dough then is divided: a portion is pressed into the baking pan to create the bottom crust, while the rest becomes the crisp, pebbly crumble topping. Apricot jam, used as the filling, can be one-dimensionally sweet, so we brighten it with a generous measure of lemon zest. (If you prefer cherry or strawberry jam, they work well, too.) Store leftovers in an airtight container for up to four days.

Don't forget to refrigerate the crumble topping while the bottom crust bakes. If it's room temperature, the bits tend to melt in the oven and the topping will be less crumbly.

Heat the oven to 350°F with a rack in the middle position. In an 8-inch square metal baking pan or glass baking dish, distribute the almonds in an even layer. Toast in the oven until lightly browned and fragrant, 3 to 5 minutes, stirring once about halfway through. Transfer to a small plate and let the almonds and the pan cool completely.

Mist the cooled baking pan with cooking spray, then line with two 7-by-14-inch pieces of kitchen parchment placed perpendicular to each other and with excess hanging over the edges of the pan. Mist the parchment with cooking spray.

In a food processor, combine the 54 grams (¼ cup) white sugar, the brown sugar and 46 grams (½ cup) of the toasted almonds. Process until finely ground, about 30 seconds. Add both flours, the vanilla, cardamom, allspice and ½ teaspoon salt. Pulse until well combined, 5 or 6 pulses. Scatter the butter over the dry ingredients and pulse until the mixture resembles wet sand, 8 to 10 pulses, then process until the dough comes together in large clumps, about 1 minute.

Transfer 265 grams (1½ cups) of the dough to a medium bowl and add the remaining 1 tablespoon sugar and the remaining almonds. Using your hands, toss, working in the sugar and almonds while also pinching the dough to form clumps the size of small grapes (it's fine if the bits are not uniform); refrigerate uncovered.

Break the remaining dough into bits, scattering them in the prepared baking pan. Using your fingers, press the dough into an even layer. Bake until lightly browned and just set, about 30 minutes. Cool on a wire rack for 20 minutes. Reduce the oven to 325°F. While the crust is baking, in a small bowl, stir together the jam, lemon zest and remaining pinch of salt.

**Start to finish: 2 hours
(40 minutes active), plus cooling**

Makes 16 bars

93 grams (1 cup) sliced almonds

54 grams (¼ cup) plus 1 tablespoon white sugar, divided

55 grams (¼ cup) packed light brown sugar

130 grams (1 cup) all-purpose flour

140 grams (1 cup) whole-wheat flour

2 teaspoons vanilla extract

1 teaspoon ground cardamom

½ teaspoon ground allspice

½ teaspoon table salt, plus a pinch

240 grams (¾ cup) apricot jam (see headnote)

1 tablespoon grated lemon zest

226 grams (16 tablespoons) cold salted butter, cut into ½-inch cubes

---

Scrape the jam mixture onto the center of the cooled crust and spread in an even layer. Remove the crumble from the refrigerator and sprinkle evenly over the jam, breaking it into pieces no larger than ½ inch. Bake until the topping is golden brown, 40 to 45 minutes. Cool completely in the pan on a wire rack, 1½ to 2 hours. Using the parchment overhang as handles, lift the bars out of the pan and set on a cutting board. Cut into 16 squares.

Lemon and Pistachio Bars

To balance the bright acidity of lemon, our take on this classic bar incorporates a small measure of fruity, savory olive oil in both the custard and crust. Buttery pistachios and fragrant lemon zest are mixed into the shortbread base, providing citrusy and nutty notes. With their subtle sweetness and vivid green hue, raw pistachios are worth seeking out. If you can't find them, the bars still are delicious made with roasted pistachios—just be sure they're unsalted. A little heavy cream in the lemon filling tamps down any harsh, brassy notes and lends a smooth, round richness. The bars hold well at room temperature for up to three days. Dust them with powdered sugar just before serving, or the sugar will dissolve.

Don't vigorously whisk the eggs and sugar when making the filling or the mixture will become aerated, which will result in a bubbled surface on the baked bars. Whisk gently and only until the eggs and sugar are combined. For incorporating the flour and liquids into the filling base, we prefer to stir with a silicone spatula to avoid additional aeration. For the cleanest cuts, allow the bars to cool completely before slicing.

To make the crust, butter a 9-by-13-inch baking pan or glass baking dish. In a food processor, process the pistachios and lemon zest until finely chopped, about 30 seconds. Add the flour, sugar and salt; process until well combined, 10 to 20 seconds. Scrape the bowl and pulse a few times to ensure no dry, floury patches remain. Scatter the butter over the mixture and drizzle in the oil, then process until large, evenly moistened clumps form, 45 to 60 seconds.

Crumble the dough clumps into the prepared pan, evenly scattering the bits. Using your fingers, press into an even layer. Lightly brush with the beaten egg white and refrigerate, uncovered, until cold and firm, about 30 minutes. Meanwhile, heat the oven to 350°F with a rack in the middle position.

Bake the crust until golden brown, 22 to 26 minutes. While the crust bakes, make the filling. In a large bowl, combine the whole eggs and yolks, sugar and lemon zest; whisk gently just until smooth (avoid aerating the mixture). Add the flour and salt; stir with a silicone spatula until combined. Stir in the lemon juice, cream and oil.

When the crust is done, remove the pan from the oven. Gently stir the filling to recombine, then pour it onto the hot crust; if any large bubbles have risen to the surface, pop them with a toothpick or skewer. Return to the oven and bake until the filling is set, 24 to 27 minutes. Cool completely in the pan on a wire rack, about 3 hours.

Start to finish: 1½ hours (30 minutes active), plus cooling

Makes 24 bars

FOR THE CRUST:

113 grams (8 tablespoons) cold salted butter, cut into ½-inch cubes, plus softened butter for the pan

145 grams (1 cup) raw pistachios (see headnote)

1 tablespoon grated lemon zest

195 grams (1½ cups) all-purpose flour

161 grams (¾ cup) white sugar

¾ teaspoon table salt

2 tablespoons extra-virgin olive oil

1 large egg white, beaten

FOR FILLING AND FINISHING:

5 large eggs, plus 3 large egg yolks

375 grams (1¾ cups) white sugar

1 tablespoon grated lemon zest, plus 1 cup lemon juice

33 grams (¼ cup) all-purpose flour

¼ teaspoon table salt

⅓ cup heavy cream

3 tablespoons extra-virgin olive oil

Powdered sugar, to serve

Using a sharp knife, cut the bars in the pan lengthwise into quarters, then crosswise into sixths, creating 24 squares. Remove from the pan with an offset spatula. Dust with powdered sugar just before serving.

VARIATION

Lemon Bars with Pistachios and Lavender

Follow the recipe to make the crust, adding **¾ teaspoon dried lavender** to the food processor with the pistachios and lemon zest. Make and slice the bars as directed. After dusting with powdered sugar, sprinkle **additional lavender** (lightly crushed) over the bars.

VARIATION

Lime Bars with Coconut and Cashews

Follow the recipe to make the crust, replacing the pistachios with **97 grams (¾ cup) roasted, unsalted cashews** and **23 grams (¼ cup) unsweetened shredded coconut** and replacing the lemon zest with an equal amount of **lime zest**. Press the dough into the pan, chill and bake the crust as directed. While the crust is baking, make the filling, substituting an equal amount of **lime zest and juice** for the lemon zest and juice. When the crust is done, remove the pan from the oven. Gently stir the filling to recombine, then pour it onto the hot crust. Bake, cool and cut as directed, dusting the bars with powdered sugar and additional grated lime just before serving.

VARIATION

Citrus Bars with Thyme and Hazelnuts

Follow the recipe to make the crust, replacing the pistachios with **130 grams (1 cup) roasted, unsalted hazelnuts**, replacing the lemon zest with an equal amount of **orange zest** and also adding **2 teaspoons fresh thyme**. Press the dough into the pan, chill and bake the crust as directed. While the crust is baking, make the filling, replacing the lemon zest with an equal amount of **orange zest** and replace the lemon juice with **¾ cup grapefruit juice** plus **¼ cup orange juice**. When the crust is done, remove the pan from the oven. Gently stir the filling to recombine, then pour it onto the hot crust. Bake, cool and cut as directed, dusting the bars with powdered sugar and **flaky sea salt, if desired,** before serving.

Index

Acknowledgments

Writing a cookbook is not unlike baking, a sometimes intimidating endeavor requiring the bringing together of disparate ingredients to achieve a delicious result. Here, those ingredients are the talented people in and around Milk Street working to create a singular well-conceived concept, from recipe idea and development through photography, editing and design. Many hands and minds make this possible.

In particular, I want to acknowledge J.M. Hirsch, our tireless editorial director; Michelle Locke, our relentlessly organized books editor; our exacting food editors Dawn Yanagihara, Bianca Borges and Ari Smolin; and Matthew Card, creative director of recipes; for leading the charge on conceiving, developing, writing and editing all of this.

Also, Jennifer Baldino Cox, our art director, and the entire design team who captured the essence of Milk Street. Special thanks to our photographer Joe Murphy, our designer, Gary Tooth, and all the photographers, stylists and art directors who have worked so hard to make Milk Street look so good.

Likewise, our talented kitchen crew, including kitchen director Wes Martin, our recipe development director Courtney Hill, recipe developers Rose Hattabaugh and Hisham Ali Hassan, our culinary support team, Kevin Clark, Elizabeth Mindreau and Hector Taborda, and the many cooks whose talent, skill and dedication have created the thousands of recipes that are the heart of Milk Street. Also Deborah Broide, Milk Street director of media relations, has done a spectacular job of sharing with the world all we do.

We also have a couple of folks to thank who work outside of 177 Milk Street. Michael Szczerban, editor, and everyone at Little, Brown and Company have been superb and inspired partners in this project. And my long-standing book agent, David Black, has been instrumental in bringing this project to life both with his knowledge of publishing and his friendship and support. Thank you, David!

Finally, a sincere thank you to my business partner and wife, Melissa. She has nurtured the Milk Street brand from the beginning so that we ended up where we thought we were going in the first place.

And, last but not least, to all of you who have supported the Milk Street project. Each and every one of you has a seat at the Milk Street table.

Christopher Kimball

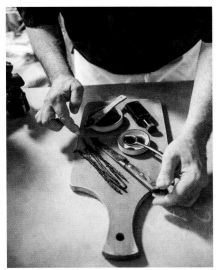

About the Author

Christopher Kimball is founder of Christopher Kimball's Milk Street, a food media company dedicated to changing the way we cook. It produces the bimonthly *Christopher Kimball's Milk Street Magazine*, as well as *Christopher Kimball's Milk Street Radio*, a weekly public radio show and podcast heard on more than 220 stations nationwide. It also produces the public television show *Christopher Kimball's Milk Street*, as well as two shows produced in partnership with Roku, *Milk Street Cooking School* and *My Family Recipe*. Kimball founded *Cook's Magazine* in 1980 and served as publisher and editorial director through 1989. He re-launched it as *Cook's Illustrated* in 1993. Through 2016, Kimball was host and executive producer of *America's Test Kitchen* and *Cook's Country*. He also hosted *America's Test Kitchen* radio show on public radio. Kimball is the author of several books, including *Fannie's Last Supper.*

Christopher Kimball's Milk Street is located at 177 Milk Street in downtown Boston and is dedicated to changing the way America cooks, with new flavor combinations and techniques learned around the world. It is home to Milk Street TV, a three-time Emmy Award–winning public television show, a James Beard Award–winning bimonthly magazine, an award-winning public radio show and podcast, a cooking school and global culinary tour provider, and an online store with more than 1,000 hard-to-find ingredients, tools and pantry products from around the world. Milk Street's cookbooks include the James Beard–winning *Milk Street Tuesday Nights*, the IACP-winning *Milk Street Vegetables*, *Milk Street 365*, *Milk Street Simple* and *Milk Street Cookish*. Milk Street also invests in nonprofit outreach, partnering with FoodCorps, the Big Sister Association of Greater Boston and the Boys & Girls Clubs of Dorchester.